The Privacy Leader Compass

Congratulations! Perhaps you have been appointed as the Chief Privacy Officer (CPO) or the Data Protection Officer (DPO) for your company. Or maybe you are an experienced CPO/DPO, and you wonder – "what can I learn from other successful privacy experts to be even more effective?" Or perhaps you are considering a move from a different career path and deciding if this is the right direction for you.

Seasoned award-winning Privacy and Cybersecurity leaders Dr. Valerie Lyons (Dublin, Ireland) and Todd Fitzgerald (Chicago, IL USA) have teamed up with over 60 award-winning CPOs, DPOs, highly respected privacy/data protection leaders, data protection authorities, and privacy standard setters who have fought the tough battle.

Just as the #1 best-selling and CANON Cybersecurity Hall of Fame winning *CISO Compass: Navigating Cybersecurity Leadership Challenges with Insights from Pioneers* book provided actionable advice to Chief Information Security Officers, *The Privacy Leader Compass* is about straight talk – delivering a comprehensive privacy roadmap applied to, and organized by, a time-tested organizational effectiveness model (the McKinsey 7-S Framework) with practical, insightful stories and lessons learned.

You own your continued success as a privacy leader. If you want a roadmap to build, lead, and sustain a program respected and supported by your board, management, organization, and peers, this book is for you.

The Privacy Leader Compass

A Comprehensive Business-Oriented Roadmap for Building and Leading Practical Privacy Programs

Dr. Valerie Lyons
Todd Fitzgerald

Foreword by Dr. Ann Cavoukian

CRC Press
Taylor & Francis Group
Boca Raton London New York

CRC Press is an imprint of the
Taylor & Francis Group, an **informa** business

Cover Illustration Credit: Imran Islam Anik

First edition published 2024
by CRC Press
6000 Broken Sound Parkway NW, Suite 300, Boca Raton, FL 33487-2742

and by CRC Press
4 Park Square, Milton Park, Abingdon, Oxon, OX14 4RN

© 2024 Dr Valerie Lyons and Todd Fitzgerald

CRC Press is an imprint of Taylor & Francis Group, LLC

ISBN: 978-1-032-46730-6 (hbk)
ISBN: 978-1-032-46731-3 (pbk)
ISBN: 978-1-003-38301-7 (ebk)

DOI: 10.1201/9781003383017

Typeset in Sabon
by SPi Technologies India Pvt Ltd (Straive)

To everyone who has inspired me, amazed me, coached me, mentored me, managed me, nudged me, and even to all those who doubted me. Thank You. You have all shaped my journey to this day. To my amazing children, my wonderful partner, and my patient friends and colleagues – I told you it would be worth it....

– Dr. Valerie Lyons

To Valerie, who moves from idea to "now we are doing this" with enthusiasm, ability, passion, and confidence – all before I can tie my shoes. To my loving father who taught me the value of hard work and respect, to my loving mother who always encouraged us to be responsible and reach higher, and to Grant and Erica, who continue to make Dad proud, and who will never read this book, but will benefit from the privacy leaders who do.

– Todd Fitzgerald

Contents

Privacy leader's insights

Figures

Tables

Foreword

Today's privacy leaders find themselves juggling a complex maze of challenges associated with privacy legislation, privacy team management, privacy technology, data protection, and much more. Privacy professionals are also acutely aware of the onslaught and increasing magnitude of data breaches and their fallout, both to the reputation of their organization and to consumer concerns. Therefore, as someone who has spent my entire career advocating for privacy, I am happy to introduce this new book, *The Privacy Leader Compass*, to anyone leading a privacy program or team. This book presents a thorough roadmap to navigate, not just for privacy leaders, but to become a truly effective privacy leader of a truly effective privacy program. This book will help privacy leaders to build and shape a strong privacy program that reflects the changing nature, scope, and challenges associated with privacy compliance, along with ever-growing societal privacy expectations.

This book brings together the expertise of two authors who have over six decades of experience in leading cybersecurity and privacy: Dr. Valerie Lyons has been leading privacy programs and teams for over ten years, and prior to that, close to 20 years leading cybersecurity teams. Not only is she a practitioner with industry privacy and cybersecurity qualifications but she is also an academic with published research and has a PhD in Information Privacy. She is considered a leading authority on the nascent topic of privacy as part of the ESG agenda. Todd Fitzgerald is a career CISO for over two decades, with industry cybersecurity and privacy qualifications. Todd is also an author in his own right, with several published books on cybersecurity leadership, the most recently being the #1 best-selling book a *CISO COMPASS: Navigating Cybersecurity Challenges with Insights from Pioneers*, aimed at helping chief information security officers and their teams, of which I was honored to contribute. Together their insights and strategies provide invaluable guidance for anyone seeking to establish or improve their privacy program.

The Privacy Leader Compass is a truly unique book, not only in the breadth and depth of the topics covered, but also in that the authors are artful collaborators who have both reached out to their networks to elicit stories, advice, and insights from key privacy leaders, in both academia and industry. There are insights included in this book from over 50 pioneers in the field of privacy. Through these insights, we get a thorough understanding of privacy – beyond regulations alone, and a real perspective of privacy on the ground and in the trenches. For instance, Daniel Solove, a highly esteemed privacy professor, discusses his taxonomy of privacy, Jules Polonetsky, CEO of the Future of Privacy forum, discusses privacy as a human right, and Dr. Johnny Ryan, privacy advocate and senior research fellow, discusses the importance of cataloging all processing purposes.

I would like to highlight several topics covered in this book, that in my view, make this book truly unique. First, to help privacy leaders demonstrate to their executive management that the privacy program they have built supports their business goals and mission, the authors have drawn upon the McKinsey 7 S model (developed to measure organizational effectiveness) as a way to measure the effectiveness of a privacy program. The application of the 7-S model in this way provides real structure to building or enhancing the privacy program. Second, given my own academic and industry background, I am delighted to see that the book starts with a comprehensive section clarifying definitions, allaying confusions, and discussing several important theories of privacy. These theories of privacy are often not included in practitioner-focused books, and yet they are fundamental to understanding how "privacy" works. This marriage of the academic perspective of privacy with the practitioner perspective is evident throughout this book, and each chapter contains comprehensive referencing, with a suggested reading section at the end of each chapter. Third, I was very pleased to see that my principles of Privacy by Design (PbD) are incorporated into the 7-S framework applied to privacy. Privacy by Design is a concept I developed back in the late 1990s to address the ever-growing and systemic effects of Information and Communication Technologies and of large-scale networked data systems. Privacy by Design is as applicable today as it was back in the 1990s and has recently been passed as an ISO standard (ISO 31700) and is also enshrined in GDPR's data protection principles ("data protection by design and by default").

Privacy by Design advances the view that the future of privacy cannot be assured solely by compliance with regulatory frameworks. Rather, privacy assurance must ideally become an organization's default mode of operation. So, I was delighted to see that "Privacy Risk Governance" has a chapter of its own as does "Privacy and Ethics". It is here that this book truly begins to contribute in a way that differentiates it from most privacy books. The chapter on "Privacy and Ethics" covers a wide range of privacy concepts such as: Privacy as a Corporate Responsibility and Privacy as a Political Activity. These activities are often overlooked by privacy program leaders as they occur in either the marketing or communications departments and often fall outside of the privacy program, since they do not primarily relate directly to personal data. However, these activities can often shape how personal data is processed and managed by an organization and are thus equally important to consider. And finally, with great introspection, the authors discuss the importance of skills beyond the technical and legal skills of the privacy leader, and present fascinating insights into privacy leadership styles plus team dynamics and their roles.

Although the book is called *The Privacy Leader Compass*, the book is not simply for privacy leaders, it is for anyone who cares deeply about privacy and wants to learn how to implement best practices to safeguard personal information. It is my hope that this book will inspire more organizations to prioritize privacy and protect the rights of both their customers and stakeholders.

I commend the authors for their dedication to privacy and for sharing their knowledge and expertise with us. May this book serve as a call to action for all privacy leaders to prioritize building a comprehensive privacy program and lead the way toward a more privacy-centric future, where privacy and innovation thrive!

Ann Cavoukian, Ph.D., LL.D. (Hon.), M.S.M.
Executive Director of the Global Privacy and Security by Design Centre,
And former three-term Privacy Commissioner of Ontario, Canada

Acknowledgments

DR. VALERIE LYONS

When I was 18, I wanted to become a veterinarian surgeon, but I didn't get the college entry points to become one. I did, however, get enough points to do a course in commercial computer programming (RPGII and COBOL, for those old enough to remember those two beautiful coding languages). And that was the start of my IT career. At the time, there was little work in Ireland. It was called the "brain drain" and many of us had to leave Ireland to go to the United States or the United Kingdom to get work. I was lucky – I got an internship at IBM in Dublin, in their Systems Engineering team. I then moved to KPMG as a programmer. I created more bugs than I fixed – so that career path was short-lived. I was, however, really good at Systems Administration (Sysadmin). This morphed into a career in systems security around 1997 at Bank of Ireland (ICS). And that led to many years in the financial services sector. During my career to date, I have worked at IBM, Gateway 2000, Revlon, JBA, Music Control, KPMG, Bank of Ireland, KBC Bank and IIB Bank, and Dublin City University. In 2012, I decided to hit "restart" on my life and seek fulfillment and contentment. Part of that re-invention was to go back to further education, something I had put on hold while I reared young kids. I had no idea about the direction I was going, but I had always found myself happier when I was in education, a happiness that was mine to control. So, I embarked on an executive master's program with the Irish Management Institute. One of the key modules was leadership theory and practice, and another was executive coaching. I was fascinated by both subjects and discovered during the coaching sessions included in these modules that 1) I wasn't fulfilled in my current career choice and was struggling to find contentment as a result and 2) I was hungry for more self-development. When I finished the master's program, in 2014, I decided to take time out from a full-time career in the financial sector to embark on a journey of discovery: I wanted to leave a stamp on the world that said "Valerie was here" – with books, and papers, and articles that would outlive me. I wanted to become an expert, to write about my expertise, and give talks on my subject of expertise. I wanted to be the go-to-person in my area of expertise.

I just didn't know what the subject of expertise was!

Then a friend of mine Frank Kennedy (thank you Frank) advised me that to answer the "what subject" question, I should talk to Professor Joseph McDonagh in Trinity College, my alma mater. Professor McDonagh suggested I look to the past, then to the future, and let my research be the funnel between the two. My past was Information Security Risk Management, the future I believed was Privacy – and my PhD, and area of expertise, became that funnel. This began the start of the journey of learning and diving deep into privacy, a journey of almost a decade that I have loved and felt privileged to take. In April 2022, after five years of study, I successfully defended my thesis and was awarded a PhD in Information Privacy. In the same year, I was included in the top women in cybersecurity in Europe, accepted into the pool of experts by the European Data Protection Board, and accepted to speak at RSA, the largest cybersecurity conference in North America. The journey to "expert" had finally begun.

The journey continues today, and the pursuit of expertise is a daily one, where development of my understanding of privacy and data protection is ongoing. I have spent the last eight years working for BH Consulting – initially as Senior Privacy Specialist, and now as we continue to grow – as Chief Operations Officer. I have loved working with BH Consulting, and I have loved working in Privacy. BH Consulting is a wonderful company whose culture is founded on balancing work, health, family, and friends – with good business and quality outputs. I never found this contentment previously. How do I measure this? For the last eight years, I have loved Mondays. Who knows what makes our boat float and why – but privacy works for me. I simply found my tribe with privacy.

I wish to acknowledge that the journey to "expert" would not have been possible without the support of my amazing PhD supervisors Professor Theo Lynn, Dr. Lisa van der Werff, and panel expert Dr. Grace Fox to whom I am eternally grateful. I could not write a book about privacy had I not spent much of the last decade researching it and these guys were instrumental in my PhD.

I want to acknowledge my parents. Although no longer here, they always instilled the belief in me that women are an incredible force and able to achieve anything they put their mind to. My father gave me the skills to navigate a world that he believed was unfair to women and did not enable them to achieve their goals more easily. While I continue to agree with him and feel that women must work harder than their male peers to get to the top positions, I want to acknowledge the men in our industry, who are unequivocal in their support of women in privacy and cybersecurity – who run panels and conferences that have fair representation of women, who consciously engage with the workforce respecting diversity, who refuse to participate in events that are not fairly represented, who don't need quotas for recruitment, and simply always choose fairly. Men like my co-author Todd, David Lynas (COSAC security conference), ISACA committee members, RSA committee members, Brian Honan, J. Trevor Hughes, Daniel Solove, Jules Polonetsky... the list goes on.

I would also like to acknowledge and thank the more than 60 contributors to this book. My mother used to say, "if you want something done, ask a busy person". Make no mistake, these are all very busy people. These pioneers, leaders, policymakers, leading academics, and researchers benevolently took the time to write a piece they hoped would bring some insight for the reader. We selected these contributors on the basis that they were not only experts in their particular field and have contributed to privacy but are also representative of the profession, its integrity, and its codes of conduct.

To my co-author and life-partner, Todd. Without sounding like Kathy Bates in the movie *Misery*, Todd is "my number one fan", and his support never falters. I would like to acknowledge how his expertise has helped sculpt and shape the book and provided me with great clarity at crucial points of its production. And finally, to my (nearly adult) children Dan and Ciara, I want to thank you both for both being there throughout this journey. I hope you keep this book on your shelves when I have departed this mortal coil.

TODD FITZGERALD

I created a presentation several years ago entitled "One Hour Privacy Primer for Security Officers" for the RSA Security Conference, one of the largest security conferences approaching 50,000 attendees annually in San Francisco. J. Trevor Hughes was giving a session at the same time on privacy and emerging technologies. I figured my session would be empty, given his session focused on the future. To my surprise, my session was packed. I ended up presenting that material, updated each year, for another five years! I knew that we were onto something – CISOs and other security leaders needed to know more about privacy.

Now here we are, almost a decade after that first session, and I am grateful to bring a comprehensive roadmap to the privacy leadership body of knowledge.

I am grateful for all the CISOs that contributed to the first book in this series, the *CISO COMPASS: Navigating Cybersecurity Leadership Challenges with Insights from Pioneers*, those who purchased that book, and selection by the CANON Cybersecurity Hall of Fame as a 2020 Winner, all resulting in the #1 Best Selling Information Security book from Taylor & Francis (2019–2022). Why is this important? In the first book, we established the application of an organizational effectiveness model (McKinsey

7-S Framework) to Cybersecurity Leadership practices and infused the knowledge of 75 Top CISOs and industry leaders. This approach resonated with readers and the success of the CISO COMPASS book set the stage for extending the organizational effectiveness model into privacy and data protection, leveraging the practical expertise and privacy education of my incredible co-author Dr. Valerie Lyons, as well as exceptional CPOs, DPOs, regulators, academics, and privacy and data protection experts. This book is not just a collection of stories nor is it the viewpoint of one or two writers – rather, it serves as a structured, organized roadmap – a collaborative roadmap for privacy leaders to build, lead, and sustain privacy and data protection programs.

Thank you to the 60+ contributors that worked diligently with us to produce the "gray boxes". Sometimes in life, we generalize or stereotype people as CPOs, DPOs, CISOs, CIOs, etc., with similar challenges. However, the one thing writing these books has taught me is that they are also people with lives, families, illnesses, and demands on their time. And yet, repeatedly, I am impressed by how people in this profession are giving and willing to share their expertise to help others. So, when you see a contributor to this book – thank them. Really thank them for sharing their insights. They collaborated for a simple purpose – to support your privacy passion and those whom you serve to protect. So please, thank them.

About the authors

Dr. Valerie Lyons

PhD, MSc, BSc, CIPP/E, CDPSE, CISSP.

Chief Operations Officer, BH Consulting (Dublin, Ireland)

Named in the top 100 women in cybersecurity in Europe, Dr. Valerie Lyons is an accomplished and driven cybersecurity and privacy leadership expert, with extensive experience at senior level in financial services, having served as Head of Information Security Risk in KBC Bank (Dublin, Ireland) for almost 15 years. Currently, Chief Operations Officer for a niche cybersecurity and privacy consulting firm, Valerie leads several consulting teams while also acting as a Senior Privacy Consultant.

Valerie holds a BSc in Information Systems (with distinction) from Trinity College Dublin. She also holds a masters in Management, a Diploma in Leadership, a Diploma in Executive Coaching, a Diploma in Cloud Computing Strategy (all from the Irish Management Institute). In March 2022, Valerie completed an award-winning PhD in Information Privacy, researching novel approaches to organizational privacy protection that engender consumer trust and loyalty. She has published several academic papers related to her PhD, and a chapter in Data Privacy and Trust in Cloud Computing (Palgrave Macmillan, 2021). She frequently lectures on Ethics, Privacy, and Cybersecurity in Dublin City University's Business School. A long serving member of the Irish Information Security Forum (IISF), she was awarded fellowship of the forum in 2001 for her work on the committee and her contribution to the information security community in Ireland. She is also a mentor and champion of the ISACA #sheleadstech forum.

While she is actively involved in both privacy and cybersecurity, privacy is her passion, where she feels she makes her greatest contribution.

Todd Fitzgerald

CIPM, CIPP/US, CIPP/E, CIPP/C, CISSP, CISA, CISM, CGEIT, CRISC, PMP, and ITILv3 certified.

Managing Director, CISO Spotlight, LLC (Milwaukee, WI, USA)

Todd Fitzgerald promotes security/privacy leadership and collaboration among security and privacy practitioners by hosting the successful SCMedia CISO STORIES weekly podcast, advisory board participation, and international speaking engagements. Todd also serves as VP of Cybersecurity Strategy, CyberRisk Alliance. Todd has authored five books, including the #1 Best-selling (2019–2022) and 2020 CANON Cybersecurity Hall of Fame Winning book entitled, *CISO COMPASS: Navigating Cybersecurity Leadership Challenges with Insights from Pioneers* (Taylor & Francis, 2019), as well as co-authoring the ground-breaking first professional organization published Chief Information Security Officer Book, *CISO Leadership: Essential Principles for Success* (ISC2 Press, 2008), and contributed to over 20 other cybersecurity books.

Named 2016–2017 Chicago CISO of the Year, Todd's global multi-industry and Fortune 500/Global 2000 company positions include CAO Information Security & Technology Risk Northern Trust, Global CISO Grant Thornton International, Ltd, Global CISO ManpowerGroup, and Senior IT/Security leadership roles in Wellpoint (Anthem)/National Government Services, Zeneca/Syngenta, IMS Health, and American Airlines.

Todd earned a BS in Business Administration from the University of Wisconsin-La Crosse and a master's degree in Business Administration with highest honors from Oklahoma State University and is an adjunct lecturer in IT Risk Management and Cybersecurity Leadership for Northwestern University McCormick School of Engineering.

Contributors

The contributors to this body of work are passionate privacy leaders who have developed and lead global, privacy programs, provided expert advice to organizations, developed privacy technologies, created some of the industry's standards and practices, or have served in a regulatory capacity to protect the privacy interests of individuals, organizations, and governments. As you examine the backgrounds of these individuals from public and private sectors and academia, it should become clear that these individuals have dealt with many of the situations facing privacy professionals today.

Many of these individuals currently hold or have held the role of Chief Privacy Officer, Data Protection Officer, or regulator roles across various industries and geographies. As you read these impressive bios, it will become clear that these contributions come from all over the world, from different jurisdictions and different approaches – all to address our common need for data protection and privacy. The opinions may differ, and that's okay. Through conversation and understanding different points of view, we can all become stronger.

We are grateful for the impressive sharing of expertise to strengthen our collective privacy and data protection needs on so many different issues. While the company names are noted in the biographies and the individual "grey boxes" in this book, it should be noted that the company names are referenced to solely provide affiliation, and the views and opinions are those of the contributor and not necessarily the position held by the company, organization, or institution to which the contributor is associated. You will notice that the contributions are almost equal in gender distribution. This was not by design – it merely reflects both an industry that is well represented by gender and the lack of implicit bias in their selection.

Dr. Susie Alegre is the author of *Freedom to Think: Protecting a Fundamental Human Right in the Digital Age* (Atlantic Books 2022), an international human rights lawyer, and an expert in digital rights. She is an associate at Doughty Street Chambers, a senior fellow at the Centre for International Governance Innovation (CIGI), and the founder of the Island Rights Initiative. She advises companies, civil societies, and public sector organizations on human rights and governance, particularly in relation to technology. With over 25 years of experience in international human rights law for international organizations including Amnesty International, the OSCE ODIHR, the UN, and the EU around the world, she understands the practical and geopolitical implications of new technologies.

Aurélie Banck has been a French privacy professional since 2006. She held different positions for the French Data Protection Authority, public institutions (like the French Interior Ministry), and private companies like BNP Paribas. The diversity of these experiences both on data controller and on regulator sides enables her to make the link between business operational constraints and the requirements of the regulator. She teaches Data Protection and Privacy laws in different programs and is certified CIPP/E and CIPM. She is the author of the *RGPD: 20* sheets to be compliant with data protection regulation, Gualino edition (5th in 2023).

João Barreiro is the Chief Privacy Officer of BeiGene, a triple-listed biopharmaceutical company with over 9,000 employees. His work at BeiGene was crucial for being recognized as 2022 Privacy Executive of the Year by the PICCASO Privacy Awards. His experience also includes privacy roles at Celgene (now BMS) and the European Medicines Agency. He also practiced in the tech industry, as the global Chief Privacy Officer of HCL Technologies, an IT services company with 210,000 employees, and the finance sector, as the Global Chief Privacy Officer of Willis Towers Watson, the third largest global insurance intermediary. João is a member of the IAPP Research Advisory Board and is a co-author of the book *Privacy Program Management*.

Amalia Barthel is a Canadian digital technology risk and privacy advisor for organizations of all sizes in the top 20 industries. She is one of the student-selected top-30 Instructors at University of Toronto School of Continuing Studies and speaks frequently at conferences in Canada, the US, and the EU. Since GDPR came into effect, Amalia had worked with several renowned multinationals to implement complex global privacy programs. Amalia holds a MSc in Computer Engineering, and she is a certified PMI, ISACA, and IAPP professional.

Ivana Bartoletti is Global Chief Privacy Officer at Wipro. She was Founder of Women Leading in AI Network. She was Cybersecurity and Privacy Executive Fellow at Pamplin Business School, Virginia Tech. Ivana is the author of *An Artificial Revolution: On Power, Politics and AI*.

Bojana Bellamy is the President of Hunton Andrews Kurth' Centre for Information Policy Leadership (CIPL), a preeminent global privacy and data policy thinktank in London, Washington, DC, and Brussels. Bojana works with global business and technology leaders, regulators, policy, and law makers to shape global data policy and practice and develop thought leadership and best practices for privacy and responsible data use. In 2019, Bojana received the IAPP Vanguard Award, which recognizes privacy professionals for outstanding leadership, knowledge, and creativity. With over 25 years of experience in privacy, data policy, and compliance, including former global privacy head at Accenture for 12 years, she sits on several industry and regulatory advisory boards and panels.

Catherine M. Boerner, JD, CHC is the President of Boerner Consulting, LLC. Since 1997, Cathy Boerner has supported compliance officers, privacy officers, and security officers. She specializes in compliance program effectiveness reviews and implementations, HIPAA Privacy Gap Analysis, and HIPAA Security Risk Analysis and Implementation. Cathy Boerner served on the Health Care Compliance Association (HCCA)'s Board of Directors from 2010 to 2013. She is a past-President of HIPAA Collaborative of Wisconsin (HIPAA COW) and has served on the Board for over 20 years.

Paul Breitbarth is an experienced data protection lawyer from the Netherlands. He works as the in-house data protection counsel for a Dutch tech scale-up, teaches at Maastricht University, and co-hosts the Serious Privacy Podcast. He is a regular speaker on topics including accountability, risk management, and cross-border data transfers. Before, Paul served as senior international officer at the Dutch Data Protection Authority. He was an active member of various Article 29 Working Party subgroups, co-authoring opinions on the data protection reform, national security and surveillance, the Privacy Shield, and others. Paul holds a Master of Laws from Maastricht University.

Julie Brill as Microsoft's Chief Privacy Officer and Corporate Vice President of Global Privacy and Regulatory Affairs, Julie Brill leads the company's work at the forefront of the tech policy, regulatory, and legal issues that underpin the world's digital transformation and is the central figure in Microsoft's advocacy for responsible data use and policy around the globe.

Building on her distinguished public service career spanning more than three decades at the federal and state levels, Brill directs Microsoft's Privacy, Digital Safety, Law Enforcement and National Security (LENS), and Telecom, Standards, Accessibility regulation, and Regulatory Governance operations and solutions. In 2018, she spearheaded Microsoft's global adoption of the European Union's General Data Protection Regulation (GDPR) and continues to lead Microsoft's advocacy around responsible approaches to privacy, data protection, and global data flows around the world.

Prior to her role at Microsoft, Brill was nominated by President Barack Obama and confirmed unanimously by the US Senate. Brill served for six years as a Commissioner of the US Federal Trade Commission (FTC).

As Commissioner, she worked actively on issues of critical importance to consumers, including privacy, fair advertising practices, fighting financial fraud, and maintaining competition in all industries with a special focus on healthcare and technology.

Brill has been elected to the American Law Institute and has received numerous awards for her work. She was named "the Commission's most important voice on Internet privacy and data security issues" and a Top Data Privacy Influencer, among other honors.

In addition to her role at Microsoft, Julie is active in civil society, serving as a board member of the International Association of Privacy Professionals, a board member of the Center for Democracy and Technology, Governor for The Ditchley Foundation, and co-chair of Business at the Organization of Economic Cooperation and Development's Committee for Digital Economic Policy.

Brill graduated, magna cum laude, from Princeton University, and from New York University School of Law, where she had a Root-Tilden Scholarship for her commitment to public service.

Dr. Ann Cavoukian is recognized as one of the world's leading privacy experts. She serves as Executive Director at Global Privacy and Security by Design Centre. She served an unprecedented three terms as the Information and Privacy Commissioner of Ontario, Canada. There she created Privacy by Design, a framework that seeks to proactively embed privacy into the design specifications of information technologies, networked infrastructure, and business practices, thereby achieving the strongest protection possible. In 2010, International Privacy Regulators unanimously passed a resolution recognizing Privacy by Design as an international standard. Since then, PbD has been translated into 40 languages.

Paul E. Clement, CIPP/US, CIPM with more than 30 years of experience as a data privacy and legal professional, Paul has worked for globally recognized law firms Hogan Lovells and Alston & Bird and at other large companies (Capital One and AOL/Time Warner). Before joining HP, Paul worked for Leidos, Inc. as a Sr. Data Privacy Analyst in their Global Privacy Office. He also worked with two different ad tech start-ups as the founding member of their legal/privacy functions.

Tim Clements, based in Copenhagen, he is Business Owner of Purpose and Means, a niche data protection consultancy with strong focus on assisting data protection leaders align their programs with business goals and strategies.

Purpose and Means is also an Official IAPP Training Partner delivering IAPP certification courses globally and Tim is also a member of IAPP's Faculty.

He supplements his privacy and data protection know-how with program management and business analysis competences applying structured approaches, pragmatism, systems thinking, visual communication, and strong stakeholder management to the privacy program context.

Besides being a Fellow of Information Privacy (FIP) with IAPP, Tim is also a Chartered Fellow of the British Computer Society (FBCS CITP) in London and holds a number of industry-standard certifications covering information risk, information security, business analysis, change management, and project & program management.

Roland Cloutier is a globally recognized security leader, author, and board member and is an expert in global protection, digital technology enablement, and security leadership. Roland's career has included Global Chief Security Officer positions at TikTok, ADP, and EMC delivering operational responsibility for cyber, data defense, privacy enforcement, operational risk, workforce protection, crisis management, and investigative operations. Roland is also the distinguished author of his book, *Becoming a Global Chief Security Executive Officer,* and has numerous industry awards, including being inducted into the IDG CSO Hall of Fame and one of the Most Influential People in Security, by *Security Magazine.*

Kate Colleary, founder and director of Pembroke Privacy, is a globally regarded privacy lawyer and DPO. She was awarded the International Association of Privacy Professionals' (IAPP) Westin Emeritus Fellow award, which is presented to world leaders in data protection and privacy, in recognition of her expertise and contribution to privacy professionals worldwide. Kate is the IAPP Country Leader for Ireland, a role which involves her traveling to global conferences where she represents the Irish privacy community. Kate has achieved the IAPP's CIPP/E & CIPM qualifications. She gained an honors degree in Law from Trinity College Dublin in 1995 and has been a qualified lawyer since 1999.

Caleb Cooper CIPM, CDPSE, CISA is a certified Privacy Executive with extensive experience implementing and leading lean privacy programs to address everchanging privacy regulations across the globe. His leadership has guided multinational organizations in addressing compliance requirements for GDPR, LGPD, PIPL, across the United States among others. Caleb is a firm believer that privacy can help an organization reach its full potential and is the new operational model for organizations. He has been working in the privacy, compliance, and risk management space for over 15 years for organizations such as Warner Media (Turner Broadcasting), Royal Bank of Scotland (WorldPay), SunTrust (Truist) Banks, and others.

R. Jason Cronk is a seasoned privacy engineer, author of the IAPP textbook *Strategic Privacy by Design* and holds CIPT, CIPM, CIPP/US, and FIP designations. His unique background includes various entrepreneurial pursuits, strong information technology and cybersecurity experience, and privacy law. Currently, Cronk serves as President of the Institute of

Operational Privacy Design and Section Leader of the IAPP's Privacy Engineering Section. He is also president and principal consultant with the boutique consulting and training firm Enterprivacy Consulting Group.

Marcin Czarnecki is the Chief Privacy Officer for PayU, one of the world's leaders in global payments and innovative fintech. Before joining PayU, Marcin was supporting Prosus group portfolio companies in developing their global privacy programs. Prior to joining Prosus, for ten years Marcin worked for an international law firm and advised on data protection, information technology, and M&A in the TMT sector. Marcin is a member of the International Association of Privacy Professionals and a frequent speaker on privacy matters.

Peter T. Davis (LL.M, CPA, CMA, CMC, CISA, CISSP, CISM, CGEIT) is the Principal of Peter Davis+Associates (http://www.pdaconsulting.com), a management consulting firm specializing in IT Governance, Security, and Audit. Prior to founding PDA, Mr. Davis' private sector experience included stints with two large Canadian banks and a manufacturing company. He was formerly a principal in the Information Systems Audit practice of Ernst & Young. In the public sector, Mr. Davis was Director of Information Systems Audit in the Office of the Provincial Auditor (Ontario), where he had overseen audit responsibilities for all Ontario crown corporations, agencies, and boards.

Emerald de Leeuw-Goggin is a globally recognized Privacy and Data Protection expert as well as an award-winning entrepreneur, advisory board member, and lecturer. At the time of the writing of this book, she was the Global Head of Privacy at Logitech.

Prior to joining Logitech, she founded a privacy-tech company, Eurocomply, for which she won various awards such as European Young Innovator of the Year in 2017 and a 30 under 30 award. She started Eurocomply after writing her master's thesis on the GDPR in 2012.

Forbes named her one of 100 European female founders to watch, and she speaks regularly at leading conferences such as TEDx and institutions such as MIT Sloan School of Business and the European Parliament. She is a Marshall Memorial fellow with the German Marshall Fund of the United States. Emerald is an advocate for female leaders and is passionate about closing the funding and pay gap for women.

Her qualifications include a Bachelor of Laws, a master's in E-Law and Intellectual Property Law, a master's in Business Information Systems. She completed her executive education at Stanford Graduate School of Business.

Colonel (Retired) Lawrence D. Dietz, US Army, ESQ is General Counsel of TAL Global, an elite security consulting and risk management firm. Prior to joining TAL Global, Dietz served in senior roles at Symantec Corporation to include Director of Market Intelligence. Legal expertise includes complex contract negotiations, NDAs, and Law of Armed Combat. His degrees include JD, Master of Strategic Studies from the US Army War College, MBA, JD, and LLM in European Law. Dietz is on the faculty of the Monterey College of Law and American Military University. He is a volunteer Public Affairs Officer and Advanced International Humanitarian Law Instructor, American Red Cross.

Dr. Chris Dimitriadis is an international authority on Digital Trust, with a proven track record in developing and managing strategy. He is working with the Board of Directors and top management of ISACA toward the continuous alignment of the organization's strategy with the changing needs of its community in 188 countries. He served ISACA as Chair of the Board for two consecutive terms and as Director of the Board for nine terms. Chris is also a former Group CEO of a global gaming solutions supplier and operator active in 42 jurisdictions. He holds a degree in Electrical and Computer Engineering and a PhD in cybersecurity.

Orrie Dinstein is the Global Chief Privacy Officer at Marsh McLennan. He has global responsibility for data protection, and he works closely with the Legal & Compliance, IT and Information Security teams, as well as other functions, on privacy and data protection matters. Prior to joining Marsh McLennan, Orrie was the Chief Privacy Officer at GE Capital.

Orrie received an LLM in Intellectual Property from the NYU School of Law and is a graduate of the Hebrew University of Jerusalem School of Law. He is a member of the New York State Bar and the Israel Bar. He is a Certified Information Privacy Professional (CIPP) and a frequent speaker on privacy, security, technology, and social media matters.

Lynn Dohm brings more than 25 years of organizational and leadership experience to the Women in CyberSecurity (WiCyS) team. Lynn is passionate about the need for diverse mindsets, skill sets, and perspectives. She aims to facilitate learning opportunities and discussions on leading with inclusion, equity, and allyship. She has successfully collaborated with businesses, non-profits, grants, and philanthropies to help produce outcomes that aligned with cybersecurity workforce initiatives. Learn more about WiCyS here: https://www.wicys.org/

Melanie Ensign is the founder and CEO of Discernible, the world's first center of excellence for security and privacy communications. After leading security, privacy, and engineering communications at some of the world's most notable tech brands, including Facebook, Uber, and AT&T, Melanie founded Discernible to help security and privacy organizations increase their influence and drive better outcomes using science-based communication techniques. For the past decade, she has also led the press department and communications strategy for DEF CON, the world's largest hacker community.

Melanie is an accomplished rescue scuba diver and brings many lessons learned in preventing, preparing for, and navigating unexpected, high-risk underwater incidents to her work in security and privacy. She holds a Master of Science degree from the College of Communication at Boston University.

Michelle Finneran Dennedy is currently the CEO & co-founder of PrivacyCode, Inc., the Privacy Engineering SaaS platform & Founding Partner at Privatus Consulting – a firm that helps businesses create data strategy and metrics. Prior to that, Michelle held several leadership roles, including VP & Chief Privacy Officer, leading security and privacy initiatives focused on regulatory compliance and privacy engineering at organizations like Cisco, McAfee, Intel Security, Oracle, and Sun Microsystems. Michelle co-authored *The Privacy Engineer's Manifesto: Getting from Policy to Code to QA to Value* and *The Privacy Engineer's Workbook*.

Linda Fletcher is the former Administrative Director of Privacy for Franciscan Alliance, Inc. with 40 years of healthcare experience. She completed her CISSP certification in 2001 and served as the first Information Security Officer (ISO) for Franciscan Alliance, Inc. She formed Franciscan's Information Security program from the ground up in 2004, serving in the ISO role for 13 years after which she transitioned to the Director of Privacy position and began maturing the Franciscan privacy program.

Elaine Fox, CIPP/E, LLM is TikTok's Head of Privacy for Europe. Based in Ireland, she leads TikTok's growing team of data protection and privacy lawyers in Europe. Prior to TikTok, Elaine worked in Facebook (Meta) as Associate General Counsel, Data Protection, where she managed a team covering privacy matters in particular in the context of gaming, bitcoin, and product development, having earned her stripes working in data protection (contentious and non-contentious) for over a decade at two leading Irish law firms prior to moving inhouse. Elaine is passionate about privacy and technology. She has a particular interest in the data protection implications of new and emerging technologies. Her work includes the utilization of innovation and technology to support privacy initiatives and driving privacy enhancing technology initiatives.

Dylan Gilbert is a Privacy Policy Advisor with the Privacy Engineering Program at the National Institute of Standards and Technology, US Department of Commerce. In this role, he advances the development of privacy engineering and risk management processes with a focus on the Privacy Framework and emerging technologies.

Prior to joining NIST, he was Policy Counsel at Public Knowledge, where he led and developed all aspects of the organization's privacy advocacy. This included engagement with civil society coalitions, federal and state lawmakers, and a broad cross-section of external stakeholders on issues ranging from consumer IoT security to the development of comprehensive federal privacy legislation.

Karen Habercoss as the Chief Privacy Officer is responsible for the strategy and operations of The University of Chicago Health System Privacy Program. Karen has master's degrees in Business Administration and Clinical Social Work with the following certifications and licensure: CCEP, CHC, CHPC, CHRC, CDPSE, and LCSW, ACSW in clinical social work. Previously, she worked in the Compliance Department at The Joint Commission and as the Corporate Compliance and Quality Officer for a healthcare start up. She is elected to the AAMC Compliance Officer Forum Steering Committee, co-leads a task group for the Health Sector Coordinating Council, and is active on a not-for-profit board. Karen speaks regularly on data use and disclosure, privacy risk management and data valuation, and joint privacy and security strategic initiatives.

Rebecca Herold has 30+ years of security and privacy experience. She is the Founder of The Privacy Professor Consultancy (2004) and Privacy & Security Brainiacs SaaS services (2021). Rebecca co-authored NIST catalogs NISTIR 7628, NISTIR 8259, SP 800-213, NISTIR 8425, and TN 2066. Rebecca has served as an expert witness for cases covering HIPAA, criminals using IoT devices, stolen personal data of retirement housing residents, and tracking app users with Meta pixels. Rebecca hosts Data Security & Privacy with the Privacy Professor. Rebecca authored 22 books and for 9.5 years was adjunct professor for the Norwich University MSISA program.

Conor Hogan is a passionate privacy advocate, trust advisor, and risk consultant with more than 15 years' experience advising clients around the world. He currently oversees BSI Group's global privacy, eDiscovery, and digital forensics teams delivering strategic advisory and operational support to clients across Europe, the Americas, and Asia. Conor is a regular industry contributor, thought leader, and privacy-by-design advocate. He holds numerous qualifications and is a member of IOPD's Standards Committee. In his spare time, Conor plays American Football, mentors at his local Coder-Dojo, and enjoys spending time with his family and going to the gym.

Jeff Jockisch is a data privacy researcher and the CEO of PrivacyPlan. He does original research, consults on privacy strategy and data governance, advises privtech startups, and hosts a live weekly show called Your Bytes Your Rights. He is the Lead Data Steward at the Data Collaboration Alliance, helping build a Collaborative Privacy community.

Jeff is unique in his work creating and managing data sets about data privacy. His independent research focuses on privacy-enhancing tech, privacy regulations, AI, and more, all in an effort to gain insight into the privacy landscape.

Before focusing on privacy and certifying as a CIPP/US, Jeff studied Organizational Behavior at Cornell and spent 20+ years in tech startups, including building mortgage information systems and search engines. His understanding of data, data science, and data governance is academic and operational, deriving from experience designing knowledge graphs, working with big data, creating taxonomies and classifiers, managing data quality, and building content management systems.

Jeff is passionate about issues such as digital identity, data brokers, and data subject access requests. He also tracks, rates, and ranks privacy podcasts and runs his own show, *Your Bytes = Your Rights*, a weekly audio event that brings experts from different disciplines together to discuss, data ownership, digital rights, and data privacy.

Odia Kagan is a Partner and Chair of GDPR Compliance & International Privacy Practice at Fox Rothschild LLP, a US national law firm. Odia has advised more than 200 companies of varying industries and sizes on compliance with GDPR, the California Consumer Privacy Act (CCPA), and other US data protection laws. With an emphasis on a pragmatic, risk-based approach, Odia provides clients with practical advice on how to design and implement their products and services in a compliant manner. Odia holds three law degrees, five bar admissions, and seven privacy certifications (CIPP/US/E, CIPM, CDPO, C-GDPR/P, FIP, PLS). You can follow her on https://www.linkedin.com/in/odiakagan/ or Twitter at @ odiakagan.

Barbara Lawler is a three-time CPO and is the President of the Information Accountability Foundation. Previously she was VP, Chief Privacy and Data Ethics Officer at Looker (Google Cloud acquisition), and CPO of Intuit and Hewlett Packard. She received the 2022 IAPP Vanguard Award and is a Westin Emeritus Fellow. She is a globally recognized executive with a track record shaping the thinking of policymakers on data policy issues, including delivering testimony to the US House and Senate, IRS, and FTC. She holds a IAPP CIPM and CIPP/US, is a graduate of San Jose State University, and is a member of the Internet Ethics advisory board to the Santa Clara University Markkula Center for Applied Ethics.

Caroline Louveaux leads Mastercard's work at the forefront of privacy and data policy, regulatory and legal compliance globally. She advises the company on issues supporting Mastercard's data and technology leadership, including privacy, cybersecurity, open banking, data flows, digital identity, blockchain, and AI.

Caroline serves on the Executive Board of the International Association of Privacy Professionals (IAPP). She is a member of the UK International Data Transfers Expert Council and the German Marshall Fund Taskforce to promote trusted data sharing. She is also a member of the ENISA Working Group on AI Cybersecurity and co-chairs the I-COM Data

Ethics Council. Caroline is a lecturer at Carnegie Mellon's School of Computer Science, Oxford Cyber Futures, and IMD Business School.

Sayid Madar is a UAE-based data protection and privacy leader with an LLM in Information Rights Law from Northumbria University. He is the Head of Operations at the ADGM Office of the Data Protection Commissioner. Sayid represents the Commissioner at the Global Privacy Assembly (GPA), the International Enforcement Cooperation Working Group (IECWG), and the Council of Europe's Convention 108. He has over a decade of experience in global privacy compliance and is designated IAPP Fellow of Information Privacy (FIP), a Certified Information Privacy Professional/Europe (CIPP/E), and a Certified Information Privacy Manager (CIPM). He was formerly the Global Privacy Lead at Etihad Aviation Group. He was also a Lead Enforcement Officer at the UK Information Commissioner's Office.

Federico Marengo is a data protection consultant who works for White Label Consultancy. He is a privacy and AI enthusiast that helps companies in the implementation of privacy programs and in the application of data protection in advanced and complex data privacy domains.

Stephen Massey is the Managing Director of Fox Red Risk, a cybersecurity and data protection consultancy in the UK. Stephen's knowledge is derived from delivering complex governance and oversight programs across defense, real estate, edtech, fintech, and financial services over the last 20 years. Stephen holds CIPP-E, CIPM, and CISSP certifications and has authored *The Ultimate GDPR Practitioner Guide*, now in its second edition. Stephen also has a passion for research and is currently working toward his PhD seeking to derive novel approaches to managing technical debt at the University of Birmingham, England.

Kirk J. Nahra is a partner with WilmerHale in Washington, DC, where he is co-chair of the firm's Cybersecurity and Privacy Practice and Big Data Practice. He assists companies in a wide range of industries and of all sizes in analyzing and implementing the requirements of privacy and security laws across the country and internationally. He teaches privacy and security law issues at several law schools, including serving as an adjunct professor at the Washington College of Law at American University and at Case Western Reserve University. He received the 2021 Privacy Vanguard Award from the International Association of Privacy Professionals in recognition of his "exceptional leadership, knowledge and creativity in privacy and data protection". He also serves as a mentor to college students and law students.

Rob Norris, CIPP/E joined Cushman & Wakefield in 2019, initially to lead its EMEA privacy program and was promoted to Chief Privacy Officer in 2021. His responsibilities are to deliver privacy compliance globally, provide expertise to colleagues, and drive a continuous improvement privacy program to support its strategy and goals. Rob previously worked as a privacy consultant, supporting clients in life sciences, financial services, and utilities. Rob has a passion for privacy combined with pragmatism and a strong delivery focus.

Chris Novak is the Managing Director of Verizon Cyber Security Consulting. He has 20+ years of cybersecurity industry experience ranging from field work to Fortune 100 C-Suite and board advisory roles. In 2022, he was appointed to President Biden's Cyber Safety Review Board and named a Top Cybersecurity Leader by *Security Magazine*. He has been featured in TV, radio, and print media. He is also a member of the Forbes Technology Council, where he frequently writes on the topic of cybersecurity. Chris holds a bachelor's degree in Computer Engineering from Rensselaer Polytechnic Institute, a CISO Certificate from Carnegie Mellon, and maintains a variety of industry certifications.

Dan Or-Hof, Adv., Esq., CIPP/E, CIPP/US, CIPM is a New York and Israeli attorney. He has founded Or-Hof Law and the Strand Alliance, an international privacy and cybersecurity alliance of top boutique firms, both with a vision to create an environment of excellence with a personal touch. He holds an LLM degree from UC Berkeley and the Tel Aviv University (summa cum laude) and he is a certified privacy professional (CIPP/E; CIPP/US, CIPM, FIP). Dan lectures at the Tel Aviv University, and he has authored guides, opinions, articles, and position papers on data privacy. He is a frequent speaker and commentator, and he is chairing and a member of privacy-related boards and forums.

Theresa Payton, a globally renowned expert on secured digital transformation. She is the Founder and CEO of Fortalice Solutions. Theresa was the first woman to serve as Chief Information Officer at the White House during the George W. Bush Administration. She is recognized globally as a strategic advisor to executives and board of directors for providing sound advice on cybersecurity topics. Theresa is the author of several books including *Manipulated: Inside the Cyberwar to Hijack Elections* and *Distort the Truth and Privacy in the Age of Big Data* being released in March 2023. Cybersecurity Ventures has named Theresa one of the 100 most influential people in cybersecurity.

Jules Polonetsky serves as CEO of the Future of Privacy Forum, a Washington, DC-based non-profit organization that serves as a catalyst for privacy leadership and scholarship, advancing principled data practices in support of emerging technologies. FPF is supported by the chief privacy officers of more than 200 leading companies, several foundations, as well as by an advisory board composed of the country's leading academics and advocates. FPF's current projects focus on AI and Ethics, Connected Cars,

Health, Research Data, Smart Communities, Ad Tech, Youth, Ed Tech, Privacy Legislation and Enforcement, and Global Data Flows.

Dr. Larry Ponemon is the Chairman and Founder of the Ponemon Institute and is considered a pioneer in privacy auditing and the Responsible Information Management or RIM framework. Dr. Ponemon was appointed to the Advisory Committee for Online Access & Security for the United States Federal Trade Commission. He was appointed by the White House to the Data Privacy and Integrity Advisory Committee for the Department of Homeland Security. Dr. Ponemon earned his PhD at Union College. He has a master's degree from Harvard University and attended the doctoral program in system sciences at Carnegie Mellon University. Dr. Ponemon earned his bachelor's degree with Highest Distinction from the University of Arizona, Tucson, Arizona. He is a Certified Public Accountant and a Certified Information Privacy Professional.

Mark Rasch is a lawyer and computer security and privacy expert and a lawyer in Bethesda, Maryland and is Of Counsel with the law firm of Kohrman, Jackson, and Krantz. He is the General Counsel of Threat Intelligence firm Unit 221B.

Rasch's career spans more than 35 years of corporate and government cybersecurity, computer privacy, regulatory compliance, computer forensics, and incident response. This includes expertise in GDPR, CCPA, and US and international privacy laws and regulations. Earlier in his career, Rasch was with the US Department of Justice where he led the department's efforts to investigate and prosecute cyber and high-technology crime, starting the computer crime unit within the Criminal Division's Fraud Section, efforts which eventually led to the creation of the Computer Crime and Intellectual Property Section of the Criminal Division. He was responsible for various high-profile computer crime prosecutions, including Kevin Mitnick, Kevin Poulsen, and Robert Tappan Morris. He was also the Chief Privacy Officer of Fortune 100 company, SAIC and Chief Security Evangelist for Verizon.

Mark is a frequent commentator in the media on issues related to information security and is the author of hundreds of articles about Internet, Internet privacy, hacking, cryptocurrency, blockchain, and ransomware and is an adjunct professor of Law at the George Washington University School of Law.

T. Andrew Reeder serves as Associate Vice President and Privacy Officer for Rush University Medical Center/Rush Oak Park Hospital and other associated entities in Chicago, IL. In this role, Andy provides leadership in achieving regulatory compliance around information protection requirements with major responsibilities including privacy incident response and investigation; privacy breach response; HIPAA privacy compliance;

coordination of patient privacy rights fulfillment; risk assessment; policy development; and awareness around top privacy risks. Andy also serves as Adjunct Faculty in the College of Computing and Digital Media (CDM) at DePaul University where he teaches topics on cybersecurity, privacy, and information assurance at the graduate and undergraduate levels.

Debbie Reynolds "The Data Diva" is a leading voice in Data Privacy and Emerging Technology. With 20+ years of experience, she is a trusted advisor and thought leader in industries such as AdTech, FinTech, EdTech, Biometrics, and IoT. As CEO of Debbie Reynolds Consulting LLC, she combines technical expertise, business acumen, and advocacy. She is a sought-after speaker, media personality, and recipient of numerous honors and awards, including the host of the #1 award-winning "The Data Diva" Talks Privacy Podcast, a spot in the Global Top Eight Privacy Experts, and the Global Top 30 CyberRisk Communicators. Debbie is dedicated to advancing the field of data privacy and shaping its future.

Dr. Johnny Ryan FRHistS is a senior fellow at the Irish Council for Civil Liberties and a senior fellow at the Open Markets Institute. He was previously Chief Policy Officer at Brave Software. He is the author of several books.

Jennifer Schack, CIPP-US/E, CIPM, FIP is an accomplished leader with over 25 years of experience in project management, compliance management, privacy, and organizational leadership. She was the Global Head of Privacy for a Fortune 500 company before turning her attention to lead on data privacy for Big 5 technology companies, including Google. At Google, Jennifer is a privacy engagement leader helping bridge the gap between privacy, technology, and business. Jennifer is also actively involved in the IAPP where she served two years on the Training Advisory Board and is now serving on the Educational Advisory Board. She has her CIPP-E, CIPP-US, and CIPM certifications and has been awarded a Fellow of Information Privacy (FIP) designation by the IAPP.

Lena Lindgren Schelin was appointed Director General of the Swedish Authority for Privacy Protection in 2018. Prior to the appointment, she was Head of the Legal Division at the Swedish Economic Crime Authority (2011–2018) and Deputy Manager of the Legal Division at the Swedish School Inspectorate (2008–2011). She has a PhD in Procedural Law from the University of Stockholm (2006).

Nubiaa Shabaka serves as Vice President, Global Chief Cybersecurity Legal and Privacy Officer for Adobe. Her responsibilities encompass overseeing all aspects of Adobe's global data protection and privacy programs and all legal aspects of Adobe's global cybersecurity and information security programs on an enterprise-wide basis. Immediately prior to joining Adobe in September 2022, Nubiaa served as Global Chief Cybersecurity

Legal and Privacy Officer for AIG. Prior to joining AIG in January 2019, Nubiaa worked at Morgan Stanley for 11 years in similar privacy and security leadership roles, including Head of Global Cybersecurity Legal and Americas Head of Privacy and Data Protection. Nubiaa started her career as a technology associate in Proskauer Rose's New York office. She earned a Bachelor of Arts, magna cum laude, from New York University and a JD from Harvard Law School. Nubiaa is based in New York.

Stuart S. Shapiro is a Principal Cyber Security and Privacy Engineer and a co-leader of the Privacy Capability in the MITRE Labs Cyber Solutions Innovation Center at the MITRE Corporation. At MITRE, he has led multiple research and operational efforts in the areas of privacy engineering, privacy risk management, and privacy enhancing technologies (PETs), including projects focused on connected vehicles and on de-identification. He has also held academic positions and has taught courses on the history, politics, and ethics of information and communication technologies. His professional affiliations include the International Association of Privacy Professionals (IAPP) and the Association for Computing Machinery (ACM).

Michael W. Smith is a Data Privacy Leader and former Chief Privacy Officer with an overall privacy experience of more than ten years. Michael's focus has been in financial services, covering US privacy laws and regulations, primarily, while evaluating worldwide privacy laws for global operations and extraterritorial impact. He helped build the central US privacy function in a large international financial institution. In addition, Michael has experience in banking compliance, operations, fraud prevention, training, and process improvement. Prior to joining corporate America, Michael spent nine years as an officer in the US Navy.

Daniel J. Solove is the Eugene L. and Barbara A. Bernard Professor of Intellectual Property and Technology Law at George Washington University Law School and author of *Understanding Privacy* (Harvard University Press 2008). He also is the founder and CEO of TeachPrivacy, a company that provides computer-based privacy and data security training to organizations around the world.

Judy Titera with more than 25 years of experience in the privacy field, Judy holds numerous privacy and related designations and certifications and earned an Executive MBA from UW-Milwaukee, her hometown. Judy is a privacy evangelist/ardent privacy campaigner who recognizes that privacy can look and feel different to each person and company. She believes that understanding one's own educated privacy philosophy and approach is critical, and she enjoys listening, learning, and sharing privacy perspectives and insights.

Patti Titus is the Chief Privacy and Information Security Officer at Markel Corporation. Previously, Ms. Titus was the Vice President and Chief

Information Security Officer (CISO) at Freddie Mac, Symantec, Unisys, and the Transportation Security Administration. Ms. Titus was awarded the CISO Connect Trailblazer Award by her peers in 2022 and received her Boardroom Certified Qualified Technical Expert from the Digital Directors Network in 2023. She serves on the Board of Directors for Black Kite and Girl Scouts for the Commonwealth of Virginia and is on the Advisory Board for The Executive Women's Forum and Glasswing Ventures.

Ian Travers, beginning his career in the Communications and Information Services of the Irish Defence Forces, he rose to the level of senior manager, where he had the privilege to lead technical teams operating and securing mission critical communication networks and systems. Since joining the private sector, he has worked with Irish-based cybersecurity and data protection advisory, BH Consulting. Working in its international client base, he delivers Chief Information Security Officer as a Service, assisting clients align cybersecurity with their business goals.

Dr. Lisa van der Werff is an associate professor of Organizational Psychology and Director of Doctoral Studies at DCU Business School. She is Co-Director of the Irish Institute of Digital Business where she leads trust-LAB, a research group focused on trust between people, people and organizations, and people and technology. Lisa is Deputy Editor in Chief of the *Journal of Trust Research* and President of FINT, an international network of multidisciplinary trust researchers (www.fintweb.org).

Fabrizio Venturelli has extensive experience on data protection matters focusing both on core GDPR issues such as Data Protection Impact Assessment, Privacy by Design, International Data Transfers, and on public policy engagements, building strong and trusted relationships with Data Protection Authorities and relevant public bodies. He has worked as DPO for European, Asian, and US multinational organizations. He has a legal background, and, among others, he is CIPP/E and ITIL v3 certified, One Trust Privacy Connect Chair, Industry Panellist for the Privacy Shield Renewal (Brussels 2018 and Washington D.C. 2019), Member of the Irish DPO Network Committee, Corporate representative of the American Chamber of Commerce Data Committee, Member of Steering Committee for the European Cloud Code of Conduct, and former IAPP Advisory Board Member.

Dr. Tim Walree is an assistant professor at the Radboud Business Law Institute and the Interdisciplinary Hub for Digitalization and Society (iHub), Radboud University (The Netherlands). He also works as Of Counsel at Freshfields Bruckhaus Deringer in Amsterdam. His doctoral thesis examined the extent to which the right to compensation (Article 82 GDPR) can help enforce data protection law in practice. Tim also worked as a privacy and data protection consultant at Deloitte.

Tom Walsh, CISSP began his career in information security in 1992 and has been a Certified Information Systems Security Professional (CISSP) in good standing since 1997. He is the Founder and Managing Partner of tw-Security, a nationally recognized healthcare security firm that began in 2003.

Tom has served as an expert witness for multiple legal firms. He was a co-author of four books on healthcare information security. He is frequently a speaker at national conventions and is often quoted in trade journals.

Amber Welch has a passion for building and improving operational privacy and data protection programs. A transplant from information security, Amber approaches privacy risk management with a collaborative inter-disciplinary style and maturity framework perspective, achieving privacy outcomes through technical controls. Amber has directed programs across the Americas, APAC, and EMEA in industries as diverse as healthcare data analytics, educational technology and publishing, and hospitality SaaS software. As a Senior Privacy Architect at Amazon Web Services (AWS), Amber helps organizations grow their understanding of how to achieve privacy and data protection outcomes in a cloud environment.

Chapter structure

The format of this book presents each chapter together with a series of stories from privacy leaders from around the globe discussing their short, personal stories of the challenges, successes, lessons learned, and sharing of their insights:

Chapter 1. "The privacy landscape: Context and challenges" begins with an outline of the evolution of the privacy landscape and of privacy legislation. It also discusses key differences in privacy terms and clarifies some differences between the US and the EU landscapes.

Chapter 2. "The McKinsey 7-S framework applied to privacy leadership" explains the framework developed in the 1980s by Tom Peters and Robert Waterman to structure our thinking around reviewing privacy program organizational effectiveness. For simplicity, this will be referred to as the 7-S Privacy Leadership Framework. To achieve this goal, the chapters in this book have been related to and organized around the 7 "Ss" of the McKinsey Framework. Ineffectiveness in anyone of these areas has the potential to impact the entire privacy program and negate investments made in other areas.

Chapter 3. "Developing an effective privacy program strategy" uses the framework defined in Chapter 2 as the privacy leader's roadmap for the rest of the book, whereby a 5-step process from creating the vision through to building an action plan is explained as well as an introduction to other techniques.

Chapter 4. "The privacy organization structure" examines the structure of key roles in privacy within the organization and focuses on the reporting structures of the CPO and the DPO.

Chapter 5. "Privacy frameworks, standards, and certifications" discusses the various frameworks and certifications that can be leveraged to help construct a privacy program.

Chapter 6. "Privacy risk governance" outlines the key factors of accountability and the systems to support accountability.

Chapter 7. "Privacy and data protection: Law and principles" explores the relevant privacy laws including the more recent EU General Data

Protection Regulation (GDPR), privacy nomenclature, data protection principles, etc.

Chapter 8. "Privacy, ethics, and responsible privacy" discusses privacy ethics and privacy as a part of the environmental, social, and governance agenda.

Chapter 9. "Forging and maintaining effective privacy teams" presents an overview of how to build and maintain team engagement and effectiveness using Belbin's Nine Team Roles, together with Beckhard's Goals Roles Processes, and the Interpersonal Behaviors (GRPI) model.

Chapter 10. "The privacy leader's key skills" explores the necessary skills that enable the privacy leader to communicate, negotiate, influence, maintain executive presence, present, listen, and achieve their goals. This chapter focuses on the assessment of and development of emotional intelligence for privacy leaders.

Chapter 11. "Privacy leadership styles" discusses key privacy leader styles via Daniel Goleman's theories of the Six Leadership Styles outlined in his seminal article "Leadership That Gets Results".

Chapter 12. "Privacy leadership: Beyond this book?" concludes the book with an overview of the next steps a privacy leader should take and the important factors beyond the 7-S Framework for the privacy leader to consider while developing a sustainable privacy program.

We summarize the chapter structures below:

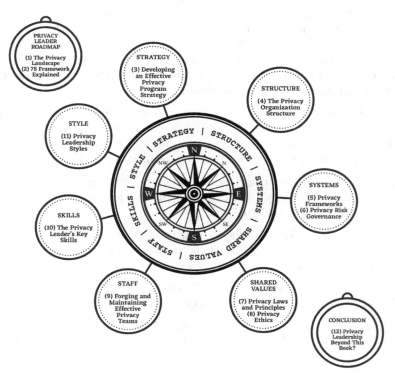

Introduction

> Many nations have developed privacy protection laws and regulations to guard against unfettered government and private use of personal information. While these protections are important first steps in protecting privacy, existing laws and their conceptual foundations have become outdated because of changes in technology.
>
> (Professor Kevin Laudon, 1944–2019)

One might be forgiven for thinking that Professor Laudon's assertions were written recently – however, they were written over 25 years ago. Today, privacy laws and data protection regulations continue to be the primary mechanism used by governments to guard against the misuse of personal data. However, despite a proliferation of privacy laws and data protection regulations globally, data breaches continue to rise in magnitude and frequency. For example, in the first quarter of 2022, data breaches were up 14% on 2021 with 20.8 million people impacted worldwide (Identity Theft Resource Center, 2022). Significant advances in technology, such as cloud computing, artificial intelligence (AI), and social media, consume large volumes of data, and are thus exacerbating the issue, for example, annual data volumes went from 2 zettabytes in 2010 to 41 zettabytes in 2019 (Statista, 2020). The costs of these breaches are also increasing, with the average cost of a data breach reaching $4.35 million in 2022, a 12.7% increase from 2021 and the highest ever noted (IBM and Ponemon Institute, 2022).

There are several challenges with the regulatory response to privacy challenges. First, the effectiveness of these laws and regulations in reducing breaches has been questioned with some studies suggesting that it is as low as 6% for preventing breaches. Second, regulations are often lagging the pace of technology by the time they are enacted. For example, the EU General Data Protection Regulation (GDPR) was in discussion for four years, before being approved by the EU Parliament in 2016, coming into force two years later. Third, the minimum regulatory requirements are often not well implemented, if at all. For example, after its 2009 breach, TJX was found to only comply with three of the 12 Payment Card Industry Data Security Standards (PCI DSS). Fourth, several recent studies have questioned the ability of privacy regulation to remain "fit for purpose", where advances such as big data and machine learning have raised not only classic concerns regarding consent, choice, and transparency but also concerns regarding due process, equal protection, data security, biased decision-making, and accountability. Finally, mandatory breach disclosure – a core element of these regulations – is predicated on detecting/prosecuting a violation after it has occurred, and the damage is done.

We, as privacy and cybersecurity leaders, need to consider revising our corporate approach to privacy by extending our lens beyond compliance to include other pillars of privacy that are equally important (e.g., privacy as a human right, privacy as an ethical and social concern, and privacy as a political and sociopolitical issue). Shifting from compliance to include these other pillars of privacy moves, the conversation beyond "doing privacy rights" and more toward "doing privacy right". This more holistic approach to privacy recognizes that useful or profitable does not equal sustainable and emphasizes responsibility over compliance. It is for this reason that we decided to write a book that considered an approach to building privacy programs that would address far more than simple regulation and incorporate all organizational activities influencing privacy risk and/or consumer attitudes.

The privacy leader's Compass is the second in the "*compass*" series of books. The first book, written by Todd Fitzgerald entitled *CISO COMPASS: Navigating Cybersecurity Leadership Challenges with Insights from Pioneers*, was the #1 best-selling book providing a comprehensive roadmap to help cybersecurity leaders navigate the challenges associated with building effective cybersecurity programs in their respective organizations.

Why did we then call this book the "The Privacy Leader Compass" and not some more exact terms such as The CPO Compass or The DPO Compass? Simply because there are so many roles that are involved in, or associated with, leading privacy, and so many variations on the title of those roles, such as "Privacy Officer", "Privacy Leader", and "Privacy Counsel". In addition to this, in certain cases, the DPO may take a senior role in privacy, depending on the context and regulatory environments. To ensure that the book reached the right audience, that is, all those responsible for leading privacy programs – we chose the term "Privacy Leaders". Why did we call the book "Compass?" This title was chosen to represent the key aim of the book – a tool/mechanism to help navigate or map challenging terrain.

The idea to write the book was born from a hunger for a body of work that would essentially represent this map, to help comprehensively navigate the world of privacy programs, and how to lead them. We searched to see what other books were already published that would fill this need and we could not find one. While we could find books that provided high-level guidance, we wanted something structured and meaty, something that would provide step-by-step guidance. Most books in the existing market outlined programs that addressed privacy as compliance. We wanted this book to extend beyond privacy as compliance – as privacy is so much more than mere compliance. We wanted to cover not just regulatory privacy, but also the ethical aspects of privacy, privacy as a corporate social responsibility (CSR), privacy as a corporate political activity (CPA), and more broadly – privacy as part of the environment, social, and governance (ESG) agenda. We also wanted a book that explained not only the key concepts of privacy and the key themes of a privacy program but also how to lead a privacy program and the attributes of the skilled leader. Both authors have assumed leadership roles in their respective careers and have amassed a wealth of experience: Todd has authored several books on Cybersecurity Leadership and led Cybersecurity Programs and developed privacy programs in partnership with privacy officers for several decades and Valerie holds a PhD in Information Privacy and a master's degree in leadership and has led cybersecurity and privacy teams for over 20 years. Most importantly, we wanted this book to highlight how privacy has the power to influence the bottom line in a positive way rather than be considered merely a cost of compliance. Agreeing that there was a gap that needed to be filled, we decided to put pen to paper and put our collective 80 years of experience together and co-author this book.

This book is groundbreaking, as it is the first to bring together leadership perspectives of European privacy and data protection from one cybersecurity and privacy leader (Dr. Valerie Lyons) with perspectives of US Privacy and Data protection from another cybersecurity and privacy leader (Todd Fitzgerald). In doing so, this book will be relevant and helpful to privacy leaders who work across jurisdictions and for privacy leadership audiences globally. Another ground-breaking contribution of this book is that Dr. Valerie Lyons brings her research to the fore on privacy as an ESG and thus presents a rather nascent lens into privacy beyond simple regulatory compliance. In this way, the reader should be able to have a comprehensive understanding of privacy across several dimensions, not just compliance. Finally, we leveraged the time-tested McKinsey7-S model for organizational effectiveness to structure our approach to building/maintaining a privacy program. This is important, as when we reviewed the current scholarship on privacy, we found it to be often "jumpy" and repetitive, particularly where there were multiple authors. We chose this model as it was applied in the CISO Compass book, and feedback from many readers of that best-selling book was that it was really an effective way to structure maturing the cybersecurity program. Thus, the focus of this book is maturing our privacy programs to incorporate the elements of the 7-S model to move to a higher level of organizational effectiveness, in this case, specifically with respect to leading a privacy program. To our knowledge, no privacy leadership book has leveraged this model or any another model geared toward managing the privacy program as a "business within a business", to present an effective privacy program to date. Finally, both authors have always also recognized the value of collaboration and the collective experience of others – as no man or woman is an island! So, we wanted this book to include contributions from key leaders in privacy and beyond. We really feel we have achieved this in this book. We wanted the book to represent the almanac of privacy, that is, if it's not in this book and it's related to leading privacy programs – we will eat our hats.

So perhaps you are a newly appointed Chief Privacy Officer (CPO) or Data Protection Officer (DPO)? Perhaps you are even a Chief Information Security Officer (CISO) or Chief Information Officer (CIO) or Chief Technology Officer (CTO) or General Counsel or Chief Legal Officer (CLO) with responsibility for privacy? Perhaps you are a consultant offering DPO or CPO advisory services? Perhaps you are a professor looking for a semester course on privacy program leadership? Perhaps you are a student studying privacy and data protection and want to understand "how it all fits together" in the workplace? Whatever journey you are on, whatever reason draws you to this book, we hope you find what you seek in the chapters within. If you take away one page that is the nugget you needed to find to make your journey easier, our job is done. While we cannot guarantee that all the answers to all your questions about privacy leadership are in here, we can guarantee that you will learn something new. How do we know this? Because, like the *CISO Compass* (the first book in this series), this book not only brings the knowledge of two experienced privacy and security authors to the fore but it also incorporates the knowledge of more than 60 pioneering privacy leaders (CPOs, DPOs, privacy and security leaders, professional association leaders, privacy standards setters, and privacy policymakers). This book provides insights from their experience to help build and lead a privacy program or to contribute to a privacy program that is already in place. Check out these privacy leaders' bios and past experiences highlighted in the contributor's section, and you will see they have done some amazing things, leading some of the most successful privacy programs in leading companies and creating today's standards and policies. Many of them heavily influenced the developing role of the privacy leader, privacy practices, and privacy legislation we have today. Each of them has taken time to share their expertise with you, the reader. Essentially, we are leveraging the principle of collaboration to incorporate the expertise others have in different aspects of leading privacy. We have enjoyed collaborating with the many experienced, incredibly skilled, knowledgeable, and talented people to put this book together, and we hope you enjoy reading it and refer to it from time to time as needed. There may also be a challenge you encounter in the future where you can reference this book as a response to provide a real, truthful, nonsalesy, straightforward, practical perspective as the leaders in this book have provided. We have brought some of the best minds in our networks to you, so please thank them for volunteering their insights when you see them speaking at a conference or in your networking travels.

Section I

The privacy leader roadmap

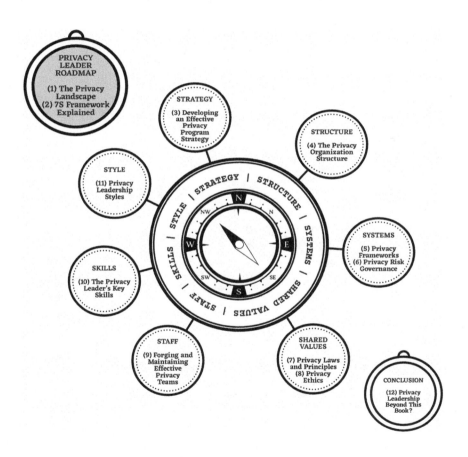

Chapter 1

The privacy landscape

Context and challenges

And I honor the man who is willing to sink
Half his present repute for the freedom to think,
And, when he has thought, be his cause strong or weak,
Will risk t' other half for the freedom to speak

James Russell Lowell, 1819–1891

WHAT IS PRIVACY?

Privacy is a construct/concept that encompasses a variety of core rights and values:

- Freedom of thought.
- Freedom of expression.
- Freedom from surveillance.
- Human dignity.
- Identity and anonymity.
- Secrecy.

Privacy is challenging not only because it is an all-encompassing concept that helps to safeguard important values such as human autonomy and dignity but also the means for achieving it can vary. For example, privacy can be achieved through seclusion, limiting observation, or individuals' control of facets of their identities (e.g., body, data, and reputation).

There is much confusion in both academia and industry about what exactly privacy is. The absence of a universally accepted definition of privacy is often attributed to the differing views toward privacy as either personal values or individual rights. There is also considerable lack of consensus as to whether privacy is a condition, a process, or a goal. Warren and Brandeis (1890) laid the foundation for the concept of privacy known as

DOI: 10.1201/9781003383017-2

"control over information about oneself", a concept endorsed by more recent classical commentators such as Alan Westin, Irwin Altman, and Stephen Margulis. For example, Westin (1967) defines privacy as the claim of individuals, groups, or institutions to control when, how, and to what extent information about them is communicated to others. Altman (1975) defines privacy as the mechanisms of control over the concealment of information, and Margulis (1977) defines privacy as the control of transactions between people rather than just information. However, the need for control over privacy is not static and evolves with time and context. Many of these definitions focus on privacy for individuals – however privacy is also valuable to social relations and society at large and regulates all our normal and ordinary social relationships: "privacy is necessary if we are to maintain the variety of social relationships with other people that we want to have, and that is why it is important to us" (Rachels, 1975). Privacy's value to society can also be understood from the perspective of democracy. Gavison (1980), for instance, argues that "privacy is also essential to democratic governance because it fosters and encourages the moral autonomy of the citizen, a central requirement for democracy". Privacy does not just place annoying restrictions on society's room for action but it is just as much an enabler of many valuable social practices. More recently, the National Institute of Standards and Technology (NIST) defined privacy in several different ways:

> "Assurance that the confidentiality of, and access to, certain information about an entity is protected".
> "Freedom from intrusion into the private life or affairs of an individual when that intrusion results from undue or illegal gathering and use of data about that individual".
> "The right of a party to maintain control over and confidentiality of information about itself".

The one theme consistent across all definitions is the concept of privacy as "control".

Roger Clarke (2006) notes how people often think of privacy as some kind of right which is problematical because it's too easy to get confused between legal rights and natural/moral rights. Clarke defines privacy as a series of interests that individuals have in sustaining "personal space", free from interference by other people and organizations. These interests are:

- Privacy of the person, sometimes referred to as "bodily privacy".
- Privacy of personal behavior.

- Privacy of personal experience.
- Privacy of personal communications.
- Privacy of personal data.

With the close coupling that has occurred between computing and communications, Clarke notes it is useful to use the term "information privacy" to refer to the combination of the final two interests: *Personal communications privacy* and *personal data privacy*. Like privacy, many of the definitions of information privacy lean on the conceptualization of "control" over the terms under which personal information is acquired and used by an organization. According to Clarke (2006), information privacy is defined as "the interest an individual has in controlling, or at least significantly influencing, the handling of data about themselves." Societal discourse equates privacy, information privacy, and data privacy – and the terms are often used interchangeably. We suspect that this is why there are so many definitions of both information privacy and data privacy that differ. In fact, NIST does not define information privacy or data privacy in its privacy framework.

The most universally accepted definition of information privacy comes from Daniel Solove (2006) who defined information privacy as an umbrella term for a set of privacy problems resulting from information collection, information processing, information dissemination, and privacy-invasion activities. Solove argued that information privacy is the relief from a range of kinds of social friction and enables people to engage in worthwhile activities in ways that they would otherwise find difficult or impossible. Solove developed "A Taxonomy of Privacy" to categorize the different harms that may arise from infringements in information privacy. Solove based this taxonomy on tort scholar William Prosser's work, who distinguished four different types of harmful activities under the privacy blanket:

- Intrusion upon the plaintiff's seclusion or solitude, or into his private affairs.
- Public disclosure of embarrassing private facts about the plaintiff.
- Publicity which places the plaintiff in a false light in the public eye.
- Appropriation, for the defendant's advantage, of the plaintiff's name or likeness.

Jason Cronk of Enterprise Consulting, in partnership with IAPP (International Association of Privacy Professionals) presents a detailed infographic on the taxonomy – see Figure 1.1.

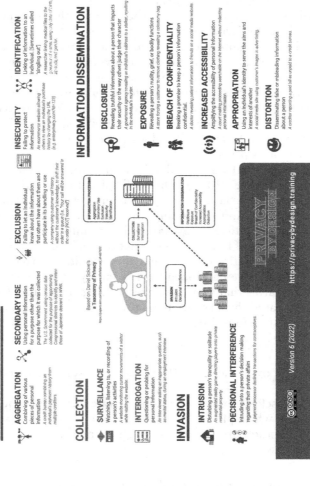

Figure 1.1 Solove's taxonomy of privacy.

(Source: Enterprise Consulting Group, Reprinted with Permission.)

UNDERSTANDING PRIVACY

Daniel J. Solove

Professor of Intellectual Property and Technology Law,
George Washington University Law School

Many attempts to conceptualize privacy do so by attempting to locate the common denominator for all things we view as private. This method of conceptualizing privacy, however, faces a difficult dilemma. If we choose a common denominator that is broad enough to encompass nearly everything, then the conception risks the danger of being overinclusive or too vague. If we choose a narrower common denominator, then the risk is that the conception is too restrictive. There is a way out of this dilemma: We can conceptualize privacy in a different way. Privacy is not one thing, but a plurality of many distinct yet related things. The focal point for a theory of privacy should be on the problems we want the law to address. Privacy problems arise when the activities of the government, businesses, organizations, and other people disrupt the activities of others. Real problems exist, yet they are often ignored because they do not fit into a particular conception of privacy. Many problems are not even recognized because courts or policymakers can't identify a "privacy" interest involved. Instead of pondering the nature of privacy in the abstract, we should begin with concrete problems and then use theory to better understand and resolve these problems.

There are four basic groups of harmful activities: (1) information collection, (2) information processing, (3) information dissemination, and (4) invasion. Each of these groups, as shown in Figure 1.2, consists of different related subgroups of harmful activities.

I have arranged these groups around a model that begins with the data subject – the individual whose life is most directly affected by the activities classified in the taxonomy. From that individual, various entities (other people, businesses, and the government) engage in *Information Collection*. The collection of this information itself can constitute a harmful activity, though not all information collection is harmful. *Surveillance* is the watching, listening to, or recording of an individual's activities. *Interrogation* consists of various forms of questioning or probing for information.

Those that collect the data (the "data holders") then process it – that is, they store, combine, manipulate, search, and use it. I label these activities *Information Processing. Aggregation* involves the combination of various pieces of data about a person. *Identification* is linking information to particular individuals. *Insecurity*

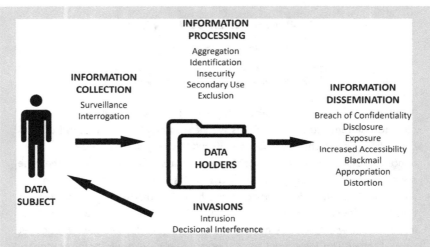

Figure 1.2 Understanding privacy: Subgroups of harmful activities.

(Source: Daniel J. Solove, Reprinted with Permission.)

involves carelessness in protecting stored information from leaks and improper access. *Secondary use* is the use of collected information for a purpose different from the use for which it was collected without the data subject's consent. *Exclusion* concerns the failure to allow the data subject to know about the data that others have about her and participate in its handling and use. These activities do not involve the gathering of data because it has already been collected. Instead, these activities involve the way data is maintained and used.

The next step is *Information Dissemination*, in which the data holders transfer the information to others or release the information. The general progression from information collection to processing to dissemination is the data moving further away from the individual's control. *Breach of confidentiality* is breaking a promise to keep a person's information confidential. *Disclosure* involves the revelation of truthful information about a person that affects the way others judge her reputation. *Exposure* involves revealing another's nudity, grief, or bodily functions. *Increased accessibility* is amplifying the accessibility of information. *Blackmail* is the threat to disclose personal information. *Appropriation* involves the use of the data subject's identity to serve another's aims and interests. *Distortion* consists of disseminating false or misleading information about individuals. Information-dissemination activities all involve the spreading or transfer of personal data or the threat to do so.

The last grouping of activities is *Invasions*, which involve impingements directly on the individual. Instead of the progression away from the individual, invasions progress toward the individual and do not necessarily involve information. Invasions, unlike the other groupings, need not involve personal information (although in numerous instances, it does). *Intrusion* concerns invasive acts that disturb one's tranquility or solitude. *Decisional interference* involves an incursion into the data subject's decisions regarding her private affairs.

I discuss the details in more depth in my book, *Understanding Privacy*, but the key point is that privacy is not one thing, but many distinct but related things. Understanding privacy in this way will hopefully help add clarity and concreteness to a concept that has been shrouded in a fog of confusion for far too long.

HOW DOES THE TERM PRIVACY DIFFER FROM DATA PROTECTION?

Each year, on 28 January, Data Protection Day (known in the United States as Data Privacy Day) is celebrated globally. It is currently observed in the United States, Canada, Nigeria, Israel, and 47 European countries. (In 2022, it was extended to Data Privacy Week, reflecting the importance of and need for time to celebrate this event and to highlight its importance.)

So how did the day come about? Back in April 2006, the Council of Europe decided to launch a Data Protection Day and it chose to commemorate the date when the Council of Europe's data protection convention, known as Convention 108, was opened for signature. Three years later, on 26 January 2009, the United States House of Representatives declared 28 January as National Data Privacy Day. The objective of the day was the same as Data Protection Day – but why would the United States call it something different? The answer to this question is key to understanding how different countries approach and interpret the safeguarding of personal data. The terms "data protection" and "data privacy" are often used interchangeably, but the context underpinning them provides an important insight into the different approaches in the EU and the US toward protecting personal data.

A cursory web search of the terms "data privacy" and "data protection" results in a myriad of widely differing and misaligned definitions. In the context of globalization and multinational data processing and data interactions, the issue of definitional ambiguity and the interchangeable use of these terms has become challenging, as their meanings are quite different in the US and the EU. Looking into the future, for a globalized and integrated digital world to operate effectively, we will need to have definitions of data protection and data privacy and to align the use of the terms across borders. In the meantime, we first address the actual definitions of these terms and our use of them in this book.

Privacy (as a right): Privacy is a fundamental right. According to Privacy International, it is

> essential to autonomy and the protection of human dignity, serving as the foundation upon which many other human rights are built. Privacy enables us to create barriers and manage boundaries to protect ourselves from unwarranted interference in our lives, which allows us to negotiate who we are and how we want to interact with the world around us. Privacy helps us establish boundaries to limit who has access to our bodies, places, and things, as well as our communications and our information.

The right to privacy is articulated in all the major international and regional human rights instruments, including:

1) United Nations Declaration of Human Rights (UNDHR) 1948, Article 12: "No one shall be subjected to arbitrary interference with his privacy, family, home or correspondence, nor to attacks upon his honor and reputation. Everyone has the right to the protection of the law against such interference or attacks."
2) International Covenant on Civil and Political Rights (ICCPR) 1966, Article 17: "1. No one shall be subjected to arbitrary or unlawful interference with his privacy, family, home or correspondence, nor to unlawful attacks on his honor or reputation. 2. Everyone has the right to the protection of the law against such interference or attacks."

The right to privacy is also included in, but not limited to:

- Article 14 of the United Nations Convention on Migrant Workers.
- Article 16 of the UN Convention on the Rights of the Child.
- Article 11 of the American Convention on Human Rights.
- Article 5 of the American Declaration of the Rights and Duties of Man.
- Article 21 of the ASEAN Human Rights Declaration.
- Article 8 of the European Convention on Human Rights.
- Privacy (as it relates to personal data).

In the EU, the right to privacy as it applies to personal data is typically referred to as "data protection". Hence, the EU GDPR is named the General Data Protection Regulation. In the US, data protection refers to the processes and controls in place to protect data, including PII, along with corporate and system data. In the US, data privacy (sometimes called information privacy) refers to not only data protection in the US interpretation of the word but also data security. In the EU, however, data protection refers to the legally required controls and processes (both privacy and security) that apply to personal data only and includes several data subject rights over personal data. Hence, the US has the California Consumer *Privacy* Act and not the California Consumer *Data Protection* Act. In fact, if the US ever creates a federal harmonized legislation in this domain, it would most likely be referred to as the Federal Consumer *Privacy* Act.

In this book, to avoid confusion, we use the term privacy in its US context, but mean data protection in its EU context.

PRIVACY AS A GATEWAY RIGHT TO FREEDOM OF THOUGHT

Dr. Susie Alegre

Digital Rights Expert, Futurist, Author, and Speaker, Alegre Consulting

The UN Guidelines on Business and Human Rights require businesses to respect human rights. Privacy is a standalone right protected in domestic and international human rights law. But it also operates as a gateway to many other fundamental rights including the absolute right to freedom of thought. The protection of personal data is key to the enjoyment of human rights in the digital age and businesses and public institutions alike need to understand how their use of data can impact on human rights more broadly.

It is not just the nature of data or who has the data that matters, it is what the data is used for. The right to freedom of thought, for example, includes the right to keep our thoughts private, not to have our thoughts manipulated, and not to be penalized for our thoughts alone. That freedom, as it relates to our inner lives, is protected absolutely so there can be no justification for violating it. But many innovations in technology involve using data to try to understand what individuals are thinking or feeling and to use that information to alter how they think or feel or to judge them based on an assessment of their emotional state or inferences about their thoughts. Using data in these ways could amount to a violation of the right to freedom of thought.

In "Freedom to Think", I identify some of the use cases that raise concerns and call for businesses, technologists, and investors in new technologies to take a proactive approach to the potential human rights implications of their work to avoid devastating unintended consequences. Understanding how your business could impact the human rights of users or the wider public is crucial, for compliance, but also for the future of all our communities. The future of innovation depends on freedom of thought, it is in all our interests to protect it, now and for the future.

HOW DOES PRIVACY DIFFER FROM INFORMATION SECURITY/CYBERSECURITY?

Although privacy and information security are different disciplines, they are also complementary. Privacy relates to any rights you have to control your personal information and how it's used. Privacy establishes a normative framework for deciding who should legitimately have the capability to access and alter information, and security implements those choices. Information security, in contrast to privacy, is the set of technological mechanisms (including, at times, physical ones) that mediates requests for access or control. Information security can be required to provide confidentiality and integrity for information that is not personal such as router port addresses, system names, and application credentials, etc. In this case, privacy is not required as the information does not relate to personal information. In this way, one can have information security without privacy but not privacy without information security.

Think, for example, of a window on a building; without it being in place an intruder can sneak in and violate both the privacy and security of the occupants. Once the window is mounted it will deter unwanted parties from getting into the building thus providing security. It won't prevent them from peeking in, thus providing no privacy protection. At least not without a curtain. The window is a security control by keeping the intruders outside, while the curtain is a privacy control by providing control to the owner of the house as to who can see inside, and when.

Then what about the difference between information security and cybersecurity? Today the term cybersecurity is often used interchangeably with the term information security; however, the two are in fact different. The word "cyber" has Greek roots (roughly meaning one who guides a boat, such as a pilot or rudder operator). In the 20th century, American mathematician and philosopher Norbert Wiener coined the word "cybernetics", borrowing from Greek roots to refer to intelligent controllers, and he indicated that they would be difficult to design and build. Fiction novelist William Gibson foresaw the space of virtual interactions in his 1984 novel Neuromancer and coined this "cyberspace", borrowing the prefix "cyber" from Wiener. In the CISM manual (as depicted in Figure 1.3), cybersecurity and information security are represented as separate entities, which overlap with "digital information".

NIST defines information security as

> the protection of information and information systems from unauthorized access, use, disclosure, disruption, modification, or destruction in order to provide confidentiality, integrity, and availability.

Where in the NIS II Directive, cybersecurity is defined as

> the activities necessary to protect network and information systems, the users of such systems and other person affected by cyber threats.

Information Security Versus Cybersecurity

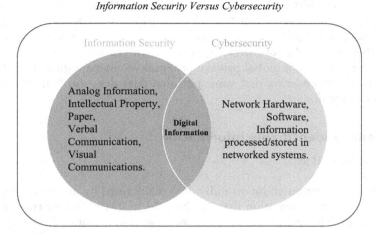

Figure 1.3 Differences between information security and cybersecurity.
(Source: ISACA Cybersecurity Fundamentals Security Guide, 3rd edition, USA, 2021.)

In 2013, Gartner acknowledged that there was confusion in the market over how the term should be used and published a research paper to help define cybersecurity as distinct from information security. The paper noted that the "use of the term Cybersecurity as a synonym for information security/IT security, confuses customers and security practitioners, and obscures critical differences between these disciplines". To help set the record straight, the paper defined the term:

> Cybersecurity encompasses a broad range of practices, tools and concepts related closely to those of information and operational technology security. Cybersecurity is distinctive in its inclusion of the offensive use of information technology to attack adversaries.

The paper further clarified that:

> Cybersecurity is a superset of the practices embodied in IT security, information security, operational technology (OT) security and offensive security.

Considering these definitions, it would seem that information security is an umbrella term describing many activities related to, among other things – cybersecurity, cryptography, mobile computing etc.

VARIOUS TERMS USED TO DESCRIBE AN INDIVIDUAL'S DATA

There is much confusion about the different terms used to describe an individual's information, and they are often used interchangeably depending on where an individual is from, for example, from the US or the EU. "Personally Identifiable Information (PII)" is often considered a US term, where the term "personal data" is often considered to be the EU equivalent of PII. Nonetheless, they do not correspond exactly with each other. It is important to highlight that in a global privacy program – understanding their differences is key to ensuring that some personal data does not "fall out of the net" so to speak.

Personally identifiable information

NIST defines PII as

> any information about an individual maintained by an agency, including (1) any information that can be used to distinguish or trace an individual's identity, such as name, social security number, date and place of birth, mother's maiden name, or biometric records; and (2) any other information that is linked or linkable to an individual, such as medical, educational, financial, and employment information.

PII can be categorized into two dimensions – Linked PII and Linkable PII. Linked PII is a piece of data that is unique to an individual and can be used as an identifier in isolation. Linkable PII is data that can't be used to track an individual on its own. One may have to combine some other data with it to be able to identify someone. Examples of such information are cookies, IP addresses, mobile IDs, postal codes, non-specific age, etc.

Personal data/personal information

In the GDPR personal data is defined as:

> any information relating to an identified or identifiable natural person ('data subject'); an identifiable natural person is one who can be identified, directly or indirectly, in particular by reference to an identifier such as a name, an identification number, location data, an online identifier or to one or more factors specific to the physical, physiological, genetic, mental, economic, cultural or social identity of that natural person.

In other countries with privacy protection laws derived from the principles outlined in the OECD privacy guidelines, the term often used is "personal information". To add confusion to this confusion – "personal information" is also defined in a section of the California data breach notification law (SB1386) as:

> an individual's first name or first initial and last name in combination with any one or more of the following data elements, when either the

name or the data elements are not encrypted: (1) Social security number. (2) Driver's license number or California Identification Card number. (3) Account number, credit or debit card number, in combination with any required security code, access code, or password that would permit access to an individual's financial account. SB1386 also notes that 'personal information' does not include publicly available information that is lawfully made available to the public from federal, state, or local government records.

Table 1.1 presents an overview of categories of personal data.

Table 1.1 Types of personal data

Category name	Information description	Examples
Name	A person's name	Elmer Fudd
Contact details	A person's addresses	Physical address, email, and telephone numbers.
Electronic identifiers	Something that uniquely identifies the person	Username, IP address, government issued ID, biometric data, GPS coordinates, and device ID.
Authentication credential	Used to authenticate an individual with something they know	Password, PIN, pet name, mothers' maiden name etc.
Public status	An individual's public life	Social status, political affiliations, interactions, communication meta-data.
Opinions and beliefs	What a person knows or believes	Religious beliefs, philosophical beliefs, thoughts.
Communication	Information communicated from or to individuals	Email, telephone recording, voice mail, and text messages.
Preferences	A person's preferences or interests	Intentions, interests, favorite food, shop, destinations, and music.
Ethnicity	A person's origin and linage	Race, nationality, ethnic origin, and language spoken.
Sexuality	Describes an individual's sexual life	Gender and preferences
Behavioral	Describes an individual's behavior or activity	Holiday destinations, browsing history, call logs, links clicked, and attitude.
Demographics	Describes an individual's characteristics shared with others	Age ranges, physical traits, income brackets, and geography.
Health	Describes an individual's health, medical conditions, or health care	Physical and mental health, drugs used, test results, disabilities, family medical history, health records, genetic data, doctors' certificates, and sick note.

(Continued)

Table 1.1 (Continued)

Category name	Information description	Examples
Physical characteristics	Describes an individual's physical characteristics	Height, weight, age, hair color, and skin tone.
Life History	An individual's personal history	Events in a person's life, wedding, and children.
Banking details	Identifies a person's financial background	Credit card number and bank account number.
Financial Ownership	Identifies what a person owns, rents, borrows, and possesses	Cars, houses, apartments, and personal possessions.
Financial transactions	An individual's purchasing, spending, or income	Purchases, sales, credit, income, loan records, transactions, taxes, spending, pension details, and salary.
Employment	About an individual's educational or professional career	Job titles, salary, work history, school attended, employee files, employment history, evaluations, references, interviews, certifications, disciplinary actions, CV, and training.
Criminal	An individual's criminal activity or conviction	Convictions, charges, and pardons.
Family background	About an individual's family and relationships	Family structure, siblings, offspring, marriages, divorces, and relationship.
Social Networks	About an individual's friends or social connection	Friends, connections, associations, memberships, and clubs.

PII vs personal data/personal information

PII has a limited scope of data which includes name, address, birth date, social security numbers, and banking information. Whereas personal data in the context of the GDPR also potentially references data such as photographs, social media posts, preferences, and location, as personal. In Australia's Privacy Act 1988, "personal information" also includes information from which the person's identity is "reasonably ascertainable", potentially covering some information not covered by PII. So, in terms of warnings about misinterpretations – make note that all PII can be considered personal data but not all personal data can be considered as PII. So, for example, a user's IP address is not classified as PII on its own but can be classified as linkable PII. Whereas in the EU, the IP address of an Internet subscriber may be classed as personal data. Cookies also by way of example are not classified as PII; however, in the EU, they have the possibility to be classified as personal data (depending on their content and the possibility to identify an individual from them).

Special category data (in GDPR)

The GDPR singles out some types of personal data as likely to be more sensitive and mandates additional measures such as a legal basis in Article 6, and Article 9, and enhanced/additional technical and organizational measures. Sensitive data include personal data:

- Revealing racial or ethnic origin.
- Revealing political opinions.
- Revealing religious or philosophical beliefs.
- Revealing trade union membership.
- Genetic data.
- Biometric data (where used for identification purposes).
- Data concerning health.
- Data concerning a person's sex life.
- Data concerning a person's sexual orientation.

Although not strictly defined as special category data, data associated with vulnerable individuals often pose a similar level of risk as special category data. Vulnerable individuals are those who may not have the capacity to act or advocate for themselves, such as by giving "explicit consent". Individuals can be vulnerable where circumstances may restrict their ability to freely consent or object to the processing of their personal data or to understand its implications.

Processing the data of vulnerable persons can thus give rise to additional or greater risks and requires that you more greatly consider their individual needs when processing their data. Most obviously, children are regarded as vulnerable to the processing of their personal data, since they may be less able to understand how their data is being used, anticipate how this might affect them, and protect themselves against any unwanted consequences. This can also be true of other vulnerable sections of the population such as:

- Individuals under the age of 16 years.
- Elderly people.
- People with mental disorders or mental health conditions (whether temporary or ongoing).
- People with disabilities.
- Injured or chronically ill people.

Even if the individuals are not part of a group you might automatically consider vulnerable, an imbalance of power in their relationship with a data controller or processor can cause vulnerability for data protection purposes – particularly if they believe that they will be disadvantaged if the processing doesn't go ahead. For instance, asylum seekers, the homeless, or most notably, employees. The European guidelines on DPIAs explain why employees could be considered vulnerable data subjects where a power imbalance means they cannot easily consent or object to the processing of their data by an employer. This type of vulnerability could also arise due to an individual's financial situation (e.g., credit rating), or even patients receiving medical care.

Processing the data of individuals who may be deemed vulnerable is one of the criteria in European guidelines for processing likely to result in high risk. If you think that your organization's processing will involve vulnerable individuals, then a DPIA will be required should any of the other criteria be engaged. (For further details on these criteria, see Chapter 6.)

DATA PROTECTION: LAWS AND POLICIES TO ADVANCE HUMAN RIGHTS

Jules Polonetsky

CEO, Future of Privacy Forum

Data protection issues are now squarely societal and human rights issues. There is a societal impact on every sector that relies on data, affecting the future of healthcare, transportation, and marketing – the list goes on. Many of these impacts will extend to the future of free speech and, ultimately, our democracy.

How? Evolving data collection and processing practices are driving digital services and socially beneficial research; however, they also pose increasing risks to individuals and communities that America's existing policies insufficiently protect. To date, the U.S. has taken a sectoral approach to privacy that has led to the creation of laws regulating specific sectors, such as surveillance, healthcare, video rentals, education records, and children's privacy.

As a result, US federal laws currently provide strong privacy and security protection for some forms of sensitive data. Still, they often leave other – sometimes similar – data (i.e., Sexual Orientation and Gender Identity data) largely unregulated. Granted the FTC's Section 5 authority does enforce against deceptive or unfair business practices, but that is limited in scope. Rightfully so, concerns have been raised about creating baseline rights and protections for personal data. State laws are starting to fill these gaps, but inconsistently – a national approach is needed.

As data protection law broadens its purview, it becomes the law of everything. We need to come to discussions with tools of not just legal and technical expertise but with a real understanding of the relevant sectors and an appreciation that these are civil rights and human rights at stake.

Businesses and consumers will benefit from clear standards that provide consumers with needed protections and the technology industry with certainty and guidance.

Rebuilding trust begins with creating uniform protections. Entering 2023, the United States remains one of the only global economic powers that lack a comprehensive national framework governing the collection and use of consumer data throughout the economy.

It is in the best interests of individuals and organizations for national lawmakers to speak in a united, bipartisan voice. To succeed, we need to bring together diverse voices – businesses, academics, civil society, policymakers, and others – to explore the real challenges posed by today's technologies. It's this multi-stakeholder approach that has helped formulate ethical norms and the advancement of responsible data practices.

Protected health information (PHI)

The Health Insurance Portability and Accountability Act (HIPAA) of 1996 is the primary law that oversees the use of access to and disclosure of PHI in the US. HIPAA defines PHI as data that relates to the past, present, or future health of an individual; the provision of healthcare to an individual; or the payment for the provision of healthcare to an individual. HIPAA regulates how this data is created, collected, transmitted, maintained, and stored by any HIPAA-covered organization. Examples are demographic information, medical histories, test and laboratory results, mental health conditions, insurance information, and other data that a healthcare professional collects to identify an individual and determine appropriate care.

HIPAA lists 18 different information identifiers that, when paired with health information, become PHI. Some of these identifiers on their own can allow an individual to be identified, contacted, or located. Others must be combined with other information to identify a person. This list includes the following:

- Name.
- Address (anything smaller than a state).
- Dates (except years) related to an individual – birthdate, admission date, etc.
- Phone number.
- Fax number.
- Email address.
- Social security number.
- Medical record number.
- Health plan beneficiary number.

- Account number.
- Certificate or license number.
- Vehicle identifiers, such as serial numbers, license plate numbers.
- Device identifiers and serial numbers.
- Web URL.
- Internet Protocol (IP) address.
- Biometric IDs, such as a fingerprint or voice print.
- Full-face photographs and other photos of identifying characteristics.
- Any other unique identifying characteristic.

PRIVACY RISK MANAGEMENT IN HEALTHCARE: IT'S NOT JUST HIPAA COMPLIANCE

Karen Habercoss

Chief Privacy Officer, The University of Chicago Medicine & Biological Sciences Division

- Clinical care and patient safety are important drivers in health care based upon system trust. Technological advances and the analyzation of ever-increasing amounts of data grow. Healthcare is impacted by globalization with the regulatory landscape rapidly evolving. The role of the healthcare privacy leader is vastly different than it was even just years ago. The path is one where data privacy responsibilities can no longer adequately be accounted for solely by the HIPAA regulation to assure trust.
- Privacy leaders in healthcare are now tasked with understanding *all* sources of data origination, collection, and processing from not only patients but also employees, professional students, human research subjects, general consumers, other third parties, as well as the impacts of *all* federal, state, and international laws that uniquely govern each. In anticipation of new technologies, network interoperability, system integrations, increasing automation, artificial intelligence and machine learning, considerable data analytics platforms, web tracking, downstream third-party servicing and more, the lens moves to a much broader privacy risk management approach well beyond HIPAA. How can this be accomplished?
- A shift must occur in healthcare privacy to a comprehensive risk management program from a "check the box" passive approach; a dynamic, wide-ranging process involving more than patients and more than just US law. The focus is on understanding the purpose behind the work and the accompanying data every department support, even outside of patient clinical care.

- In addition to already active partnerships with information security, legal, and corporate compliance, the privacy office strategically and holistically positions and embeds itself into every aspect of the system including patient clinical care, safety, and experience but also finance, revenue cycle, digital health and information technology, business intelligence, supply chain, records management, public safety, marketing, human resources, employee relations and benefits, research, education, etc. Data inventory and flow mapping are essential for the recognition of all potential privacy obligations aside from HIPAA.
- Key leader stakeholders are surveyed to gain extended awareness of the entire universe of privacy risk considerations beyond just patient care. Through this, gaps can be identified, risks ranked and prioritized, and ultimately a privacy framework used for management of the entire privacy ecosystem of enterprise data as a continuous process. Not a novel approach but a wider scope than contemplated.

Inferential data

Inferential/derived data are created by the data controller based on the data "provided by the data subject". For example, the outcome of an assessment regarding the health of a user or the profile created in the context of risk management and financial regulations (e.g., to assign a credit score or comply with anti-money laundering rules) cannot in themselves be considered as "provided by" the data subject. The European Data Protection Board (EDPB) considers that both inferential/derived data are classified as personal data (e.g., the outcome of a medical assessment regarding the health of a user or a risk management profile). Examples could range from simple categorization (such as when a person says that they live in postcode 10963, Germany, and their file is automatically tagged with "Berlin") to cases where there are human comments (such as when a doctor examines a patient and writes "symptoms of bronchitis" in the file). It could be a car navigation service that classifies a person as a "fast" driver, based on observed behavior, in order to estimate driving times for that individual; it could be a tag to indicate that someone has a propensity to be susceptible to food-related advertising if presented before 9 am. Numerous applications drawing potentially beneficial or potentially troubling inferences about individuals and groups have emerged in recent years. Facebook, for example, can infer protected attributes such as sexual orientation, race, as well as political opinions and imminent suicide attempts, while third parties have used Facebook data to decide on the eligibility for loans and infer political stances on abortion. Susceptibility to depression can similarly be inferred via usage data signals from social media sites such as Instagram and Twitter. These signals are taken from the posting and behavioral history of users on these apps. By sifting through data on the physical movements of computer users from millions of internet searches, a study from Microsoft found links between some behaviors – such as tremors when using a mouse, repeat queries and average scrolling velocity, and Parkinson's disease. The Microsoft study leveraged artificial intelligence (AI) to identify which of the metrics separated a control group from those searching for Parkinson's disease symptoms.

Other recent invasive "inferential applications" include the assessment of users' satisfaction based on mouse tracking, and China's Social Credit Scoring system. Scoring is not a new concept. Data brokers such as Experian trace the punctuality in which we pay our debts, giving us a score that's used by lenders and mortgage providers. More social-style scoring is conducted on those shopping online; for example, eBay has a rating on shipping times and communication, while Uber drivers and passengers both rate each other. China's social credit system expands that idea to all aspects of life, judging citizens' and organizations' behavior and trustworthiness. The People's Bank of China and the Chinese government compile data about individuals and businesses through various mediums, including financial and government records and online credit platforms. These data are then analyzed, and everyone, business, and government entity are given a social credit score. If caught jaywalking, don't pay a court bill, don't pay your creditors on time, play music too loud – certain rights and freedoms can be lost, such as the ability to use public infrastructure or to travel.

DOES PRIVACY IN CHINA MEAN THE SAME IN WESTERN COUNTRIES?

João Barreiro

Chief Privacy Officer (Global), Executive Director, BeiGene

Views on privacy differ widely between Chinese and Western cultures. In China, privacy concerns as a human right are second-order factors, where the ethical and business dimensions are first-order factors. Moreover, in the light of the collectivism principle of the prevailing ethics, collective interests and individual interests are both important, but comparatively speaking, collective interests are more important than individual interests. BeiGene is a triple-listed global company with over 9,000 employees but most of its employees are in China. When implementing the China Personal Information Protection Law (PIPL) requirements, I quickly understood that the correct narrative was needed to successfully get our China-based employees to adhere to our privacy program. Implementing a compliance program is not just adhering to legal requirements, not just a tick the box exercise. Therefore, simply arguing that the law requires companies to comply with privacy controls and imposes hefty fines was not the right approach. If I wanted to successfully implement the China PIPL requirements, a cultural shift needed to happen in the way BeiGene employees perceive privacy. I then realized that ethics and business are two core elements of the Chinese cultural identity that could be leveraged. By incorporating those two concepts into BeiGene's new privacy program vision, mission, and logo, I was able to get our colleagues in China onboard. Employees now understand that complying with privacy is an ethical imperative and benefits business. When we receive data from our patients, there is an expectation that we will process it in good faith and in an ethical way. Moreover, employees endorse the statement that privacy is a business enabler and a competitive advantage. For instance, having robust and clear privacy notices during our clinical trials enables us to collect and generate more usable health data, including for secondary research projects, aimed to discover and commercialize new medicines for our patients.

If inferences are deemed to be personal data, the data protection rights enshrined in GDPR should also equally apply. Unfortunately, European data protection law and jurisprudence currently fails in this regard. The data subjects' rights to being informed, rights to rectification, right to object to processing, and right to portability are significantly reduced when data is not "provided by the data subject", for example, in their guidelines on the rights to data portability, the EU Working Party (WP) 29 notes that

> though such data may be part of a profile kept by a data controller and are inferred or derived from the analysis of data provided by the data subject, these data will typically not be considered as 'provided by the data subject' and thus will not be within scope of this new right.

Similarly, the GDPR provides insufficient protection and remedies against sensitive inferences (the creation of sensitive data from standard personal data), or the decisions based on them, for sensitive data collection and processing – GDPR typically requires consent (with obvious exceptions, for instances, such as statutorily mandated information, life and death decisions, and/or criminal justice reasons). However, individuals are typically not aware of the creation of the inference/profile or its use for decision or prediction. Thus, their right to access and to being fully informed can often be overlooked.

Accountability also becomes an issue, when an organization can more readily conceal the creation and processing of sensitive data inferred by themselves rather than declared by the data subject. In addition to these challenges, the interpretation of GDPR regarding inferential sensitive data has been inconsistent. For example, in August 2022 the Court of Justice of the EU (CJEU) issued a ruling on a Lithuanian case concerning national anti-corruption legislation. As part of this case, the CJEU assessed whether personal data that can indirectly reveal the sexual orientation of a person falls under GDPR's protections for "special category data". The question was centered around the publication of the name of a spouse. The interpretation taken by the CJEU was that processing personal data liable to disclose sexual orientation constituted processing of special categories of data. In another words, if my name is Deborah and my spouse's name is Linda, then it is reasonably easy to infer my sexual orientation. Prior to this, Norway's data protection authority fined Grindr for breaches of GDPR, as someone using Grindr inferentially indicates their sexual orientation, and therefore this constitutes special category data. Surprisingly, Spain's data protection authority did not concur and found that Grindr did not process any special category information.

Anonymized, pseudonymized personal data

Pseudonymization of data means replacing any information which could be used to identify an individual with a pseudonym, or, in other words, a value which does not allow the individual to be directly identified. An example of pseudonymized data can be found in Table 1.2.

Anonymized data on the other hand is where individuals are no longer identifiable. It is important to note that a person does not have to be named to be identifiable, that is, if there is other information enabling an individual to be connected to data about them, which could not be about someone else in the group, they may still "be identified". In this context, it is important to consider what "identifiers" (pieces of information which are closely connected with a particular individual, which could be used to single them out) are contained in the information held.

In determining whether a person can be distinguished from others in a group, it is important to consider what "identifiers" are contained in the

Table 1.2 Example of pseudonymization of data

	Student name	Student number	Course of study
Original Data	Joe Smith	12345678	History
Pseudonymized Data	Candidate 1	XXXXXXXX	History

Source: from www.dataprotection.ie

information held. Identifiers are pieces of information which are closely connected with a particular individual, which could be used to single them out. Such identifiers can be "direct", like the data subject's name or image, or "indirect", like their phone number, email address, or a unique identifier assigned to the data subject by the data controller. As a result, removing direct identifiers does not render data sets anonymous. Data which are not identifiers may also be used to provide context which may lead to identification or distinction between users – for example, a series of data about their location or perhaps their shopping or internet search history. Indeed, these kinds of data series on their own may be sufficient to distinguish and identify an individual.

However, just because data about individuals contains identifiers does not mean that the data subjects will be identified or identifiable. This will depend on contextual factors. Information about a child's year of birth might allow them to be singled out in their family but would probably not allow them to be distinguished from the rest of their school class if there are many other children with the same year of birth. Similarly, data about the family name of an individual may distinguish them from others in their workplace, but might not allow them to be identified in the general population if the family name is common.

On the other hand, data which appear to be stripped of any personal identifiers can sometimes be linked to an individual when combined with other information, which is available publicly or to a particular individual or organization. This occurs particularly in cases where there are unique combinations of connected data. In the above case, for instance, if there was one child with a particular birthday in the class, then having that information alone allows identification.

Where data have been anonymized, the original information should be securely deleted to prevent any reversing of the "anonymization" process. In most cases, if this deletion does not take place, then the data is classified as "pseudonymized" rather than "anonymized" and is still considered personal data.

In 2021, the European Data Protection Board (EDPB) and the European Union Agency for Cybersecurity (ENISA) published technical guidance on pseudonymization techniques, covering asymmetric encryption, ring signatures, group pseudonyms, chaining mode, pseudonyms based on multiple identifiers, pseudonyms with proof of knowledge, and secure multi-party computation. It then applies some of these techniques in healthcare to discuss possible pseudonymization options in different example cases. A link to this guidance is included in the suggested reading.

PRIVACY-ENHANCING TECHNOLOGIES (PETs)

Privacy-enhancing technologies (PETs) are technologies that embody fundamental data protection principles by minimizing personal data use, maximizing data security, and empowering individuals. PETs allow online users to protect the privacy of their personal data which is often provided to and handled by services or applications. Generally speaking, PETs can be categorized as hard and soft privacy technologies. Soft privacy technologies are used where it can be assumed that a third party can be trusted for the processing of data. This model is based on compliance, consent, control, and auditing. Example technologies are access control, differential privacy, and encryption. Hard privacy technologies are used where no single entity can violate the privacy of the user. The assumption here is that third parties cannot be trusted. Data protection goals include data minimization and the reduction of trust in third parties, for example, VPNs. In the remainder of this section, we discuss the most common types of PETs, namely; Hashing, Data Masking, Tokenization, Encryption, and Differential Privacy (while pseudonymization is also a common PET – it is discussed in the previous section).

Hashing

A hash is a one-way algorithm used to compare an input with a reference without compromising the reference. It is very much an "integrity" check rather than a privacy function. However, the requirement to ensure that personal data is accurate now mandates more considered use of hashing. A very naive and simple hash is "The first 3 letters of a string". That means the hash of "abcdefg" will be "abc". This function can obviously not be reversed which is the entire purpose of a hash. However, note that "abcxyz" will have exactly the same hash, this is called a collision. So again, a hash only proves with a certain probability that the two compared values are the same. Modern hash-algorithms are designed to keep the number of collisions as low as possible, but they can never be completely avoided. A rule of thumb is the longer your hash is, the less collisions it has. An obvious example of hashing is the letter at the end of many social insurance numbers such as "5111795 P". The P, in this case, equates to an algorithmic sum of the previous seven numbers. The system or application will be able to detect that the number or letter has been keyed incorrectly as the algorithm application will not match the letter/number combination.

Data masking

Data masking, sometimes called data obfuscation, substitutes realistic but false data for original data to ensure privacy. Using masked out data, testing, training, development, or support teams can work with a dataset without putting real data at risk. Data masking goes by many names. You may have heard of it as data scrambling, data blinding, data shuffling, or data sanitization. There is no algorithm to recover the original values of masked data. This is a common technique used during the development or testing of a new system. Old data is taken, and the identifiers are masked (e.g., customers are changed to fictitious names and addresses – in a previous organization I worked for – we used names such as Mickey Mouse, Donald Duck, Elmer Fudd, etc.).

Tokenization

Tokenization substitutes sensitive data with a value that is meaningless. This process is unable to be reversed. However, unlike data masking – you can map the token back to the original data. Tokenized data supports operations like running a credit card payment without revealing the credit card number. The real data never leaves the organization and can't be seen or decrypted by a third-party processor.

Data encryption

Data encryption is what happens when you take the text or data you use and convert it to a code (also called "ciphertext") that can't be understood by those who do not have the correct key. For the data to be usable, it must be changed back or decrypted. The more complex the data encryption algorithm, the safer the data will be from unauthorized access. Encryption allows us to send relevant and often-sensitive information digitally across the internet and through electronic means without unauthorized people seeing it. For the data to be decrypted, it needs a key, which authorized users will have. However, keep in mind that even encrypted data can sometimes be decrypted by those with enough skills or resources, some of whom may have malicious intent. Encryption generally prevents the theft or sharing of important data, whether it's the movies we watch, which use digital rights management (DRM) to prevent illegal copying, or the banking login passwords we type into the bank's website.

The three major encryption types are DES, AES, and RSA (most of the others are variations of older types, and some are no longer supported or recommended).

> DES ENCRYPTION: Accepted as a standard of encryption in the 1970s, Data Encryption Standard (DES) is no longer considered to be a safe encryption standard. It encrypts just 56-bits of data at a time, and it was found to be easily hacked not long after its introduction. It has, however, served as the standard upon which future, more-secure encryption tools have been based. A more modern Triple Data Encryption Standard (3DES) is a version of block cipher used today. Instead of using a single 56-bit key, it uses three separate 56-bit keys for triple protection. The drawback to 3DES is that it takes longer to encrypt data. Many banks and businesses still use this form of encryption, but newer forms are likely to phase 3DES out.

AES ENCRYPTION: Advanced Encryption Standard (AES) is used by governments and security organizations as well as everyday businesses for classified communications. AES uses "symmetric" key encryption. Someone on the receiving end of the data will need a key to decode it. AES differs from other encryption types in that it encrypts data in a single block, instead of individual bits of data. The block sizes determine the name for each kind of AES encrypted data (AES-128 encrypts blocks of a 128-bit size, AES-192 encrypts blocks of a 192-bit size, and AES-256 encrypts blocks of a 256-bit size). In addition to having different block sizes, each encryption method has a different number of rounds: AES-128, for example, uses 10 rounds, and AES-256 uses 14 rounds.

RSA ENCRYPTION: One of the most popular encryption standards is "Rivest–Shamir–Adleman" or RSA. It is widely used for data sent online and relies on a public key to encrypt the data. Those on the receiving end of the data will have their own private key to decode the messages.

Differential privacy

Differential privacy represents a system for publicly sharing information about a dataset by describing the patterns of groups within the dataset while withholding information about individuals in the dataset. The idea behind differential privacy is that if the effect of making an arbitrary single substitution in the database is small enough, the query result cannot be used to infer much about any single individual, and therefore provides privacy. Another way to describe differential privacy is as a constraint on the algorithms used to publish aggregate information about a statistical database which limits the disclosure of private information of records whose information is in the database. For example, differentially private algorithms are used by some government agencies to publish demographic information or other statistical aggregates while ensuring the confidentiality of survey responses, and by companies to collect information about user behavior while controlling what is visible even to internal analysts.

Benefits of differential privacy
- It assumes all information is identifying information, eliminating the challenging (and sometimes impossible) task of accounting for all identifying elements of the data.
- It is resistant to privacy attacks based on auxiliary information, so it can effectively prevent the linking attacks that are possible on de-identified data.
- It is compositional – this means that meaningful guarantees about privacy can be made even when releasing multiple analysis results from the same data. Techniques like de-identification are not compositional.

Table 1.3 Overview of differential privacy use cases over the last decade

Year deployed	Deployed by	deployed for
2008	U.S Census Bureau	Showing commuting patterns
2014	Google's RAPPOR	Telemetry such as learning statistics about unwanted software hijacking users' settings
2015	Google	Sharing historical traffic statistics
2016	Apple	iOS 10 to improve its intelligent personal assistant technology
2017	Microsoft	For telemetry in Windows
2020	Social Science One and Facebook	A 55 trillion cell dataset for researchers to learn about elections and democracy
2021	The US Census Bureau	Uses differential privacy to release redistricting data from the 2020 Census.

These advantages are the primary reasons why a privacy practitioner might choose differential privacy over some other data privacy technique. A current drawback of differential privacy is that it is rather new, and robust tools, standards, and best-practices are not easily accessible outside of academic research communities. Table 1.3 presents an overview of differential privacy use cases over the last decade.

Evolution of the privacy landscape

We are currently experiencing the fourth industrial revolution. The first Industrial Revolution used water and steam power to mechanize production. The second used electric power to create mass production. The third used electronics and information technology to automate production. The fourth builds on the third and is characterized by a fusion of technologies that is blurring the lines between the physical, digital, genetic, and biological spheres. See Table 1.4 for a brief description of these revolutions.

Each revolution has been accompanied by a privacy legislation wave, linking its governance to the accelerating pace of change. So, we find

Table 1.4 Industrial revolutions

Revolution	Year	Information
1	1784	Steam, Water, and Mechanical Production Equipment
2	1870	Division of Labor, Electricity, and Mass Production
3	1969	Electronic, IT, and Automated Production
4	?	Cyber-Physical Systems

Source: World Economic Forum.

ourselves in the fourth privacy wave, where technological changes outpace regulation, causing consumer fear and digital distrust and resulting in strong ethical arguments for aggressive improvements in organizations' privacy practices.

To establish and understand how privacy has come to the point it is at today, we need to understand the evolutionary trajectory of privacy and the programs we build in response to that evolution. While societal concerns regarding privacy have evolved into societal concerns regarding information privacy, organizations' strategic responses toward information privacy have also evolved. Initially, their responses were primarily compliance based, and over time have extended from being solely a legal compliance requirement to also being recognized as a market imperative and critical enabler of trust and consumer engagement. Westin (2003) presents the evolution of these responses over four decades, beginning in the sixties, into three broad categories: political, societal, and legal. Such responses, he suggests, evolved from events such as wiretapping, nation state surveillance, and media invasions of privacy.

The period spanning 1961 to 1979 is described as the first era of contemporary information privacy development, during which discretionary frameworks such as Fair Information Privacy Practices (FIPPS) emerged. These frameworks combined privacy standards with due process, consumer rights, and equality protections. In this period, privacy emerged as an explicit social, political, and legal issue. In the second era, spanning 1980 to 1999, fair monitoring ethical codes in the financial and telecommunication industries were introduced, with increased privacy protections for the wider stakeholder community such as employees. In the third era, spanning 2000–2010, Westin (2003) suggests that information privacy first became a social and political issue in response to, among others, the bombing of the twin towers, the Internet, the cell phone, the human genome project, data mining, and the automation of government public records.

The evolution continues into a fourth era, spanning from 2010 to the present day, during which societal privacy concerns have emerged in response to advancing technologies such as Big Data, Facial Recognition, National Surveillance, and Artificial Intelligence. These evolving societal concerns have given rise, in part, to privacy activities exceeding an organization's legal, financial, and ethical responsibilities (such as Privacy by Design standards, developing open privacy standards, or collaborating with privacy advocacy groups). Privacy by Design (PbD), covered in more detail in Chapter 7, is a framework of seven foundational principles that embed privacy into the design/operation of IT systems, networked infrastructure, and business practices (Cavoukian, 2011). Thus, this era sees organizations' privacy activities being shaped as Environmental, Social, and Governance (ESG) activities, that is, as social and/or political activities rather than simply compliance ones, covered in more detail in Chapter 8.

AI AND A NEW ERA FOR PRIVACY PROFESSIONALS

Julie Brill

*Chief Privacy Officer and Corporate Vice President, Global
Privacy and Regulatory Affairs, Microsoft*

Advanced technologies, like artificial intelligence, can drive new advances that help overcome the challenges that people, organizations, and countries face. At the same time, powerful technology like AI brings both opportunities and challenges for privacy professionals who have a responsibility to ensure data is used responsibly. Often times that work must happen while regulations are still evolving.

At Microsoft, I led the company's program implementing the European Union's General Data Protection Regulation (GDPR) requirements. I continue to lead our approach to regulatory governance and advocacy around the globe. Along the way, we've learned a lot about how companies can approach robust regulatory governance for AI and privacy:

1) **Establish principles to guide your approach**: Microsoft has internal standards based on core principles that guide our responsible development of our products. For example, our AI standard focuses on fairness, privacy and security, safety, inclusivity, transparency, and accountability. This Responsible AI standard then also connects with our privacy and digital safety standards to provide actionable guidance for protecting user data, keeping people safe, respecting user privacy, and using artificial intelligence responsibly.

2) **Take an iterative approach and share learnings across domains**: More mature domains like cybersecurity and privacy have a lot to teach an organization grappling with newer areas like AI. For instance, consider how privacy impact assessments can be used to help ensure accountable AI systems. Our responsible AI governance program has effectively borrowed this tool from our privacy governance system, and we now require our teams who design and deploy different AI tools and products to undertake a holistic impact assessment to identify any potential risks and take appropriate mitigation measures. These assessments are made from development to deployment and updated frequently to reflect any material changes to the product.

3) **Ensure accountability through concrete requirements**: Customers, regulators, and other stakeholders expect a high level of concrete accountability from business leaders. Microsoft's Responsible

AI Standard includes concrete requirements for data governance, human oversight, and impact assessments. These accountability obligations are part of a larger and holistic risk management and governance framework.

Privacy professionals have the skills and accountabilities to operate a trustworthy system and will play an increasingly critical role in AI governance going forward. We need privacy leaders within organizations, civil society, and government to work together to ensure new innovations have a beneficial impact for everyone and earn trust from all of society.

Models and theories of privacy

While in industry we refer little to these theories, in academic contexts, they are used to help understand privacy more deeply and to structure research theoretically on how organizations, consumers, employees etc. behave and respond to privacy. We therefore don't need to know these theories to do our jobs as privacy leaders, however they are immensely helpful in guiding our understanding of how, as human beings, we respond and behave toward invasions of privacy, and toward privacy activities that engender feelings of trust.

These theories are rarely, if ever, referenced in industry-specific books, and we have included them here early in the book as a prompt to perhaps evaluate them further if you have not come across them before. It is the firm view of the authors, particularly given one of the authors has a PhD in Privacy, that academic understanding of privacy and the practitioners understanding of privacy need to become more closely aligned, and the gap between the two needs to be bridged. Privacy leaders should develop a multidisciplined understanding of privacy that incorporates privacy from a legal, governance, anthropological, psychological, and philosophical perspectives. For example, one could have perceived decisions regarding Schrems I and Schrems II as   legal decisions with legal outcomes such as the implementation of enhanced Standard Contractual Clauses (SCCs) and Transfer Impact Assessments (TIAs). But if the privacy professional starts understanding privacy from the cultural and historical differences between Europe and the US in terms of their expectations toward privacy, we become better at identifying and addressing the potential gaps for employees and consumers. For instance, in the case of Schrems I and Schrems II, we might have started the engagement with the third-party transfer by addressing their cultural differences toward privacy first. Perhaps that culture perceives certain data subject rights as an unfair cost or burden on the organization? A multidisciplined understanding of privacy will enable us to think philosophically about privacy rather than legally, that is, the processing of this data was "cheap" beforehand, and all that data subject rights legislation does is to remedy that cheapness to make the playing field fairer. A multidisciplined approach to privacy also enables one to understand not only the different perspectives of privacy for the consumer but also our own team members. Some of our team may, for instance, have a greater propensity toward privacy than others ("a private person"), a greater propensity toward privacy risks (risk-takers) etc. We urge privacy leaders to seek an understanding of privacy beyond their compliance program, and hope that these theories we discuss in the remainder of this section will help. The key theories we have identified as being important to understand are outlined with a brief summary of them in Table 1.5.

Table 1.5 Key theories of privacy

Theory	*Summary*
The APCO Model of Privacy	Factors leading to privacy concern and outcomes of privacy concern. Individual factors, contextual factors, and macro factors are modeled in the APCO model as antecedents. Beliefs and behaviors are modeled in the APCO model as outcomes.
Privacy Calculus	Explains how we trade our privacy for benefits. This calculus is influenced by several factors.
The Privacy Paradox	A largely misunderstood phenomenon regarding users who while are concerned about privacy, their behaviors do not mirror those concerns.
Social Contract Theory of Privacy	Privacy is regulated by social contracts governing that organizations use individuals' data according to social norms regarding what, by whom, why, and how, and that individuals have some level of control over that use.
The Power Responsibility Equilibrium (PRE) Model of Privacy	If organizations are not seen to be responsible, a consumer's privacy concern is likely to increase, leading to defensive measures by a consumer or negative measures by other stakeholders, such as regulators.
Nissenbaum's Theory of Privacy as Contextual Integrity	We are surrounded by all kinds of information flows that threaten our privacy but are also necessary or useful. The appropriateness of a particular flow of information can be determined by whether "context-relative informational norms" are respected.
Westin's Theory of Segmentation	A segmentation of the American public into three groups: The privacy fundamentalists (high privacy concern and high distrust in government, business, and technology), the privacy pragmatists (mid-level concern and distrust), and the privacy unconcerned (no/low concern and distrust).

The antecedents to privacy concerns and outcomes (APCO) model of privacy

The APCO model (Smith et al., 2011) presents a macro-micro model of privacy-related concepts and is divided into three main categories: Antecedents (A), Privacy Concerns (PC), and the Outcomes (O). In other words, what causes users' privacy concerns, and what are the potential consequences of those concerns? In the existing literature, most of the studies harness "privacy concerns" as the proxy to examine privacy, as privacy itself is an abstract construct that is difficult to measure. Privacy concerns are personal perceptions that will ultimately influence how the individual perceives a situation involving personal information. Figure 1.4 presents a high-level overview of the APCO model.

Privacy decisions are determined by many factors such as, but not limited to age, gender, race, culture, propensity to trust, privacy concerns, perceived benefits, perceived risks, perceived enjoyment, perceived usefulness, privacy-invasion experience, privacy regulations and so on. However, depending on the context, some factors overpower others. For example, in online banking, trust, usefulness, and ease of use are much more significant than privacy concerns or perceived enjoyment with the bank's website/app. The APCO model provides a useful way to summarize the previous scholarly work regarding antecedents to, and outcomes of, privacy concern. Individual factors, contextual factors, and macro factors are modeled in the APCO model as antecedents. Beliefs and behaviors are modeled in the APCO model as outcomes. Of course, we can identify many aspects that may be missing, for example, political orientation or benevolence. However, the APCO model provides a strong understanding of the key factors that determine privacy concerns (called "antecedents") and the key outcomes of privacy concern. Over time, the APCO model has continued to be extended by further research and a recent example is presented in Figure 1.5.

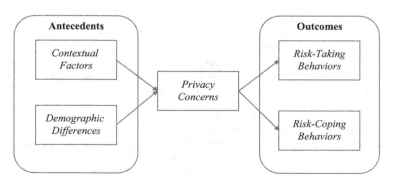

Figure 1.4 The APCO model of privacy.

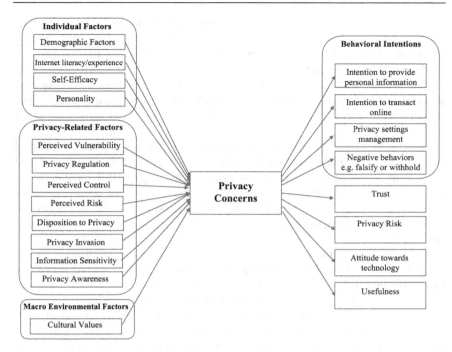

Figure 1.5 The extended APCO model of privacy.

Privacy calculus

The privacy calculus is a rational comparison of the risks (privacy concerns) and benefits of a behavior such as information disclosure. If the individual perceives the benefits outweigh the risks, they will engage in the behavior and vice versa. Often, the perceived benefits are deemed greater. If the benefits are guaranteed, that is the person will avail themselves of a free service, receive personalization etc., then they tend to outweigh the concerns or risks. Consider the privacy calculus as a way to explain how we trade our privacy for benefits.

The privacy calculus suggests that when individuals are asked to reveal personal information to others, they deliberate on the risks involved and the potential benefits received. However, this description may be limited as users may not be able to fully deliberate on the risks and benefits of a disclosure decision due to (1) cognitive limitations and a finite amount of time to make the decision and (2) the role that levels of uncertainty, ambiguity, and behavioral biases play in behavioral outcomes.

The privacy paradox

The privacy paradox is a dichotomy in how a person intends to protect their online privacy versus how they actually behave online. In other words, users have a tendency toward privacy-compromising behavior online which eventually results in a dichotomy between privacy attitudes and actual behavior (Acquisti, 2004). The first mention of the term "privacy paradox" is attributed to Hewlett-Packard employee Barry Brown (2001), who used it regarding the use of supermarket loyalty cards by customers despite their concerns about privacy. In 2006, professor and author Susan B. Barnes studied the concept in relation to teenagers freely giving up personal information on social networks.

In "The Privacy Paradox – Investigating discrepancies between expressed privacy concerns and actual online behavior", Barth and De Jong analyzed more than 30 different papers and theories on the alleged "Privacy Paradox". Their analysis finds that (1) consumer decisions on use of data-dependent services were not always rational, (2) such decisions may be based on the limited understanding of the consequences of the decision, (3) erroneous valuation of risk and benefit, (4) old habits inhibiting engagement in privacy management tools, and finally (5) little or no risk assessment at all. A more recent study from Chen et al. (2021) would suggest that the privacy paradox is more linked to digital demand – in other words that even when privacy concerns are high, the need for the digital technology in question is stronger.

While we know that there are multiple factors involved in the privacy paradox, the need to understand the causal factors has never been more important as the presence of this disconnect between stated concerns and consumer behaviors is often used as evidence to argue either:

1) That consumers' privacy concerns are not credible.
2) That privacy is no longer achievable in the age of the data economy.

Social contract theory of privacy

Extending beyond the privacy calculus theory, the social contract theory (SCT) assumes that individuals will enter a social contract with an organization once they perceive that the benefits of this relationship outweigh the risks. Consumers form contracts based on their perceptions about firms' contractual obligations. The social contract theory of privacy maintains that privacy is governed by social contracts governing that organizations use individuals data according to social norms regarding what, by whom, why, and how (Martin, 2016), and that individuals have some level of control over that use. These norms include not only the type of information expected but also who will be able to see and use the information as well as the transmission principles associated with the information. Consumer privacy concerns can be viewed through this theory as an outcome of the violation of perceived contracts between consumers and organizations. The social contract (and consequently trust) is breached if a consumer perceives that a particular organization has failed to meet its obligations or has failed to deliver on the contractual agreement. An excellent example of this is the now infamous Facebook/Cambridge Analytica scandal. In this breach, personal data belonging to millions of Facebook users were collected without their consent by Cambridge Analytica, predominantly to be used for political advertising. The data was collected through an app called "This Is Your Digital Life". The app consisted of a series of questions to build psychological profiles on users and collected the personal data of the users' Facebook friends. The app harvested the data of up to 87 million Facebook profiles. Cambridge Analytica used the data to provide analytical assistance to the 2016 presidential campaigns of Ted Cruz and Donald Trump. Information about the data misuse was disclosed in 2018 by whistleblower Christopher Wylie, a former Cambridge Analytica employee, in interviews with The Guardian and The New York Times. Interestingly, often the only time we get to know that the social contract has been breached, is when there is a data breach or whistleblower – as this is often the first window of opportunity to have transparency over the collection and misuse of personal data.

Being aware of the implications of the privacy specific social contract is very important when consumer trust in the protection of their personal data is currently so low across industries. The 2022 Thales Consumer Digital Trust Index: A Consumer Confidence in Data Security Report, conducted by the University of Warwick, found that social media companies (18%), the government (14%), and media and entertainment organizations (12%) had the lowest levels of consumer trust when it came to safeguarding their users' personal information. In 2022, Twitter reached a proposed $150 million settlement with the Federal Trade Commission (FTC) to resolve allegations that the company deceptively used nonpublic user contact information obtained for account security purposes to serve targeted ads to Twitter users.

The power responsibility equilibrium (PRE) model of privacy

Developed based on the Power Responsibility Equilibrium (PRE) theory, the PRE Model of Privacy (Lwin et al., 2007), outlined in Figure 1.6, holds that consumers who perceive that organizations are acting responsibly in terms of their privacy practices are expected to have greater trust and confidence in organizations and show less concern for privacy. The model classifies organizations and government on one side, that is, the powerholders who are expected to show responsibility. They classify consumers on the other side, i.e., the information providers who expect responsible use of control/power. Consumers will take defensive actions when corporations and governments fail to promote equality in an information exchange and effectively manage privacy protection. These consumer actions are driven by deficits in privacy protection by powerholders. The three key actions in the PRE Model of Privacy are "fabricate, protect and withhold"; however, there are a wide range of other actions that a consumer can undertake such as promote bad press, stop transacting, discontinue a relationship, discontinue use of

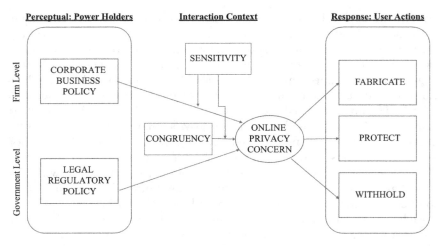

Figure 1.6 The PRE model of privacy.

(Source: Lwin et al., 2007)

a system, etc. Therefore, when an organization does not treat information fairly by being transparent about their information strategy and practices, a consumer can decide to leave or not provide any further information.

If organizations are not seen to be responsible, a consumer's privacy concern is likely to increase, leading to defensive measures by a consumer or negative measures by other stakeholders, such as regulators. Facebook, for instance, had to pay a $5 billion penalty and submit to new restrictions and a modified corporate structure that will hold the company accountable for the decisions it makes about its users' privacy to settle Federal Trade Commission charges that the company violated a 2012 FTC order by deceiving users about their ability to control the privacy of their personal information. The FTC accused Facebook of repeatedly using deceptive disclosures and settings to undermine users' privacy preferences in violation of its 2012 FTC order. These tactics allowed the company to share users' personal information with third-party apps that were downloaded by the user's Facebook "friends". The FTC alleged that many users were unaware that Facebook was sharing such information and therefore did not take the steps needed to opt-out of sharing. Inversely, where an organization is seen to have consumer-friendly privacy practices, they are perceived as responsible and thus will lessen privacy concerns.

More recently, in 2023, the Irish Data Protection Commissioner fined WhatsApp €5.5million and directed WhatsApp to bring its data processing operations into compliance within a period of six months. In advance of 25 May 2018, the date on which the GDPR came into operation, WhatsApp updated its Terms of Service and informed its users that if they wished to continue to have access to the WhatsApp service following the introduction

of the GDPR, existing (and new) users were asked to click "agree and continue" to indicate their acceptance of the updated Terms of Service.
WhatsApp considered that, upon accepting the updated Terms of Service, a
contract was entered into between WhatsApp and the user. It also took the
position that the processing of users' data in connection with the delivery of
its service was necessary for the performance of that contract, to include the
provision of service improvement and security features, so that such processing operations were lawful by reference to Article 6(1)(b) of the GDPR
(the "contract" legal basis for processing). It was argued however that by
making the accessibility of its services conditional on users accepting the
updated Terms of Service, WhatsApp was in fact "forcing" them to consent
to the processing of their personal data for service improvement and
security.

PRE theory does not presume that only one party can be the powerholder,
although the literature most often presumes the organization as such. Other
possible powerholder combinations could be shareholders over organizations, employers over employees, etc. The PRE theory also recognizes that
legislation may affect the level of power that an organization can exercise
over privacy. For instance, the stringency of GDPR over privacy has restricted
the use and collection of data, thus reducing the power that organizations
must extract utility from this information. Most importantly, GDPR introduced the concept of statutory data subject rights for the first time. These
rights enable a data subject to have powers such as GDPR's right to be
deleted. This results in consumers becoming powerholders on one side, by
demanding deletion of their data, while organizations on the other side have
legitimate needs to retain data in line with predetermined schedules. Thus,
privacy can be considered an exchange between not just two but several
parties in which all parties' need for control are considered so that the outcomes are "just" for all involved parties. Balance is achieved when both the
individual's and organization's expectations are met.

Nissenbaum's theory of privacy as contextual integrity

Helen Nissenbaum observes that we are surrounded by all kinds of information flows that, on the one hand, may threaten our privacy, but, on the other
hand, are also necessary for many essential or useful services. Nissenbaum
argues that information should flow in appropriate ways. The appropriate-
ness of a particular flow of information can be determined by analyzing
whether "context-relative informational norms" are respected (Nissenbaum,
2009, p. 129). Privacy is respected when information flows without breaching context-relative informational norms. Consider the norm: "US residents are required by law to file tax returns with the US Internal Revenue
Service containing information, such as, name, address, SSN, gross earnings,
etc. under conditions of strict confidentiality". If the US Internal Revenue

Service, then sends this data to private institutions for the purpose of matching tax declarations with spending (for fraud purposes), then this would represent a breach of contextual integrity.

Westin's theory of segmentation

Alan Westin proposed a segmentation of the American public into three groups: The privacy fundamentalists (high privacy concern and high distrust in government, business, and technology), the privacy pragmatists (mid-level concern and distrust), and the privacy unconcerned (no or low concern and distrust).

Some people feel very strongly about privacy matters. They tend to feel that they have lost a lot of their privacy and are strongly resistant to any further erosion of it. These were called privacy fundamentalists and amounted (in 1999) to about a quarter (25%) of all adults. "Privacy Fundamentalists see privacy as an especially high value, rejecting the claims of many organizations to need or be entitled to get personal information for their business or governmental programs, thinks more individuals should simply refuse to give out information they are asked for, and favors enactment of strong federal and state laws to secure privacy rights and control organizational discretion...".

At the other extreme, there were those who have no real concerns about privacy and who have far less anxiety about how other people and organizations are using information about them. These were called privacy unconcerned, and they amounted to about 20% of all adults. "This group doesn't know what the 'privacy fuss' is all about, supports the benefits of most organizational programs over warnings about privacy abuse, has little problem with supplying their personal information to government authorities or businesses, and sees no need for creating another government bureaucracy ... to protect someone's privacy...".

The third, and by far the largest group, now almost two-thirds of all adults (55%) were called privacy pragmatists, who have strong feelings about privacy and are very concerned to protect themselves from the abuse or misuse of their personal information by companies or government agencies. However, they are – to a far greater degree than the privacy fundamentalists – often willing to allow people to have access to, and to use, their personal information where they understand the reasons for its use, where they see tangible benefits for so doing, and when they believe care is taken to prevent the misuse of this information. "Privacy Pragmatists weigh the value to them and society of various business or government programs calling for personal information, examines the relevance and social propriety of the information sought, wants to know the potential risks to privacy or security of their information, looks to see whether fair information practices are being widely enough observed, and then decides whether they will agree or disagree with specific information activities—with their trust in the particular industry or company involved a critical decisional factor. The pragmatists favor voluntary standards and consumer choice over legislation and government enforcement. But they will back legislation when they think not enough is being done— or meaningfully done—by voluntary means".

Since 1999, the numbers in each segment have varied somewhat. Privacy pragmatists have increased from 55% to 64%, while the privacy unconcerned have declined from 22% to 10% of all adults. In 2018, a further analysis of the segmentation model from Westin was conducted by Elueze and Quan-Haase, and extended to five rather than three categories, namely: fundamentalists, cynical experts, intense pragmatists, relaxed pragmatists, and marginally concerned.

There has been much debate regarding the methodology used by Westin (a three-question survey) and the reliability of the scales used, particularly the one he used to measure privacy concerns. Most of the studies harness "privacy concerns" as a proxy to examine privacy because privacy is a rather abstract and difficult-to-measure construct. Privacy concerns are defined as personal perceptions that will ultimately influence how the individual perceives a situation involving personal information (Malhotra et al., 2004). There are many factors that may create privacy concerns including, unauthorized access, secondary use, and interception of personal information and misuse of such information. More recent than Westins segmentation measurements, the most common measurements today for privacy concerns are (1) the consumer privacy concern scale, (2) the Mobile Users Interpret Privacy Concerns (MUIPC) scale, and (3) the Internet Users' Information privacy concerns (IUIPC) scale. In Westin's favor, however, the theory that the population is comprised of people who differ fundamentally in the levels of privacy concern they feel and their responses is undisputed.

SUGGESTED READING

Acquisti, A. (2004). Privacy in electronic commerce and the economics of immediate gratification. *Proceedings of the 5th ACM Conference on Electronic Commerce*, 21–29.

Altman, I. (1975). *The Environment and Social Behavior: Privacy, Personal Space, Territory, Crowding*. Monterey, CA: Brooks/Cole.

Barth, S., and de Jong, M. (2017). The privacy paradox: Investigating discrepancies between expressed privacy concerns and actual online behavior - A systematic literature review. *Telematics and Informatics*, 34(7), 1038–1058.

Brown, B. (2001). Studying the internet experience. HP Laboratories Technical Report (HPL-2001-49).

Brunon-Ernst, A. (2013). *Beyond Foucault: New Perspectives on Bentham's Panopticon*. London: Routledge.

Cavoukian, A. (2011). Privacy by design. https://www.ipc.on.ca/wp-content/uploads/resources/7foundationalprinciples.pdf

Clarke, R. (2006). What is privacy?. http://www.rogerclarke.com/DV/Privacy.html

Chen, L., Bolton, P., Holmström, B. R., Maskin, E., Pissarides, C. A., Spence, A. M., Sun, T., Sun, T., Xiong, W., Yang, L., Huang, Y., Li, Y., Luo, X., Ma, Y., Ouyang, S., & Zhu, F. (2021). *Understanding Big Data: Data Calculus in the Digital Era*. Luohan Academy Report.

De Choudhury, M., Gamon, M., Counts, S. & Horvitz, E. (AAAI, 2013). Predicting depression via social media. *ICWSM*, 2, 128–137.

Developing a Common Understanding of Cybersecurity. (2015). https://www.isaca.org/resources/isaca-journal/issues/2015/volume-6/developing-a-common-understanding-of-cybersecurity

Developing a Common Understanding of Cybersecurity. (n.d.). https://www.isaca.org/resources/isaca-journal/issues/2015/volume-6/developing-a-common-understanding-of-cybersecurity

EDPB & ENISA. (2021). Advanced techniques and use-cases for pseudonymisation. https://www.enisa.europa.eu/publications/data-pseudonymisation-advanced-techniques-and-use-cases

Elueze, I., & Quan-Haase, A. (2018). Privacy attitudes and concerns in the digital lives of older adults: Westin's privacy attitude typology revisited. *American Behavioral Scientist*, 62(10), 1372–1391.

EU ART 29 WP. Guidelines on the Right to Data Portability (2017). https://ec.europa.eu/newsroom/article29/items/611233

EU Court of Human Rights Case Of b v. France. (57/1990/248/319) JUDGMENT STRASBOURG. (24 January 1992). http://www.pfc.org.uk/caselaw/B%20vs%20France.pdf

EU Guidelines on Data Protection Impact Assessment (DPIA) (wp248rev.01). (n.d.). https://ec.europa.eu/newsroom/article29/items/611236/en

Five Loopholes in GDPR (including Inferred Data). (2017). https://medium.com/mydata/five-loopholes-in-the-gdpr-367443c4248b#_ftn2

Fourth Industrial Revolution: What It Means, How to Respond. (2016). https://www.weforum.org/agenda/2016/01/the-fourth-industrial-revolution-what-it-means-and-how-to-respond/

Friedewald, M., Finn, R., and Wright, D. (2013). Seven Types of Privacy. In: Gutwirth, S., Leenes, R., deHert, P., Poullet, Y. (eds). *European Data Protection: Coming of Age*. Dordrecht: Springer.

Gavison, R. (1980). Privacy and the limits of law. *The Yale Law Journal*, 89(3), 421–471.

Guidance Note on Anonymization and Pseudonimization. Data Protection Commissioner Ireland. (n.d.). https://www.dataprotection.ie/en/dpc-guidance/anonymisation-and-pseudonymisation

Identiq (2020). e-Book how providerless technology is changing online identity validation. https://go.identiq.com/providerless-ebook

Illustration of the Solove's Taxonomy of Privacy. (2018). *Enterprise Consulting Group*. https://iapp.org/resources/article/a-taxonomy-of-privacy/

Lawrence et al. v. TEXAS, The Court Of Appeals Of Texas, Fourteenth District No. 02-102. (2003): http://supreme.justia.com/cases/federal/us/539/558/case.html

Lwin, M. Wirtz, J., and Williams, J. (2007). Consumer online privacy concerns and responses: A power–responsibility equilibrium perspective. *Journal of the Academy of Marketing Science*, 35(1), 572–585.

Malhotra, N., Kim, S. and Agarwal, J. (2004). Internet users' Information privacy concerns (IUIPC): The construct, the scale and a causal model. *Information Systems Research*, 15(4), 336– 355.

Margulis, S. (1977). Conceptions of privacy: Current status and next steps. *Journal of Social Issues*, 33(3), 5–21.

Martin, K. (2016). Understanding privacy online: Development of a social contract approach to privacy. *Journal of Business Ethics*, 137(1), 551–569.

Near, J., Darais, D. and Boeckl, K. (2020). Differential privacy for privacy-preserving data Analysis: An introduction to our blog series. https://www.nist.gov/blogs/cybersecurity-insights/differential-privacy-privacy-preserving-data-analysis-introduction-our

Nissenbaum, H. (2009). *Privacy in Context: Technology, policy, and the Integrity of social Life*. Stanford, CA: Stanford Law Books.

Privacy Indexes: A Survey of Westins Studies. (2005). http://reports-archive.adm.cs.cmu.edu/anon/isri2005/CMU-ISRI-05-138.pdf

Rachels, J. (1975). Why privacy is important. *Philosophy and Public Affairs*, 4(4), 323–333.

Reece, A. and Danforth, C. (2017). Instagram photos reveal predictive markers of depression. *EPJ Data Science*, 6, 1–34.

Schofield, P. (2009). *Bentham: A Guide for the Perplexed*. London: Continuum.

Smith, H., Dinev, T. and Xu, H. (2011). Information privacy research: An Interdisciplinary review. *MIS Quarterly*, 35(4), 989–1015.

Solove, D. (2006). A taxonomy of privacy. *University of Pennsylvania Law Review*, 154(3), 477–564.

Taylor, H. (2003). Most people are privacy pragmatists who while concerned about_privacy will sometimes trade it off for other benefits. https://www.researchgate.net/publication/268342423_Most_People_Are_Privacy_Pragmatists_Who_While_Concerned_about_Privacy_Will_Sometimes_Trade_It_Off_for_Other_Benefits

Thales Consumer Digital Trust Index. (2022). https://cpl.thalesgroup.com/data-trust-index

Tsugawa, S. (2015). Recognizing depression from twitter activity. In *Proc. ACM Conference on Human Factors in Computing Systems (CHI)*. 3187–3196 (ACM, 2015).

Warren, S. and Brandeis, L. (1890). The right to privacy. *Harvard Law Review*, 4(5), 193–220.Warren, S. and Brandeis, L. (1890). The right to privacy. *Harvard Law Review*, 4(5), 193–220.

Westin, A. (1967). *Privacy and Freedom*. New York: Athenbaum.

Westin, A. (2003). Social and political dimensions of privacy. *Journal of Social Issues*, 59(1), 431–453.

Woodruff, A., Pihur, V. and Consolvo, S. (2014). Would a privacy fundamentalist sell their DNA for $1000…if nothing bad happened as a result? The Westin categories, behavioral intentions, and consequences. *Symposium on Usable Privacy and Security (SOUPS)*. https://www.usenix.org/system/files/conference/soups2014/soups14-paper-woodruff.pdf

Yazdavar, A., Mahdavinejad, M., Bajaj, G. and Romine, W. (2020). Multimodal mental health analysis in social media. *PLoS One*, 15(4), 1–27.

Chapter 2

The McKinsey 7-S framework applied to privacy leadership

> Chaos often breeds life, when order breeds habit
> Henry [Brooks] Adams 1838–1918

THE MCKINSEY 7-S FRAMEWORK FOR ORGANIZATIONAL EFFECTIVENESS

The 7-S Framework (known as the McKinsey 7-S Framework and named for the two creators who were consultants for McKinsey & Co. at the time) has been around since the first publication of the concept several decades ago (Waterman et al., 1980) as a method to examine organizational effectiveness. At the time, it was believed that when organizations had difficulty in executing their strategy, they could hire external consultants skilled in organizational design and resolve the issues by changing the organizational structure. Waterman et al. (1980) in their paper "Structure is not Organization", asserted that there were more factors involved in executing a successful strategy than just re-organizing the workforce around a new structure. The structure of the organization follows the strategy, but the strategy, they believed, rarely dictated specific structural solutions. The main problem, they observed, in failing to execute the strategy was not in the structure of the organization, albeit that was one piece, rather the real issue was "getting it done". Organizations are slow to adapt to change and the reason is explainable by more than two variables (strategy and structure) and are usually attributed to a) systems that have outdated assumptions, b) management styles at odds with the strategy, c) absence of a stated goal (i.e., vision) that binds the organization together to achieve a common purpose, and d) not dealing with people problems and opportunities.

THE MCKINSEY 7-S FRAMEWORK APPLIED TO PRIVACY LEADERSHIP

The 7-S framework was used as the basis for this book to examine and incorporate privacy program effectiveness. The chapters are organized into

DOI: 10.1201/9781003383017-3

sections relating to each of the components of the 7-S framework. The following chapters examine privacy program leadership through the 7-S framework lens, a powerful way to examine organizational effectiveness, so we as an industry can have richer conversations about effectiveness. After all, the privacy leader "raison d'être" is to run effective organizations with respect to privacy programs. Before delving into the application of the model to privacy program leadership, let's briefly examine the 7-S framework or model.

THE 7-S FRAMEWORK DEFINED

The 7-S model asserts that effective organizational change depends upon the relationship between each of the 7 "S" s depicted in Figure 2.1. The 7 "S" s stands for structure, strategy, systems, style, skills, staff, and shared values (originally called 'superordinate goals'). The premise is that organizational effectiveness is the result of the interaction between these factors, and some

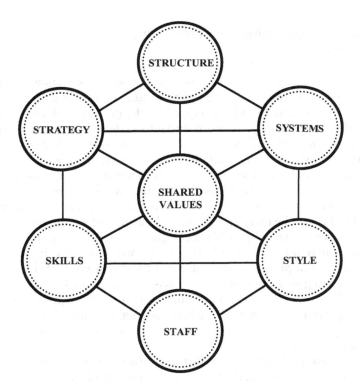

Figure 2.1 McKinsey 7-S framework.

(Source: Adapted from Waterman, Jr., R. and Peters, T., Structure Is Not Organization, June 1980, *Business Horizons*.)

are not obvious and thus are often under analyzed. The figure demonstrates several ideas: 1) there are multiple factors for organizational effectiveness, but many organizations only seem to spend time on structure and strategy, 2) the factors are all interconnected, and thus a change in one of the areas has an impact on another, and 3) the shape of the diagram is important – there is no starting point or hierarchy, each is an important factor to achieve organizational effectiveness. At different times, different factors may be the driving force for change in the organization at the time.

The "S"s in the top half of the figure are known as the "hard" factors, including strategy, structure, and systems. These are called hard factors due to their feasibility and being easier to identify. Strategy documents, corporate plans, organizational charts, and other documentation make it easier to identify. The four soft factors are skills, staff, style, and shared values as these are continuously changing. It becomes much harder to plan on these factors, even though they have a great influence on the ability to be successful with the other three elements of strategy, structure and systems.

THE 7-S FRAMEWORK APPLIED TO PRIVACY LEADERSHIP

While the McKinsey 7-S model was geared toward examining an overall organization and creating changes that would succeed in delivering upon the strategy, this model can be leveraged by the privacy leader to build and lead an effective privacy program, referred to as the 7-S Framework Applied to Privacy Leadership. If we think about it carefully, each privacy leader is running a business with stakeholders, customers, management, and staff to produce products and services. We can therefore leverage the model to organize the activities of the privacy leader and ensure we are proving ample coverage and attention to the areas of most concern. The 7-S Framework Applied to Privacy Leadership becomes a holistic tool for the privacy leader to evaluate what is missing within the organization. When the strategy is not working, it may not be due to having an incorrect strategy, but rather the right skills are not present to carry it out or the organizational shared values may be showing that the same level concern is not owned by the organization and there is more work to do. The 7-S Framework Applied to Privacy Leadership can be very powerful when building and sustaining the privacy program. Figure 2.2 shows an illustration of how the 7-S Model is applied to Privacy Leadership.

Let's examine each of the seven factors of the framework (structure, strategy, systems, style, skills, staff, and shared values) applied to privacy leadership and how they are presented within the content of the rest of this book. The 7-S Framework Applied to Privacy Leadership topics in this book are provided in Table 2.1.

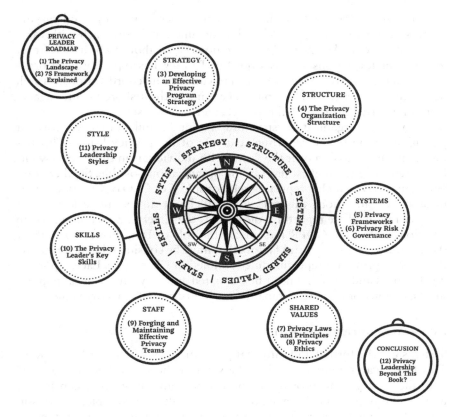

Figure 2.2 McKinsey 7-S framework applied to privacy leadership.

Privacy program strategy

Strategy embodies those actions an organization plans to execute in response to, or from, anticipated changes in the external environment (i.e., new technology or new/enhanced regulation), customers (i.e., new applications, methods of service, products), and competitors. The organization also must be looking to improve their competitive position by adding more value, lowering the cost, and increasing sales – or the competition will. The privacy leader must also build a vision and strategy to protect personal data at the lowest cost, assisted by tools and methods to develop and maintain the strategy. Emerging technologies need to be understood, so that proper investments can be made to leverage these technologies for maximum privacy protection.

Privacy organization structure

Organizations are structured to divide the tasks and provide coordination of activities. Over the years, organizations have had centralized functions, decentralized functions, specialized activities (such as privacy), and varying degrees of organization by product line or functional area, each with varying spans of control. Matrixed organizations came about to be able to react to different formations of areas quickly. Privacy has typically been organized in a central area due to the need to concentrate coordination and skill development. This model is rapidly changing with offshore talent, engagement of external firms, global presence, and remote users.

The privacy organization structure cannot be fully discussed without paying attention to the reporting structure of the privacy leader. This has fueled much discussion over the years, with individuals in those roles wanting to report to the highest level in the organization possible. Smaller companies may have a higher reporting relationship (i.e., CEO or COO), whereas in larger organizations this role may still be at an executive level, with another intermediate reporting role such as the Chief Legal Counsel, etc. In addition to this, the GDPR introduced the role of Data Protection Officer (DPO) and prescribes several factors that must be considered in determining the most appropriate reporting line (outlined in Chapter 4). Each reporting line has pros and cons that must be evaluated and may vary by legal requirements, conflict of interest, company size, industry, and maturity state.

Privacy program systems

Systems are the formal and informal procedures by which work gets done. This factor can dominate all the others and if the systems are not aligned with the strategy and provide the necessary information, they can have a detrimental impact on achieving the strategy. Take for example, the organization that fails to select an appropriate privacy framework, a "system for the privacy leader", to measure maturity over time, or worse yet, the organization that picks 2–3, and changes the approach every other year. In either case, the organization will find it difficult to achieve an effective strategy as the "product du jour" is implemented without a sense of what currently exists or what the current level and expected levels of maturity are there. In other words, without following a consistent system or approach, attaining the strategic goals related to effectiveness may be a struggle. Finally, the risk management processes are key in any privacy program to determine the appropriate level of risk and mitigation strategies, and in GDPR the fundamental component of the risk-based approach are Data Protection Impact Assessments (DPIAs).

Privacy program shared values

Shared values, originally named superordinate goals, refer to the higher order goals of the organization or a set of aspirations and guiding concepts that are sometimes unwritten and may not be in the formal statements of objectives, but which represent ideas around which a business is built. A shared value binds the company together and is a way of thinking. Tim

Cook, CEO at Apple, echoed the need for these values, stating "My belief is that companies should have values, like people do" in response to being challenged at an investors meeting to only make moves that would be profitable for the company. To infuse privacy values into the organization, we first need to define what the values are. Here, we are not talking about the systems to achieve the results, such as those noted in the privacy program systems section (such as leveraging the incidents of others and considering the maze of privacy frameworks), as these explain how we accomplish advancing the privacy posture of the organization by evaluating risk, applying privacy frameworks, and reducing the likelihood of a breach. The privacy program shared values, on the other hand, represent the higher-level values of the organization and are related to a) laws and regulations that organizations are subject to, b) an organization's concern for and approach to data protection and privacy, and c) meaningful policies and procedures stating the expectations of the organization, and organizational risk appetite.

As shown in Figure 2.1 for the 7-S framework, the privacy shared values are at the center, connecting the strategy, structure, staff, skills, and style factors, as they impact the delivery of each of those factors. For example, if privacy is not taken seriously within the organization as a core shared value, it is doubtful resources will be hired (staff), with appropriated privacy knowledge (skills), or there will be a function focused on privacy or data protection (structure). Introduce a law, regulation, and policies to the contrary, and the shared values of the organization may shift, embracing stronger protection of personal information, as focus is placed on these regulations to become compliant.

Privacy program staff

The 7-S Framework posited that organizations maintain two different views of staff: 1) people are treated in "hard" terms of salaries, performance measurement systems, and formal training programs or 2) a focus on the "soft" terms of morale, attitude motivation, and behaviors. The model asserts that top executives dislike either approach, as the first one leads the company to put the human resources department in charge of ensuring people are treated appropriately while the later gives visions of psychologists analyzing the moves of the employees. The model indicates top organizations focus on their talent from the time they are hired and throughout their career, many times allocating new hires to key departments where they can grow and make a difference, as well as promoting to higher-level positions early in their career (early mid-thirties). Top companies try and understand their talent and provide training to become effective managers and spend time continuing to develop their top managers.

We present and discuss Meredith Belbin's nine team roles to understand individuals within a team and what their key strengths in the team dynamic will be. Thus, helping to understand, respect, and appreciate the differences between team members, making for a more productive team environment.

We also discuss Beckhard's GRPI Model (Goals, Roles, Processes, and Interpersonal Relationships) as a tool to help build high performing teams.

Privacy program skills

We characterize organizations not by their strategies or structures, but rather by what they do best. Skills are clearly important as the strategy of the organization shifts into new markets and services or faces increased competition to fend off new disruptive startups aiming to cut into the business. In this chapter, we present two sets of skills based on the responsibilities of two key privacy leader roles, that is, the traditional CPO versus the DPO. Because the privacy leader maintains such a pivotal role for the organization, the focus here is on both the technical skills of the privacy leader and the softer skills required by the privacy leader.

Privacy leadership style

There are many books on leadership development for developing employees and managers. Different leaders have different styles and can still be effective. Each leader chooses to spend their time in different ways and must understand the organization culture to know what is important. Some leaders manage by "walking around" to know their staff, peers, and other department staff, while others are holding meeting after meeting. Each leader's style has an impact on the workforce, and in this section, we present Daniel Goleman's Harvard Business Review research article on leadership styles "Leadership that gets results".

Table 2.1 McKinsey 7-S framework applied to privacy leadership

7-S factor	Privacy topic	Chapter	Coverage
ROADMAP	Privacy leadership and the McKinsey 7-S Framework	2	7-S Framework is defined. 7-S Framework applied to privacy leadership.
STRATEGY How do we intend to meet our objectives?	Developing the privacy strategy Success factors for the privacy strategy	3	Privacy tools and techniques. Emerging technologies to consider.
STRUCTURE How is the team divided? What is the organizational hierarchy? How do team members align themselves? Is decision-making centralized?	CPOs and DPOs CPO responsibilities DPO responsibilities	4	Privacy leadership functions. Determining best fit. Reporting lines.

(Continued)

Table 2.1 (Continued)

7-S factor	Privacy topic	Chapter	Coverage
SYSTEMS What systems does the privacy leader use to run the privacy organization? What controls are in place to ensure they are being managed (maturity)? What is the impact of external incidents influencing the control development?	Privacy framework maze Privacy risk governance and oversight	5 6	Privacy frameworks explained. Privacy certifications explained. Accountability. DSARs. Privacy risk management. Privacy Risk Assessments
SHARED VALUES What are the core privacy values shared across the organization (policies, procedures, standards, laws, ethics? How strong are these values? Does the culture support the mission of the privacy leader?	Privacy laws Privacy ethics Privacy as an ESG	7 8 8	Privacy laws and regulations. Emerging legislation. Data protection key components. Privacy by design (PbD). Privacy laws and common principles. Privacy as a CSR. Privacy as an ESG. GRI and ISO standards.
STAFF What are the differences between team members, team dynamics, and how does this impact managing the team?	Team formation theories Team dynamics Team roles	9	Leadership implications. Belbin's team roles Beckhard's GRPI model.
SKILLS What skills does the privacy leader need? What are the innate preferences of the privacy team and what are the implications for leadership?	CPO skills DPO skills Privacy leadership soft skills	10	Talking vs listening. Soft skills (influencing, negotiating, writing, presenting, networking, etc.). Technical excellence vs organizational enablement. Value of certifications. Talking to the board.
STYLE How effective is the privacy leader with the board? What is the role of the board with respect to privacy?	The privacy leader's style of leadership and its influence on team effectiveness and engagement	11	Goleman's 6 leadership styles

SUGGESTED READING

Fitzgerald, T. (2019). *CISO Compass: Navigating Cybersecurity Leadership Challenges with Insights from Pioneers*. Boca Raton: Auerbach Publications.

Fortune. (2018). 100 best companies to work for. http://fortune.com/best-companies/list

Leswing, K. (2016). Apple CEO Tim Cook: 'Companies should have values, like people do'. *Business Insider, U.K.* http://uk.businessinsider.com/apple-ceo-tim-cook-companies-should-have-values-like-people-2016-8?r=US&IR=T

Peters, T. (1982). *In Search of Excellence: Lessons from America's Best-Run Companies*. Harpers and Row.

Think Marketing (2016). Have you ever read about Apple's core values? (January 11). https://thinkmarketingmagazine.com/apple-core-values/

Waterman Jr., R., Peters, T., Phillips, J. (1980). Structure is not organization. http://tompeters.com/docs/Structure_Is_Not_Organization.pdf

Section II

Strategy

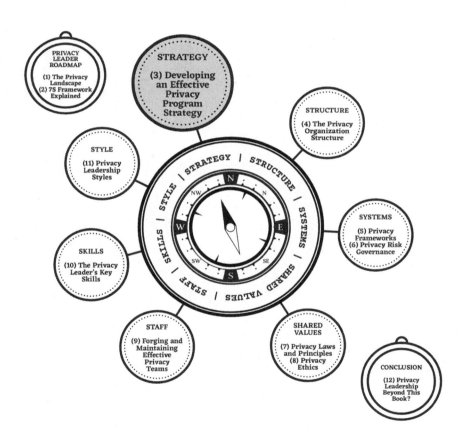

Chapter 3

Developing an effective privacy program strategy

Strategy without tactics is the slowest route to victory. Tactics without strategy is the noise before defeat.

Sun Tzu 544–496 BC

John Kotter best summarized the process of strategy by stating, "Leaders establish the vision for the future and set the strategy for getting there". This very succinctly sums up two key components of strategy: 1) setting a vision and 2) creating a mechanism to attain the vision. Both are necessary, or the target will not resonate with the team charged with implementing the strategy and the methods for getting there will be left to chance. A privacy strategy is about more than just legal compliance and ensuring adherence to a good privacy policy. A well-managed privacy strategy helps to embed privacy into the overall business practices of the organization and can serve many functions including maintaining quality and value of data, enhancing brand reputation, engendering increased consumer trust, meeting consumer expectations, safeguarding data against attacks and threats, meeting the expectations of business partners and clients, and meeting regulatory compliance. If done well, a privacy strategy can positively influence the organization's bottom line!

FOUR WAYS ORGANIZATIONS DEVELOP A PRIVACY STRATEGY

Commonly, the need for a privacy program "appears one day" as the result of an incident, public disclosure of information, a new law or regulation which must be complied with, or an inquiry from a member of senior management that was reading about a privacy incident that was experienced by one of their competitors in the news. This scenario is depicted in Figure 3.1.

What follows is that someone is assigned to resolve the incident or come up with what needs to be done for the privacy program. The assigned individual then takes this assignment on, in addition to his/her other responsibilities, and starts fixing the problem at hand. After a series of small successes

DOI: 10.1201/9781003383017-5

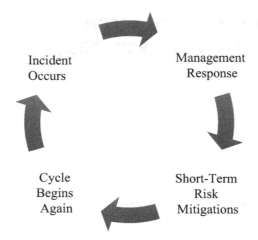

Figure 3.1 Incident-driven privacy approach.

and a further understanding of the broader scope of privacy, the person charged with addressing privacy requests more resources, and is initially met with resistance. A few more projects are taken on, and problems tackled, increasing the visibility of the privacy function. In this scenario, the strategy is the result of looking in the rear-view mirror and articulating the accomplishments of what has been completed to gain more funds to further initiatives. The focus becomes that of a) attempting to prevent the next incident and b) responding to the next incident in a more organized, timely manner. Since limited privacy expertise was most likely available within the organization, the focus of this strategy development is tilted toward fixing privacy so the reported incident which first initiated the program is resolved.

One could argue that using an immediate privacy incident to spur the organization into action is not developing a strategy at all and is more akin to "running by the seat of your pants" or managing by chaos. The reality is that organizations do not always have the foresight or the knowledge within the organization to recognize the role that privacy should play within the business. They may not have an advocate for privacy that can articulate how implementing or expanding this function can be good for the business by reducing costs, increasing market share, creating a competitive advantage, etc. Imagine also that a privacy incident is occurring, and the person assigned says, "We should create a strategy to develop and implement a privacy program to deal with this". Using the nomenclature put so well within the book, Good to Great – there may not be a seat on the next bus for that individual! When there are urgent business problems to solve, the first order of action is to put out the fire and then work on the fire suppression equipment, safety procedures, install additional smoke/carbon monoxide detectors, buy fire extinguishers, and so forth. The same principle applies to privacy incidents, while they may spur us into action and get the ball rolling, we must address the immediate issue at hand first.

A second approach is to proactively perform an assessment of the privacy practices that are in place, usually by partnering with an external firm to conduct an objective review, creating a vision, mission, and short and long-term multi-year plans for addressing the problem areas, concentrating on the areas of highest risk first as illustrated in Figure 3.2. This top-down approach is beneficial in that it provides broad coverage for all the domains and can be established without focusing on an immediate trigger, as in the incident-driven privacy strategy approach. The top-down approach also takes into consideration the risks of the privacy domains and areas evaluated and future business projects and opportunities versus focusing on the issue that is getting the most visibility at the time.

The third approach, as shown in Figure 3.3, is the bottom-up privacy strategy approach, whereby the privacy leader examines the infrastructure, various regulations, and privacy frameworks and begins to fill in the gaps based on those presenting the highest risk to the organization. Initially, the privacy leader may perform this activity without much involvement or buy-in from senior management, thus the characterization of a bottom-up approach. This approach usually entails an analysis of the current environment and focuses on "what's missing today" vs. expending energy on "where are we going tomorrow". The value in this approach is that it can inform the future direction and movement to a greater level of maturity driven by a subsequent top-down approach. Many organizations start the analysis using

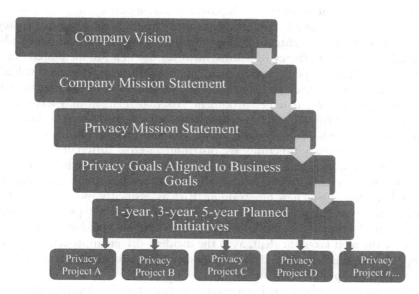

Figure 3.2 Top-down privacy strategy approach.

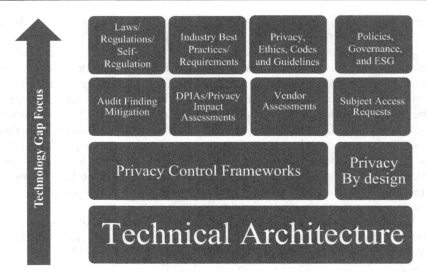

Figure 3.3 Bottom-up privacy strategy approach.

a bottom-up approach to understand the current state before engaging senior management to explore the expectations of how privacy practices can protect and enable the business. The focus typically begins with the gaps in the technical infrastructure and becomes the de facto strategy as projects are added to fill in the gaps.

A fourth type of strategy development is performed by not consciously creating a strategy at all. Organizations that could be classified as privacy unaware fall into this category. They are the organizations that have individuals performing privacy functions, however not in a pre-meditated manner. Privacy "just happens" within these organizations as different individuals are assigned the various privacy functions, whether it is called that or not. For example, in a regulated environment, risk management may have communicated the "rules", whereby these rules subsequently trickle down to administrators who comply with them, and the process involves privacy requirements. Privacy functions are distributed across different individuals within the organization without a master plan of what should be performed or anyone specifically "at the helm". Human resources provide guidance on confidentiality during new hire training. Risk assessments and reviews of the latest privacy regulations are usually non-existent in this type of organization. Plans for upcoming initiatives are sparse and new initiatives are generated by the next large incident, as in the incident-driven approach. This can impact continued access to data (availability), inappropriate access to data, or unintended public disclosure.

So whatever method has been used to initiate the development of a privacy strategy, whether leveraging the privacy incident in the incident-driven approach, the pre-planned, systematic top-down vision-driven approach, the structured bottom-up privacy approach, or by the accidental privacy approach, it should be recognized that all organizations have a privacy strategy, deliberate or not. The more planned the strategy is, the more likely that the strategy will be one that meets the needs of the business and is properly aligned with the business strategy. The incident-driven and accidental privacy strategy approaches have a relatively slim chance of meeting the needs of the business, as privacy incidents, problems of the day, or third-party vendors tend to drive what the privacy response will be vs a thought-out plan. The bottom-up approach is where companies usually begin the formal process before senior management has embraced the program.

PRIVACY AS A CORE BUSINESS STRATEGY ISSUE

Kirk J. Nahra

Partner, WilmerHale

When I first became involved in privacy issues, it was a niche issue of importance only to a handful of industries (mainly health care and financial services). Today, with the explosion of privacy and data security laws around the country (and around the world), privacy obligations now apply to almost every company in every industry around the world.

Even more than merely a "compliance" issue, privacy should also now be viewed as a core strategy issue for a wide range of companies, particularly (but not exclusively) start-up companies. And while privacy and security compliance may not always be at the top of mind, understanding the risks and opportunities in an increasingly complicated privacy framework is essential for a growing number of companies. These issues affect a broad range of critical topics for start-ups, including business partnerships, overall business plan issues, market opportunities, and of course realistic acquisition opportunities. Start-ups failing to think about these issues from the beginning may be missing opportunities and reducing their chances for future success.

These issues are particularly sensitive now because of the complexity of the US privacy regulatory eco-system. The United States has a large (and growing) number of laws and regulations at the state and federal levels (and even some international laws to be worried about). These laws have (to date) been specific by industry segment (e.g., health care, banking), by practice (e.g., telemarketing), or by data category (biometrics, genetic data, children's data). Today, there is no generally applicable US privacy law at the federal level covering all industries and all data (although that may be changing), but there is increasing complexity within the regulatory environment because of this multiplicity of laws. We also are beginning to see state-level laws (such as the California Consumer Privacy

Act) that apply across industries on a "comprehensive" level. In addition, we are seeing a new set of "specialty" privacy laws dealing with emerging technologies like facial recognition and location data. The Dobbs decision and various aggressive regulatory enforcement matters (particularly the FTC's GoodRx case) are increasing regulatory and enforcement risk. These US principles are mirrored and often expanded internationally, where a growing number of countries have privacy and data security laws. Where these laws exist (and they exist in a growing number of countries), the rules usually are tougher, meaning that they are more protective of individual privacy.

This means that it is critical for companies to be thinking about these issues as they are planning their overall business activities. For example, given that current U.S. law is primarily sectoral, determining where your company fits into these sectors is crucial. In the health care space, if your business model is direct to consumer, you typically have modest legal obligations today. If you partner with health insurers or hospitals, you are likely subject to the HIPAA privacy and security rules as a service provider to these entities – with different legal obligations and risks and opportunities to use personal data. Thinking about where your business operates also matters in evaluating whether you are subject to laws in other countries or state-specific laws. These principles matter for overall compliance, product design, customer and vendor relationships, marketing opportunities, and, critically, mergers and acquisition activity, given that purchasers now are drilling down into data assets, data rights, and privacy and security compliance.

So, what should companies be thinking about? A few key questions are listed below, but make sure your company is considering how privacy law can apply to what you want to do as a business.

Companies should answer the questions below when thinking about business operations, right from the start or as your business evolves:

- Data flows – what personal data are we generating?
- From where are we obtaining other personal data? Did we (or our source) have the right permissions and rights?
- Are we collecting or using sensitive data categories, including health, financial, genetic, biometrics, facial recognition, location, etc.?
- Can we "aggregate" data for analytics or product improvement?
- Can we legally or practically de-identify the data?
- What are we doing with our data?
- What rights do we have in the data?
- Are we interested in selling the data?

- What happens to relevant data at the end of a client relationship?
- Who are our customers and partners?

The privacy area is rapidly evolving and likely will continue to do so for the foreseeable future. A growing number of states are passing broad-based privacy laws. The federal government likely will pass a national privacy law in the next few years. New technologies raise concerns as does the use of artificial intelligence and algorithms. Legal developments – the Dobbs decision, an activist Federal Trade Commission, and international challenges – are dictating new paths. Start-ups should plan for these issues from the beginning – it does not take much to think about these issues, but it will mean real risks and missed opportunities to not think about them at all.

HOW TO BUILD A PRIVACY STRATEGY

An oft-asked question by privacy leaders is where do I begin to develop the strategy? Is there a guide I can use? What is the preferred strategy? Because businesses have different challenges, operate in different industry verticals, are subject to different regulations, are facing similar/different threats, are in different geographical regions, are protecting different types of information assets, and have differing levels of resources available to commit to privacy – the strategies are inherently different. Each consulting firm will have their own proprietary methodology to assist in building the privacy strategy. While one organization may be more efficient and have a thought-out structured process for developing the strategy, there is no proprietary "secret sauce" in these strategies and the results really come down to the extent the firm is able to quickly digest the business initiatives of the company and match privacy policies, processes, and technology to the protection and detection of critical information asset compromise and envision the future. While competent staff that understand the options are required, equally important is the engagement of business staff internally to articulate the concerns, products, and services on the horizon and significant business changes. The overall process for developing a privacy strategy is shown in Figure 3.4.

Step One – Determine why you were hired

Before developing the privacy strategy, it is useful to step back and ask, "why was I hired for this position?" Was I the first privacy leader? 2nd? 3rd? Was there an issue that needed to be solved and I had a specific skill set they needed? Or why did I decide to take this job? More than a fleeting moment

Figure 3.4 Privacy strategy development framework.

should be taken with these questions. While we would like to think that we were hired because of our education, knowledge, and ability to run a privacy program for the hiring company, these factors are most likely, in truth, merely table stakes. To put it another way, it is expected that we know the right privacy practices or they would not have invited us to the party to be interviewed. The question of – why you were hired – goes deeper than the list of requirements in the job description. There was most likely some trigger event at the organization which prompted the hiring. The privacy leaders' position may be the first position being filled after a regulation has caught management's attention. The previous privacy leader may not have been a good fit with the culture, they may have left the organization due to a lack of privacy investment by the organization, or the organization may have recruited them to satisfy a regulatory or "privacy" checkbox. Alternatively, the previous privacy leader may have simply left to move to a new role.

Why is this important? This is important because understanding the conditions by which the privacy leader is hired helps understand what may be possible in executing a new strategy. For example, if the prior privacy leader moved on to another role due to a very public privacy incident, the new privacy leader may have much more latitude to change the existing program and secure greater resources and investments. If this role is the first privacy leader hired, the time to implement the strategy may be longer as the executive culture adjusts to the requests to invest additional money to build the privacy program in an environment where a privacy breach has not previously occurred (that they are aware of). If a longtime incumbent running a bare bones privacy program has left the company, the new privacy leader may be challenged with a "not broken, don't fix it" mentality and limited to the predecessor's budget, even though the focus may have been solely on basic privacy compliance and little more.

By listening to the stakeholders and understanding their needs during this period, a strategy can reflect the values of the organization and truly be in alignment with the business objectives. If after reviewing the interview questions and talking with people it is still unclear as to the "real" reason you were hired, just ask! The real answer may or may not be provided in response, and may vary by whom is asked, and that can be telling as to the motivations for the position as well.

Before developing the privacy strategy, the person responsible for developing the strategy needs to understand the organization's past experiences with privacy. Organizations tend to have long memories with projects that failed and relatively short-term memories with projects that were successes and had little visibility. Failure may have been due to not enough resources applied, lack of available technical expertise, failure to communicate project vision, lack of management support, etc. Alternatively, it may have had more to do with clashes of personality of the individual responsible for the implementation utilizing an autocratic approach vs a collaborative approach.

Many privacy leaders will echo the sentiment, that "there is nothing like a good privacy incident". While it is true that the first incident raises the level of awareness and importance that adequate controls be in place and many times does provide the necessary funding, the problem is that the second, third, and fourth times-the "sky is falling" message is given. The response from senior management is likely to be – find a way to prevent the issue from reoccurring with the resources that have already been provided. It is much more effective however to have a privacy strategy roadmap or plan laid out which provides concrete enhancements to the business to deal with the threats facing the organization. This is not to assert that incidents in the news of others should not be leveraged, as this is a good approach. The privacy leader needs to be strategic and judicious in the use of these incidents.

Step Two – Create a privacy vision statement

A vision statement is a written declaration clarifying an organization's meaning and purpose for stakeholders, especially employees. It describes the desired long-term results of the company's efforts. Most organizations today have a vision statement to direct the company employees to conduct business in a way that meets the overall goals of the organization. Vision statements are generally very short so that employees can easily grasp the essence of the strategy and behave in a manner that is consistent with the strategy. This is helpful to determine the right course of action in the absence of a documented policy. Just as the overall business needs to have a vision, mission statement, goals, and action plans, so does the privacy program if it is to sustain long-term viability and be effective in meeting the needs of the business. The vision is about the goals of the privacy program or team and how to achieve them. The privacy vision statement reflects the organization's core values toward privacy and supports the mission of the organization. A vision should get people excited or inspired to move in the direction necessary.

The vision should motivate the team to make a difference and be part of something bigger than themselves. Why do the privacy role(s) exist? If the privacy leader could wave a wand, what would the perfect future look like? Paint that vision. Help people understand why the privacy team is there (or person!) and the value added to the organization, as well as what are the roles and responsibilities of everyone in the company to achieve this vision. These should be succinct statements that inspire action. We shouldn't fall into this trap of explaining what we do in a vision statement, these are left to individuals' goals, objectives, and plans to accomplish the vision.

Step Three – Examine internal and external environment constraints

Companies work within the context of a much larger environment and are subject to external circumstances beyond what is created by them. These include the regulatory environment, strategies of the competitors, being aware of the emerging threats, knowing the cost structures, and leveraging the external independent research that is available.

Regulatory

Each organization should understand the regulatory environment within which they participate. Is the organization transacting business subject to the GDPR? Are they transacting business subject to the California Consumer Privacy Act (CCPA)? Do they process biometric information subject to state laws such as the Illinois Biometric Privacy Law (BIPA)? Do they process sensitive information that requires additional security or privacy measures? Do they maintain Protected Health Information (PHI) and subject to the Health Insurance Portability & Accountability Act (HIPAA)? Are they complying with disclosure notification laws? Many non-privacy specific regulations also influence privacy. For example, several financial regulations mandate information to be safeguarded and its integrity assured. Specific internal security controls need to be identified to protect these data, auditing must take place. Crossovers exist in regulations such as Digital Operational Resilience Act (DORA), the Digital Services Act (DSA) and the Digital Markets Act (DMA). Additionally, is the company subject to a regulatory body to operate, such as Finance Codes and Markets in Financial Instruments Directive (MIFID) and are there specific privacy requirements for that sector regulation? Are they processing credit cards and subject to the Payment Card Industry Data Security Standards (PCI DSS)?

The regulatory landscape for every organization is completely different; however, typically there is a base landscape from which most organizations in a particular section operate.

ADAPTING YOUR APPROACH WHEN COMMUNICATING PRIVACY CHALLENGES ACROSS BORDERS AND CULTURES

Sayid Madar

Head of Operations, Office of the Data Protection Commissioner, UAE, Abu Dhabi's International Financial Center, ADGM

Receiving an email from senior leadership following a discussion with their department is a common occurrence. However, when the email starts with *"What do you mean we can't...."* is rarely a good start. This was unfortunately my first misstep as a former EU regulator moving into a commercial environment in the Middle East where I was responsible for overseeing global privacy. The issue at hand here was a proposed global email campaign to approximately 8 million individuals in over 60+ countries. While I identified immediately that the *"send to all"* suggested approach would likely be non-compliant as electronic marketing and data collection rules are not aligned across jurisdictions, there are better ways of conveying this.

So, with the benefit of hindsight, it's important to recognize that projecting your expertise in applying laws like the GDPR or ePrivacy Regs doesn't necessarily translate to results across borders. Solution? Start with an explanation of the issue. In this case, why do jurisdictions enact rules governing electronic marketing and privacy? To provide individuals with a choice over receiving unsolicited marketing.

Ask probing questions like:

(1)   How did you collect the email addresses?
(2)   Where were they located at the time of the collection?
(3)   What were they informed?

Unsurprisingly, the responses showed that some were opt-in, some were inferred, and some were collected in the course of a sale of a service. We undertook research and analyzed jurisdictions which we then categorized as: (a) Strict Jurisdictions; (b) Moderate Jurisdictions; and (c) Relaxed Jurisdictions. The categorization supported the creation of rules allowing the business to target recipients based on the way consent was gathered and their location.

This method can be applied to other issues and departments. When dealing with legal, you will most likely get a positive response by applying a legalistic approach by citing regulations, case laws, and guidance from regulators on its interpretation. When dealing with IT, they may be more receptive to data quality or security implications. Always adapt communication styles and consider how best to present your advice to teams who may be unfamiliar with their obligations or may view you as an obstacle.

Competition

Most board of directors want to know how the privacy strategy and investment compares with that of their competitors. The objective in many companies is to spend no more and no less than that of their competitors, unless privacy is seen to provide a competitive advantage that is worth the additional investment. It can be very difficult, in practice, to ascertain what the competitors are spending on privacy (although for some large organizations, we do get some insight from disclosures such as CSR reports and annual corporate reports), as this information is not generally shared. Companies may also have information from other employees that were hired away from competitors. Intelligence, whether formal or informal, is obtained at some level by an organization, hopefully through ethical means, to enable the organization to differentiate their products and services to obtain a competitive advantage.

The reason organizations prefer to spend the same amount on privacy as their competitors is that an organization must allocate funds across the different business units in a way that maximizes profitability. Spending more on a function such as privacy, which is traditionally viewed as a cost of compliance (i.e., doesn't increase revenue), would normally be viewed as money that is not available to grow the business. This assumption makes privacy investment a hard sell in most organizations; however, being able to articulate competitor investments in developing the strategy is one way to garner support for the strategy. This is especially true if the competitor will be using this knowledge to bid on or obtain, new business that the company is also pursuing. Spending the same amount in this context provides the Board of Directors with the comfort that they are not overspending, while at the same time, providing the comfort that they are exercising due diligence in funding the privacy efforts. If a privacy incident occurs in the future and they are subject to external governmental review or a lawsuit, they can provide justification that they spent an appropriate amount on the protection of personal data given the business climate in which they operated.

DON'T OVERLOOK EMERGING TECH PRIVACY RISKS

Rebecca Herold

CEO, Privacy & Security Brainiacs SaaS Services and the Privacy Professor Consultancy

Capable privacy pros understand privacy basics and legal requirements. Outstanding privacy pros, who bring noticeable and measurable values to the business also have this understanding, and additionally, the ability to identify privacy and security risks created by new tech, often overlooked until after a privacy breach occurs. To be an outstanding and valuable privacy pro, you need to be confident in your capabilities and willing to act upon your curiosity. Don't be constrained by finite lists or established rules and compliance requirements. Privacy risks always exist with new technology products within the business environment even when no legal requirements govern them and in the absence of lists.

My entire career I've identified security and privacy risks with new technologies and associated practices. A few examples:

Created and implemented my Fortune 200 corporation employer's first anti-malware program, as well as the remote access solution, in the early 1990s.

Led the first-ever privacy impact assessment (PIA) for the US Smart Grid and then co-authored the NISTIR 7628 Smart Grid Guidelines for Cybersecurity and Privacy, the NIST Privacy Framework and associated supporting resources, and co-authored the NIST IoT Cybersecurity SP 800-213 and NISTIR 8259 documents, along with the NISTIR 8425 Profile of the IoT Core Baseline for Consumer Products.

A few years ago, I was sitting in my musculoskeletal physician's treatment center, surrounded by many types of medical devices. Curious to see if there were open access points, I used the Wigli app on my new phone and found over a dozen open access points. My doctor and the CISO were surprised when I told them this, and as I explained that I could see all the servers on the network, and all the data, with huge amounts of cleartext patient data being transmitted. Ultimately, it was determined that the medical devices had not been included in the clinic's annual risk assessment procedures, resulting in increasingly more vulnerabilities over several years.

New technologies currently creating many new undetected privacy risks and legal compliance challenges include Internet of Things (IoT) products, artificial intelligence (AI) tools, large language model (LLM) tools (e.g., ChatGPT), 5G technology, supply chain tech, mesh networks, embedded tracking tech (e.g., web beacons), and blockchain.

Stay aware of all emerging tech being incorporated into your business environment to be a valued and effective privacy pro. If you don't, you will experience security incidents and privacy breaches, and data protection regulation non-compliance penalties.

Emerging threats

In building the privacy strategy, emerging threats need to be considered. As discussed further in Risk Management, certain types of information will need more protection focus than others and will need further protection strategies. For example, an organization that processes credit card information or handles social security numbers will want to know where that information is located via the data classification activities. This information is more likely to be the subject of a targeted attack than other, non-proprietary or non-sensitive information within the company and will need to be protected appropriately. Or an organization who is considering the use of AI to infer new personal data or to assist in decision-making processes, for instance, by using AI text assistants such as ChatGPT. Threats that were typically considered cyber threats such as ransomware have now migrated into the privacy space, as they impact the integrity of, and access to, personal data.

Another emerging threat to consider is the use of AI and Facial Recognition software. In 2022, Hungary's Data Protection Authority (NAIH) levied a fine of HUF 250 million (EUR 675,675) against a bank for the shortcomings of its automatic AI analysis of the recordings of customer service calls, which included assessing the emotional state of the speaker and other characteristics. Another emerging threat emanates from the Internet of Things (IoT). The IoT refers to the network of physical devices, vehicles, home appliances, and other items that are connected to the Internet. These devices can collect a vast amount of personal data, including location, activity, and usage patterns. While IoT devices can greatly improve convenience and efficiency, they also pose significant risks to privacy, as the data collected by these devices can be used to track and monitor individuals without their knowledge or consent.

Social media platforms and big data analytics pose significant growing risks to privacy, as they can be used to collect vast amounts of personal data and use that data to target individuals with personalized marketing and advertising campaigns. Additionally, social media platforms have been criticized for their handling of user data, with concerns over the potential misuse or mishandling of personal information. The use of big data and social media when combined with AI leads to another emerging threat which is referred to as "data scraping" – an activity which is typically considered to have no standing under GDPR. For example, Clearview AI built its facial recognition database using images scraped from the Internet and was consequently served enforcement notices by several data protection regulators in 2022.

DATA PRIVACY PROGRAMMING IMPLICATIONS OF AI

Jeff Jockisch

CEO, Data Privacy Researcher, Privacy Plan

The startling success and rapid evolution of generative AI models in text-to-image and chat have brought with it many concerns, including that of data privacy.

Many different privacy implications can arise during the use of AI and machine learning models. Let's look first at the Corpi, the data used to train the models. Three injection points offer opportunities for issues.

Base Training Data (The privacy of data in the base training corpus) Chat AI, (*ChatGPT, Bard*) text dataset used to generate the Large Language Model or LLM. The text-to-image AI (*Dall-E, Midjourney, Stable Diffusion*) image dataset used to create a GAN or VAE, or another model.

The primary question: Where did the training data come from? Does it contain PII? And what can be done if the data turns out to be personal, biased, and/or inaccurate? How was the data gathered or scraped? Does it violate consent or copyright?

There will be lawsuits around these questions for years to come I suspect, but I doubt it will stop the coming innovation wave. LLMs, for instance, use vast quantities of scraped data, and only a very small portion of that data could be considered personal. In contrast with Clearview AI, who is scraping all our faces, our biometric info, to generate facial recognition models.

Interaction Data (The privacy of data gleaned from us while interacting) Services collecting and processing data from you when you interact with the model. What questions do you ask? What input do you provide? What images do you create? This data can be highly sensitive. The prompts you provide while interacting with AIs, in addition to your login information or a digital fingerprint, can connect it all to you. Is it being stored? Is it being used to retrain the model? Is it being sold?

There is the possibility that employees will share proprietary, confidential, or trade secret information when having "conversations" with a Chat AI. In fact, some corporations have banned usage while they evaluate the business risk.

What happens if a company shares client data with an AI? Where does the data go? Does it cross borders as a transfer? Is it stored indefinitely? Can it be deleted in response to a DSAR?

Proprietary Data (The privacy of private data sources we provide access to) AI models are trained with based data. Their value is often enhanced by exposure to new data sources. This can happen in a number of ways.

Let's suppose I link it to a project dataset so that it can answer questions about that data. I get a lot of value from this. I might then be able to query the AI about project tasks, deadlines, who is going to be late, who has extra capacity, etc. But what risks have I taken? If I link it to my product and sales data, that seems really cool. If I link it to my human resource data, that sounds very risky.

When we link AI to private datasets, are they sucking up all of that data for the enrichment of their models? Data transfer and DSAR issues now arise as above, as well as potential IP and privacy concerns.

These are just a few of the issues that I've seen with AI and privacy. New speech recognition AI models, which might sound passé compared to the tech above, could have even more profound impacts on our data privacy. This AI will create truly cheap, effective, and accurate transcriptions of our voice. This means voice commands will just work. Every video will be transcribed. Every voice will be recognized.

Think about the implications of everything you say being transcribed and turned into text. It's now searchable and attributable. Your boss can analyze your meeting input. Your teacher can analyze your class interactions. Your government can more effectively surveil you. This tech will bring more of our content, more of our interactions, and more of our offline actions into the digital realm. And make them potential privacy problems.

It's a brave new world. Be safe with your data.

External independent research

For an up-to-date understanding of privacy challenges and solutions, there are several key organizations that privacy professionals can turn to. The range of supports on offer can range from the provision of data for research purposes to the certification of privacy professionals. The list in Table 3.1 is not meant to be exhaustive but simply meant to offer insight into the range of supports available.

The International Association of Privacy Professionals (IAPP) was founded in 2000 to define, promote, and improve the privacy profession globally. It provides a credential program in information privacy (CIPP and CIPM), as well as educational and professional development services and hosts yearly conferences on privacy. "In late 1999 several of the large IT companies began hiring CPOs", said J. Trevor Hughes, CEO of the International Association of Privacy Professionals (IAPP), an organization of privacy officials that was formed in 2000. Today, IAPP has more than 50,000 members. And while the private sector leads that growth, government employees now represent a fair number of IAPP members, according to Hughes.

The Members of the European Privacy Officers Forum (EPOF) include data protection compliance officers and counsel from Europe. Members exchange information regarding data protection compliance, and the forum serves as a means for data protection authorities and business representatives to interact and discuss issues of mutual concern. Members in the European Privacy Officers Network (EPON) include data protection professionals who work for organizations that operate in more than one country. It meets three times a year to discuss privacy issues related to cross-border data flows.

The internal company culture

The company's external environment is clearly important to privacy strategies, as they represent how the world is interacting with our organizations. The internal company culture has a great impact on how successfully our

Table 3.1 Range of privacy supports

Organization	Offering
Enterprise Consulting	• Illustrations for privacy taxonomy.
Information is Beautiful	• Visualization of some of the largest data breaches in the world.
ISACA	• Privacy in practice report. • Certifications for CDPSE. • Advisory and guidance materials. • Privacy conferences.
Maastricht European Centre on Privacy and Cybersecurity Research	• Ethical approaches to privacy. • Professional masters on cybersecurity and privacy. • Certified DPO. • Privacy as CSR framework and research.
NOYB.EU (none of your business)	Schrems I and II. Advocacy
PrivacyRights.Org	• Laws overview. • Data breach chronology. • Databrokers database. • Definitions.
Privacy Rights Clearinghouse (PRC)	• A not-for-profit that maintains a database of data breaches since 2005.
PEW Research Center	• Privacy surveys of the US population.
The Future of Privacy Forum (FPF)	• Advisory and guidance materials. • Advocacy.
The Identity Theft Resource Center (IDRC)	• Database of data breaches in the US.
The International Association of Privacy Professionals (IAPP)	• Certification for CIPP, CIPM, CIPT etc. • Advisory and guidance materials. • Privacy Conferences. • Advocacy.
The Ponemon Institute (& IBM)	• Cost of a data breach report.
Verizon	• Data breach Investigations Report (DBIR).

security programs will be received. While it would be nice to be able to copy another organization's security strategy, implement the strategy as ours, and call it a day, unfortunately no two organizations have the same "norm of operation" and a security strategy that may work for one company may not work for another. The following are areas to give some thought to. It may not even be clear how the organization is operating and may need the perspective of several individuals at different management/end user levels to achieve an accurate assessment.

Risk appetite

A community banking organization may have a low-risk appetite and will tend to make very risk-averse decisions. A small retail company, for example, may use data in such a way to simply provide online transactions.

Whereas a large social media company may use data to infer trends and patterns and sell such data regarding trends and patterns to advertising or other interested companies, which is obviously a higher risk strategy. Risk-averse organizations will tend to have more rigid interpretation of privacy rules and less likelihood to grant exceptions. On the other hand, innovative organizations promoting creativity or research will tend to allow more creativity. This is not to say that one organization cares about privacy and another does not, however what often differs is the internal approach to privacy and the level of investment in the controls that provides protection in line with the culture, business operations, and management direction, and at the same time provides an adequate level of protection from unauthorized users. For instance, many years ago – Google's then CEO Eric Schultz famously said that "Google gets right up to the creepy line but never cross it". This illustrated clearly at that point, that Google had a high-risk appetite, but one that remained within the confines of the law.

Some organizations view the implementation of privacy enhancing technologies (PETs) or extended privacy programs in a similar way to prescription drug research and are willing to invest the money in multiple initiatives knowing that several will fail, understanding there will be one that is successful and will make up for the others. Pharmaceutical companies, for instance, spend hundreds of millions on research and clinical trials for new drugs, knowing that most of these drugs will fail in the testing process. The prices for the drugs which are viable and effective then carry the costs of the research for the failed drugs. Likewise, large organizations can invest larger amounts in privacy because they can spread their costs across many more users, systems, or products and services. If the solution does not turn out to be effective within a few years, the same organization will invest funds to replace it with a better solution. The smaller organization is more likely to select a product, service, or process that will last for a longer period. So, we find large public sector organizations investing in more recent PETs such as Differential Privacy where smaller organizations continue to rely on older, less-effective techniques.

Speed

Organizations move at different speeds, some acquiring one business and then acquiring another before the first acquisition is fully implemented. How long do privacy projects typically take? Weeks? Months? Years? An 18-month implementation will not be very well received in an organization that typically implements projects in a three-month timeframe. The privacy strategy needs to mirror the speed culture of the organization.

Leadership Culture: Collaborative vs Authoritative

Organizations structured in a command-control type organization where the subordinates are expected to follow the directives of their immediate supervisors tend to operate in an authoritative manner. Individuals may be encouraged within the organizations to suggest improvements to existing practices or suggest new processes; however, the decision-making authority in this case typically resides within the superior manager and is pushed down through the organization. Privacy policies and procedures are introduced via directives and established at higher levels within the company. Alternatively, collaborative organizations tend to request input and more discussion prior to the decisions made. Decisions are made collectively by a team or steering committee to achieve consensus on a direction. Privacy Risk Councils/Committees are very well received within this type of organization, and privacy policies are less likely to emerge solely as directives from one department.

Knowing who are the individuals in an authoritative structure whose opinions shape most of the company actions and plans would be beneficial to know. Time would be well spent with these individuals early in the strategy planning process to get them behind the strategy. In the collaborative organization, the senior executive may be looking for clues that opinions were solicited from others within their organization before they will agree to the strategy.

Trust level

An organization with low trust levels is a very difficult organization to work within, as it is unclear as to whom the message needs to be communicated to for it to be effective and who is ultimately in control. In this type of organization, it may be necessary to increase the number of stakeholders that need to accept the privacy strategy. By garnering broader support, it will be harder for a single individual acting on their own to undermine the security strategy. The trust level can be evaluated by matching up the statements made, and the actions observed. Two-way trust is obviously preferred to exist at the beginning of strategy development; the privacy leader may have to take the first step by implementing projects within the committed timelines and functionality promised to build the trust over time.

Individuals may also have hidden agendas related to their own advancement that the privacy leader should be conscious of. If a privacy strategy is viewed as adding time to a project that the individual is responsible for implementing or it is perceived that the project may not meet the deadline because of a new privacy policy, the individual may not fully support the implementation. The worst case may come when the manager appears to support the privacy initiative publicly, meanwhile does little to advance the effort. The manager could also not like the constraints that the privacy strategy places on their operations. Whatever the reason, it is important to understand which individuals are advocates for the privacy program and which individuals will serve as detractors.

Growth seeker or cost-cutter

Stocks can be classified in many ways, such as large capitalization stocks (greater than $10 billion revenue), mid-cap stocks ($2–$10 billion), small capitalization stocks (less than $2 billion), domestic, international, or by the sector or industry they operate in. Stocks are also classified as to whether they are considered a growth stock or a value stock. A growth stock is one in which there appear to be significant opportunities for the stock to grow in the future. These stocks typically represent either new start-ups or innovative established companies with product ideas that have not reached their full potential. Value stocks are those stocks where companies are perceived to be worth more than their book asset value, but for some reason, have been beaten down by the market and are now out of favor. These stocks are purchased in the hopes that someday the negative events pushing down the stock price are changed, and the stock will rise in value.

All companies want to increase revenues and cut costs. The distinction that is important here is that growth companies tend to invest more money than value companies in future product development and are more likely to embrace a growth privacy strategy that projects initiatives into the future that may not have immediate payback. Value companies, on the other hand, may be out of favor and are looking for significant cost reductions to increase the stock value. Projects may be cut and layoffs may be the norm to regain financial viability. If an organization is in the cost-cutting mode, and the privacy leader suggests a project with a large financial commitment with a payoff several years into the future, this may be embraced by a growth-oriented company that is willing to take the risk and has the investment projects for growth, but not by the value-oriented company that is searching for new ways to cut costs. There needs to be an immediate or short-term payback to gain the support of leadership with the cost-cutting company.

Company size

Large companies tend to be more willing to invest in more initiatives as noted earlier, in large part because the total impact of the budget of the organization will be less when initiatives do not work out as anticipated. In other words, the larger organization can hedge their bets. On the flip side, larger organizations are sometimes more bureaucratic, with more buy-in and management approval necessary before the initiative can move forward. Privacy strategies need to take this into account when establishing timeframes for implementation. Whereas a smaller organization may accept a contract more readily from a vendor without challenging it due to the lack of legal support or leverage with the large vendor, a large organization may require a couple of months to move the contract through the legal negotiation process. Similarly, a small organization may not need the level of documentation that a large organization may need to conduct business.

For example, a small organization with little or no staff turnover may not require the same amount of privacy awareness training as a large organization where turnaround is higher. A healthcare organization of any size, on the other hand, may require specific privacy protections such as encryption for all information, a large organization processing little personal information may not. Typically, however, the small organization still needs to address each of the domains within the privacy strategy albeit the degree of definition, documentation, and approach to satisfying the domain will be vastly different.

Outsourcing posture

The privacy strategy should consider the company's inclination to outsource functions or processing. What has the history of the company been? Is someone else currently providing the ICT, Payroll, Privacy, DPO, or Compliance services for the organization? Is processing occurring outside of the local legislative landscape? The outsourcing posture has implications not only for how the privacy organization should be managed as a function (employees, contractors, or outsourcing of pieces of the privacy function) but also for the controls which must be put in place for personal data being processed by another company or beyond company's borders. If the cost savings are significant or if the quality of work is viewed to be superior to the work that could be done internally, the privacy strategy must be written to incorporate processes and controls that legitimate the processing. Quite often, the outsourcing decisions are made at a very high company level with limited detailed input of costs at the time of agreement, as they tend to be kept very confidential. Few individuals are in the loop at this juncture. As the privacy program matures and the privacy leader becomes the trusted partner, involvement in the mergers and acquisitions discussion should increase. However, since leakage of these mergers can have significant consequences, involvement and information flow is typically limited to a select few. In either case, the privacy leader needs to be prepared to provide high-level estimates and processes, either during or shortly after the business partner engagement.

The privacy strategy needs to ensure that contractual obligations are established, and it is clear how the external functions will be managed. Take the case of outsourcing the internal email systems to a cloud-based provider. The question that should be addressed by the privacy strategy is who is responsible for ensuring the adequacy of the controls over the information? Or in the case of the privacy function being outsourced, is the outsourcer responsible for the DPO role? Is the outsourcer responsible for performing Data Protection Impact Assessments? Auditing? Testing? Identity management? Subject Access Requests? Nothing is inherently wrong with outsourcing functions, where it typically goes wrong is when expectations are not clear. Without proper strategy and agreements in place, such as Data

Processing Agreements (DPAs), and Service Level Agreements (SLAs), privacy expectations can be unclear. For instance, response times to Data Subject Access Requests (DSARs) may not happen in a reasonable timeframe and privacy awareness training may not occur as frequently or comprehensively as expected. Most notably – responsibilities for dealing with breaches and the responsibilities for addressing any disclosure and reporting requirements can be unclear.

THE CONVERGENCE OF DATA PROTECTION AND TECHNICAL DEBT

Stephen Massey

CISO & Outsourced DPO, Fox Red Risk

When I talk to IT departments about technical debt (TD), they mostly know what I am talking about. I'm speaking their language! But when I talk to fellow data protection leaders about technical debt, I get blank expressions. There is little awareness about the technical debt outside IT, all the while poorly managed technical debt has major impacts on data protection. So, what is TD and why should data protection leaders care about it?

Let's set the scene, you're a plucky developer working on a new healthcare app. You're under pressure to deliver and so quickly write messy code. But, hey it works – kind of. You know the code will not scale and only works under very specific conditions. You add comments to the code reminding yourself to rewrite (refactor) that code later – that future rewrite is now on the credit card as "technical debt" to be repaid one day. Before you get around to repaying that debt, your fellow developers start building on your code and soon their code becomes heavily dependent on your messy code. If you now change your code, their code will be impacted too. You now have a technical debt with accumulating interest! Months later, a new data protection regulation is introduced. It should have been a cinch to make the necessary changes to the app, but all that messy code has made, what was a one-day job, into a yearlong, unavoidable project – the bank is calling in all that debt and interest all at once because you have failed to manage your debt repayment! The leadership are now massively frustrated because paying down this debt is now materially deviating developer time away from revenue-generating activities. All because this technical debt was not effectively managed.

It doesn't have to be this way though. Data protection leaders can help by being part of the technical debt conversation. Here's how:

1) Understand the technical debt your organization and its vendors hold.

2) Work with IT and others to assess how future regulatory changes may impact the organization's technology roadmap.

3) Educate business leaders on how poorly managed technical debt can affect compliance activities – and the bottom line.

4) Advocate for effective technical debt management

To wrap up, every organization holds technical debt. Make sure data protection is a consideration when deciding how and when that debt is repaid.

Mergers and acquisitions posture

Does the organization undertake mergers and acquisitions or is it in a growth phase and buying smaller or ancillary organizations? Consideration of data protection and other associated issues in an M&A context is essential in developing a privacy strategy. Unlike employment or IP matters, privacy teams and leaders may lack well-established precedents for how to approach privacy risks that arise in M&A. For example, it is common practice in M&A transactions for the parties and their legal/financial advisors to exchange information about the target company during the due diligence process through a virtual data room ("VDR"). Information and documentation which contains personal data may be required to be uploaded to this data room, for example, contracts of employment, customer contracts, etc. This exchange of personal data would be deemed "processing" and as such must comply with the requirements of local and international privacy and data protection regulations among others. The EDPB has previously stated that it is essential to assess longer-term implications for the protection of economic, data protection, and consumer rights whenever a significant merger is proposed.

PRIVACY ADVICE IN THE M&A PROCESS AND RELATED COMMUNICATIONS

Marcin Czarnecki

Chief Privacy Officer, PayU

Mergers and acquisitions – a topic distant for many privacy and compliance specialists due to the dynamics of M&A transactions and the distinct imperatives to look at risks in a constructive way. Methods of work characteristic to M&A require fast, precise assessment of present and future risks, frequently based on limited information and common sense. This makes us – privacy professionals – feel uncomfortable. Even when we identify risks, we ask ourselves: How can I ensure that a risk is managed in such a fast-paced process? What should I communicate to make my advice pragmatic?

Referring solely to "likelihood and impact" driven risk assessments – while appropriate in a compliance world – might not easily match the reality of M&A transactions, which focus on price as its main parameter. The approach that I use to answer the above questions involves assigning value to as many aspects of privacy advice as possible, whether it's a recommended measure or a potential consequence. This allows the stakeholders (M&A teams, finance teams) to use the valuation directly in price or budget planning.

Let's look at some examples to illustrate that – imagine discovering that an acquired business has gaps in basic privacy compliance, for example, it's missing records of processing activities. While it's difficult to precisely quantify the potential regulatory exposure, a privacy professional can deliver an accurate indication of costs and efforts necessary to fill in the gap (e.g., costs of employing a privacy specialist), which can then be budgeted.

Another example can be that of a business that goes up for sale and is affected by new privacy laws coming into force after the transaction. Privacy leaders should be able to quantify the efforts needed to implement new controls prescribed by such regulatory changes. Moreover, such changes might affect the operations of the business, which should be communicated to the M&A team for them to evaluate the impact.

Although the application of this method might not allow us to quantify all the risks, it allows privacy leaders to influence the way M&A teams manage privacy risks during a transaction and makes us trusted partners for M&A activity.

Prior privacy breaches/incidents, audits

Evaluation of prior privacy incidents can be of great value in developing a privacy strategy. Did an end user leave a box of confidential information in his car with the engine running, only to have it stolen? Did an executive share her password with her administrative assistant so she could access his email? Was the business strategy sent unencrypted across the Internet? Was a data subject sending the wrong details in their subject access request response? Incidents provide a wealth of information as to what actions are not being performed within the company. Privacy incidents are like mice – where you see one, there must be many more that are not seen. The question to ask when building the privacy strategy is, do I have a stated control in place, as evidenced by the existence of a policy, procedure, and implemented activity which serves to mitigate or reduce the likelihood or impact of this event occurring? If the answer is no, then this item needs to be included in the privacy strategy. The tendency to evaluate how important an incident is by the number of occurrences that should be avoided, as there may only be one incident, but the potential impact may be large.

Internal and external audits also provide significant knowledge as to the process breakdowns within an organization. For instance, companies may do a very good job in documenting the policies and procedures but may do a very poor job of executing them. Is the problem one of communication (awareness) or culture (do as we do, not do as we say)? Is the problem one of misinterpretation? Or is there a personal disagreement with the standard or lack of supporting technical controls to support the policy? Audits should be reviewed, and unresolved findings should be used to enhance the privacy strategy. Previously resolved findings can also provide input as an issue may have been resolved by a quick fix to remove the finding, but a better long-term solution may be warranted and should be reflected within the privacy strategy.

External audits may or may not provide recommendations to mitigate the audit issue depending upon the nature of the audit (some firms will not provide recommendations in the post-Enron era as this may be viewed as a conflict of interest as it could possibly be viewed as providing consulting services). If they are providing an attestation of the controls, they are not supposed to provide advice. However, many auditors will informally be willing to provide their opinions outside of the formal written report as to what types of actions would have made the situation a non-issue and not result in a finding. This information can be very valuable in constructing the strategy, as the auditors are exposed to many different solutions across industries and companies.

If the organization is in the business of contracting work to other organizations, the government, or a parent company, other formal reviews of past performance should be reviewed. Reviews of past performance may include metrics such as ratings, quality, timeliness, meeting project deadlines, etc.

Step Four – What and where are the crown jewels?

Without knowing what to protect, we end up trying to protect everything at the same investment level. None of our companies have the resources to achieve this. Therefore, we need to identify exactly what we are protecting. Different industries will have different assets needing protection. This is a great exercise to engage the business areas, as any one organization may have hundreds or thousands of asset types needing protection, however, only a few will be considered "the crown jewels" of the organization. The privacy leader should have a good handle on what the crown jewels are and where they are. Crown jewels will be those systems, applications, databases, files, and folders etc. that contain or process personal data which if lost, compromised, inaccessible/unavailable, or disclosed would have the largest financial impact or damage to the brand (reputation). Figure 3.5 shows some examples of the "Crown Jewels" an organization may need to protect. In fact, under GDPR – a record of processing activities (ROPA) and data maps may be mandated ensuring that the privacy leader knows exactly what

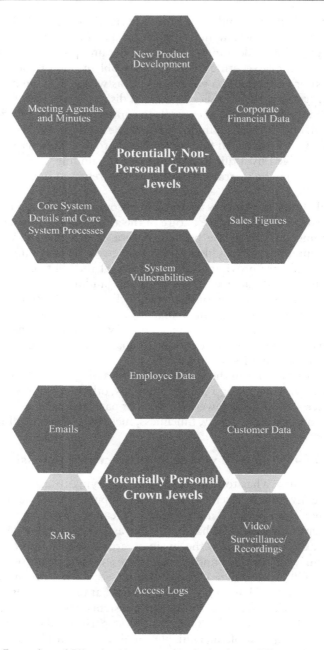

Figure 3.5 Examples of PII-related crown jewels (and non-PII crown jewels).

data is where and under what legal basis it is processed. Further details on assessing the Crown Jewels via a ROPA can be found in Chapter 4.

Step Five – Planning the next 12 months, 24 months, and 3–5 years

A good privacy strategy enables a privacy program to be planned that encompasses the management of privacy concepts, policies, procedures, and programs at the organizational level. It begins with establishing a privacy program framework and considers the vast responsibilities of the privacy leader. The full scope of a privacy program is all the activities within your business that touch and manage personal client information – from the first step of collection to the end-of-cycle deletion. The aspects of a successful program include support from senior management, ongoing team training, and a culture of solid privacy protection. Privacy programs should undergo regular reviews, with room for adjustments, and continual improvement.

Taking a global approach to privacy program management is not a new concept, however, it has changed with the introduction of data protection and privacy regulations such as the GDPR and the CCPA. Global organizations need to consider not just national/state but federal and international emerging privacy laws on the horizon to ensure that their privacy programs are being managed effectively and compliantly. They also need to consider beyond just privacy laws such as the ePrivacy regulation, cookie regulations, digital regulation, critical networks regulations, health-data specific regulations etc.

Developing a framework can help you to take global privacy obligations into account and set a benchmark for protecting personal data to the highest standard possible. Building a comprehensive privacy framework for your organization should also go beyond the collection of personal data and ensure that personal data is being stored and maintained securely throughout its lifecycle with your organization. This means that collaborations with other business functions are a must for privacy program management.

Budget cycles are determined on an annual basis in most organizations and typically consume 3–5 months of a year to determine. By having a 12- to 24-month cycle, progress can be shown and changes in the environment can be reacted to in a sufficient timeframe. As shown in Figure 3.6 Sample Privacy Plan 2025–2030, the initiatives to advance privacy are mapped to a control framework, in this case the NIST Privacy Framework, and progress to new states of maturity is shown in 12-month, 24-month, and three to five-year horizons. This permits communication within the organization to see the short-term goals (12–24 months) as well as the long-term goals taking 3–5 years. If additional funding becomes available or a threat is deemed to have a higher risk level, then the strategy can be adjusted. While this charge shows the maturity related to a framework, the same mapping can be done by replacing the NIST categories with the business processes, products,

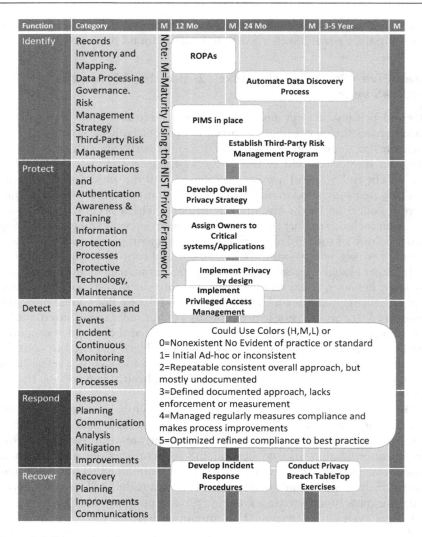

Function	Category	M	12 Mo	M	24 Mo	M	3-5 Year	M
Identify	Records Inventory and Mapping. Data Processing Governance. Risk Management Strategy Third-Party Risk Management		ROPAs		Automate Data Discovery Process			
			PIMS in place		Establish Third-Party Risk Management Program			
Protect	Authorizations and Authentication Awareness & Training Information Protection Processes Protective Technology, Maintenance		Develop Overall Privacy Strategy					
			Assign Owners to Critical systems/Applications					
			Implement Privacy by design					
			Implement Privileged Access Management					
Detect	Anomalies and Events Incident Continuous Monitoring Detection Processes							
Respond	Response Planning Communication Analysis Mitigation Improvements							
			Develop Incident Response Procedures		Conduct Privacy Breach TableTop Exercises			
Recover	Recovery Planning Improvements Communications							

Note: M=Maturity Using the NIST Privacy Framework

Could Use Colors (H,M,L) or
0=Nonexistent No Evident of practice or standard
1= Initial Ad-hoc or inconsistent
2=Repeatable consistent overall approach, but mostly undocumented
3=Defined documented approach, lacks enforcement or measurement
4=Managed regularly measures compliance and makes process improvements
5=Optimized refined compliance to best practice

Figure 3.6 Strategic privacy plan example.

or services which will be rolled out and the initiatives used to protect those business imperatives.

Once there is consensus on what needs to be protected and the approaches for protection, alternatives can be produced with cost estimates for management approval. Business cases may need to be developed according to organizational templates and processes for approval. Approval for these initiatives may be very time consuming in larger organizations and can take months to go through the socialization and acceptance process. The privacy leader needs to ensure the time for approval is built into any multi-year projections, as well as understanding the timing of the budget cycle. These business cases sometimes may request Return on Investment (ROI) calculations, as the business must decide on privacy investments in conjunction with other company investments. These calculations are very often difficult to project, as the privacy function does not in itself generally produce revenue and is viewed as a cost. However, costs can be associated with products and services being brought to market, the protection of the revenue streams from those products, and the reduction of risk.

Success factors for the privacy strategy

There are three things that are essential within an organization to ensure that a privacy strategy is successful, outlined below. Bear in mind that an organization's adoption of a new privacy program is not likely to succeed if any single one of these three elements is missing.

1. Executive Support
   When developing the privacy strategy, setting, and revising goals, approval from senior leadership is important. More than that, having visible, significant support from the C-Suite is key to overall success. When a company's executive team makes it clear that customer and client privacy is important to them, that significance permeates through the entire team and into the culture. Similarly, if senior leaders don't care about privacy, then the rest of the team will not be able to make it a priority.
2. Team Training
   Another way to emphasize the gravity and significance of maintaining strict privacy controls is through team training. The company's overall philosophy on maintaining privacy controls and meeting regulatory requirements should be outlined here so that all team members understand the "why" behind the privacy guidelines. Then, employees should consider what data they have access to and how a possible breach could take place. All team members should know what to do in the case of a privacy breach and how to report and escalate issues correctly. In addition, the proper handling of devices can be covered in training.
3. A Culture of Privacy Protection
   With senior management support and consistent team training, the privacy leader is on the path to building a culture that recognizes the importance of protecting privileged data. Maintaining strong privacy protocols and protecting against breaches and phishing scams is another way to keep privacy top of mind among team members. In addition, team culture can be infused with the importance of privacy by making sure to mention it in team documents, such as the employee handbook and other materials. In addition, marketing and/or public

relations may want to tout the organization's rigorous standards for handling matters of customer privacy as a point of differentiation for the business. All these factors add up to create a strong company culture steeped in privacy protection.

STEERING ORGANIZATIONS TOWARD HUMAN-CENTRIC DATA PRIVACY

Debbie Reynolds
CEO, Debbie Reynolds Consulting, LLC

The privacy challenge: Seeing data privacy as a bottom-line benefit to organizations.

Newsflash: Customer data is a valuable asset that belongs to the customer, and businesses must respect that by acting as responsible stewards.

The story: As the privacy advisor to large corporations, I ensure that companies comply with data privacy regulations while operationalizing the protection of customer data. However, in one instance, I soon realized that my role was much more complex than I initially thought. The company's existing data privacy policies were outdated and did not reflect customers' growing concerns.

I faced resistance from the leadership team and other departments, who saw data privacy as a burden and a hindrance to the company's growth. They were reluctant to change how they had been operating for years, even though I could see the clear benefits of a human-centric approach to data privacy.

I was determined to advise the company in a new direction and clarify how important customer trust is with data privacy. We researched, engaged with customers, and made a case to the leadership team for why a change was necessary.

Despite the challenges, I successfully secured buy-in from the leadership team and implemented several changes to the company's data privacy operations. These changes helped restore customer trust in the brand and made the company stand out as a leader in data privacy.

The company's sales and customer base improved greatly, and I was proud of the difference I had made. The company's reputation for privacy and trust has become a key differentiator, and customers chose this brand over the competition.

Five Takeaways

1. As a privacy leader, you may need to navigate resistance to change within the organization.

2. Engaging with customers and researching helped me build a strong case for data privacy-related changes.
3. Being able to articulate the benefits of a human-centric approach to data privacy to secure buy-in from the leadership team is key.
4. Building buy-in from the leadership team will be critical to the success of any data privacy initiative.
5. A human-centric approach to data privacy can result in improved customer trust, increased sales, and a competitive advantage in the marketplace.

7-S framework applied to privacy leadership strategy

The premise of the 7-S Model as articulated in Chapter 2 is that an organization is not just a structure, and organization effectiveness consists of seven elements – strategy, structure, systems, the "3 hard elements", and four "soft elements" style (culture), staff, skills, and shared values developed and expanded upon by Peters and Waterman in the early 1980s. The 5-step strategy process satisfies the "Strategy S" portion of the 7-S Framework applied to privacy leadership, and the other 6 Ss need to be evaluated as well to support the strategy. For example, identification and protections of the crown jewels and recording these in the ROPA will lead to identification of certain systems, or processes necessary to protect them, such as utilizing data analytics to determine who has been accessing the information over the past month and the business areas they represent. Upon reviewing the skills as part of the framework, a gap in available skills may be identified to enable this job to be performed well. So, while the protections may be in place, without the right skill set to setup the right rules and understand the information being reviewed, a change would need to be made to the strategy to recruit (or outsource) such capability, amplifying the importance of the interrelationships between the other 6 "S"s in constructing a viable privacy strategy.

Alternative strategy development techniques

There are other approaches for developing the strategy "S" of the privacy program as well. These techniques can be used as the basis for increasing the maturity of the program or can be used as tools to analyze different aspects of the program. For example, a SWOT analysis could be leveraged to determine the state of the overall program or could be leveraged to analyze the ability to provide business resiliency in the core systems and where improvements could be made in the future.

When businesses are embarking on a new business venture, a SWOT (strengths, weaknesses, opportunities and threats) analysis is typically used

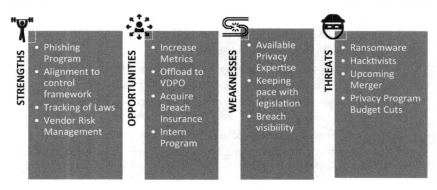

STRENGTHS	OPPORTUNITIES	WEAKNESSES	THREATS
• Phishing Program • Alignment to control framework • Tracking of Laws • Vendor Risk Management	• Increase Metrics • Offload to VDPO • Acquire Breach Insurance • Intern Program	• Available Privacy Expertise • Keeping pace with legislation • Breach visibility	• Ransomware • Hacktivists • Upcoming Merger • Privacy Program Budget Cuts

Figure 3.7 Example of a SWOT analysis.

to determine the organization's current ability to compete in that marketplace. The process involves a facilitated brainstorming discussion whereby a box is drawn divided into four quadrants (each representing one of the four dimensions of the SWOT acronym) and each quadrants is then evaluated by the team. An example SWOT analysis for a privacy program is shown in Figure 3.7. In practice, much time is usually spent on defining the strengths and weaknesses as these appear to be easier to grasp as they tend to be based upon past observations of performance within the organization. Opportunities require an understanding of items that are more abstract, such as possibilities of the future without necessarily being currently equipped to develop the product or service. Threats are those actions which may serve to derail our future or disrupt our existing environment.

Applied to privacy strategy development, the SWOT process can illuminate areas where privacy could make a positive, proactive impact to the organization (opportunity), but to date has not acted. For example, creating and deploying a Data Subject Access Request management system would benefit the business process and the data subject experience by making it more efficient. Other benefits could be added to the privacy strategy such as the reduction in time to respond to a Data Subject Access Request or the length of time to complete a Data Protection Impact Assessment. Each of these would represent an opportunity for the business.

Another tool that can be used is the Balanced Scorecard. The Balanced Scorecard was developed by Kaplan & Norton and gained popularity after the idea was published in the Harvard Business Review. Essentially, the Balanced Scorecard approach encourages organizations to not only examine the financial measures of profitability but rather also to continuously examine the measurements of how well the customer, process (quality), and learning perspectives are being attained. Each of these processes eventually contributes to the financial measures and by focusing upon these other measures as well as the financial measures, the overall financial profitability of the organization will be improved.

Some organizations identify a few key measures such as growth in the number of customers, non-conformance to processes, or the percentage of staff which have acquired a new skill. Other organizations drive the Balanced Scorecard concept to an individual employee level, whereby goals are created for each employee and rolled up into higher-level goals (or vice versa). Driving the Balanced Scorecard to the employee level enables a valuable discussion regarding the tasks each employee performs and if it is truly contributing to the overall company strategy. Everyone in the organization should be able to determine which tasks are more important in attaining the company objectives. The downside of this approach is it is very labor intensive and can become an exercise in compliance if the intent is not valued. Organizations which structure tasks at the higher levels track the metrics and often base the annual bonus on these numbers, thus making them meaningful at the company and department levels. Some employees may not feel connected to the overall strategy. In either case, the Balanced Scorecard provides an excellent mechanism to review the progress of the organization in meeting their goals. As the quality guru Deming is frequently credited with saying by many, "if you can't measure it, you can't improve it".

BUILDING A GLOBAL PRIVACY PROGRAM

Ivana Bartoletti

Global Chief Privacy Officer, Wipro

To lead privacy at a global scale effectively means grasping dancing with legislation that is both diverging and converging. While nations are finding common ground on many aspects, from data subject rights to fair processing of data, they also present us with many areas of divergence. For example, data localization is a challenge across several jurisdictions and what constitutes sensitive data varies, too.

Identifying the common denominators and then making tweaks to allow for divergence might seem an obvious approach to take but it is not a winning strategy. It does not deal with the complexity of the legal evolution of privacy – and other intertwined issues. A global chief privacy officer must try to master all aspects at the intersection between privacy and technology, some prime examples being AI, algorithmic decision-making, virtual reality, or blockchain technology.

While privacy is recognized as a human right across much of the world, different governments and societies mean different things by that. A truly "global" attitude means exploring and working within the constraints of these differences of approach. Yes, any corporation must operate swiftly and smoothly across borders, but privacy does not flow as simply as, say, financial currency. It is a messier, less-convenient substance that is ultimately about people, their life, and their dignity and no realist will ignore how differently it may be perceived around the globe. For example, financial details are deemed as sensitive data in some jurisdictions, but not in others.

Practically speaking, a good global program is a combination of the following: Culture, agility, stability, technology, and metrics for success.

> **A culture of privacy** must be fostered and grown, and that works if it is embedded into the local realities where the organization operates, not presented as an abstract universal approach. You need to root it in local experiences.
>
> **Agility** means that programs need to be able to swiftly adapt to legal changes and developments. This means that they must be built on solid ground. For example, China gave almost no time (just one month!) for companies to comply with its new data protection rules whereas generally, lead-in times to adapt are much longer.
>
> **Metrics for success** are very important as they enable business buy-in – make sure you prepare the metrics in a way that the senior management would understand. Ultimately, well-honed privacy is a competitive edge, so challenge yourself to measure your success in those terms, which may mean stepping outside of your usual mindset!
>
> **Technology** here means tools that allow right access, segregation, user control, obfuscation, and the use of all the privacy enhancing tools that can help unleash the value of data.
>
> **Stability** means organization-wide traction and support, a recognition that in a data-driven organization, the privacy team must be part of the business bedrock for the business to thrive. Turnover, attrition, and lack of skills (especially at the intersection between engineering and the law) are all problems that need solving. Give your team the exposure to cutting edge privacy and data protection that keeps them engaged.

No single element guarantees success – a global program is a combination of all the above. What I can guarantee is that it will be a constant struggle. So, make it one you relish and thrive on!

SUGGESTED READING

Collins, J. (2001). *Good to Great: Why Some Companies Make the Leap and Others Don't*. New York: Harper-Business.

EDPB Opinion. (n.d.). Privacy Implications During Mergers. https://edpb.europa.eu/our-work-tools/our-documents/statements/statement-privacy-implications-mergers_en

Kaplan, J. et al. (2011). Meeting the cybersecurity challenge. *McKinsey & Co*. June 2011. https://www.mckinsey.com/business-functions/digital-mckinsey/our-insights/meeting-the-cybersecurity-challenge

Kaplan, Robert S. and Norton, David P. (1996). *The Balanced Scorecard, Translating Strategy Info Action*. Boston, MA: Harvard Business School Press.

Ropa Template. (n.d.). https://www.cnil.fr/en/record-processing-activities

Section III

Structure

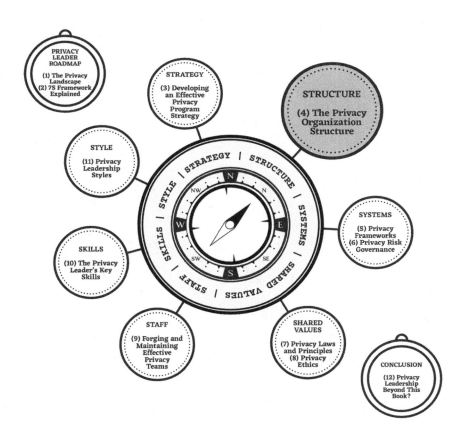

Chapter 4

The privacy organization structure

> A councilor ought not to sleep the whole night through, a man to whom the populace is entrusted, and who has many responsibilities.
>
> Homer c. 700 B.C.

The most common key roles directly involved in leading privacy are Chief Privacy Officers (CPOs), Data Protection Officers (DPOs), Chief Information Security Officers (CISOs)/Chief Security Officers (CSOs), and Chief Information Officers (CIOs). There are other roles involved in privacy programs without doubt, such as privacy officers and privacy champions but they are not typically involved in leading privacy programs, rather they are either operationally involved or are involved in its implementation. ISACA's 2023 Privacy in Practice Report suggests that the role accountable for leading the enterprise privacy program varies considerably: 21% of respondents say that the CPO is accountable for the privacy program, 16% of respondents say that the CIO is accountable for privacy, and 14% say the executive-level security officer – for example, CISO or CSO – is accountable for the privacy program.

While the CISO and CSO focus on data governance and infrastructure, others such as the DPO and the CPO focus on personal information and how that information is collected, stored, shared, and transmitted, as well as compliance with a complex set of domestic and foreign regulations. Because the CSO's and CISO's responsibilities toward privacy are so comprehensively covered in the first book in the series (*CISO Compass: Navigating Cybersecurity Leadership Challenges with Insights from Pioneers*), in this chapter we outline why an organization may have a CPO or a DPO, or both. We also outline the difference in the reporting structures for those roles.

DOI: 10.1201/9781003383017-7

SHOULD THE CISO ALSO TAKE ON THE ROLE OF DATA PROTECTION?

Patti Titus

Chief Privacy and Information Security Officer, Markel Corporation

The convergence of cybersecurity and data protection is creating a change in the responsibilities shouldered by the Chief Information Security Officer (CISO). This next-generation thinking shifts the responsibility from the risk and privacy officers to the CISO. In all, honestly, this move is going to be the best way to accelerate the success of the privacy program and shift the movement of data protection to an organization that can be singularly responsible for both privacy and security. Of course, the ultimate goal will be to lower the systemic risk data poses to every organization.

When I first volunteered to take ownership for privacy, it was during the release of the GDPR in the EU. At the time, there seemed to be a trend for the CISO to add data protection to their portfolio of responsibilities. NOTE: Some advice for CISOs thinking about taking on privacy – do not ask for more than you can take on, because you will own that for your career at that company. As the months passed, I realized that it made perfect sense to combine security and privacy with two fundamental realizations. The CISO is responsible for applying the data protection controls and the regulations lay out the require-ments. Where the challenge is in data protection is determining where to start. Typical advice is to use at least a few of the NIST CSF 5 pillars: Identify, Protect, Detect, Respond. Hopefully, you won't have to use the recover pillar and can avoid a breach.

Far too often, I've witnessed firsthand that organizations try to boil the ocean, creating mounds of remediation plans. This in turn makes the privacy program an emerging risk area. The unfortunate part is then the remediation plans get passed over for new functionality, innovation, and digital transforma-tion. A far better way to approach this is to assess your nonpublic information, determine which data is the most critical, and use that data as the starting point. Clearly, the things that get you in the most trouble with fines and oversight will be the regulated data like PII or PHI. Databases and document management systems which are high-value targets are another starting point. The key take away is *to get started*, develop a plan, and start attacking the problem. But realize there is only so much one team can accomplish without fully disrupting your business operations.

WHAT IS A CHIEF PRIVACY OFFICER (CPO)?

In 1991, Jennifer Barrett, at the consumer database marketing company Acxiom, is most often cited as the first CPO, followed by Ray Everett (the Internet advertising technology firm AllAdvantage) in 1999. However, the role of the CPO was not solidified within the US corporate world until November 2000 with the naming of Harriet Pearson as the Chief Privacy Officer for IBM Corporation. By 2002, the position of CPO and similar privacy-related management positions were sufficiently widespread to support the creation of professional societies and trade associations to promote training and certification programs. In 2002, the largest of these organizations, the Privacy Officers Association and the Association of Corporate Privacy Officers, merged to form the International Association of Privacy Officers, which was later renamed the International Association of Privacy Professionals (IAPP). The IAPP holds several conferences and training seminars each year around the world, hosting association members from major global corporations and government agencies, with executives seeking certification programs in privacy management practices. In 2019, it reportedly had more than 50,000 members globally, which its leadership attributed to companies' responses to new laws like the GDPR.

The CPO is a senior-level executive responsible for managing risks related to and ensuring compliance with information privacy laws. The role exists in an increasing number of corporations, public agencies, and other organizations. The CPO role may not necessarily be labeled CPO. Some organizations may use different designations, such as Data Protection Lead, Privacy Counsel, Chief Privacy Counsel etc. To simplify the discussion, we will refer to these titles collectively as CPO. What the different job titles have in common is that they refer to a role organized in the first line of the defense of the organization and are directly involved in the management of privacy risks. This notion of three lines of defense was advocated for by many accounting firms after the dot.com failures and the Enron scandal in the early 2000s, whereby there is separation between the operations management, oversight, and independent assurance of the organizational activities. The model, as shown in Figure 4.1 Three Lines of Privacy Defense, is favorable as the variety and complexity of the risks are rising rapidly, roles can be clarified within the organization, and the board of directors and audit committee can be provided with assurance that people are working together to avoid gaps in risk management and duplication of efforts are being avoided. The first line of defense is the day-to-day operational area responsible for identifying, assessing, mitigating, and reporting on the risks. The second line provides risk oversight and designs and implements a risk program, developing a framework to be supported by the first line to manage risk. Overall governance is provided as this group evaluates the risks across operational areas. As such, this provides a top-down view of the risk profile relative to the strategy and the acceptable risk appetite. Privacy is just one

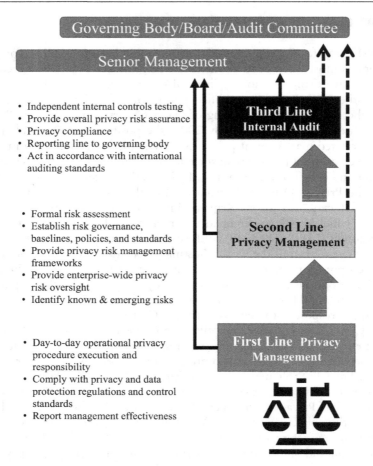

Governing Body/Board/Audit Committee

Senior Management

- Independent internal controls testing
- Provide overall privacy risk assurance
- Privacy compliance
- Reporting line to governing body
- Act in accordance with international auditing standards

Third Line
Internal Audit

- Formal risk assessment
- Establish risk governance, baselines, policies, and standards
- Provide privacy risk management frameworks
- Provide enterprise-wide privacy risk oversight
- Identify known & emerging risks

Second Line
Privacy Management

- Day-to-day operational privacy procedure execution and responsibility
- Comply with privacy and data protection regulations and control standards
- Report management effectiveness

First Line Privacy
Management

Figure 4.1 Three lines of privacy defense.

of the organizational risk areas within the organization and may be providing input to an overall corporate enterprise risk management team. The third level of defense is internal audit, which is to be fully independent and objective and conduct audits and reviews of a sample of the activities of the first and second lines to ensure controls are designed and operating effectively. This balance of controls provides multiple checks to ensure the controls are operating as planned.

In practice, the activities are not as clear-cut as shown in Figure 4.1 and the operational or business areas in the first line of defense may not have the ownership of the risk issues and look to the second line to provide those, taking away from second-line activities, which should be spending time providing deeper insights into the risk areas. New regulations have also increased the burden on the second-line oversight areas, spreading their time across more activities. The audit process conducted by the third line is also still predominantly a manual process, limiting the number of areas that may be audited. Even with these constraints, the organization should develop an RACI model (Responsible, Accountable, Informed, and Consulted) to define which area performs which activity in line with the three-line defense model to identify areas of oversight weakness.

The CPO role evolved as a response to increasing consumer concerns over the use of personal information, including medical data and financial information along with laws and regulations. In particular, the expansion of information privacy laws and new regulations governing the collection, protection, and use of personal data, such as the EU GDPR, raised the profile and increased the frequency of having a senior executive as the leader of privacy-related compliance efforts. In addition, some laws and regulations (such as the HIPAA Security and Privacy Rule) require that certain organizations within their regulatory scope must designate a privacy compliance leader.

The CPO directs the company's privacy strategy, steering the business through the complex array of different data protection regulations that affect the organization. They also look for ways in which privacy can add value to the business, using it in a positive way to gain a competitive advantage. Appointing any role to the C-Suite level is a strategic action that sends signals to both internal and external stakeholders about the strategic importance of a role. The appointment of a CPO can also help the organization to connect with external stakeholders, to obtain more external resources, and to improve its reputation. Organizations are then positioned to deepen the involvement of top management in privacy stewardship rather than simple leadership.

WHAT DATA BREACHES TELL US ABOUT PRIVACY

Chris Novak

Managing Director, Cybersecurity Consulting, Verizon

I had the unique opportunity to be part of the team that created the first Verizon Data Breach Investigations Report back in 2008, as well as every edition since then. Drawing from my own personal experiences, I have helped hundreds of organizations investigate, mitigate, and recover from some of the ugliest data breaches that you can imagine. That has allowed me to form some interesting views and perspectives on the changing landscape of data breaches and privacy.

Having been in the industry for over 20 years, I find the data breach and data privacy conversations almost to be like a chicken and egg dilemma – which came first? How different are they? This is a great debate to have at a bar while at a security or privacy conference, as you are sure to get dozens of lively and impassioned responses. What I have seen is that plenty of organizations exist that have a CISO, but do not have a CPO. Conversely, you can also find many organizations that have a CPO, but do not have a CISO.

What may be even more fascinating is that from my experience, bigger and more damaging breaches have happened to organizations that lack either a CISO or CPO – and typically the biggest and worst breaches happened to organizations that lacked both. I'm not saying the lack of one or both causes breaches, but I feel that whether an organization is missing one or both of those roles is a strong indicator of their underlying culture toward security and privacy. You need the CPO role and associated authority and support to drive the understanding of what sensitive data the organization handles and their associated protection requirements. As a complement, the CISO role should ideally set the organization's strategy for how appropriate controls are put in place to satisfy the protection requirements and ensure that they can be enforced and continuously monitored.

So, which came first, security or privacy? Both!

CPO responsibilities

As the leader of a corporate privacy program, a CPO has several essential responsibilities, including:

- Keeping on top of the latest developments on the evolving data privacy landscape.
- Managing, monitoring, and continually improving data protection measures.
- Guiding and managing the company's policies, procedures, and data governance.
- Driving privacy-related awareness and training among employees.
- Leading incident response, including data breach preparedness.
- Communicating privacy goals and values both internally and externally.
- Designing controls for managing privacy compliance.
- Assessing privacy-related risks arising from existing products and services.
- Conducting Privacy Impact Assessments to identify risks in new/changed activities.

- Monitoring the effectiveness of privacy-related risk mitigation/compliance measures.
- Driving privacy awareness within your organization.
- Often includes liaising with the media in relation to privacy matters.
- Building trust with privacy-conscious consumers.
- Collaborating with other stakeholders in the organization, including engineers and product managers (for privacy impacts to products and services), human resources (for privacy impacts to employee data), legal teams (for monitoring and interpretations of applicable laws and compliance measures), procurement and vendor management, and information technology and information security teams etc.

Reporting line of the CPO

Unlike the DPO role, there is much more flexibility for the organization to decide how the CPO role should be organized, and much depends on how the role is defined. A major component of the role is compliance and, sometimes, the CPO is also responsible for incident response. In this case, it becomes a risk management function.

With the role being more operationally focused, you will often see the Chief Privacy Officer report to the 1) the General Counsel/Legal Director or 2) the CEO or Corporate Affairs Officer or 3) the Risk/Compliance/Corporate Governance Director. It will vary depending on the existing organizational split of responsibility from organization to organization and the tasks that will make up the key components of the role of the CPO, where the role is best placed.

Where the role is mostly expected to be involved in day-to-day advice and counselling around operational data protection matters, it would make most sense to position the role in the legal function. This is because the landscape of privacy regulation is becoming more and more complex. Not only does the function need to deal with privacy specific legislation but also with cybersecurity legislation with privacy requirements or industry-specific privacy requirements. If the role is expected to take a more prominent role in raising awareness, training of the organization, and development of governance, then it would make more sense to place the role with compliance or corporate governance in case data processing is a fundamental part of the core activities of the organization, and customer trust in the data processing activities of the organization is critical for the long-term success of the organization, it would make most sense for the CPO to report to the CEO or the Corporate Affairs Officer. The IAPP-EY 2022 Annual Privacy Governance Report shows that 30% of "privacy leaders" report to the General Counsel, 18% to the CEO, and 16% to the Chief Compliance Officer.

WHERE SHOULD THE CPO REPORT?
Orrie Dinstein
Global Chief Privacy Officer, Marsh McClennan

When I was hired for my first in-house privacy role, I was placed in legal, reporting to the General Counsel (GC). After a while, there was a corporate reorg, and in the process, I was moved over to the Chief Compliance Officer (CCO). As part of that journey, I had a dotted line to the Chief Information Officer (CIO). When I switched jobs to a new company, I found myself reporting once more to the CCO but after a while there was a reorg (a bit of a theme in the corporate world) and I was moved over to report to the CIO. Some years later, another reorg put me back under the CCO and after yet another reorg I was back in legal. Through all these changes, I have come to learn and develop some core ideas about the CPO reporting line.

I'll start by addressing my experience with the different functional reporting lines:

Reporting into Legal – the biggest advantage is that (assuming you are a lawyer) you can provide legal advice, not just general guidance. Also, legal tends to be closely aligned with the business and its primary mission is to support the business so you are treated as a partner. And therein lies the biggest challenge – as a partner, it is harder to push back on things.

Reporting into Compliance – the biggest advantage is that compliance is often treated as an internal watchdog and, as such, more likely to raise concerns and second-guess business decisions. On the other hand, because of the nature of the role, compliance doesn't always have a seat at the table and is not regularly included in business discussions; so, it's harder to know what is going on or be viewed as a valued partner. Additionally, and this is especially true in financial services, members of the compliance team cannot practice law or give legal advice and that's another limitation.

Reporting into the CIO – to me this was always the preferred mode as it gave me a front row seat to all things IT related. That means you don't have to wait for someone to say "lets consult with Legal" or "maybe we should run this by Compliance" – you're there. And you build trust with the IT teams. They are more likely to work with you and accept your guidance as you're not an outsider. The challenge of course is that it can be more difficult to challenge decisions. But with the right relationships, this can work and for me it worked the best in terms of my reporting lines.

Moving to some broader thoughts about reporting lines:

1. Functional alignment can be a formality in some industries but in financial services it can be critical. This is because there is typically a strict separation between the first, second, and third lines of defense and it is not possible to report across lines. There's also typically a clear split between legal and compliance that makes it impossible to straddle that line. So here the functional placement of the CPO is very important. But even with these "fences" it is important to identify and maintain partnerships and proper work dynamics with the key stakeholders and you can definitely make this work despite the inherent barriers.

2. Speaking of key stakeholders, regardless of where you report, it is critical that you have a strong relationship with and regular access to the CIO and the CISO. Most decisions about data are made in IT and impacted by the InfoSec team and unless you're working closely with the CIO and CISO, you will not be effective in your job. Having a quarterly or even monthly catch-up is not sufficient. Regular and ongoing interaction is the key.

3. Ultimately regardless of who you report to, you need to have proper access and visibility to senior business and functional leadership so that you can be effective in your job. Personal data doesn't have borders or reporting lines and you must be able to roam the organization to "follow the data" in order to be successful in your role.

Bottom line – there's no "correct answer" to the question "where should the CPO report" and many CPOs are very successful in their roles despite being in different reporting lines and industries. What dictates whether a CPO will succeed in their job is the support they get and their access to the key stakeholders.

WHAT IS A DPO?

A DPO is a role within a company or organization whose responsibility is to ensure that the company or organization is correctly protecting individuals' personal data according to current legislation. A DPO ensures, in an independent manner, that an organization applies the laws protecting individuals' personal data. The designation, position, and tasks of a DPO within an organization are described in Articles 37, 38, and 39 of the EU GDPR., and 39 of the EU GDPR.

The purpose of the role is to provide the organization with the capabilities to use personal data in accordance with the laws and regulations and the expectations of individuals. Similar roles (although with varying titles) are also required by Canada's Personal Information Protection and Electronic Documents Act (PIPEDA) and South Africa's Protection of Personal Information Act (POPI). In general, the DPO shall i) advise/inform their organization of applicable legislation and standards, ii) advise on risk assessments and DPIAs, and iii) act as a liaison to the supervisory authority and data subjects. The organization who appoints a DPO has a legal obligation to provide the DPO with the appropriate resources, knowledge, information, and support to carry out their duties effectively.

TRAINING EMPOWERS THE BUSINESS

Paul Breitbarth

Senior Visiting Fellow and In-House Data Protection Counsel, Maastricht University

"But we are not allowed to do so because of GDPR". If only I had received a euro for every time, I had heard that statement. The thing is: Many people have heard about some of the concepts of data protection and privacy laws, but many have no idea about the variety of options data protection laws offer to actually get some processing done.

If you look at the modern generation of data protection and privacy laws, the rules are far less restrictive than is often assumed. Data protection and privacy laws generally are not black and white, allowing room for interpretation. Not all organizations are willing to be the best student in compliance class all the time. Sometimes, they want to use a more lenient interpretation of the laws and take a bit of risk to make the business grow. In principle, this is fine. But if you do, you need to make sure you understand what you are doing, so you can also explain it in case of questions asked.

It is not without reason that a whole new field of compliance lawyers – data protection officers (DPOs) – has developed in the past couple of decades. DPOs are the go-to advisors for anything you want to do with personal data within an organization. But not every single data processing operation an organization undertakes can be dependent on the DPO's recommendation. It would simply cause too much delay if every new plan has to be submitted for an assessment.

That is where training comes in. I'm not talking about the basic training about key concepts of data protection law or how to report a data breach if something goes wrong during daily work. Of course, those are important. But the trainings I would like to see much more of are the ones empowering the business. They focus on the risk appetite of the organization. They explain the boundaries within which the business is free to experiment with data. They illustrate how the internal policies and procedures related to data use should be applied. They clarify when the DPO or other compliance teams should be involved. And of course, they spell out what has to be documented, because training is also a part of the organization's accountability requirement.

Proper training explains how to work with personal data, and at the same time alleviates the work of the DPO, empowers the organization, and helps to make the business grow.

DPO responsibilities

- Advising staff on their use of personal data.
- Monitoring the organization's data protection policies and procedures.
- Advising management on whether DPIAs are necessary.
- Serving as the point of contact between organization and supervisory authority.
- Serving as the point of contact for individuals on privacy matters.

THE PATH TO DPO SUCCESS IS ENGAGING BUSINESS PARTNERS EARLY ON

Fabrizio Venturelli

DPO, Workday

I have been in DPO positions for most of my career, mostly in multinational companies.

Many people think the most challenging part of the DPO role is understanding the applicable laws, regulations, and guidelines. However, it can also be understanding how to apply them to your specific company unless you prioritize your responsibilities with the corporate and business partners to make your plan work in the company you are part of.

Starting to assess and then deploy a DPO oversight function may seem like a hurdle: Broad scope, blurred geographical boundaries as standards, given the nature of the GDPR may apply well beyond the EU, and finally, many diverse stakeholders inside and outside the organization.

So, the biggest and overarching challenge to me has always been: How to find the right balance between all of those factors? Obviously, I can only mention what worked for me personally, given my specific experience and the great mentors I was lucky to encounter on my path.

First, adopt an international privacy principle-based framework (e.g., OECD privacy principles) that you can leverage across your organization entities, and drill down into national specifics as a following step.

Second, start early in embedding privacy requirements into your organization's processes and products, building strong relationships with the relevant business functions, and deploying a business-enabler privacy program.

Third, develop a robust and holistic training program and, if possible, build a network of privacy stewards (or champions) across your organization. They will greatly help to make a DPO oversight and monitoring function more effective "on the ground".

Fourth, bring to the attention of the senior management potentially high privacy risks to coordinate both company goals and regulatory requirements.

Fifth, have roles and responsibilities clearly defined across the privacy function, it will streamline decision-making.

These are a few of the lessons I have learned that still help me greatly every day. It is a never-ending learning experience though, so I will never stop updating the list!

Reporting line of the DPO

The requirements in the GDPR and the subsequent decisions by various supervisory authorities put certain restrictions on how and where the DPO can be organized. The GDPR requires that the DPO exercises its functions independently and that he or she "shall directly report to the highest management level". This doesn't mean the DPO has to be directly managed at this level but they must have direct access to give advice to senior managers who are making decisions about personal data processing.

This structure helps to facilitate the DPO's mandate to advise senior management on these matters. Rather than being a member of the senior management team, the DPO advises at this level. A senior management position implies decision-making on the purposes and means of the processing of personal data. This is a competence that is restricted to the data controller and its representative bodies (e.g. compliance committee etc.). Further, management positions often lack the so-called "arm's length" distance to their organization which may impact the data subjects negatively. Each Member State in the EU has a supervisory authority (also known as Data Protection Authority) with the task of supervising GDPR compliance. So, for example, the French supervisory authority, Commission Nationale de l'Information Liberte (CNIL), states that the function of the DPO cannot be both judge and jury.

Smaller and most medium-sized organizations will often find it challenging to establish an independent DPO role that reports directly to the executive management of the organization. It is however possible to solve the reporting line requirement of the GDPR by other means. The DPO can be placed within several organizational functions such as legal, compliance, and even security, as long as: 1) there is a clear mandate that establishes the rights and independence of the DPO and 2) the DPO – as mentioned above – is not involved in tasks relating to determining the purposes or means of the processing of personal data.

The DPO function can also in many of these cases be outsourced. This is often the most profitable solution as you get an experienced and competent specialist who can make GDPR-related decisions quickly and can be held accountable for them. The increasing demand for the services of a DPO has given rise to an offering called "DPO as a Service" (DPOaaS). DPOaaS is a solution for organizations lacking the requisite expertise to fulfil their DPO duties or unable to recruit someone part time into the role. The DPO service provider offers direct and fast access along with expert advice and data protection law guidance by outsourcing DPO tasks. DPOaaS which follows the "aaS" models is typical of cloud computing environments and reflects a flexible arrangement where an organization purchases several days of a DPO per week or month over the course of a fixed period such as 6 months to a year. DPOaaS can be delivered remotely or on premises, depending on client requirements. However, when delivered remotely the DPOaaS is often referred to as a virtual DPO.

The DPO may be a member of staff dedicated to a single organization. But where maintaining a full-time position may not be cost justified, within reason, they can act on behalf of other organizations at the same time. They can also undertake other responsibilities – provided these don't conflict with their DPO duties.

CONFLICT OF INTEREST

A DPO and CPO have many overlapping privacy management responsibilities. However, the scope of the CPO's work is broader, more strategic, and more aligned to organizational objectives. The tasks and duties of the DPO must not result in a conflict of interest, meaning that the DPO cannot hold a position or perform tasks within the organization that leads her or him to influence the use of personal data. Article 38(6) GDPR states that:

> The data protection officer may fulfil other tasks and duties. The controller or processor shall ensure that any such tasks and duties do not result in a conflict of interests.

This impacts how the DPO is appointed and how data governance is organized. This means that the specific role of the DPO must be defined in a service contract (external DPO) or a job description (internal DPO) and communicated internally within the organization.

The decision of which reporting line to adopt in a company is likely to depend also on the company's size, taking into consideration that the reporting line should not produce any conflict of interest, and a function being able to provide sufficient support to the DPO. As most of the positions set out above refer to reporting to the top management, the board or the CEO (whether directly or indirectly) reporting to a function not directly connected to the Board or the CEO may not fit with the spirit of the GDPR.

The Article 29 Working Party (the pre-2018 EU advisory board on data protection compliance, now called the European Data Protection Board (EDPB)) has published guidelines on appointing a DPO. It notes that, although some job roles were likely to create a conflict of interest, it is not always clear-cut. This is because organizations will handle personal data in different ways depending on their structure. Although it is considered acceptable that the person appointed as DPO may have other tasks and duties alongside the DPO role, those functions should not give rise to conflicts of interests. The guidelines note:

> that the DPO cannot hold a position within the organization that leads him or her to determine the purposes and the means of the *processing* of personal data. Due to the specific organizational structure in each organization, this has to be considered case by case.

The guidelines go on to set the out the positions that typically are conflicting positions with the DPO role as:

- Senior management positions.
- Chief executive officer.
- Chief operating officer.
- Chief financial officer.
- Chief medical officer.
- Head of the marketing department.
- Head of human resources.
- Head of the IT department.
- Other roles lower down in the organizational structure if such positions or roles lead to the determination of purposes and means of processing.

To ensure that the DPO can remain independent and free from pressure exerted to satisfy competing agendas within the organization, a company should not assign the DPO role to legal counsel that is involved in potential or actual litigation or regulatory action against the company. In addition, the DPO may be required to provide frank advice on the adequacy of the company's IT and security systems – that is, some of the organizational and technical measurers in place to mitigate privacy risk – so, the following roles may also present conflicting functions:

- Chief Information Officer (CIO) – who defines the IT strategy, where the data resides, accessed by who, and how and on what infrastructure to use.
- Chief Information Security Officer (CISO) – who create security strategies with certain prioritizations.
- Chief Legal Officer/Head of Legal – who balances the interests of their organization against what is permissible and/or possible under applicable law.

Not considering the conflict requirement of the DPO role adequately has resulted in several fines from supervisory authorities. For example, a Belgian company was fined EUR 50,000 because its DPO had a conflicting role as Director of Audit, Risk, and Compliance. The Litigation Chamber of the Belgian supervisory authority (the "APD"), found that the Head of Compliance role created a conflict of interest and constituted an infringement of Article 38(6) of the GDPR. The company argued that the Head of Compliance function was advisory, and that the person did not take any decisions regarding the purposes and means of the processing of personal data. The APD chose to issue a fine, rather than to order an alternative DPO appointment, because of the conflict of interest, although unintentional, constitutes serious negligence by the organization. In 2022, the Berlin Commissioner for Data Protection and Freedom (BInBDI) fined a retail group €525,000 for violating the conflict-of-interest principle (Article 38(6) in GDPR. The DPO of the retail group (the controller) was also the MD of two service companies (providing customer services) which processed data on behalf of the controller. The DPO was required by GDPR to monitor compliance with data protection laws by the service companies while also being responsible for making managerial decisions within it. This, and other similar cases, led to a 2023 ruling (February) from the CJEU that DPOs should "be in a position to perform their duties and tasks in an independent manner" but "cannot be entrusted with tasks or duties which would result in him or her determining the objectives and methods of processing personal data on the part of the controller or its processor". The CJEU also noted that this is "a matter for the national court to determine, case by case, on the basis of an assessment of all the relevant circumstances". This conflict-of-interest challenge is likely to present a real challenge for many organizations where a DPO wears many different hats. It is imperative to keep in mind that the purpose of the DPO role as such is to act as the representative of the data subjects of which the organization processes data. At the same time, the DPO cannot perform tasks relating to determining the purposes or means of the processing of personal data.

Once organizations grow larger, they will often see the need to establish other similar functions, for example, compliance and internal audit, that have direct reporting lines to either the executive management or board of directors. Where internal committees have been established to receive recurring reporting from functions – other than the DPO – it will typically be easier to establish a direct reporting line for the DPO.

How to avoid creating a conflict of interest

A DPO can be chosen from within internal resources or fulfilled through a service contract by an external consultant. A word of warning: where appointed, an external DPO fulfilling the function of DPO based on a service contract as a consultant can have a different conflict of interest. For example, the consultant must always be vigilant and observant of any relationships or situations with other clients and counterparties that may create a conflict of interest with the DPO appointment. It is also not advisable to have the external DPO represent their organization in court in cases regarding data protection issues. The service contract should include an obligation on the consultant to observe any conflict of interest and regulate how to manage such issues during the appointment as DPO.

Irrespective of how the DPO function is fulfilled, it is considered best practice to:

- Identify positions within the firm that are incompatible with the DPO function.
- Draw up internal rules to avoid DPO conflict of interest.
- Declare that the DPO has no conflict of interest regarding its function as a DPO to raise awareness of the requirement of independence.
- Include safeguards in the internal rules to ensure that in the event of a vacancy of the DPO function, the vacancy is filled with the appropriate resource.
- To provide the DPO with a budget and ability to retain its own legal advice in case of an alternative opinion to the organization is needed.
- The DPO shall report to the highest management, preferably in the form of a compliance committee with representation from the highest management (including the board of directors).

It is important to note that where the role of DPO is outsourced – the conflict-of-interest factor must continue to be sustained. This means considering who internally is managing the relationship with the external party and if there is any conflict of interest.

When does a DPO need to be appointed?

While the introduction of GDPR brought international visibility to the idea of a formal DPO position, the concept has existed in more than a few privacy-conscious organizations for some time. The DPO role is specifically required for certain organizations falling under the jurisdiction of the EU GDPR. Article 37 of the GDPR provides that a DPO "shall be designated on the basis of professional qualities and, in particular, expert knowledge of data protection law and practices and the ability to fulfil the tasks referred to in Article39".

DPOs have very specific roles, requirements, and expectations and those include a level of required independence and organizational separation that make it very different from a CPO. The DPO is the steward of data protection implementation and data privacy strategy within an organization. They are charged with facilitating a culture of data protection throughout the company. The language of GDPR indicates that the size of an organization is not what compels the need for a DPO, but rather the size and scope of data handling and the risks to the data subject. Under the GDPR, an organization is required to appoint a designated DPO where:

- The processing is carried out by a public authority/body.
- The core activities of the controller/processor consist of processing operations, which require regular and systematic monitoring of data subjects on a large scale.
- The core activities of the controller/processor consist of processing on a largescale of special categories of data or personal data relating to criminal convictions and offences.

The notion of regular and systematic monitoring of data subjects is not defined in the GDPR, but clearly includes all forms of tracking and profiling on the Internet, including for the purposes of behavioral advertising. However, the notion of monitoring is not restricted to the online environment. The Article 29 Working Party, an independent European working party that dealt with issues relating to the protection of privacy and personal data until 25 May 2018 and subsequently adopted the name European Data Protection Board (EDPB), interpreted "regular" as meaning one or more of the following:

- Occurring at intervals for a particular period.
- Recurring or repeated at fixed times.
- Constantly or periodically taking place.

The Article 29 WP also interpreted "systematic" as meaning one or more of the following:

- Occurring according to a system.
- Pre-arranged, organized, or methodical.
- Taking place as part of a general plan for data collection.
- Carried out as part of a strategy.

Examples: Operating a telecommunications network; providing telecommunications services; email retargeting; profiling and scoring for purposes of risk assessment (e.g. for purposes of credit scoring, establishment of insurance premiums, fraud prevention, detection of money-laundering); location tracking, for example, by mobile apps; loyalty programs; behavioral advertising; monitoring of wellness, fitness and health data via wearable devices; closed circuit television; and connected devices, for example, smart meters, smart cars, home automation, etc.

THE DPO ROLE – BEYOND ARTICLE 39 OF THE GDPR!
Aurélie Banck
Group Data Protection Officer, Europcar mobility group

When I started as a privacy professional 17 years ago, the DPO role didn't exist. A few companies had legal counsels with a background in data protection at the bottom of Legal Department (when they had one) and I was worried about finding a position which would meet my expectations as a student.

The GDPR was a tremendous opportunity for privacy professionals like me, as the appointment of DPO became mandatory for many organizations, creating major job market opportunities.

At the start of 2018, DPO positions were mainly held by legal experts, but now the profiles can be broader (risk, cybersecurity etc.). Today the DPO role is becoming a strategic position for companies in industry B to C or for tech companies.

DPOs are evolving in a challenging landscape of privacy regulations with different conceptions around the world and in a challenging digital world. The raise of the enforcement of GDPR in Europe and CCPA in the US, and the increasing awareness of data subjects about their rights, is going to raise the risk of fines, civil litigation, and collective actions (what is likely the next major threat for organizations).

In-house DPOs could struggle between data protection authorities' positions and business's objectives and the requirement to interplay data protection, contract, consumer law, and competition regulations.

A DPO has to be of course an expert in data protection and have appetence for technology. The DPO needs to be a manager and a strategist with the capability to communicate its vision across the organization, to bring clarity on complex topics, to expose and manage risks, and to be pragmatic.

Agility is also a key skill with a high capability to work under pressure and to be resilient.

My best advice is to ask questions – if the project is not crystal clear for you, it will certainly not be for the data protection authority or for your clients – and do not be afraid of complicated questions or to challenge the status quo! (e.g., *Is this processing activity necessary or only useful? Do you really need to process that personal data? What are the alternative options and are you able to demonstrate there are insufficient to reach the purpose? What will be the impacts to change this service provider....*).

And remember DPO is a job with purpose!

SUMMARY

The primary difference between the DPO and the CPO roles (summarized in Table 4.1) is the possibility to represent the organization's data processing interests and participate actively in developing solutions for the data processing needs of the organization. In practice, this will mean that the CPO will have the possibility to engage with internal stakeholders on the design of the solution, be the data protection expert "of the organization", and thereby take an active role in providing arguments and proposals for how the organization can justify and explain data processing activities.

While both DPOs and CPOs address a company's privacy responsibilities, the drivers behind the two roles are very different. While DPOs act as independent compliance-safeguards, CPOs have a broader, more strategic role. Another key difference between the DPO and the CPO roles is that the DPO is an advocate for data subjects' rights, acting as an independent and impartial advisor on GDPR compliance (i.e., legally they cannot be fired for meeting their responsibilities) where a CPO, on the other hand, is more that of a traditional company or public sector employee, acting in the interests of the organization.

Table 4.1 Summary of the differences between DPO and CPO

	Data protection officer (DPO)	Chief privacy officer (CPO)
Alternative titles	None	Privacy leader or privacy counsel
Key role	Ensure compliance with GDPR	Direct company-wide privacy strategy
Scope	Specific to GDPR	Data protection and privacy
Advocates for	Data subject rights under GDPR	The organization's privacy objectives and business objectives
External stakeholder interactions	Regulatory supervisory authorities Data subjects (general public)	The media (in relation to general privacy matters)
Legislative mandate	Yes (under certain circumstances as outlined in GDPR)	Not specifically as "CPO" (some legislation mandates the appointment of a privacy officer however)
Experience/ qualifications/ background	Tends to have a data protection and business background	Tends to have a legal background

SUGGESTED READING

Articles 37 and 38 of GDPR. Summary of GDPR (n.d.). https://www.gdprsummary.com/author/gdpr-summary/

EDPB (Art 29 Working Party) Guidelines on Data Protection Officers. (n.d.). https://ec.europa.eu/newsroom/article29/items/612048

ISACA's. (2023). Privacy in practice report. https://www.isaca.org/resources/reports/privacy-in-practice-2023-report

Pfeiffer, N. (2020). The privacy organization of tomorrow. https://whitelabelconsultancy.com/2020/02/the-privacy-organization-of-tomorrow/

Pfeiffer, N. (2022). CPO or DPO? https://whitelabelconsultancy.com/2022/01/chief-privacy-officer-or-data-protection-officer/

The IAPP-EY. (2022). Annual privacy governance report. https://iapp.org/resources/article/privacy-governance-report/

Section IV

Systems

Chapter 5

Privacy frameworks, standards, and certifications

Nothing is more dangerous than an idea, when it's the only one we have.
Émile Auguste Chartier 1868–1951

A privacy framework describes a set of standards or concepts around which a company bases its privacy program. Typically, a privacy framework does not attempt to include all privacy-related requirements imposed by law or account for the privacy requirements of any particular legal system or regime. Instead, the framework attempts to establish a privacy program that is separate and apart from the legal requirements of one, or more, specific jurisdictions. Privacy frameworks can be based on standards, principles, legislation, or technology vendor products. The following are the standards and frameworks most commonly used for privacy; ISO 27701 (Privacy Information Management System, or PIMS certification), US Homeland Security Fair Information Practice Principles, Generally Accepted Privacy Principles (GAPP), Privacy Maturity Model, The OECD Privacy Framework based on the OECD Guidelines for the Protection of Privacy and Transborder Flows of Personal Data, and the NIST Privacy Framework. Legislative frameworks, for example, are the General Data Protection Regulation (GDPR), the California Consumer Privacy Act (CCPA), and the Health Insurance Portability and Accountability Act (HIPAA). TrustArc is an example of a technology vendor privacy framework (TrustArc acquired the Privacy Data Governance Accountability Framework when they acquired Nymity).

After the OECD Privacy Guidelines, sector-specific privacy frameworks began to emerge which addressed privacy or data protection. Those frameworks used the OECD Privacy Guidelines as their key reference. On a European level, three distinct private international non-profit organizations are officially recognized by the EU as being responsible for developing and defining voluntary standards or frameworks: 1) The European Telecommunications Standards Institute, 2) The European Committee for Standardization, and 3) the European Committee for Electrotechnical Standardization. In Asia, the APEC Privacy Framework provides privacy principles and implementation guidelines, forming the basis for a regional system called the APEC Cross-Border Privacy Rules. A more recent development was the

DOI: 10.1201/9781003383017-9

adoption of the ASEAN Data Management Framework in January 2021. In the US and internationally, NIST and ISO/IEC have produced privacy frameworks. Another prominent global organization in the field is the Standards Association of the Institute of Electrical and Electronics Engineers (IEEE) which has developed many industry standards for privacy and security architectures. There are also national privacy standards, for example, the newly developed standards for data privacy assurance by the Bureau of Indian Standards and the German standard data protection model (SDM). The SDM is a procedure that translates the legal requirements of the GDPR into concrete technical and organizational measures).

It is not always clear which framework to choose, if any. Or what motivates the selection of one over the other. Just as this book is written using a framework (the 7-S model) to guide its structure, many books are written without such frameworks. Using the book as an example, the problem with writing a book without a framework is that authors can miss chunks of information, be a bit jumpy from one topic to the next, and can be either too vague or too generic. We use theoretical frameworks to prevent these issues. And the same applies to privacy. We can apply frameworks to help guide how we approach the privacy program. But which one should we choose? Much of the choice is personal or organizational. For instance, you may have used a particular framework before and be very familiar with it, or the organization may choose a particular framework that they align with. The industry sector may also be an attribute to consider and often the sector can dictate the framework required. We accept the purist criticism that some of the frameworks we present here are in fact standards, and as such can be attested to/independently assessed. However we present them here as frameworks on the basis that many organizations use standards as frameworks without any intention of attesting to them, but rather to align with them instead.

A word of warning on frameworks. It should not be assumed that implementing a framework or reaching a high level of maturity using a maturity model equates to a high level of compliance. An organization's processes might be comprehensively defined and implemented, but where privacy is not embedded into the culture of the organization, final decisions on data processing activities may unduly favor the organization over the data subject and result in unfair processing of data. That said, frameworks help to structure the approach to building and maintaining the privacy program in an organization and common sense would indicate that aligning to a privacy framework will most likely bring the organization closer to a compliance position. Aligning to frameworks can also bring comfort to consumers that the organization adheres to a particular set of auditable and actionable standards. It can provide assurance to potential third-party alliances.

Except for certifications, in most cases the frameworks reflect the same thing, just differently packaged. One can see this as like taking an enchilada, refolding it a little differently and calling it a burrito. It's still pretty much the same thing.

The remainder of this chapter presents the most common privacy frameworks/guidelines:

- The OECD Privacy Framework.
- Fair Information Practice Principles.
- National Institute of Standards and Technology (NIST) Privacy Framework.
- ISO27701 (Privacy Information Management System).
- Generally Accepted Privacy Principles (GAPP) Maturity Model.

OECD PRIVACY GUIDELINES/FRAMEWORK

The OECD developed a set of privacy guidelines (principles) representing international consensus on personal data protection in the public and private sectors. These guidelines influenced the development of national legislation and model codes within OECD member countries and beyond. The guidelines also influenced the development of the APEC Privacy Framework, expanding their reach beyond the OECD membership, and are the most widely accepted privacy principles. This framework is most commonly referred to as the OECD framework as the OECD privacy guidelines (which form Chapter 1 of the framework) are its cornerstone. The OECD principles are:

Collection limitation principle

There should be limits to the collection of personal data and any such data should be obtained by lawful and fair means and, where appropriate, with the knowledge or consent of the data subject. In many cities, video cameras are used by businesses and law enforcement to record movement. An example of complying with this principle would be to ensure that the data subject has knowledge by posting a sign communicating the video surveillance. A company collecting driver's license information or fingerprint biometrics when someone is paying cash at a grocery store would be an example of excessive collection of personal data.

Data quality principle

Personal data should be relevant to the purposes for which they are to be used, and, to the extent necessary for those purposes, should be accurate, complete, and kept up to date. If an organization maintains personal data on an individual, they have an ongoing responsibility to ensure the data is correct. Consider the case of a credit reporting agency that fails to keep records up to date or stores misinformation on subjects applying for credit and then using that information to determine their credit worthiness. This would not be viewed as a fair practice on behalf of the consumer.

Purpose specification principle

The purposes for which personal data are collected should be specified not later than at the time of data collection and the subsequent use limited to the fulfillment of those purposes or such others as are not incompatible with those purposes and as are specified on each occasion of change of purpose. Ever sign up for a product and then start receiving emails from companies that no business relationship existed prior? Or junk mail starts piling up in the snail mailbox? Information collected by companies must state the purposes for which they will be using the information. Some companies try to broaden the definition to include future business areas they may want to venture into. In 2013, Art. 29 WP (now the European Data Protection Board) proposed an opinion to help clarify the meaning of the purpose limitation principle, indicating that such statements in the privacy notices indicating broad and vague purpose statements such as: "improving user experience" or "marketing purposes" is not sufficient to rise to the standards of a "specified, explicit and legitimate" processing requirement. To determine the acceptability of an acceptable purpose, the following four factors need to be taken into consideration:

- The relationship between the data collection purposes and further processing purposes.
- The context in which data has been collected and the reasonable expectations of the data subjects regarding further use of the data.
- The nature of the data and the impact of the further processing on the data subjects.
- The safeguards put in place by the data controller to ensure fair processing and prevent undue harm to the data subjects.

The Art 29 WP also reviewed the impact of Big Data with respect to purpose limitation. In the scenario where Big Data was being used to analyze trends and detect correlations in the information, the Art 29 WP indicated that the data controller needed to be able to ensure technical and organizational safeguards for the information to ensure confidentiality of the information, as well as provide functionally separate processing environments. In the scenario where the use of Big Data directly affects individuals such as conducting profiling using behavioral advertising, location-based advertising, and tracking digital research, opt-in consent would almost always be necessary. Furthermore, organizations need to provide data subjects with easy access to their profiles and disclose the decision criteria.

The purpose needs to be stated when the information is collected, at the point when individuals are providing their consent through opt-in or opt-out mechanisms.

Use limitation principle

Personal data should not be disclosed, made available, or otherwise used for purposes other than those specified in accordance with the Purpose Specification Principle above except a) with the consent of the data subject or b) by the authority of law. This principle works in concert with the purpose specification principle to ensure that the ongoing usage of the personal data is used for the purposes specified at collection unless there has been a positive affirmation of consent by the individual or the information is needed and requested through the appropriate procedures by law enforcement.

Security safeguards principle

Personal data should be protected by reasonable security safeguards against such risks as loss or unauthorized access, destruction, use, modification, or disclosure of data. The term "reasonable safeguards" is always open for debate as it depends upon the state of technology, the state of the industry, and most importantly, what are other companies in the same industries doing to reduce the risk of disclosure. This clause is the one, in the absence of any other industry specific regulation, that widens the requirement for privacy and security to every organization collecting, processing, using, or storing personal data. In other words, this is the clause applicable to almost every organization requiring the implementation of appropriate administrative, technical, and operational safeguards.

Openness principle

There should be a general policy of openness about developments, practices, and policies with respect to personal data. Means should be readily available of establishing the existence and nature of personal data, the main purposes of their use, as well as the identity and usual residence of the data controller. This clause promotes transparency of the operations and where the information is being processed. Individuals have a right to know how their information is being used. The organization can make information publicly available, such as the posting of their privacy notices on the websites along with contact information for questions. Information should be made available in different formats for different audiences, such as policies and procedures online along with downloadable PDF files for users.

CIPP/E, LLM: PRIVACY FOR TEENS
Elaine Fox
Head of Privacy Europe, TikTok

In 2021, TikTok kicked off a new internal project designed to create a series of easy-to-understand videos that explain how data is collected and shared on the TikTok app. Known as Privacy Highlights for Teens, and available on both the TikTok app and TikTok Web app, the series explored GDPR privacy topics such as legal basis (e.g., contractual necessity, legitimate interests, and consent) as well as providing information on user rights.

KEY LEARNINGS

The project was a cross-functional effort requiring a number of teams working collaboratively to design and develop the video series. Collaboration was key, as this project, like many others, required us to balance several considerations. For example, the videos needed to be attractive in terms of design, but also language agnostic so they could be used in different regions. They needed to be long enough to deliver the key information, but short enough to ensure that users watched them to the end. The language needed to be simple so that they could easily be understood by teenagers but also needed to accurately explain complex legal constructs from the GDPR – no small task.

There are logistical and technical challenges which also present themselves when designing a video series particularly one available in over 20 languages. When it comes to composing text and video scripts for this type of project, it is essential to consult a broad range of stakeholders including child development experts, communications professionals, and UX writers to ensure that the language used achieves the overall goal of meaningful transparency for teens. Finally, given the burden on resources both in terms of cost and people hours across numerous departments within the company, senior executive sponsorship is a critical element to the success of this type of project.

The principle of transparency and finding novel and engaging ways to explain how personal data is processed have always been interests of mine. Transparency is a key concept which exists beyond GDPR. Around the world, we are increasingly seeing the importance and significance of this core data protection principle take center stage. Through Privacy Highlights for Teens, we took a significant step forward in addressing how we encourage people and, in particular, younger teenage users (aged 13–18) to explore more about how their data is processed.

Individual participation principle

Individuals should have the right: to obtain from a data controller, or otherwise, confirmation of whether the data controller has data relating to them, to have communicated to them, data relating to them, to be given reasons if a request made under subparagraphs (a) and (b) is denied, and to be able to challenge such denial, and to challenge data relating to them and, if the challenge is successful to have the data erased, rectified, completed, or amended.

This principle allows the individual to see what information has been captured on their behalf and who had access to the information. Hospital environments control access to information through the logging of access via Electronic Medical Record (EMR) Systems. The benefit of capturing this information electronically is tremendous, as all the individuals interacting with the patient can see the full medical situation with the patient. The downside may be that sometimes hundreds of people may be involved with a person's care – from the physicians to the person reading and interpreting the charts, nurses, and the billing office. While each of these individuals most likely has a legitimate need to view this information, the patient has the right to understand what records have been accessed and retrieve these for a reasonable cost. Consider the case of a divorce where the ex-spouse still works at the healthcare provider and the patient wants to ensure their privacy is still being protected – they have the right to request this information at a reasonable cost. Sometimes it may be difficult to determine who the records were disclosed to or the costs may be excessive, in which case the data controller has the responsibility to provide the information on all individuals to whom the information may have been disclosed to. Also consider the case of a credit reporting agency where information is kept on the consumer. The consumer has a right to understand what information has been collected and be afforded the opportunity to modify information if the information was deemed inaccurate. Credit reports may be obtained from each of the major credit reporting agencies (Equifax, TransUnion, and Experian) once a year free of charge to review the information maintained by them and could challenge the information stored by providing contrary evidence.

Accountability principle

A data controller should be accountable for complying with measures which give effect to the principles stated above. The data controller cannot abdicate their responsibilities for maintaining accountability for personal data throughout the data life cycle. They are responsible for all stages, including the collection, usage, disclosure, transfer to third parties for processing, etc. Many organizations will appoint a Chief Privacy Officer to assume this role to guide the program and demonstrate that the organization is taking privacy seriously. Policies and procedures also provide data organization with the mechanism to carry out their accountability.

FAIR INFORMATION PRACTICE PRINCIPLES (FIPPS)

The Fair Information Practices (FIPs) are also known as the Fair Information Practice Principles (FIPPs) and are a set of eight principles regarding data usage, collection, and privacy: Many organizations use these principles as guidance for how to handle personal data. Several of the principles listed in FIPPs are included in important privacy frameworks like the GDPR and CCPA.

FIPPs were initially proposed and named by the US Secretary's Advisory Committee on Automated Personal Data Systems in 1973 – in response to the growing use of automated data systems containing information about individuals. The central contribution of the Advisory Committee was the development of a code of fair information practices for automated personal data systems. The Privacy Protection Study Commission also may have contributed to the development of FIPPs principles in its 1977 report, Personal Privacy in an Information Society.

As privacy laws spread to other countries in Europe, international institutions took up privacy with a focus on the international implications of privacy regulation. In 1980, the Council of Europe adopted a Convention for the Protection of Individuals with regard to Automatic Processing of Personal Data. At the same time, the Organization for Economic Cooperation and Development (OECD) proposed similar privacy guidelines in the OECD Privacy Guidelines on the Protection of Privacy and Transborder Flows of Personal Data. The OECD Privacy Guidelines, Council of Europe Convention, and European Union Data Protection Directive relied on FIPPs as core principles. All three organizations revised and extended the original US statement of FIPPs, with the OECD Privacy Guidelines being the version most often cited in subsequent years. Although these principles are not laws, they form the backbone of privacy law and provide guidance in the collection, use, and protection of personal information.

Currently the FTC version of FIPPs are only recommendations for maintaining privacy-friendly, consumer-oriented data collection practices, and are not enforceable by law. The enforcement of and adherence to these principles is principally performed through self-regulation. The FTC has, however, undertaken efforts to evaluate industry self-regulation practices, provide guidance for industry in developing information practices, and use its authority under the FTC Act to enforce promises made by corporations in their privacy policies.

The eight FIPPs are:

1. Collection Limitation Principle. There should be limits to the collection of personal data and any such data should be obtained by lawful and fair means and, where appropriate, with the knowledge or consent of the data subject.
2. Data Quality Principle. Personal data should be relevant to the purposes for which they are to be used, and, to the extent necessary for those purposes, should be accurate, complete, and kept up to date.
3. Purpose Specification Principle. The purposes for which personal data are collected should be specified not later than at the time of data collection and the subsequent use limited to the fulfillment of those purposes or such others as are not incompatible with those purposes and as are specified on each occasion of change of purpose.
4. Use Limitation Principle. Personal data should not be disclosed, made available, or otherwise used for purposes other than those specified in accordance with the Purpose Specification Principle except a) with the consent of the data subject or b) by the authority of law.

5. Security Safeguards Principle. Personal data should be protected by reasonable security safeguards against such risks as loss or unauthorized access, destruction, use, modification, or disclosure of data.

6. Openness Principle. There should be a general policy of openness about developments, practices, and policies with respect to personal data. Means should be readily available for establishing the existence and nature of personal data, the main purposes of their use, as well as the identity and usual residence of the data controller.

7. Individual Participation Principle. An individual should have the right:
   a. To obtain from a data controller, or otherwise, confirmation of whether the data controller has data relating to him/her.
   b. To have communicated to him/her, data relating to him/her within a reasonable time; at a charge, if any, that is not excessive; in a reasonable manner; and in a form that is readily intelligible to him.
   c. To be given reasons if a request made under subparagraphs (a) and (b) is denied and to be able to challenge such denial.
   d. To challenge data relating to him/her and, if the challenge is successful to have the data erased, rectified, completed, or amended.

8. Accountability Principle. A data controller should be accountable for complying with measures which give effect to the principles stated above.

FIPPs provide a framework of principles for balancing the need for privacy with other public policy interests, such as national security, law enforcement, and administrative efficiency. Striking that balance varies among countries and among types of information (e.g., medical or employment information). For example, the balance between the need for privacy and the need for national security differs between the US context to the EU context (these differences have essentially resulted in Schrems I and II).

NIST PRIVACY FRAMEWORK

The NIST Privacy Framework is a voluntary tool developed in collaboration with stakeholders intended to help organizations identify and manage privacy risk to build innovative products and services while protecting individuals' privacy. According to ISACA's 2023 Privacy in Practice survey results, 61% of respondents in the United States use the NIST Privacy Framework. The NIST Privacy Framework can be used for multiple applications:

• Mapping to Informative References in Other Frameworks.
• Strengthening Accountability.
• Establishing or Improving a Privacy Program.
• Applying to the System Development Life Cycle.
• Informing Buying Decisions.

A roadmap is included which consists of several "Areas for Development, Alignment and Collaboration" namely

- Privacy Risk Assessment.
- Mechanisms to Provide Confidence.
- Emerging Technologies.
- De-Identification Techniques and Re-identification Risks.
- Inventory and Mapping.
- Technical Standards.
- Privacy Workforce.
- International and Regulatory Aspects, Impacts, and Alignment.

NIST PRIVACY FRAMEWORK

Dylan Gilbert

Privacy Policy Advisor, NIST

Our online, connected world is mind bogglingly complex. It's no wonder that individuals face significant challenges in safeguarding their privacy as they interact with the vast array of systems, products, and services that collect and use their data. Similarly, it can be a struggle for organizations to understand the full extent to which privacy problems for individuals and communities can have consequences for their trustworthiness, bottom lines, and future growth. Given their complexity, privacy problems are ill-suited to one-size-fits-all solutions.

In response to these challenges, NIST collaborated with stakeholders in an open and public process to produce the Privacy Framework, a voluntary, law and technology-neutral tool to help organizations better manage their privacy risks. The NIST Privacy Framework takes a flexible, risk and outcome-based approach to privacy. Privacy risk management supports ethical decision-making in the design and deployment of products and services to maximize the benefits of data while protecting privacy. It likewise avoids privacy becoming a box-checking exercise that does little to address privacy's broad and shifting nature.

The Framework is helping organizations meet their privacy needs in myriad ways. Some organizations use it in high-level conversations with leadership about how their privacy programs are organized and where they need to go. Other organizations use it to integrate both privacy and security considerations into their overall risk management program. Organizations with complex regulatory obligations use it to develop a foundational privacy program that they can tailor for different jurisdictions.

NIST continues to work with stakeholders to create tools, guidelines, and resources such as our quick start guide for small and medium businesses to help organizations achieve more effective privacy outcomes and keep pace with technological advances.

The NIST Privacy Framework follows the structure of the Framework for Improving Critical Infrastructure Cybersecurity (the Cybersecurity Framework) to facilitate the use of both frameworks together. Like the cybersecurity framework, the privacy framework is composed of three parts: Core, profiles, and implementation tiers. Each component reinforces how organizations manage privacy risk through the connection between business or mission drivers, organizational roles and responsibilities, and privacy protection activities.

The core tier

The core tier is a set of privacy protection activities and outcomes that allow for communicating prioritized privacy protection activities and outcomes across an organization from the executive level to the implementation/operations level. The core is further divided into key categories and subcategories – which are discrete outcomes – for each function. These categories and subcategories are outlined in Table 5.1.

Profile tier

A profile represents an organization's current privacy activities or desired outcomes. To develop a profile, an organization can review all the outcomes and activities in the core to determine which are most important to focus on based on business or mission drivers, data processing ecosystem role(s), types of data processing, and individuals' privacy needs. An organization can create or add functions, categories, and subcategories as needed. Profiles can be used to identify opportunities for improving privacy posture by comparing a "Current" profile (the "as is" state) with a "Target" profile (the "to be" state). Profiles can be used to conduct self-assessments and to communicate within an organization or between organizations about how privacy risks are being managed.

Implementation tiers

Implementation tiers provide a point of reference on how an organization views privacy risk and whether it has sufficient processes and resources in place to manage that risk. Implementation tiers reflect a progression from informal, reactive responses to approaches that are agile and risk informed. When selecting implementation tiers, an organization should consider its target profile(s) and how achievement may be supported or hampered by its current risk management practices, the degree of integration of privacy risk into its enterprise risk management portfolio, its data processing ecosystem relationships, and its workforce composition and training program.

However, NIST recognizes that for many small- to medium-sized organizations, the NIST framework is too "labor intensive" and complex and they

Table 5.1 NIST privacy framework core tier categories

Function	Category	Subcategory
IDENTIFY: Develop the organizational understanding to manage privacy risk for individuals arising from data processing.	**Inventory and Mapping**: Data processing by systems, products, or services is understood and informs the management of privacy risk.	Systems/products/services that process data are inventoried.
		Owners or operators (e.g., the organization or third parties such as service providers, partners, customers, and developers) and their roles with respect to the systems/products/services and components (e.g., internal or external) that process data are inventoried.
		Categories of individuals (e.g., customers, employees, or prospective employees, and consumers) whose data are being processed are inventoried.
		Data actions of the systems/products/services are inventoried.
		The purposes for the data actions are inventoried.
		Data elements within the data actions are inventoried.
		The data processing environment is identified (e.g., geographic location, internal, cloud, third parties).
		Data processing is mapped, illustrating the data actions and associated data elements for systems/products/services, including components; roles of the component owners/operators; and interactions of individuals or third parties with the systems/products/services.
	Business Environment: The organization's mission, objectives, stakeholders, and activities are understood and prioritized; this information is used to inform privacy roles, responsibilities, and risk management decisions.	The organization's role(s) in the data processing ecosystem are identified and communicated.
		Priorities for organizational mission, objectives, and activities are established and communicated.
		ID.BE-P3: Systems/products/services that support organizational priorities are identified and key requirements communicated.

Risk Assessment: The organization understands the privacy risks to individuals and how such privacy risks may create follow-on impacts on organizational operations, including mission, functions, other risk management priorities (e.g., compliance, financial), reputation, workforce, and culture.	Contextual factors related to the systems/products/services and the data actions are identified (e.g., individuals' demographics and privacy interests or perceptions, data sensitivity and/or types, visibility of data processing to individuals and third parties).
	Data analytic inputs and outputs are identified and evaluated for bias.
	Potential problematic data actions and associated problems are identified.
	Problematic data actions, likelihoods, and impacts are used to determine and prioritize risk.
	Risk responses are identified, prioritized, and implemented.
Data Processing Ecosystem Risk Management: The organization's priorities, constraints, risk tolerance, and assumptions are established and used to support risk decisions associated with managing privacy risk and third parties within the data processing ecosystem. The organization has established and implemented the processes to identify, assess, and manage privacy risks within the data processing ecosystem.	Data processing ecosystem risk management policies, processes, and procedures are identified, established, assessed, managed, and agreed to by organizational stakeholders.
	Data processing ecosystem parties (e.g., service providers, customers, partners, product manufacturers, and application developers) are identified, prioritized, and assessed using a privacy risk assessment process.
	Contracts with data processing ecosystem parties are used to implement appropriate measures designed to meet the objectives of an organization's privacy program.
	Interoperability frameworks or similar multi-party approaches are used to manage data processing ecosystem privacy risks.
	Data processing ecosystem parties are routinely assessed using audits, test results, or other forms of evaluations to confirm they are meeting their contractual, interoperability framework, or other obligations.

(Continued)

Table 5.1 (Continued)

Function	Category	Subcategory
GOVERN: Develop and implement the organizational governance structure to enable an ongoing understanding of the organization's risk management priorities that are informed by privacy risk.	**Governance Policies, Processes, and Procedures:** The policies, processes, and procedures to manage and monitor the organization's regulatory, legal, risk, environmental, and operational requirements are understood and inform the management of privacy risk.	Organizational privacy values and policies (e.g., conditions on data processing such as data uses or retention periods, individuals' prerogatives with respect to data processing) are established and communicated.
		Processes to instill organizational privacy values within system/product/service development and operations are established and in place.
		Roles and responsibilities for the workforce are established with respect to privacy.
		Privacy roles and responsibilities are coordinated and aligned with third-party stakeholders (e.g., service providers, customers, and partners).
		Legal, regulatory, and contractual requirements regarding privacy are understood and managed.
		Governance and risk management policies, processes, and procedures address privacy risks.
	Risk Management Strategy: The organization's priorities, constraints, risk tolerances, and assumptions are established and used to support operational risk decisions.	Risk management processes are established, managed, and agreed to by organizational stakeholders.
		Organizational risk tolerance is determined and clearly expressed.
		The organization's determination of risk tolerance is informed by its role(s) in the data processing ecosystem.
	Awareness and Training The organization's workforce and third parties engaged in data processing are provided privacy awareness education and are trained to perform their privacy-related duties and responsibilities consistent with related policies, processes, procedures, and agreements and organizational privacy values.	The workforce is informed and trained on its roles and responsibilities.
		Senior executives understand their roles and responsibilities.
		Privacy personnel understand their roles and responsibilities.
		Third parties (e.g., service providers, customers, and partners) understand their roles and responsibilities.

Monitoring and Review: The policies, processes, and procedures for ongoing review of the organization's privacy posture are understood and inform the management of privacy risk.

Privacy risk is re-evaluated on an ongoing basis and as key factors, including the organization's business environment (e.g., introduction of new technologies), governance (e.g., legal obligations, risk tolerance), data processing, and systems/products/services change.

Privacy values, policies, and training are reviewed, and any updates are communicated.

Policies, processes, and procedures for assessing compliance with legal requirements and privacy policies are established and in place.

Policies, processes, and procedures for communicating progress on managing privacy risks are established and in place.

Policies, processes, and procedures are established and in place to receive, analyze, and respond to problematic data actions disclosed to the organization from internal and external sources (e.g., internal discovery, privacy researchers, professional events).

Policies, processes, and procedures incorporate lessons learned from problematic data actions.

Policies, processes, and procedures for receiving, tracking, and responding to complaints, concerns, and questions from individuals about organizational privacy practices are established and in place.

(Continued)

Table 5.1 (Continued)

Function	Category	Subcategory
CONTROL: Develop and implement appropriate activities to enable organizations or individuals to manage data with sufficient granularity to manage privacy risks	**Data Processing Policies, Processes, and Procedures**: Policies, processes, and procedures are maintained and used to manage data processing consistent with the organization's risk strategy to protect individuals' privacy.	Policies, processes, and procedures for authorizing data processing (e.g., organizational decisions, individual consent), revoking authorizations, and maintaining authorizations are established and in place.
		Policies, processes, and procedures for enabling data review, transfer, sharing or disclosure, alteration, and deletion are established and in place.
		Policies, processes, and procedures for enabling individuals' data processing preferences and requests are established and in place.
		A data life cycle to manage data is aligned and implemented with SDLC
	Data Processing Management: Data are managed consistent with the organization's risk strategy to protect individuals' privacy, increase manageability, and enable the implementation of privacy principles (e.g., individual participation, data quality, data minimization).	Data elements can be accessed for review, transmission, disclosure, alteration, deletion. Data are destroyed according to policy.
		Data are transmitted using standardized formats.
		Mechanisms for transmitting processing permissions and related data values with data elements are established and in place.
		Audit/log records are determined, documented, implemented, and reviewed in accordance with policy and incorporating the principle of data minimization.
		Technical measures implemented to manage data processing are tested and assessed.
		Stakeholder privacy preferences are included in algorithmic design objectives and outputs are evaluated against these preferences.
	Disassociated Processing: Data processing solutions increase disassociability consistent with the organization's risk strategy to protect individuals' privacy and enable implementation of privacy principles (e.g., data minimization).	Data are processed to limit observability and linkability.
		Data are processed to limit the identification of individuals (e.g., de-identification privacy techniques, tokenization).
		Data are processed to limit the formulation of inferences about individuals' behavior or activities (e.g., data processing is decentralized, distributed architectures).
		System or device configurations permit selective collection or disclosure of data elements.
		Attribute references are substituted for attribute values.

COMMUNI-CATE- Develop and implement appropriate activities to enable organizations and individuals to have a reliable understanding and engage in a dialogue about how data are processed and associated privacy risks.	**Communication Policies, Processes, and Procedures:** Policies, processes, and procedures are maintained and used to increase transparency of the organization's data processing practices (e.g., purpose, scope, roles and responsibilities in the data processing ecosystem, and management commitment) and associated privacy risks.	Transparency policies, processes, and procedures for communicating data processing purposes, practices, and associated privacy risks are established and in place.
		Roles and responsibilities (e.g., public relations) for communicating data processing purposes, practices, and associated privacy risks are established.
	Data Processing Awareness: Individuals and organizations have reliable knowledge about data processing practices and associated privacy risks, and effective mechanisms are used and maintained to increase predictability consistent with the organization's risk strategy to protect individuals' privacy.	Mechanisms (e.g., notices, internal or public reports) for communicating data processing purposes, practices, associated privacy risks, and options for enabling individuals' data processing preferences and requests are established and in place.
		Mechanisms for obtaining feedback from individuals (e.g., surveys or focus groups) about data processing and associated privacy risks are established and in place.
		System/product/service design enables data processing visibility.
		Records of data disclosures and sharing are maintained and can be accessed for review or transmission/disclosure.
		Data corrections or deletions can be communicated to individuals or organizations (e.g., data sources) in the data processing ecosystem.
		Data provenance and lineage are maintained and can be accessed for review or transmission/disclosure.
		Impacted individuals and organizations are notified about a privacy breach or event.
		Individuals are provided with mitigation mechanisms (e.g., credit monitoring, consent withdrawal, and data alteration or deletion) to address impacts of problematic data actions.

(Continued)

Table 5.1 (*Continued*)

Function	Category	Subcategory
PROTECT: Develop and implement appropriate data processing safeguards.	**Data Protection Policies, Processes, and Procedures**: Security and privacy policies (e.g., purpose, scope, roles and responsibilities in the data processing ecosystem, and management commitment), processes, and procedures are maintained and used to manage the protection of data.	A baseline configuration of information technology is created and maintained incorporating security principles (e.g., concept of least functionality). Configuration change control processes are established and in place.
		Backups of information are conducted, maintained, and tested.
		Policy and regulations regarding the physical operating environment for organizational assets are met.
		Protection processes are improved. Effectiveness of protection technologies shared.
		Response plans (Incident Response and Business Continuity) and recovery plans (Incident Recovery and Disaster Recovery) are established, in place, and managed.
		Response and recovery plans are tested.
		Privacy procedures are included in human resources practices (e.g., deprovisioning, personnel screening).
		A vulnerability management plan is developed and implemented.
	Identity Management, Authentication, and Access Control (PR.AC-P): Access to data and devices is limited to authorized individuals, processes, and devices, and is managed consistent with the assessed risk of unauthorized access.	Identities and credentials are issued, managed, verified, revoked, and audited for authorized individuals, processes, and devices.
		Physical access to data and devices is managed.
		Remote access is managed.
		Access permissions and authorizations are managed, incorporating the principles of least privilege and separation of duties.
		Network integrity is protected (e.g., network segregation, network segmentation).
		Individuals and devices are proofed and bound to credentials, and authenticated commensurate with the risk of the transaction (e.g., individuals' security and privacy risks and other organizational risks).

Data Security: Data are managed consistent with the organization's risk strategy to protect individuals' privacy and maintain data confidentiality, integrity, and availability.

- Data-at-rest are protected.
- Data-in-transit are protected.
- Systems/products/services and associated data are formally managed throughout removal, transfers, and disposition.
- Adequate capacity to ensure availability is maintained.
- Protections against data leaks are implemented.
- Integrity checking mechanisms are used to verify software, firmware, and information integrity.
- The development and testing environment(s) are separate from the production.
- Integrity checking mechanisms are used to verify hardware integrity.

Maintenance: System maintenance and repairs are performed consistent with policies, processes, and procedures.

- Maintenance and repair of organizational assets are performed and logged, with approved and controlled tools.
- Remote maintenance of organizational assets is approved, logged, and performed in a manner that prevents unauthorized access.

Protective Technology: Technical security solutions are managed to ensure the security and resilience of systems/products/services and associated data, consistent with related policies, processes, procedures, and agreements.

- Removable media is protected and its use restricted according to policy.
- The principle of least functionality is incorporated by configuring systems to provide only essential capabilities.
- Communications and control networks are protected.
- Mechanisms (e.g., failsafe, load balancing, hot swap) are implemented to achieve resilience requirements in normal and adverse situations.

have simplified the framework into a simple model of five privacy risk management areas: identify, govern, control, communicate, and protect. These are presented in Table 5.2.

Table 5.2 The five privacy risk management areas

Risk area	Action
Identify	Identify the data you are processing (such as collecting, using, sharing, and storing) and map out its flow through your systems throughout the full data lifecycle – from collection to disposal. This doesn't have to be comprehensive, especially at first, but it's a foundation for understanding your privacy risks.
	Conduct a privacy risk assessment by using your data map to assess how your data processing activities could create problems for individuals (like embarrassment, discrimination, or economic loss). Then assess the impacts to your organization if those problems occurred (like loss of customer trust or reputational harm) that can negatively affect your bottom line.
	Ask about options for contracts and the products and services you use to run your business to ensure that they are set up to reflect your privacy priorities.
Govern	Privacy culture starts at the top. Determine which privacy values (e.g., autonomy, anonymity, dignity, transparency, and data control) your organization is focused on. Connect your organization's privacy values and policies with your privacy risk assessment to foster trust in your products and services.
	Know your privacy-related legal obligations so that you can build compliant products and services.
	Help your workforce know their roles and responsibilities so that they can make better decisions about how to effectively manage privacy risks in the design and deployment of your products and services.
	Regularly reassess to see if your privacy risks have changed. This can happen when you make improvements to your products and services, change your data processing, or learn about new legal obligations.
Control	Are you collecting, sharing, or keeping data that you don't need? Consider how your policies help you or other organizations maintain control over data and how individuals might have a role as well.
	Take your privacy risks and legal obligations into account when deciding on the functionality of your systems, products, or services. Consider a flexible design so that you can respond more cost-effectively to shifting customer privacy preferences and a dynamic legal environment.
	What kinds of data processing do you do? The more you can disassociate data from individuals and devices, the greater the privacy gains. Consider how different technical measures such as de-identification, decentralized data processing, or other techniques could allow you to meet your business or agency objectives while protecting privacy.

(Continued)

Table 5.2 (Continued)

Risk area	Action
Protect	Control who logs on to your network and uses your computers and other devices.
	Use security software to protect data.
	Encrypt sensitive data, at rest and in transit.
	Conduct regular backups of data.
	Update security software regularly, automating those updates if possible.
	Have formal policies for safely disposing of data and old devices.
Communicate	Craft policies for communicating internally and externally about your data processing activities.
	Increase transparency and customer understanding by providing clear and accessible notices and reports or implementing alerts, nudges, or other signals to inform individuals about your data processing activities and their choices.
	Do you conduct surveys or focus groups to inform your product or service design? Include privacy so that you learn more about customer privacy preferences.
	Consider what you will do in case of a data breach. How will you provide notifications or any remedies such as credit monitoring or freezes?

Source: NIST.

ISO/IEC 27701

The EU GDPR and various data protection acts require organizations to take measures to ensure the privacy of any personal data that they process. However, the legislation does not provide much guidance on what those measures should look like. The ISO (the International Organization for Standardization) and the IEC (International Electrotechnical Commission) developed this standard as a way to provide that guidance.

ISO/IEC 27701:2019 is a privacy extension to ISO/IEC 27001. The ISO/IEC 27001 Information Security Management Systems Requirements provide a model for establishing, implementing, operating, monitoring, reviewing, maintaining, and improving an Information Security Management System (ISMS). ISO 27001 was originally constructed around 114 controls in 14 groups but was recently revised to 93 controls across 4 groups. The four groups of controls are: Organization, Physical, People and Technological.

The standard has been used for several years to provide assurance to external parties of the security practices in an organization. Granted, the scope could be specified as very small and the risk tolerance high for an organization, and then the certification would not mean much. However, many organizations going down the ISO27001 path do so to provide assurance and improve the existing security practices.

While ISO/IEC 27001 provides controls for general security measures, ISO/IEC 27701 focuses on new requirements and controls, along with implementation guidance, directed specifically at protecting PII. The design goal is to enhance the existing Information Security Management System (ISMS) from ISO 27001 with additional requirements to establish, implement, maintain, and continually improve a Privacy Information Management System (PIMS). ISO 27701's approach also expands on the clauses of ISO 27001 and controls that relate specifically to data privacy, as well as providing two additional sets of controls specific to data controllers and data processors. The standard outlines a framework for Personally Identifiable Information (PII) Controllers and PII Processors to manage privacy controls to reduce the risk to the privacy rights of individuals. The language is clearly designed around an American audience, as PII is not a typical term used in Europe.

A robust PIMS has many potential benefits for PII Controllers and PII Processors, with at least three significant advantages:

- First, achieving compliance with privacy requirements (particularly laws and regulations, plus agreements with third parties, plus corporate privacy policies, etc.) across multiple landscapes is a challenge. A managed approach eases the compliance burden where a single compliance requirement can address multiple jurisdictions.
- Second, achieving and maintaining compliance with applicable requirements is a governance and assurance issue. Based on the PIMS (and, potentially, its certification), privacy or data protection officers can provide the necessary evidence to assure stakeholders such as senior management, owners, and the authorities that applicable privacy requirements are satisfied.
- Third, PIMS certification can be valuable in communicating privacy compliance to customers and the wider stakeholder community particularly investors. Under GDPR, controllers are required to assure themselves that processors privacy management system adheres to applicable privacy requirements. A uniform evidence framework based on international standards can greatly simplify such communication of compliance transparency, especially when the evidence is validated by an accredited third-party auditor.
- Lastly, PIMS certification can potentially serve to signal trustworthiness to consumers and the wider stakeholder community.

GAPP/AICPA/CICA PRIVACY MATURITY MODEL

Maturity models are assessment systems that allow organizations to evaluate their current state of progress in each area. Developed in the field of quality management, they are now used in a wide variety of domains such as software development, human resources, learning, marketing, and cybersecurity (and now privacy). The most common maturity model, transposed to privacy, is based on the AICPA's Generally Accepted Privacy Principles (GAPP). The Generally Accepted Privacy Principles (GAPP) have been developed from a business perspective, referencing several significant local, national, and international privacy regulations. GAPP converts complex privacy requirements into a single privacy objective supported by ten privacy principles. Each principle is supported by objective, measurable criteria (73 in all) that form the basis for effective management of privacy risk and compliance. Illustrative policy requirements, communications, and controls, including their monitoring, are provided as support for the criteria. GAPP was developed to help management create an effective privacy program that addresses privacy risks and obligations as well as business opportunities. GAPP can also be a useful tool for boards and governance bodies, as it enables oversight of privacy risk at the macro level. It includes a definition of privacy and an explanation of why privacy is a business issue and not solely a compliance issue. Also illustrated are how these principles can be applied to outsourcing arrangements and the types of privacy initiatives that can be undertaken for the benefit of organizations, their customers, and related persons. The ten principles that comprise GAPP are outlined in Table 5.3.

Using GAPP, the American Institute of Certified Public Accountants (AICPA) and the Canadian Institute of Chartered Accountants (CICA) have developed the AICPA/CICA Privacy Maturity Model (PMM) to assist organizations in strengthening their privacy policies, procedures, and practices. The Privacy Maturity Model is a recognized means by which organizations can measure their progress against established benchmarks while also recognizing that:

- Becoming compliant is a journey and progress along the way strengthens the organization, whether the organization has achieved all the requirements.
- Not every organization, or every application, needs to be at the maximum for the organization to achieve an acceptable level of security or privacy.
- Creation of values or benefits may be possible if they achieve a higher maturity level.

Table 5.3 GAPP principles

Principle	Definition
Management	The entity defines, documents, communicates, and assigns accountability for its privacy policies and procedures.
Notice	The entity provides notice about its privacy policies and procedures and identifies the purposes for which personal information is collected, used, retained, and disclosed.
Choice and consent	The entity describes the choices available to the individual and obtains implicit or explicit consent with respect to the collection, use, and disclosure of personal information.
Collection	The entity collects personal information only for the purposes identified in the notice.
Use, retention, and disposal	The entity limits the use of personal information to the purposes identified in the notice and for which the individual has provided implicit or explicit consent. The entity retains personal information for only the minimum amount of time necessary to fulfill the stated purposes or as required by law or regulations and thereafter appropriately disposes of such information.
Access	The entity provides individuals with access to their personal information for review and update.
Disclosure to third parties	The entity discloses personal information to third parties only for the purposes identified in the notice and with the implicit or explicit consent of the individual.
Security for privacy	The entity protects personal information against unauthorized access (both physical and logical).
Quality	The entity maintains accurate, complete, and relevant personal information for the purposes identified in the notice.
Monitoring and enforcement.	The entity monitors compliance with its privacy policies and procedures and has procedures to address privacy-related complaints and disputes.

The PMM uses five maturity levels, and these are outlined in Table 5.4. Each of the 73 GAPP criteria is broken down according to these five maturity levels. This allows entities to obtain a picture of their privacy program or initiatives both in terms of their status and, through successive reviews, their progress.

While the PMM can be used to set benchmarks for organizations establishing a privacy program, it is designed to be used by organizations that have an existing privacy function and some components of a privacy program. The PMM provides structured means to assist in identifying and documenting current privacy initiatives, determining status, and assessing it against the PMM criteria. Start-up activities could include the following and we highly recommend using this as a "checklist" for initiating a privacy program:

- Identifying a project sponsor (e.g., Chief Privacy Officer or equivalent).
- Appointing a project lead with sufficient privacy knowledge and authority to manage the project and assess the findings.

Table 5.4 The PMM five maturity levels

Maturity description	What it looks like
Ad hoc	Procedures or processes are generally informal, incomplete, and inconsistently applied.
Repeatable	Procedures or processes exist; however, they are not fully documented and do not cover all relevant aspects.
Defined	Procedures and processes are fully documented and implemented and cover all relevant aspects.
Managed	Reviews are conducted to assess the effectiveness of the controls in place.
Optimized	Regular review and feedback are used to ensure continuous improvement toward optimization of the given process.

Source: AICPA.

- Forming an oversight committee that includes representatives from legal, human resources, risk management, internal audit, information technology, and the privacy office.
- Considering whether the committee requires outside privacy expertise.
- Assembling a team to obtain and document information and perform the initial assessment of the maturity level.
- Managing the project by providing status reports and the opportunity to meet and assess overall progress.
- Providing a means to ensure that identifiable risk and compliance issues are appropriately escalated.
- Ensuring the project sponsor and senior management are aware of all findings.
- Identifying the desired maturity level by principle and/or for the entire organization for benchmarking purposes.

(IM)PERFECT PRIVACY PRINCIPLES
Michael W. Smith
Data Privacy Leader/Chief Privacy Officer, Financial Services

If you are in a large, multi-state or multi-national company, you know how difficult it is to meet the many privacy laws impacting your organization. From states to federal governments, from industry sectors to regional agreements, the list of laws, regulations, and obligations is long and ever-changing. It can feel incredibly challenging to deal with all these requirements – because it *is* incredibly challenging.

Many organizations use principle-based decision-making to meet the many requirements, looking at the strictest laws and setting policies to meet them. This approach is completely reasonable and would likely be recommended by many privacy professionals, including me. Principle-based policies allow the organization to focus less on keeping track of every law and, instead, to group common privacy law themes within the principles. Now, when evaluating a new or changing law, the privacy team can look to see whether the law exceeds the principle-based procedures already in place. If not, the law requires no change in processes.

If using principle-based policies solved all our problems, privacy professionals would probably not be needed. The reality is that enough variation and contradictions exist across privacy laws to require that we look deeper.

A simple example is to examine varying state breach notification laws in the United States and the requirements for when and how either the impacted individual or the state government is notified. If we write our policy that we will provide breach notification based on the strictest of the laws, this seemingly makes the company's job simple. In a large breach, all individuals involved would be treated equally and on the same timeline. In reality, a strict adherence to this principle could mean a rushed timeline for notification, notification to individuals and states who don't require notification, increased customer queries, unnecessary expense, and lots of unhappy internal customers.

Stick to these rules:

Set a principle-based policy for ensuring your company meets common privacy requirements. Allow the policy for risk-based decisions to be made when situations don't fit strictly within the principles.

Train and communicate how the principle-based logic drives the policy and help colleagues to know what they need to do.

Stress that the privacy team should be included in decisions, as not every situation will fit within the principles.

Using privacy maturity models

The aim of the maturity level is not necessarily to reach level 5 maturity. Maturity models can be used not only as an assessment mechanism but also as guidance mechanism or a way to structure an organization's approach to their privacy program or a way to highlight specific challenges. The organization's appetite for risk, the quantity or category of data they process, the local legislative landscape they operate in, and the resources they assign to privacy shape the maturity level the organization should be aiming for. For instance, organizations operating in the clinical health research space who receive very few data subject access requests may want to reach a security maturity level of 5 but an access maturity level of 2.

Other privacy maturity models have emerged in recent years, developed by consulting firms or regulators, based on soft or hard law. Some organizations even develop their own in-house system. The government of New Zealand published a Privacy Maturity Assessment Framework. The Office of the Privacy Commissioner of Canada and the Offices of the Information and Privacy Commissioners of Alberta and British Columbia also took a similar approach in their "Getting Accountability Right with a Privacy Management Program". The most common of these was released in 2021 by CNIL, the French data protection authority. CNIL's model "transposes the maturity levels defined in international standards [based on the CMM] to data protection management" and "allows organizations to assess their own level of maturity and determine how to improve their management of data protection". [Links to the CNIL commentary on its maturity model can be found in the suggested reading section.] The CNIL self-assessment provides a description of the five levels of maturity (ad hoc, repeatable, defined, managed, and optimized) for the eight following items: define and implement privacy procedures; pilot privacy governance; maintain a data inventory; ensure legal compliance; training and awareness; handle data subjects requests; manage security risks; and manage data breaches. The CNIL explains that its maturity model can be used as a basis to build an action plan to reach the desired level of maturity but reminds that this methodology does not aim at ensuring compliance. Instead, it is meant to create conditions favorable to the implementation of lasting privacy activities.

GDPR CERTIFICATIONS

The GDPR seeks to encourage the demonstration by organizations of their compliance with the provisions of the GDPR. Articles 42 and 43 of the GDPR deal with data protection certification and allow for organizations to demonstrate and account for any compliance measures they have in place. In the context of GDPR, a key part of certification is a "certification scheme". Such schemes specify the mechanisms in place for the processing of personal data and how appropriate controls and measures are implemented. These schemes may then be assessed by an accredited certification body. If satisfied, a certification body may then validate and confirm (i.e., independently certify) that appropriate controls and measures have been implemented by the organization and that their processes or services fulfill the scheme's requirements and data protection criteria. Certified organizations are subsequently reviewed and monitored by the relevant certification body, to ensure that the criteria continue to be met.

There has been much discourse regarding these certification schemes, or more importantly the lack of these schemes up to now. This is largely because despite its implementation in 2018, no certification schemes emerged until late 2022. However, GDPR is still in its first decade of adoption and certification mechanisms were always expected to emerge once GDPR started to mature and become more embedded. In this regard, it may be prudent that Europe has taken a slow but methodical approach to build certification schemes, as they will become fundamental assurance mechanisms going forward. Hence, they need these schemes to be robust and well-planned.

What exactly does "Certification" mean?

The GDPR does not define "certification mechanisms, seals or marks" and uses the terms collectively. The European Data Protection Board (EDPB) notes that a certificate is a statement of conformity, where a seal or mark is a logo or symbol whose presence indicates that the object of certification has been independently assessed and conforms to specified requirements. The International Organization for Standardization (ISO) provides a universal definition of certification as "the provision by an independent body of written assurance (a certificate) that the product, service or system in question meets specific requirements". Certification is also known as "third party conformity assessment" and certification bodies can also be referred to as "conformity assessment bodies" (CABs). In the context of certification under Articles 42 and 43 of the GDPR, the EDPB notes in their guidelines that certification shall refer to "third party attestation related to processing operations by controllers and processors".

Why is "Certification" so important?

Certification provides a public-facing accountability instrument that allows an organization to demonstrate compliance measures to individuals, as well as to other organizations that it engages with, and to supervisory authorities. The implementation of a certification mechanism can promote transparency and compliance to the GDPR and allow data subjects to better determine the degree of protection offered by services, processes, or systems used or offered by the organizations that process their personal data. In short, certification helps to demonstrate that controllers and processors' processing operations comply with GDPR requirements. EDPB Chair, Andrea Jelinek, said: "The main aim of certification mechanisms is to help controllers and processors demonstrate compliance with the GDPR. Controllers and processors adhering to a certification mechanism also gain greater visibility and credibility, as it allows individuals to quickly assess the level of protection of the processing operations".

Another equally important benefit of certification schemes is to mitigate the risk of organizations offering "GDPR certified" services, or offering GDPR compliant applications, etc. (as many do currently) without having valid mechanisms or adequate qualifications/to do so.

GDPR-CARPA Certifications

GDPR-CARPA (Certified Assurance Report Based Processing Activities) is the first certification scheme to be adopted under the GDPR. GDPR-CARPA was developed by Luxembourg's National Data Protection Commission (Commission Nationale pour la Protection des Données – CNPD) together with input from various audit firms and other supervisory authorities, and a final opinion from the EDPB. Luxembourg's CNPD adopted this certification mechanism on 13th May 2022. The EDPB notes that the CNPD has been a driving force behind the progress made by the EDPB in the field of certification, notably as rapporteur for the adopted guidance or as a help to the EDPB in issuing formal opinions on this novel subject. To date, the CNPD is the only European supervisory authority to have developed a GDPR certification mechanism. Companies, public authorities, associations, and other organizations (i.e., data controllers and processors) established in Luxembourg will now have the possibility to demonstrate that their data processing activities comply with the GDPR.

Under the GDPR-CARPA certification criteria, interested organizations may be certified by competent certification bodies. These certification bodies will be approved by the CNPD. In this way, the CNPD accredits the entities that will issue the GDPR certifications. It is expected that the CNPD will publish a list of such certification bodies in the future. The accreditation criteria for these certification bodies developed by the CNPD are based on ISAE 3000 (audit), ISCQ1 (quality control of auditing organizations), and ISO 17065 (licensing of certification entities). The EDPB notes that "The unique feature of the CNPD certification mechanism is the fact that it is based on an ISAE 3000 Type 2 report that allows for the issuing of an opinion on the correct implementation of the control mechanism, while the auditor is formally held responsible". This guarantees a high level of confidence, a key factor in building trust in the processing of personal data covered by the certification scheme.

The criteria are divided into three sections. The first section relates to data governance within the applying entity (e.g., policies and procedures, records of processing activities, data subjects' rights, DPO, recording and reporting of data breaches, etc.). The second relates to entities acting as data controllers to check compliance with the main data protection principles under Article 5 GDPR. Finally, the third section relates only to entities acting as data processors (contracts with controllers and subcontracting, security, transfer of personal data to third countries).

The certification process consists of several steps:

- The application for/applicability of the certification is assessed.
- Certification audits are performed by the certification body based on the norm ISAE 3000.
- The decision to certify the organization is made in consideration of the GDPR-CARPA criteria and the decision is communicated to the CNPD.
- The certificate is issued by the certification body.
- Compliance with the GDPR-CARPA criteria is monitored.

The GDPR-CARPA certification scheme is a general scheme, which does not focus on a specific sector or type of processing. GDPR-CARPA focuses on the responsibility of controllers/processors who must implement a governance system that allows them to define and implement information management (data protection and security) measures for the processing activity within its scope. Only data processing operations can be certified (e.g., a company could certify a data processing operation linked to the products/ services it is selling).

GDPR-CARPA certification is not considered suitable:

- For certifying the processing of personal data specifically targeting minors under the age of 16.
- For certifications of processing activities under joint control.
- For processing activities under Article 10 of the GDPR (i.e., processing of personal data relating to criminal convictions and offences).
- For entities that have not formally appointed a DPO (Article 37 of the GDPR).
- For use as "appropriate safeguards" for transfers of personal data to third countries as referred to under Article 46(2) (f) GDPR.

Europrivacy

In 2022, Europrivacy was approved by EDPB as the European Data Protection Seal to assess and certify the compliance of all sorts of data processing with the GDPR and complementary national data protection regulations. It enables applicants to identify and reduce their risks, to demonstrate and value their compliance, and to enhance their reputation and market access. It is the only GDPR certification officially recognized in all EU Member States.

Developed through the European Research Program Horizon 2020, it is continuously updated by the European Centre for Certification and Privacy (ECCP) in Luxembourg and its International Board of Experts in data protection. It is licensed to qualified certification bodies and consulting firms committed to protect personal data.

Europrivacy has been developed based on ISO/IEC 17065 and Article 42 of the GDPR "for the purpose of demonstrating compliance with this Regulation of processing operations by controllers and processors". It provides a comprehensive set of online resources and services to effectively implement, enhance, and demonstrate data protection compliance. It is supported by a community of qualified partners, an online academy, a community website, and online tools. It presents numerous benefits and advantages.

Scope and applicability

Europrivacy enables assessing, documenting, certifying, and valuing compliance with the GDPR and complementary data protection regulations. It assists businesses and enterprises to:

- Identify and reduce legal and financial risks of non-compliance.
- Document compliance.
- Assess and certify compliance.
- Value and communicate compliance.

Europrivacy is eligible to both data controllers and data processors. While the Europrivacy methodology can be applied to diverse targets of evaluations, under Art. 42 GDPR, only data processing activities can be certified. Therefore, for EU jurisdictions, it is not possible to certify a whole company at once or even its whole management system under the GDPR. The positive side of this element is that compliance can be progressively certified, starting with priority data processing activities and extending the certification step by step to more data processing. Validity: Certificates are valid for renewable periods of three years.

Europrivacy can be used in any place to assess compliance with the GDPR. However, the deliverance of certificates is not applicable to jurisdictions that do not provide adequate and sufficient guarantees for the rights and freedoms of data subjects. The European Commission has so far recognized Andorra, Argentina, Canada (commercial organizations), Faroe Islands, Guernsey, Israel, Isle of Man, Japan, Jersey, New Zealand, Republic of Korea, Switzerland, the United Kingdom under the GDPR and the LED, and Uruguay as providing adequate protection. With the exception of the United Kingdom, these adequacy decisions do not cover data exchanges in the law enforcement sector which are governed by the Law Enforcement Directive (Article 36 of Directive (EU) 2016/680).

Europrivacy certification process

The certification procedure can be divided into the following major steps:

- Prepare and document compliance with the Europrivacy criteria with the support of the Europrivacy Welcome Pack of resources and tools.

- Certify data processing compliance with a qualified certification body. The certification body must be authorized by ECCP and have a valid accreditation with a competent national authority. The certificate is published on the official Europrivacy Registry of Certificates to enable its authentication by third party and to prevent forgery.
- Maintain and enhance your compliance using online resources and tools, including continuous updates on compliance requirements, and yearly surveillance audits.

HITCHING A RIDE ON YOUR PRIVACY JOURNEY

Amber Welch

Senior Privacy Architect, Amazon Web Services

You've probably been there too… you have a global presence, international subsidiaries, and a tight budget. How do you operationalize privacy with such strained resources? By hitching a ride with other teams, of course! Embedding your privacy efforts into existing processes can stretch your budget beyond what you could achieve with standalone initiatives or expensive privacy-specific tooling.

A first stop on your journey should be a privacy framework. If you have been using a law as a framework, such as the GDPR, consider the benefits of instead adopting a companion or extension control framework to partner with your security team's approach. The NIST Privacy Framework shares control with the NIST Cybersecurity Framework, with one of the five functions shared between the two. If you are using ISO 27001, consider adding ISO 27701. Even sector-specific frameworks like HITRUST can be expanded to incorporate privacy controls. This will save time and effort in setting up the structure of your privacy program management.

You will also need some way of managing compliance documentation such as assessments and data mapping. Other teams with enterprise-wide functions may have existing inventories available. For example, your disaster recovery team may have comprehensive business impact assessments, including RACI charts. That could be your data mapping entry point, and if you're lucky, you might be able to embed all your requirements directly in their existing system.

If you need to deploy website privacy requirements such as cookie consent tools and privacy policies across a universe of websites, connect with your web architecture team. They are probably tracking other critical domain information in a format you can use. Similarly, the teams managing vendor risk will have processes naturally positioned to capture some key details on data processors for your records of processing activities, cross-border transfers, and impact assessments. SOC teams can build privacy use cases for your SIEM, security can support privacy threat modelling and enterprise-level risk assessment, and you can surely find other areas of collaboration with some charisma and diplomacy. Support your enterprise teams in return and enjoy the road trip together!

SUGGESTED READING

Article 29 Working Party Opinion on Purpose Limitation. https://ec.europa.eu/justice/article-29/documentation/opinion-recommendation/files/2013/wp203_en.pdf

CNIL Commentary on its Maturity Model. https://www.cnil.fr/fr/la-cnil-propose-une-autoevaluation-de-maturite-en-gestion-de-la-protection-des-donnees

Europrivacy Certification. https://www.europrivacy.org/

Guide to ISS maturity – ANSSI. https://www.ssi.gouv.fr/guide/guide-relatif-a-la-maturite-ssi/

ISO/IEC 29190:2015 – Information technology – Security techniques – Privacy capability assessment model – ISO. https://www.iso.org/obp/ui/fr/#iso:std:iso-iec:29190:ed-1:v1:en

NIST Privacy Framework Crosswalks. https://www.nist.gov/privacy-framework/resource-repository/browse/crosswalks

Siegel, Bob. (2021). Choosing a privacy framework (Privacy Ref.com). https://privacyref.com/blog/choosing-a-privacy-framework/

Software Capability Maturity Model (CMM) – IT Governance https://www.itgovernance.eu/fr-fr/capability-maturity-model-fr

Starting Guide for NIST Privacy Framework. https://www.nist.gov/system/files/documents/2021/01/13/Getting-Started-NIST-Privacy-Framework-Guide.pdf

The AICPA-CICA Privacy Maturity Model. https://iapp.org/media/pdf/resource_center/aicpa_cica_privacy_maturity_model_final-2011.pdf

The OECD Privacy Framework. https://www.oecd.org/sti/ieconomy/oecd_privacy_framework.pdf

The SDM Methodology. https://www.datenschutzzentrum.de/uploads/sdm/SDM-Methodology_V2.0b.pdf

Chapter 6

Privacy risk governance

> This time, like all times, is a very good one, if we but know what to do with it.
>
> Ralph Waldo Emerson 1803–1882

PRIVACY RISK IN CONTEXT

Obviously, privacy is a risk (and is a potentially large risk to an organization); however, it is important to keep the perspective of "this is one more risk the organization must evaluate and reduce to an acceptable level". Organizations face many risks including financial, operational, risks of an upcoming merger, introduction of a new product or service, and performance risks. Risks are managed daily, and decisions are made on a big picture level by the CEO, and daily within each of our jobs. We make decisions on how long it will take to develop a product and recognize that we may not introduce the product to market before our competitors as part of the organizational and [7-S Framework Applied to Privacy Leadership] strategy factor. We take risks with the staff we have, deciding they are the right staff with the right skills (two other 7-S Framework Applied to Privacy Leadership factors), or we supplement the staff with external expertise. We buy businesses and sell others, all assuming we have formulated the right vision for our organization. Each of these events contributes to ensure that the organization can sustain itself with a stream of income and manageable expenses. These decisions are "opinions" based on past results and attempts to predict a better future for the company, employees, shareholders, and the public. Privacy risk is one of the risks managed similarly. It is important to recognize this, as the senior executives may view privacy as one of the many risks they need to address, and if they are presented with only "the sky is falling" scenarios, the attention may turn to other risks communicated by other departments containing deeper analysis on the probability and impact of a "very bad thing" happening and the steps to mitigate it.

When considering privacy risk, the context of the organization is important. For example, if the organization is a health insurance company and is

DOI: 10.1201/9781003383017-10

comfortable calculating the probability of occurrence of an event happening based upon the likelihood of someone needing diagnosis-based surgery vs the likelihood of someone avoiding surgery based upon that individual using a chosen drug, they are going to want to see a similar analysis for privacy. Such an analysis may be expected to follow the rigor of actuaries using statistical analysis. Alternatively, an organization may be used to a red–green–yellow or high–medium–low method of communicating and will more readily understand risks communicated in this way. The privacy leader will need to "read the room" on this one.

PRIVACY RISK CONSIDERATIONS

R. Jason Cronk

President, Consultant, Lawyer, and Engineer, Institute of Operational Privacy Design

We're all familiar with the stop-light approach to risk: Green (low), yellow (medium), red (high). But could you imagine if your insurance company were limited to rating risk into three very crude buckets? Your house is high risk: Uninsurable. Your house is low risk: we can't make money from this. Your house is medium risk: just right, pay us $1,000 per month. Even expanding into five categories, adding very low and very high categories, would be insufficiently granular for an insurer. Qualitative approaches to risk suffer dozens of deficiencies (Krisper, 2021): irrelevance, correlations, non-linear behavior, range compression, ambiguity, human bias, inconsistency, just to name a few. Yet, this is the norm in privacy and information security, though the latter is moving more quickly toward quantitative approaches. Privacy must do the same, but how? Privacy is so contextual, subjective, and personal. Here are some considerations when developing a privacy risk model:

- **Privacy is an externality** – Like pollution, privacy is what economists call an externality. The costs are borne by individuals outside of the organization. Companies profit from data use, but consumers, employees, bystanders, and others bear the risks. Privacy risk should not be measured in terms of organizational risk but the likelihood and impacts on individuals (EU GDPR, Article 25).
- **Privacy harms are not necessarily tangible** – While we're all familiar with the financial harms of identity theft or embarrassment of leaked racy photos, privacy risk need not have tangibility. There is also a probability that someone will covertly surveil us in a short-term rental. It's not just harms of embarrassment or blackmail that are problematic, but this moral harm of covert monitoring that we, as a society, find distasteful and

wish to avoid. Quantifying the risk to the individual of privacy invasions regardless of tangible consequences can help us uncover mitigations.

- **Privacy is a subjective expectation that society is willing to recognize** – Just as there is the probability of covert surveillance in the rental, there is a probability that someone will surveil us in a cafe. Neither will necessarily have tangible impact on us and both are creepy situations we may want to avoid. But notice the disparity in severity of these two types of surveillance. Monitoring us in our rental, a private space, is way more creepy. We can use surveys of social norms to measure this "ick" factor and quantify the risks of being surveilled in a cafe versus a rental.
- **Comparison is key** – Risk measures don't exist in a vacuum. Even risk measured in currency incorporates our innate sense of the value of that currency and the context. A million dollars a year may seem like a lot of risk, unless you're a multinational with billions in liquidity. Quantifying the covert rental surveillance as "17" may not seem like much but if I tell you that's compared to the cafe scenario's (which most people would see as tolerable) measure of 1, the former seems huge and intolerable. You can compare risk to other situations, residual risk after controls are put in place or to previously ascertained tolerance levels.
- **Zero risk is impractical** – Most people want zero risk. No one should be covertly surveilled in their rental. But zero risk is impractical. No auto manufacturer wants people dying in their vehicles. But that fact is, though safety is paramount, people die in cars. A manufacturer insisting on zero risk wouldn't be in business. Privacy professionals need to help business develop reasonable levels of risk tolerance.

Privacy risk governance

This organizational context may also influence the privacy governance model in place, which will most likely be either decentralized or centralized, and these are discussed below.

Decentralized privacy governance model

The most common privacy governance model is the decentralized or local model. In the decentralized model, business owners within an organization bear responsibility for data protection matters within their scope of operations. They need to be educated about general GDPR requirements and trust the organization's privacy team to help them achieve their goals and stay compliant, by giving the right advice and being proactive when solving issues.

Centralized privacy model

Another privacy governance model is a centralized model. It is a common model that fits well in organizations used to utilizing single-channel actions with planning and decision making completed by one team. A centralized privacy governance model will leave one team or person responsible for privacy-related affairs, and this person is usually a CPO or DPO. This means that all GDPR-related matters will flow through this single point.

ACCOUNTABILITY AND ETHICS ARE KEY FOR RESPONSIBLE AND TRUSTED DATA-DRIVEN INNOVATION

Bojana Bellamy

President, Centre for Information Policy Leadership

At the time of unprecedented transition to digital economy and society, businesses need a new roadmap to deliver responsible and trusted uses of data and technology and ensure long-term business sustainability and growth. Risk-based organizational accountability provides business leaders with guidance for the uncharted waters of digital transformation. It enables them to foster growth through responsible innovation and address proactively and systematically the business' impact on the interests and rights of people and wider society.

Accountability, which requires companies to maintain privacy and data management programs, can also be leveraged for all the areas of responsible development and use of technology and digital regulatory compliance, from AI, emerging technologies, to online safety, children's protection, and competition and platform regulation. The governance, rules, and tools are transferrable and provide a repeatable and systematic roadmap for the business to follow when they encounter new requirements, risks, and expectations.

Accountability is not an add-on. It is embedded in and closely linked to business digital strategy. It supports that strategy by establishing the following elements and expected outcomes, without prescribing how to do it:

Establish leadership and oversight for data protection and the responsible use of data.

Assess and mitigate the risks that data use may raise to individuals, including weighing the risk of the information use against its benefits.

Establish internal policies, procedures, and tools that operationalize legal requirements, including the use of technologies, such as PETs.

Provide transparency to all stakeholders internally and externally about the organization's data privacy program and control.

Provide training and communications for employees to raise awareness of the program, its objectives, requirements, and the implementation.

Monitor and verify the implementation and effectiveness of the program and internal compliance through regular internal or external audits and redress plans.

Implement response and enforcement procedures to address inquiries, complaints, data breaches, and otherwise enforce internal compliance.

Accountability is firmly linked to companies' values and the code of business ethics and ethical decision making is an integral part of each of the elements above.

By establishing proper accountability, businesses will be able to anticipate, adapt, and advance faster. They will create lasting digital trust with their consumers and business customers and enhance their brand and reputation. Responsible data practices will also generate confidence and trust with external stakeholders, such as investors and regulators. Finally, accountable businesses will be able to innovate and move faster, as they will have the tools and culture to engage in broader beneficial uses of data while minimizing risks to individuals and society and demonstrating compliance with applicable laws and regulations. These are all prerequisites for long-term sustainable business!

Accountability

The jurisdictional context may also influence accountability requirements within that governance model. Accountability is a principle in the OECD Privacy Guidelines and has been included in numerous data protection laws over the past 40 years. While the principle is not new, there is growing interest in how the principle can be better used to promote and define organizational responsibility for privacy protection. The development of better privacy (and security) practices and more basic considerations of privacy within organizations in response to data breach legislation indicates an evolution in accountability, for instance accountability is the cornerstone of the risk-based approach to data protection enshrined in GDPR.

Accountability ensures that an organization is responsible for complying with privacy and data protection legislation and that compliance can be evidenced and demonstrated. Appropriate technical and organizational measures to meet the requirements of accountability need to be evidenced. There are several measures that can provide accountability, including:

- Adopting and implementing data protection policies; outlining how you meet data subject rights.
- Putting written contracts in place with organizations that process personal data on your behalf.
- Maintaining documentation of your processing activities (see section on ROPA).
- Recording and, where necessary, reporting personal data breaches.
- Ensuring that the data subject rights are supported and fully informed.
- Carrying out data protection impact assessments for uses of personal data that are likely to result in high risk to individuals' interests.
- Adhering to relevant codes of conduct and signing up to certification schemes.

(NOTE: A privacy management framework can help build accountability measures and create a culture of privacy across the organization. See Chapter 5 for a discussion of these frameworks.)

Policies

A data protection policy sets out how your organization deals with data. This includes all the safeguards put in place and how to help people who request access to their data on your systems. A data protection policy (now sometimes called a privacy policy) is a document, much like a home office policy or an equal opportunities policy, which outlines certain recommendations for and requirements of your employees. In this case, a data protection policy deals with how you monitor, manage, and standardize the use of data.

While organizations previously published "privacy policies" according to the UK Information Commissioner's Office (ICO), the terminology in GDPR suggests that privacy notice is the more effective term. In fact the ICO publish a template for a "Privacy Notice" for use by the public that looks like what is traditionally a privacy policy. Adding more confusion to this matter, the Irish Data Protection Commissioner's website call this "a data protection statement", where the ICO on the other hand calls it a "data protection notice". If this is not confusing enough – now add in different uses of these terms in the US versus the EU and things really heat up. For instance, Cloudian (a company based in the US) note that "a privacy policy is a document that explains to customers how the organization collects and processes their data. It is made available to the public by organizations required to comply with privacy regulations. A data protection policy is an internal document created for the purpose of establishing data protection policies within the organization. It is made available to company employees, as well as third parties, responsible for handling or processing sensitive data".

While these varying definitions can be argued as to right and wrong, for the purpose of allaying confusion during the course of this book – the term "privacy policy" will be used to describe where the principles and rights of data subjects, and how the organization handles data (the right to be informed) are published. These publications can be internal or external, that is, a privacy policy for employees or a privacy policy published on a website for customers. [In truth – they should not be that different – except that an internal policy may also include dos and don'ts handling policies, together with organizational hierarchy policies related to data processing signoffs and agreements.] The term "privacy notice" will be used to describe those information clips delivered before or at data collection point that further inform the data subject – such as moments online where you hover, for example, over a field and are informed in a small online box of the required information. We could argue ourselves that this is incorrect, but for the purpose of picking a middle ground of these many mixed definitions and "sticking to it", this is how we will progress. You should however use whatever term applies in your organization to describe these documents.

THERE IS NO SUCH THING AS A "SIMPLE" PRIVACY POLICY: TIPS FROM A LAWYER ON WRITING PRIVACY POLICIES

Mark Rasch

Of Counsel, Kohrman Jackson & Krantz LLP

Sometimes, the simplest things are the most challenging. Lawyers are often called upon to write website privacy policies for clients – which are almost always "cookie cutter" affairs which involve cutting and pasting from clauses used in previous privacy policies. But this approach is dangerous for both lawyers and clients alike, as it fails to consider the subtlety and nuance associated with each individual company – and each individual website – data collection and use practices. For example, when queried, most companies will reply that they do not collect ANY personally identifiable information on their website. However, invariably, they collect configuration and IP information, which they may later use to track unique users. They may or may not use persistent cookies, tracking cookies, or apps from sites like Facebook (Meta), Google, or Amazon to track individual identified users. Credit card payment data, shipping and delivery data, order data, and similar data are "personally identifiable" and the use, sharing, accuracy, and access to such data should be included in your website privacy policy. Even if you allow people to opt out of the use of data, the collection and use of the "opt out" list is itself personal information. So, the most important thing to do when drafting a privacy policy is to take a good hard look at ALL of the data you ARE collecting, all of the data you MAY later collect, and ALL of the data you may get from third parties and consider any current or possible future use of those data by your company, partners, affiliates, subsidiaries, and even any company which may acquire or team with you. This can make your privacy policies somewhat future proof. Finally, write in simple, easy to understand sentences without legalese. While privacy policies are rarely read and even more rarely understood, they should be presented in a form that is capable of being understood.

Privacy policies are often written, distributed, and communicated by way of a box ticking compliance exercise. However, privacy policies can in fact be leveraged to engender trust, to brand privacy as a value-addition, and to encourage cultural change. We suggest following the process outlined in Figure 6.1 to ensure that privacy policies don't gather dust but become

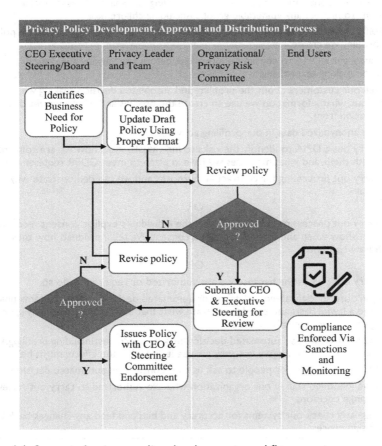

Figure 6.1 Suggested privacy policy development workflow.

embedded at all levels of the organization as a cultural expectation rather than a compliance check.

Before writing those policies, the checklist presented in Table 6.1, adapted from the UK ICO, is also very helpful to determine what needs to be in place to establish baseline compliance with GDPR:

Table 6.1 Checklist for baseline compliance to GDPR

- We have a lawful basis to carry out profiling and/or automated decision-making and document this in our data protection policy.
- We send individuals a link to privacy statement when collecting their personal data indirectly.
- We explain how people can access details of the information we used to create their profile.
- We tell people who provide us with their personal data how they can object to profiling.
- We have procedures for customers to access the personal data input into the profiles so they can review and edit for any accuracy issues.
- We have additional checks in place for our profiling/automated decision-making systems to protect any vulnerable groups (including children).
- We only collect the minimum amount of data needed and have clear retention policy for profiles we create.
- We carry out a DPIA to consider/address risk before starting any automated decision-making or profiling.
- We tell our customers about the profiling and automated decision-making we carry out, what information we use to create the profiles and where we get this information from.
- We use anonymized data in our profiling activities.
- We carry out a DPIA to identify the risks to individuals, show how we are going to deal with them, and what measures we have in place to meet GDPR requirements.
- We carry out processing for contractual purposes and we can demonstrate why it's necessary.

OR

- We carry out processing because we have the individual's explicit consent recorded. We can show when and how we obtained consent. We tell individuals how they can withdraw consent.

OR

- We carry out processing because we are authorized or required to do so.
- We don't use special category data in our automated decision-making systems unless we have a lawful basis and can demonstrate what that basis is. We delete any special category data accidentally created.
- We explain that we use automated decision-making processes, including profiling. We explain what information we use, why we use it and what the effects might be.
- We have a simple way for people to ask us to reconsider an automated decision.
- We have identified staff in our organization who are authorized to carry out reviews and change decisions.
- We regularly check our systems for accuracy and bias and feed any changes back into the design process.

TRANSPARENT, TRANSLUCENT, OPAQUE: YOUR PRIVACY DISCLOSURES NEED AN URGENT WINDOW CLEANING TREATMENT, AND NO STREAKS

Odia Kagan

Partner and Chair of GDPR Compliance and International Privacy, Fox Rothschild LLP

"Can you just send me a privacy notice template that I can use to be GDPR/CCPA compliant?" is a question that I often get asked by clients and one that you may have asked your attorneys too.

Here I explain why the answer is "no", why asking this question would lead you into trouble, and what to do next instead.

The answer is "no" because a privacy disclosure is only one aspect of compliance under any of the data protection laws and it can't "make" you compliant. It's also "no" because a notice only reflects what you do, it doesn't create a reality. Finally, the answer is "no" also because the privacy disclosure needs to be precise and accurately reflect your practices. It cannot be a generic, general document.

Using a generic vague template will lead you into trouble because: Your clients care. Recent surveys show that consumers are increasingly basing their decisions whether to do business with you on whether they trust how you handle their data, and they look to your privacy disclosure for this. It will land you in trouble because the regulators, on both sides of the Atlantic, are very vigilant about this issue. The recent Meta cases, decided by the Irish Data Protection Commission and the European Data Protection Board, show to the tune of nine-digit fines and a violation of the transparency principle of GDPR that disclosures should be clearly understood by individuals rather than lead them through a maze of documents just to stay confused. This principle is stated clearly also in the new US privacy laws. Finally, it will lead you into trouble because your competitors are watching you, as are NGOs and plaintiffs' attorneys, ready to file a class action lawsuit or a complaint with the regulators.

What to do now?

- Make sure you understand all the personal data you collect (both online and offline and both direct identifiers and things like cookie ID and device fingerprinting), where you get it, what do you use it for, who do you share it with, why you share it, and for how long do you need to keep it
- Get good privacy counsel who can draft the disclosure in a way that includes all the legal requirements, matches your company's voice, AND is understood by real human beings.
- Review it to make sure that it is accurate and do that every time you start a new processing operation as well as every year.

Contracts

The data protection contract (called a Data Processing Agreement in GDPR) should set out details of the processing and include:

- The duration of the processing;
- The nature and purpose of the processing;
- The type of personal data involved;
- The categories of data subject;
- The controller's obligations and rights.

The contract or other legal act should also include clauses that:

- The processor must only act on the controller's documented instructions, unless required by law to act without such instructions;
- The processor must ensure that people processing the data are subject to a duty of confidence;
- The processor must take appropriate measures to ensure the security of processing;
- The processor must only engage a sub-processor with the controller's prior authorization and under a written contract;
- The processor must take appropriate measures to help the controller respond to requests from individuals to exercise their rights;
- Considering the nature of processing and the information available, the processor must assist the controller in meeting its privacy and data protection obligations in relation to the processing, the notification of personal data breaches, and data protection impact assessments;
- The processor must delete or return all personal data to the controller (at the controller's choice) at the end of the contract and the processor must also delete existing personal data unless the law requires its storage; and
- The processor must submit to audits and inspections. The processor must also give the controller whatever information it needs to ensure they are both meeting their Article 28 obligations.

Records of processing activities (ROPAs)

Records of processing activities (ROPAs) allow you to make an inventory of the data processing that takes place in your organization (hence they are sometimes referred to as a data inventories) and to have an overview of what you are doing with that personal data. ROPAs are mandated under certain conditions by Article 30 of the GDPR, that is, entities with less than 250 employees are not obliged to keep such a record. However, they must keep records from the moment that:

- The data processing is non-occasional (e.g., salary management, customer management/prospect and supplier, etc.);

- The data processing is likely to involve a risk for people's rights and freedom (e.g., geolocation systems, video surveillance, etc.);
- The data processing concerns sensitive data (e.g., health data, breach, etc.).

ROPAs are fundamental building blocks of any privacy program and as such are vital to get right from the outset. While your organization may not be obligated to produce them, it is highly recommended here that you do as the ROPAs enable you to precisely identify, among others:

- The actors involved (controller, processors, representative, joint controller, etc.) in the data processing;
- The categories of data processed;
- The purpose of the processing (what you do with the collected personal data), who has access, and who are the recipients of the personal data;
- For how long the personal data will be retained;
- The technical and organizational security measures implemented.

A template for conducting a ROPA, adapted from the CNIL ROPA self-assessment tool, is presented in Figure 6.2a and Figure 6.2b.

What needs to be included in the record of processing?

CNIL recommends keeping two records:

1. One for the personal data processing that you are responsible by yourself.
2. Another one for the processing you perform as a processor.

Controllers Records of Processing Activities

The controller's record must make an inventory of all the processing implemented by your organization. For each processing activity, the ROPA must include at least the following details:

1. If necessary, the name and contact details of the processing supervisor;
2. The processing's aim and the reason why you have collected these data;
3. The category of personal data (e.g., identity, familial, economic and financial situation, banking data, connection data, localization data, etc.);
4. The category of recipient personal data is sent to or will be sent to, including the processor you resort to;

Example of a completed record of

This example is based on a fictitious processing and should not to be repeated as it is, but to be adapted according to your processing (cf. tab 3).

1-Example

Description of the processing operation

Name of the processing operation	Payroll management
N° / REF	1 - Example
Data of creation of the processing	May 26, 2018
Update of the processing	May 13, 2019

Stakeholders	Name	Address	ZIP Code	Town	Country	Phone number	Email address
Controller	Louise DUPONT	1 rue Rivoli	75001	Paris	France	01 xx xx xx xx	example1@ets.com
Data protection officer	Martin HENRI	1 rue Rivoli	75001	Paris	France	01 xx xx xx xx	example2@ets.com
DPO's Organisation (if external DPO)	N/A						

Purpose(s) of the data processing

Main purpose	Payroll management
Sub-purpose 1	Calculation of remuneration
Sub-purpose 2	Calculation of the amount of payments made to social security organisations
Sub-purpose 3	Transfer orders to the bank

Categories of personal data	Description	Data retention period
Marital status, ID, identification data, images...	Last names, names and addresses	5 years from the payment of the salary
Economic and financial information (income, financial situation, tax situation, etc.)	Bank account details	5 years from the payment of the salary
Social Security Number (or NIR)	Social security numbers of the employees	5 years from the payment of the salary

(a)

Figure 6.2 Template for ROPA.

(Source: CNIL)

Categories of data subjects	Description	Details
Catégorie de personnes 1	Employees	

Recipients	Type of recipient	Details
Recipient 1	Internal department that processes the concerned data	Administrative and Financial Department
Recipient 2	Institutional or commercial partners	Social organisations
Recipient 3	Recipients in third countries or international organisations	

Security measures	Type of security measure	Details
Security measure 1	Software protection measures	
Security measure 2	Data backup	
Security measure 3	User access control	

Transfers to third countries or international organisations	Recipient	Country	Type of guarantees	Links to the related documents
Recipient organisation 1	Bank of Andorra	Andorra	Standard contractual clauses (SCC)	Agreement dated January 23, 2011.

(b)

Figure 6.2 (Continued)

5. Personal data transfers to another country or to an international organization, and, in some specific cases, the guarantee provided for these transfers;
6. The period provided for the erasure of several data categories; in other words, the preservation length or the criterion allowing to determine this length;
7. Insofar as possible, a general account of technical and organization security measures you will implement.

The Processor Records of Processing Activities

The ROPA for the processor must make an inventory of all types of processing activities operated in place of your customers. For each type of activity conducted by your customers, it must include at least the following details:

1. The name and contact details of each customer, processor, for who you process data, and, if necessary, the name and contact details of their representative;
2. The name and contact details of the processor you have recourse to in this activity;
3. The types of processing operated in place of each of your customers, in other words, the operations performed for them (e.g., for the category "market research sending service", it can be mail address collect, secured messages sending, subscription cancellation management, etc.);
4. Personal data transfer to another country or to an international organization. In some very particular cases, mentioned in the 2nd paragraph of Article 49.1 (lack of balance decision in virtue of Article 45 of GDPR, lack of guarantees appropriated set in the Article 46 of GDPR, and non-practicability of the exceptions provided in the first paragraph of Article 49.1), and the guarantees foreseen to frame the transfers must be mentioned;
5. Insofar as possible, a general account of technical and practical security measures you will implement.

FRHISTS: PURPOSE SPECIFICATION/LIMITATION: THE IMPORTANCE OF CATALOGING ALL PROCESSING PURPOSES

Dr. Johnny Ryan
Senior Fellow, Irish Council for Civil Liberties

To protect data that your organization uses you must first know what the organization does with the data and why it does it. A person should be able to anticipate the reasons their data will be used. The organization must be able to account for what is done to the data for each reason.

The question is, how granular does this get? Processing purposes cannot be vague. European enforcers agreed guidelines in 2013 that each purpose must be "detailed enough to determine what kind of processing is and is not included within the specified purpose, and to allow that compliance with the law can be assessed and data protection safeguards applied".

In 2018, they produced guidance that gave the following examples of insufficiently clear processing purposes: "We may use your personal data to develop new services" and "We may use your personal data to offer personalized services". California now follows a similar model.

This means understanding what diverse parts of the organization do with data.

For example, if the organization's marketing team sends email campaigns, there may be more processing purposes involved than the mere sending of an email: Does the marketing email request a tracking pixel when the recipient's email client renders it? Does it contain text links that incorporate tracking parameters? Do the pages the recipient is taken to on clicking those links contain further tracking technologies? If so, the processing purposes include not only the sending of email, but also the counting of the number of times the email is opened, of whether the recipient clicks each link, and what they then do on the Web after they have clicked it.

Cataloging all processing purposes within the organization is the essential step at which all other data protection actions are built. When I was the data protection officer for a technology firm, this was the biggest challenge. Without tackling it, everything else becomes irrelevant.

But once the organization has itemized every processing purpose and can account for who does what, to which data, and for what reason, it now has supreme command of its data use.

The alternative is a data free-for-all.

Responding to a data subject exercising their rights

Article 8 of the EU Charter of Fundamental Rights states that data protection is a fundamental right notably; everyone has the right to the protection of personal data concerning him or her. Such data must be processed fairly for specified purposes and based on the consent of the person concerned, or some other legitimate basis laid down by law. Everyone has the right of access to data which has been collected concerning him or her, and the right to have it rectified. This means that every individual is entitled to have their personal information protected, used in a fair and legal way, and made available to them when they ask for a copy. These rights are enshrined in GDPR as data subjects' rights and are outlined in Figure 6.3.

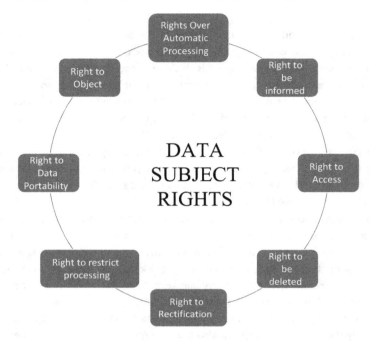

Figure 6.3 Data subject rights.

To process personal data, organizations must also have a lawful reason. The lawful reasons for processing personal data are set out in Article 6 of the GDPR. The six lawful reasons for processing personal data are presented in Figure 6.4. Any one of the six reasons given can provide a legal reason for processing personal data.Any one of the six reasons given can provide a legal reason for processing personal data.

Data Subject Access Request (DSAR)

An individual (or someone acting on their behalf) can exercise the right to access personal information:

- With a company of which he/she is a customer, for example, to obtain a copy of his/her customer file or of a telephone conversation with customer service which has been recorded.
- With their employer to access the data in their administrative file.
- From their doctor to obtain a copy of the data in their medical file.
- With an administration to obtain confirmation that data relating to it is being processed.

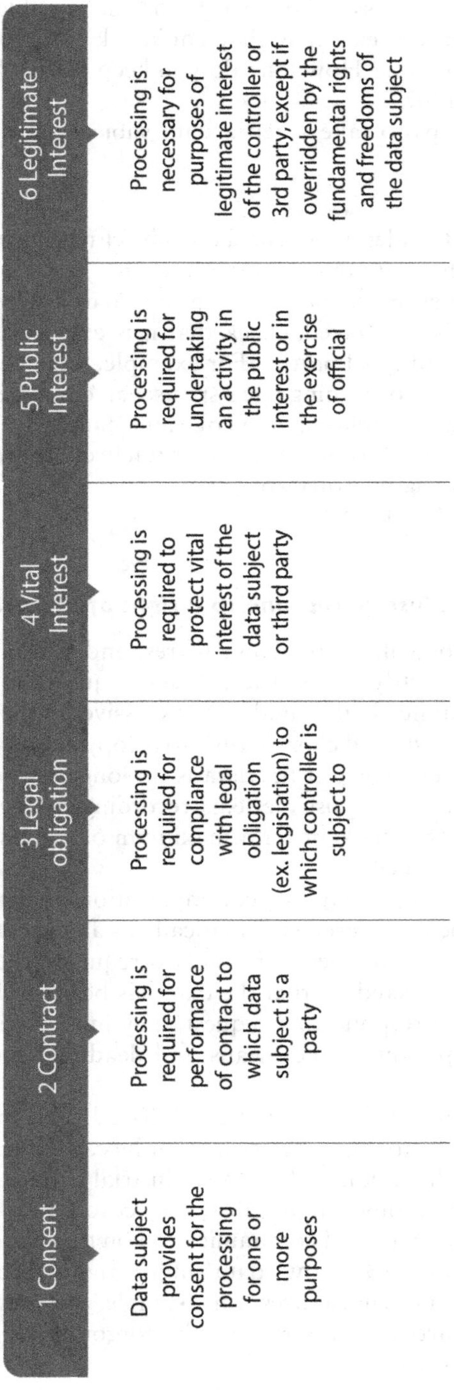

1 Consent	2 Contract	3 Legal obligation	4 Vital Interest	5 Public Interest	6 Legitimate Interest
Data subject provides consent for the processing for one or more purposes	Processing is required for performance of contract to which data subject is a party	Processing is required for compliance with legal obligation (ex. legislation) to which controller is subject to	Processing is required to protect vital interest of the data subject or third party	Processing is required for undertaking an activity in the public interest or in the exercise of official	Processing is necessary for purposes of legitimate interest of the controller or 3rd party, except if overridden by the fundamental rights and freedoms of the data subject

Figure 6.4 Legal bases for processing.

An individual may ask for access to information on the possible processing of data concerning them. For example, they could ask "Do you have any data concerning me? What for? How long do you keep them? Who do you transmit the information to?".

There are four key steps to take when a data subject access request is received:

1. If necessary, verify the identity of the data subject making the request.
2. If necessary, ask what data the request relates to.
3. Check that the request does not concern a third party. When a request for a right of access is received, check that it is exercised in compliance with the rights of third parties. For example, it is not possible to request access to data concerning one's spouse; an employee of a company cannot obtain data relating to a colleague. Similarly, the right of access may not infringe business secrecy or intellectual property such as copyright protecting the software.
4. Respond to demand on time.

Can a data controller refuse to respond to a right of access?

In some cases, a data controller can refuse to respond to right of access requests, but will have to justify this decision. Access requests do not require a response if they are manifestly unfounded or excessive by their repetitive nature (e.g., multiple requests and close in time to a copy already provided). Access requests can also be denied if the data is no longer stored/has been deleted. In this case, access is impossible (e.g., recordings made by a video surveillance device are normally kept for a maximum of 30 days. They are destroyed at the end of this period).

Note: The fact that a person requests communication of data which he already has should not be considered systematically as an excessive request. It is necessary to assess the time between the two requests, the possibility that new data has been collected, or that the data has been modified, etc. If a data controller does not respond to a request, they must justify the decision and inform the applicant of the means and deadlines for appealing against this decision.

The exercise of the right of access is not conditioned. This means that a person does not have to justify his request and that he can exercise his right of access in parallel with litigation (before the industrial tribunal, for example) or administrative proceedings in progress, subject to not to infringe the rights of third parties. The refusal of communication on this basis would not be valid. The GDPR (Article 23) allows data subject rights to be restricted by national law in certain circumstances, for example, the prevention and detection of crime. In particular, the right to be forgotten will not apply where processing is necessary for:

- Exercising the right of freedom of expression and information;
- Compliance with a legal obligation, the performance of a task carried out in the public interest, or in the exercise of official authority;
- Reasons of public interest in the area of public health (See Article 9(2) (h) and (i) and Article 9(3), GDPR);
- Archiving purposes in the public interest, scientific or historical research purposes, or statistical purposes;
- Establishment, exercise, or defense of legal claims.

Who can make this request?

The data subject themselves or the person wishing to access their personal data can give a mandate to a person of his choice to exercise his right of access. In this case, the chosen person must submit a letter specifying: the purpose of the mandate (exercise of the right of access), the identity of the principal (identity of the applicant who exercises his right of access to the data concerning him), and the identity of the agent (his identity). It must prove its identity and that of the applicant. For minors and adults unable to exercise their rights, it is, depending on the case, the parents, the holder(s) of parental authority, or the guardian who carries out the procedure.

What proof of identity should be asked for?

To exercise their rights, the individual must prove their identity. In principle, this justification can intervene "by any means". Thus, it is not necessary to attach a photocopy of an identity document in the event of the exercise of a right – if the identity of the person is sufficiently established (e.g., by providing information additional to those relating to identity, such as a customer or member number, etc.). Moreover, in a digital environment, exercising their rights from a space where the person has authenticated may be sufficient, depending on the digital identity data requested. However, if there is a "reasonable doubt" about the applicant's identity, they can be asked to attach any other document to prove their identity, such as, if necessary, a photocopy of an identity document. The level of checks to be carried out may vary depending on the nature of the request, the sensitivity of the information communicated, and the context in which the request is made. There are circumstances where organizations have implemented far more stringent validation procedures for DSARs than for financial transactions and online banking. Be reasonable if you are going to validate an individual and remember this is an opportunity to engender/enhance stakeholder trust.

What are the deadlines for responding to a request?

Under most legislations, it is around a 4–6 weeks for a simple request. The maximum is 3 months for a complex request (e.g., if a person requests a copy of all of their data). For instance, GDPR is a one-month timeframe and CCPA is a 45-day timeframe. In certain countries, for example, France, health data demands a lesser timeframe and is typically set to eight days. Whatever the situation, the person must be informed of the consequences within the maximum timeframe. In the case of GDPR, there is a possibility of extending the period by two months, "taking into account the complexity and the number of requests", provided that the data subject is informed within one month of the receipt of the request.

Is it possible to request reproduction fees?

In most cases, individuals cannot be required to pay a fee to make a subject access request. Only in certain very limited circumstances, per Article 12(5) GDPR, where the initial request is "manifestly unfounded or excessive" (which the controller must prove), can a controller charge a "reasonable fee" for the administrative costs of complying with the request. Controllers are also allowed to charge a reasonable fee, based on administrative costs, where an individual requests additional copies of their personal data undergoing processing.

How can data be communicated?

Requests can be made on site or in writing, postal, or electronic.

- If the request is made on the spot and you cannot respond immediately, you must give the requester a date and signed acknowledgment of receipt.
- If the request is made electronically, the information is provided in a commonly used electronic form, unless the data subject requests otherwise. In this case, pay attention to the methods of transmission of information which must be done in a secure manner.
- If the request is made in writing and you need clarification or additional information to respond to it, you must contact the applicant (postal or electronic mail).
- If you send personal data by post, it is advisable to do so by registered mail with acknowledgment of receipt.
- If the data is communicated by USB key, you can deliver the USB key personally to the person who contacted you or send it by post. You must take appropriate measures to protect the data contained on this medium if it concerns sensitive data. To prevent this data from being accessible to everyone, it is thus possible to encrypt it. The decryption code must then be communicated in another letter or by another means (SMS, email, etc.).

A checklist for preparing to deliver on Data Subject Rights is presented in Table 6.2, based on the guidelines from the Information Commissioners Office, the UK. While these are no doubt skewed in favor of GDPR

Table 6.2 Checklist for Delivering Data Subject Rights

Preparing and Complying for Requests for Deletion

- We know how to recognize a request for erasure, and we understand when the right applies.
- We have a policy for how to record requests we receive verbally.
- We understand when we can refuse a request and are aware of the information we need to provide to individuals when we do so.
- We have processes in place to ensure that we respond to a request for erasure without undue delay and within one month of receipt.
- We are aware of the circumstances when we can extend the time limit to respond to a request.
- We understand that there is a particular emphasis on the right to erasure if the request relates to data collected from children.
- We have procedures in place to inform any recipients if we erase any data, we have shared with them.
- We have appropriate methods in place to erase information.

Preparing and Complying for Requests for Restriction

- We know how to recognize a request for restriction, and we understand when the right applies.
- We have a policy in place for how to record requests we receive verbally.
- We understand when we can refuse a request and are aware of the information we need to provide to individuals when we do so.
- We have processes in place to ensure that we respond to a request for restriction without undue delay and within one month of receipt.
- We are aware of the circumstances when we can extend the time limit to respond to a request.
- We have appropriate methods in place to restrict the processing of personal data on our systems.
- We have appropriate methods in place to indicate on our systems that further processing has been restricted.
- We understand the circumstances when we can process personal data that has been restricted.
- We have procedures in place to inform any recipients if we restrict any data, we have shared with them.
- We understand that we need to tell individuals before we lift a restriction on processing.

Preparing and Complying for Requests for Data Portability

- We know how to recognize a request for data portability, and we understand when the right applies.
- We have a policy for how to record requests we receive verbally.
- We understand when we can refuse a request and are aware of the information we need to provide to individuals when we do so.
- We can transmit personal data in structured, commonly used and machine-readable formats.
- We use secure methods to transmit personal data.

(Continued)

Table 6.2   (Continued)

- We have processes in place to ensure that we respond to a request for data portability without undue delay and within one month of receipt.
- We are aware of the circumstances when we can extend the time limit to respond to a request.

Preparing and Complying to Objections to Processing

- We know how to recognize an objection and we understand when the right applies.
- We have a policy in place for how to record objections we receive verbally.
- We understand when we can refuse an objection and are aware of the information we need to provide to individuals when we do so.
- We have clear information in our privacy notice about individuals' right to object, which is presented separately from other information on their rights.
- We understand when we need to inform individuals of their right to object in addition to including it in our privacy notice.
- We have processes in place to ensure that we respond to an objection without undue delay and within one month of receipt.
- We are aware of the circumstances when we can extend the time limit to respond to an objection.
- We have appropriate methods in place to erase, suppress or otherwise cease processing personal data.

Preparing and Complying with Requests for Rectification

- We know how to recognize a request for rectification, and we understand when this right applies.
- We have a policy for how to record requests we receive verbally.
- We understand when we can refuse a request and are aware of the information we need to provide to individuals when we do so.
- We have processes in place to ensure that we respond to a request for rectification without undue delay and within one month of receipt.
- We are aware of the circumstances when we can extend the time limit to respond to a request.
- We have appropriate systems to rectify or complete information or provide a supplementary statement.
- We have procedures in place to inform any recipients if we rectify any data, we have shared with them.

Preparing and Complying with Subject Access Requests

- We know how to recognize a subject access request and we understand when the right of access applies.
- We have a policy for how to record requests we receive verbally.
- We understand what steps we need to take to verify the identity of the requester, if necessary.
- We understand when we can pause the time limit for responding if we need to ask for clarification.
- We understand when we can refuse a request and are aware of the information we need to provide to individuals when we do so.
- We understand the nature of the supplementary information we need to provide in response to a subject access request.

(Continued)

Table 6.2 (Continued)

- We have suitable information management systems in place to allow us to locate and retrieve information efficiently.
- We have processes in place to ensure that we respond to a subject access request without undue delay and within one month of receipt.
- We understand how to perform a reasonable search for the information.
- We understand what we need to consider if a third party makes a request on behalf of an individual.
- We are aware of the circumstances in which we can extend the time limit to respond to a request.
- We understand how to assess whether a child is mature enough to understand their rights.
- We understand that there is a particular emphasis on using clear and plain language if we are disclosing information to a child.
- We understand what we need to consider if a request includes information about others.
- We are able to deliver the information securely to an individual, and in the correct format.

How to Deliver on the Right to be Informed

We provide individuals with all the following privacy information:

- The name and contact details of our organization.
- The name and contact details of our representative (if applicable).
- The contact details of our data protection officer (if applicable).
- The purposes of the processing.
- The lawful basis for the processing.
- The legitimate interests for the processing (if applicable).
- The categories of personal data obtained (if the personal data is not obtained from the individual it relates to).
- The recipients or categories of recipients of the personal data.
- The details of transfers of the personal data to any third countries or international organizations (if applicable).
- The retention periods for the personal data.
- The rights available to individuals in respect of the processing.
- The right to withdraw consent (if applicable).
- The right to lodge a complaint with a supervisory authority.
- The source of the personal data (if the personal data is not obtained from the individual it relates to).
- The details of whether individuals are under a statutory or contractual obligation to provide the personal data (if applicable, and if the personal data is collected from the individual it relates to).
- The details of the existence of automated decision-making, including profiling (if applicable).

Source: UK ICO.

implementations, they do provide a comprehensive overview of how to respond generally to DSARs regardless of jurisdiction.

Personal data breaches

A personal data breach can be broadly defined as a security incident that has affected the confidentiality, integrity, or availability of personal data. In short, there will be a personal data breach whenever any personal data is accidentally lost, destroyed, corrupted, or disclosed; if someone accesses the data or passes it on without proper authorization; or if the data is made unavailable, and this unavailability has a significant negative effect on individuals. However, the definition of a personal data breach is broadening in line with breaches of unavailability such as those enabled by attacks such as ransomware attacks or just systems/hardware failures.

Personal data breaches can include:

- Access by an unauthorized third party;
- Deliberate or accidental action (or inaction) by a controller or processor;
- Sending personal data to an incorrect recipient;
- Computing devices containing personal data being lost or stolen;
- Alteration of personal data without permission; and
- Loss of availability of personal data.

A breach can have a range of adverse effects on individuals, which include emotional distress, physical, and material damage. Some personal data breaches will not lead to risks beyond possible inconvenience to those who need the data to do their job. Other breaches can significantly affect individuals whose personal data has been compromised. These need to be assessed on a case-by-case basis, looking at all relevant factors. For example, the theft of a customer database, whose data may be used to commit identity fraud, would need to be notified, given its likely impact on those individuals who could suffer financial loss or other consequences. But you would not normally need to notify the supervisory authority, for example, about the loss or inappropriate alteration of a staff telephone list.

DISSECTING A PERSONAL DATA BREACH NOTIFICATION. UNDERSTANDING FROM A REGULATOR'S PERSPECTIVE

Sayid Madar

Head of Operations, Office of the Data Protection Commissioner, UAE, Abu Dhabi's International Financial Centre, ADGM

A personal data breach is inevitable. It happens. You should be concerned if your organization claims it has never had a personal data breach. When the incident meets the threshold for notifying a regulator, there are certain things which you should know. I spent several years as a Lead Enforcement Officer at the UK ICO where my sole responsibility was to investigate breaches and where necessary, take enforcement action. There are hundreds of notifications a week to regulators. At any one time, I had approximately 25+ cases in my queue. Therefore, notifications are normally triaged before it reaches the Enforcement Dept. This allows us to focus on cases which were more likely to result in formal action. This triage is a key factor in whether a case will likely be closed with advice or be subject to further investigation.

So, what should you know?

(1) **Be transparent.** There is no scenario that a regulator hasn't seen before. If your notification is not clear or transparent, it indicates to the case officer that something is withheld. You'll likely be triaged for further investigation. While it may be embarrassing, awkward, or bizarre, trust me, we've seen worse. One case I still remember was the destruction of physical healthcare files. The files were destroyed by effluent.

(2) **Get straight to the point.** Time is important. Don't tell a story. There is a time and place for that! You'll likely be triaged for further investigation if you are not direct.

(3) **Be reasonable and pragmatic regarding the potential risk to individuals.** Nothing rubs a regulator the wrong way more than a Controller heavily downplaying potential risks to individuals. Ask yourself, if this was a loved one's personal data, how would they feel about it? Distress and nonmaterial damage should also be considered.

(4) **Avoid legalese** – don't cite the law. You'd be surprised how many times I've had lawyers attempting to define "personal data" or what relevant sections mean in practice to the regulator. It is of course wise to seek external legal advice but you're responsible for their output.

When do we need to tell individuals about a breach?

If a breach is likely to result in a high risk to the rights and freedoms of individuals, the organization must inform those concerned directly and without undue delay. In other words, this should take place as soon as possible. A "high risk" means the requirement to inform individuals is higher than for notifying the supervisory authority. Again, you will need to assess both the severity of the potential or actual impact on individuals because of a breach and the likelihood of this occurring. If the impact of the breach is more severe, the risk is higher; if the likelihood of the consequences is greater, then again, the risk is higher. In such cases, you will need to promptly inform those affected, particularly if there is a need to mitigate an immediate risk of damage to them. One of the main reasons for informing individuals is to help them take steps to protect themselves from the effect of a breach.

Assessing the severity of a breach is really very difficult. Getting it right can mean the difference between having to notify the supervisory authority or having to notify the data subject. To help calculate the severity, ENISA proposed a methodology to quantify the severity of a breach (link in the suggested reading section). This is a tool that we have used all the time. We are always surprised by the number of people who don't know about it or use it. ENISA produced the following formula to calculate the severity level:

$$SE = DPC \times EI + CB$$

Where SE is the overall severity, DPC is data processing context, EI is ease of identification, and CB is circumstances of the breach. ENISA also produced an associated table containing values that can be used to qualify the quantitative results and these are outlined in Table 6.3.

The final score shows the level of severity of a certain breach, considering the impact to the individuals. If you decide not to notify individuals, you will still need to notify the supervisory authority unless you can demonstrate that the breach is unlikely to result in a risk to an individual's data rights and freedoms.

Table 6.3 Quantitative metrics for severity of data breach

SE < 2	Low	Individuals either will not be affected or may encounter a few inconveniences, which they will overcome without any problem (time spent re-entering information, annoyances, irritations, etc.).
2 ≤ SE < 3	Medium	Individuals may encounter significant inconveniences, which they will be able to overcome despite a few difficulties (extra costs, denial of access to business services, fear, lack of understanding, stress, minor physical ailments, etc.).
3 ≤ SE< 4	High	Individuals may encounter significant consequences, which they should be able to overcome albeit with serious difficulties (misappropriation of funds, blacklisting by banks, property damage, loss of employment, subpoena, worsening of health, etc.).
4 ≤ SE	Very High	Individuals may encounter significant, or even irreversible, consequences, which they may not overcome (financial distress such as substantial debt or inability to work, long-term psychological or physical ailments, death, etc.).

Source: ENISA.

RESPONDING TO LAWSUITS OR REGULATORY AGENCIES MONTHS OR YEARS AFTER A BREACH

Linda Fletcher

Administrative Director, Privacy, Franciscan Alliance, Inc

Lawsuits and requests for additional information about a breach can come months or years after the fact. With key personnel turnover and significant time elapses, it is important to have effective methods to respond accurately and in a timely manner. Lawsuits generally take time to come to the attention of the organization and in some cases even the regulatory agencies are behind with contacting organizations for additional details they need to complete their review of an incident. The turnover of personnel directly involved in the incident leaving with their detailed knowledge of the incident poses additional challenges. Not having detailed documentation became very critical to our success when preparing for litigation or responding to regulatory agencies. It seems very simple and logical but remembering to take the time each day to document can be a challenge. Detailed documentation that will position you for success includes the following:

- Breach notification, supplemental notification, dates when key players became involved.
- Notes of those interviewed who had facts about the incident.
- Decisions made by your leadership or legal team after being presented with the facts.
- How breach analysis was performed (decisions about what is a reportable breach vs. low probability of harm factoring).
- A single timeline document with chronological notes of daily activities and key milestones.
- Artifacts such as what data about an individual was involved, a master list of impacted individuals, incident call center call logs including complaints that were escalated, breach letter versions, which individuals received which version of the notification letter, total number of impacted individuals by category of data disclosed, number of individuals by state of residence, copies supplemental notices to the media, copies of supplemental notifications, reports submitted to regulatory agencies, etc.

After experiencing the scramble to get answers in a timely manner, I developed a methodology that would allow the organization to be ready to respond, regardless of whether the personnel involved were still working for the organization. With turnover of personnel, it was imperative to create a central repository for each incident, where everyone involved could store their individual notes, email messages, and artifacts discussed above. When an incident begins, thinking forward and anticipating the information that you will need is key. This forward thinking at the beginning will ensure you are prepared to respond quickly without missing a beat.

Data protection impact assessment (DPIA)

Central to the accountability principle and the risk-based approach enshrined in GDPR, the DPIA is a key and central process in demonstrating accountability and risk oversight. DPIAs can help organizations develop a "culture of privacy", build trust, and assist with legal compliance, among other benefits. They promote cohesion between privacy and security communities within the organization. They can also minimize costs in the longer term since fixing privacy problems after the fact can be very costly for organizations. The DPIA underpins the risk assessment process in many privacy and data protection regulations. While DPIAs are similar to a privacy impact assessment, they can often be misreferred to as a data privacy impact assessment. For this reason, we explain the two and their differences.

A DPIA is an (ongoing) process designed to describe the processing, assess its necessity and proportionality, and help manage the risks to the rights and freedoms of natural persons resulting from the processing of personal data by assessing them and determining the measures to address them. The DPIA report is supposed to show the characteristics of the treatment, the risks and the measures adopted. DPIAs can be used to identify and mitigate data protection–related risks (arising from a project, process, or system) which may affect an organization or the individuals it engages with. DPIAs are important tools for demonstrating compliance with the GDPR and as such DPIAs should be undertaken following a structured and consistent approach.

Privacy impact assessments (PIAs) evolved in the 1990s as a means of systematically assessing risk to anticipate and mitigate privacy problems. A PIA is a process that analyzes the activities of a business/project/system and determines how those activities might pose a risk to the privacy of individuals or to the legal obligations of the organization. It considers the personal data collected and processed and evaluates whether the activities under examination will present a risk to that personal data. Therefore, the primary goal of a PIA is to minimize and eliminate risks to personal data.

Key differences between PIA and DPIA

Many privacy experts claim that a PIA and a DPIA are different terminology to describe the same thing. While the key commonality between these two terms is that they are assessing privacy risk, we would like to highlight that there are three key differences between a PIA and a DPIA. First, and most importantly – the DPIA is not only focused on the risks to the protection of personal data but also the risks to a data subject's rights. Second, DPIAs are mandated under certain conditions outlined in GDPR, regardless of whether an organization is governmental or private sector, where PIAs are advised under other legislation. For example, the US E-Government Act of 2002 mandates PIAs for all federal IT systems that "collects, maintains, or disseminates personally identifiable information (PII), or for any new aggregation of information that is collected, maintained, or disseminated using information technology". Alberta's Health Information Act requires that a PIA be carried out under certain circumstances. Similarly, the European Commission recommendation on Radio Frequency Identification (RFID) requires operators to conduct an assessment of the implications of an RFID application implementation for the protection of personal data and privacy, including whether the application could be used to monitor an individual. Third, the DPIA is an ongoing process rather than a point in time assessment. However, the authors recognize that the terms DPIA and PIA are often used interchangeably. In fact, CNIL – France's Data Protection Supervisory Authority – produced a DPIA tool called a PIA tool. For the purpose of this book, this chapter will use the term DPIA to describe both interchangeably.

The DPIA requirements mandated by GDPR are quite comprehensive and this has resulted in a growing need for competency in understanding and undertaking effective DPIAs. However, on a weekly basis, we encounter badly designed DPIAs, inconsistent risk evaluation, and a complete lack of understanding of "high risk". This chapter aims to address this gap.

Before we outline the requirements for and how to conduct a DPIA, we would like to first take a step back and highlight seven principles for managing privacy risks, as outlined in Figure 6.5. You can do the best DPIA in the world; however, without these high-level principles being in place/addressed before conducting a DPIA, it is unlikely your DPIA will be effective. For example, your DPIA may address the privacy risks to data subjects and your organizational obligations. However, if privacy awareness training is not being conducted on a regular basis, new employees are likely not to understand or be aware of 1) the privacy controls in place and 2) the DOs and DO Nots embedded into the privacy culture. The DPIA will also expect that the organization has already quantified the impact of privacy threats, so that these metrics can be used in the privacy risk assessment stage of the DPIA. We highly recommend that the privacy leader ensures that each of these principles are addressed well in advance of any DPIAs.

Creating a DPIA

The DPIA is an iterative cycle of four sequential stages as presented in Figure 6.6.

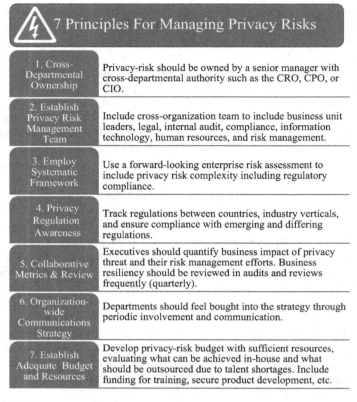

7 Principles For Managing Privacy Risks

1. Cross-Departmental Ownership	Privacy-risk should be owned by a senior manager with cross-departmental authority such as the CRO, CPO, or CIO.
2. Establish Privacy Risk Management Team	Include cross-organization team to include business unit leaders, legal, internal audit, compliance, information technology, human resources, and risk management.
3. Employ Systematic Framework	Use a forward-looking enterprise risk assessment to include privacy risk complexity including regulatory compliance.
4. Privacy Regulation Awareness	Track regulations between countries, industry verticals, and ensure compliance with emerging and differing regulations.
5. Collaborative Metrics & Review	Executives should quantify business impact of privacy threat and their risk management efforts. Business resiliency should be reviewed in audits and reviews frequently (quarterly).
6. Organization-wide Communications Strategy	Departments should feel bought into the strategy through periodic involvement and communication.
7. Establish Adequate Budget and Resources	Develop privacy-risk budget with sufficient resources, evaluating what can be achieved in-house and what should be outsourced due to talent shortages. Include funding for training, secure product development, etc.

Figure 6.5 Seven principles for managing privacy risks.

Threshold Assessment

• Is a DPIA really required? If Yes, move to the next phase.

Discovery Phase

• Controller: Establish details of the project
• Processor: Investigate any 3rd party involved in the project

Assessment Phase

• Lawful Processing: Decision on legal basis, proportionality and necessity
• Risk & Mitigation: Perform a risk assessment

Implementation Phase

• Signoff & Implementation: Implement mitigation actions or risk acceptance

Figure 6.6 DPIA phases.

There is no strict form a DPIA must take; instead, what is appropriate will depend (among other things) upon the nature and complexity of the processing, the potential risks posed by the processing, the resources of the employer, and any further guidelines that may be put in place (e.g., any guidelines related to a specific industry sector). We present the four phase processes below.

Phase I Threshold assessment: When to undertake a DPIA?

Understanding when to undertake and, more importantly, when not to undertake a DPIA is very important for anyone providing data protection advice to clients, anyone fulfilling the Data Protection Officer role (as mandated in certain circumstances by the GDPR), or anyone working in Information Risk or Compliance.

To demonstrate compliance with the GDPR, appropriate measures need to be implemented that provide assurance that "the risks of varying likelihood and severity for the rights and freedoms of natural persons" are addressed. DPIAs are not mandatory where the processing is unlikely to result in a high risk to the rights and freedoms of natural persons or when the nature, scope, context, and purposes of the processing are similar to the processing for which DPIAs have already been carried out or where a processing operation has a legal basis which states that an initial DPIA does not have to be carried out. Several European supervisory authorities have established whitelists which present scenarios where a DPIA may not be required. Many of these scenarios are subject to further caveats set out by the specific recommendation. For instance, the Belgium supervisory authority has published the following processing operations not subject to DPIA:

- Processing operations carried out by private organizations which are necessary for compliance with a legal obligation to which the organization is subject, provided that the law sets out the purposes of the processing, the categories of personal data to be processed, and provides safeguards to prevent abuse or unlawful access or transfer.
- Processing for the purposes of the administration of salaries of people who work for or on behalf of the controller.
- Processing exclusively for the purposes of administration of personnel who work for or on behalf of the controller, where that administration is required by law or regulation, but only to the extent that the processing does not involve health data, special categories of personal data, data concerning criminal convictions or infractions, or data to be used to evaluate data subjects.
- Processing exclusively for the purposes of the controller's accountancy practices. The processing must be limited to the data subjects and the data categories which are necessary for the controller's accountancy practice.

- Processing in relation to the administration of shareholders and associates. The processing must be limited to the data subjects and the data categories which are necessary for that administration.
- Processing undertaken by a foundation, association, or any other nonprofit organization carrying out its day-to-day activities, but only where the data was not obtained from third-party databases and where the processing concerns:
  - Personal data about its own members;
  - People with whom the controller regularly interacts and the beneficiaries of the organization.
- Processing in relation to the registration of visitors for the purposes of a sign-in or check in procedure, although data must be limited to certain information such as the name and professional address of the visitor and information identifying their vehicle.
- Processing by educational institutions for the management of their relationship with their own pupils or students (past, present, or potential) in the context of their educational duties.
- Processing exclusively in relation to the management of an organization's clients or suppliers (past or present), as long as the processing does not involve data such as "special category personal data" or data concerning criminal convictions or infractions.

Even if there is no specific indication of likely high risk, it is good practice to do a DPIA for any major new project involving the use of personal data. Non-compliance with DPIA requirements can lead to fines imposed by the competent supervisory authority.

The obligation for controllers to conduct a DPIA in certain circumstances should be understood against the background of their general obligation to appropriately manage risks presented by the processing of personal data. Article 35 refers to a likely high risk "to the rights and freedoms of individuals". The reference to "the rights and freedoms" of data subjects primarily concerns the rights to data protection and privacy but may also involve other fundamental rights such as freedom of speech, freedom of thought, freedom of movement, prohibition of discrimination, right to liberty, conscience, and religion. In line with the risk-based approach embodied by the GDPR, carrying out a DPIA is not mandatory for every processing operation. Instead, a DPIA is only required where a type of processing is "likely to result in a high risk to the rights and freedoms of natural persons". The mere fact that the conditions triggering the obligation to carry out DPIA have not been met does not, however, diminish controllers' general obligation to implement measures to appropriately manage risks for the rights and freedoms of data subjects. In practice, this means that controllers must continuously assess the risks created by their processing activities to identify when a type of processing is "likely to result in a high risk to the rights and freedoms of natural persons".

To provide a more concrete set of processing operations that require a DPIA due to their inherent high risk, the following criteria should be considered.

1. Evaluation or scoring, including profiling and predicting, especially from "aspects concerning the data subject's performance at work, economic situation, health, personal preferences or interests, reliability or behavior, location or movements". Examples of this could include a financial institution that screens its customers against a credit reference database or against an anti-money laundering, counter-terrorist financing (AML/CTF), or fraud database; a biotechnology company offering genetic tests directly to consumers to assess and predict the disease/health risks; a company building behavioral, marketing profiles based on usage or navigation on its website.

2. Automated decision making with legal or similar significant effect: Processing that aims at taking decisions on data subjects producing "legal effects concerning the natural person" or which "similarly significantly affects the natural person". For example, the processing may lead to the exclusion or discrimination against individuals, such as the use of AI algorithms, inherently biased, in border control systems.

3. Systematic monitoring: Processing used to observe, monitor, or control data subjects, including data collected through networks or "a systematic monitoring of a publicly accessible area". This type of monitoring is a criterion because the personal data may be collected in circumstances where data subjects may not be aware of who is collecting their data and how the data will be used. Additionally, it may be impossible for individuals to avoid being subject to such processing in public (or publicly accessible) space(s). Systematic and extensive profiling "Any systematic and extensive evaluation of personal aspects relating to natural persons which is based on automated processing, including profiling, and on which decisions are based that produce legal effects concerning the natural person or similarly significantly affect the natural person". The Irish Data Protection Commission guidelines state that "systematic" means that the processing 1) occurs according to a system; 2) is pre-arranged, organized, or methodical; 3) takes place as part of a general plan for data collection; or 4) is carried out as part of a strategy. For example, a large retail website who uses algorithms to monitor the searches and purchases of its users and, based on this information, offers recommendations to them. As this takes place continuously and according to predefined criteria, it can be considered as regular and systematic monitoring of data subjects on a large scale.

4. Sensitive data or data of a highly personal nature: This includes special categories of personal data (e.g., information about individuals' political opinions), as well as personal data relating to criminal convictions

or offenses. An example would be a general hospital keeping patients' medical records or a private investigator keeping offenders' details. Beyond these provisions of the GDPR, some categories of data can be considered as increasing the possible risk to the rights and freedoms of a strategy. In a "publicly accessible area" (i.e., any place open to any member of the public, for example, a piazza, a shopping center, a street, a market place, a train station, or a public library), additional care must be given to the protection of personal data. Whether the data has already been made publicly available by the data subject or by third parties may also be relevant. The fact that personal data is publicly available may be considered as a factor in the assessment if the data was expected to be further used for certain purposes, such as determining an individual's political orientation. This criterion may also include data such as personal documents, emails, diaries, notes from e-readers equipped with note-taking features, and very personal information contained in life-logging applications.

5. Data processed on a large scale: The GDPR does not define what constitutes large scale. However, according to the European Data Protection Board ("EDPB"), the following factors should be considered:
   • The number of data subjects concerned – either as a specific number or as a proportion of the relevant population.
   • The volume of data and/or the range of different data items being processed.
   • The duration of the data processing activity.
   • The geographical extent of the processing activity.

   The EDPB also suggest the following as examples of large-scale processing:
   • Processing of travel data of individuals using a city's public transport system (e.g., tracking via travel cards);
   • Processing of real-time geolocation data of customers of an international organization for statistical purposes by a processor specialized in these activities.
   • Processing of customer data in the regular course of business by an insurance company or a bank.
   • Processing of personal data for behavioral advertising by a search engine.
   • Processing of data (content, traffic, location) by telephone or internet service providers.

6. Matching or combining datasets, for example, originating from two or more data processing operations performed for different purposes and/or by different data controllers in a way that would exceed the reasonable expectations of the data subject.

7. Data concerning vulnerable data subjects: The processing of this type of data is a criterion because of the increased power imbalance between the data subjects and the data controller, meaning the individuals may

be unable to easily consent to, or oppose, the processing of their data, or exercise their rights. Vulnerable data subjects may include children (they can be considered as not able to knowingly and thoughtfully oppose or consent to the processing of their data), employees, more vulnerable segments of the population requiring special protection (asylum seekers applying for social welfare, or the elderly applying for pensions, patients applying for mental health services, etc.).

8. Innovative use or applying new technological or organizational solutions, like combining use of fingerprint and facial recognition for improved physical access control, etc. The GDPR makes it clear that the use of a new technology, defined in "accordance with the achieved state of technological knowledge", can trigger the need to carry out a DPIA. This is because the use of such technology can involve novel forms of data collection and usage, possibly with a high risk to individuals' rights and freedoms. Indeed, the personal and social consequences of the deployment of a new technology may be unknown. A DPIA will help the data controller to understand and to treat such risks. For example, certain "Internet of Things" applications could have a significant impact on individuals' daily lives and privacy; and therefore, require a DPIA. This is because through the passive nature of many IoT devices, it can be difficult for individuals to be informed that their personal information is being collected/processed. Devices in public spaces can collect information automatically, sometimes relying on individuals to opt out if they do not want their information collected. Users may not be aware that their information is being collected, let alone that they can opt out of that collection. IoT devices frequently do not have interfaces such as screens or input mechanisms such as keyboards, making it difficult for IoT devices to provide clarifying information like privacy policies. The DPIA will address things like – how will the application using IoT devices inform the data subject of the data collection and purpose? How will privacy policies be communicated? How will data subject rights be supported?

9. When the processing in itself "prevents data subjects from exercising a right or using a service or a contract". This includes processing operations that aims at allowing, modifying, or refusing data subjects' access to a service or entry into a contract. An example of this is where a bank screens its customers against a credit reference database to decide whether to offer them a loan. In most cases, a data controller can consider that a processing meeting two criteria would require a DPIA to be carried out.

10. One can also add to the list "is there a transfer of personal data taking place outside the EU" (particularly in the context of the Schrems II decision). In this case, a Transfer Impact Assessment (TIA) should be undertaken as part of the DPIA. A TIA is a type of risk assessment that enables organizations to determine if the Standard Contractual

Clauses (SCCs) (or other transfer mechanisms under Article 46 of the GDPR, that they intend using for transferring personal data outside the EU) provide an adequate level of protection in the specific circumstances of that transfer. The TIA must evaluate whether the laws and practices in the country outside the EU (i.e., third country) where the personal data is being transferred to or accessed from, provides "essentially equivalent" protection and does not impinge on the effectiveness of the SCCs or other mechanism under Article 46 of the GDPR used to facilitate the data transfer. If the outcome of the TIA is that the laws and practices in the third country impinge on the effectiveness of the GDPR Article 46 mechanism, the organization must identify and adopt supplementary measures to bring the level of protection for the transferred personal data up to the EU level of protection.

In general, the more criteria are met by the processing, the more likely it is to present a high risk to the rights and freedoms of data subjects, and therefore to require a DPIA, regardless of the measures which the controller envisages to adopt. However, in some cases, a data controller can consider that a processing meeting only one of these criteria requires a DPIA. Why? Since the adoption of GDPR in 2018, many countries have amended local and national legislations to reflect GDPR, and in some cases, these revisions make DPIAs mandatory in other circumstances not covered by GDPR – regardless of the assessment of risk to the data subject. For example, The Irish Data Protection Act 2018 (Section 36(2) (Health Research) Regulations 2018 (S.I. No. 314/2018)) mandates that certain clinical research institutions, hospitals, research units, and academic research centers need to undertake a DPIA for every research project processing personal data regardless of the "high risk" criteria.

Generally, there is no unified "large scale" definition by GDPR or other general data protection laws. However, such definitions are provided by the supervisory authorities of each country. Paul Breitbart provides a wonderful summary of these (a summary of some of these is outlined below), noting that if you match at least one of these you are processing data on a "large scale":

Estonia: In case of processing of special categories of personal data and/or data related to criminal convictions and offenses, the threshold lies at 5,000 persons. This threshold doubles to 10,000 persons in case data is processed related to financial and payment services; digital trust services like e-signatures; communication data; real-time geolocation data; and data related to profiling with legal effect. These data are considered by the Estonian Data Protection Authority to have an elevated risk. Finally, for all other data, the large-scale threshold is set to 50,000 persons, meaning that any database covering over 50,000 people will trigger the DPIA requirement.

The Netherlands: Data processing by hospitals, pharmacies, general practice centers, and care groups are always considered to be large scale. For smaller general practices or pharmacists working solo and specialist medical care centers, data processing is large scale if more than 10,000 patients are registered with the practice or more than 10,000 patients are treated on a general basis and all patient files are maintained in a single filing system.

Czechia: Above 10,000 data subjects is considered large-scale processing. However, processing by more than 20 processing branches or by more than 20 employees is considered to be large scale. Organizations will need to consider if data processing is at the regional level or at the (inter)national level, with the latter being more likely to be large scale.

Germany: Any data processing operations covering more than 5 million people or those covering at least 40% of the relevant population. The latter threshold is thus dependent on the type of data that is being processed as well as the data subjects involved in the processing operation.

Poland: No number provided but examples are of data processing operations that should be considered to be large scale are suggested, including the processing of medical records; employee documentation; systems in which a processor processes data from multiple data controllers; and databases collecting a wide range of data about web pages browsed, completed purchases, and/or TV or radio programs watched/listened to.

The United Kingdom: No number provided but the guidance is that large scale includes the duration, or permanence, of the data processing activity, the number or proportion of data subjects involved, the volume of data, and/or the range of different data items being processed as well as the geographical extent of the processing activity. Examples provided include data processing by a hospital, tracking individuals using a city's public transport system, as well as the processing of customer data by banks, insurance companies, and phone and internet service providers.

The following template (based on guidelines from the EDPS) outlined in Table 6.4 can be used to conduct a threshold assessment.

Phase 2 Discovery and definitions

In conducting a DPIA, organizations should ask themselves the following questions:

- What does the processing activity involve and what is its purpose?
- Is it necessary and proportionate given the risks involved?
- Does the planned processing help to achieve your purpose?
- Is there any other reasonable way to achieve the same result?

Table 6.4 DPIA threshold assessment

Mandatory grounds to conduct a DPIA – SECTION A	Yes	No
1. Will the project/system/application use systematic/extensive profiling to make significant decisions about people?		
2. Will the project/system/application process special category/criminal offence data on a large scale?		
3. Will the project/system/application systematically monitor publicly accessible places on a large scale (e.g., CCTV)?		
4. Will the project/system/application use new technologies e.g., biometrics, genetics, facial recognition or a major new piece of software?		
5. Will the project/system/application use profiling of special category (sensitive) data or criminal offence data to decide on access to services, opportunity or benefit?		
6. Will the project/system/application combine/compare/match data from multiple sources?		
7. Will the project/system/application process personal data without providing a privacy notice to the individual e.g., scraping/mining personal data for research.		
8. Will the project/system/application process personal data in a way which involves tracking individuals' online/offline location/behavior & meets one/more of the Section A criteria?		
9. Will the project/system/application process children's personal data for profiling/automated decision-making/marketing/ or offer online services directly to them?		
10. Will the project/system/application process data that might endanger the individual's health or safety in the event of a security or data breach?		

Advisory grounds to conduct a DPIA – SECTION B	Yes	No
11. Will the project/system/application involve transfer of personal data outside of the EEA?		
12. Will the project/system/application involve large scale processing of personal data?		
13. Will the project/system/application involve profiling or monitoring or automatic decision making?		
14. Does the project/system/application involve Special category (sensitive data) or criminal offence data or the use of the personal data of vulnerable individuals (including children)?		

If any of the questions 1–10 are a YES, then it is a legal requirement to conduct a DPIA. If any of questions 11–14 are a YES, then it is strongly recommended that you conduct a DPIA.

Full DPIA required?

DPIAs should include how data protection compliance is ensured, which will in turn provide a good measure of necessity and proportionality. They should include relevant details of:

- The lawful basis for the processing; this should reflect what is already outlined in the Records of Processing Activity (ROPA), if they exist and should contain at least one legal basis for processing (as per Article 6) for personal data and at least one legal basis for processing (in both Article 6 and Article 9) for sensitive personal data.
- How function creep will be prevented?
- How data quality will be addressed?
- How data minimization will be assured?
- How privacy information will be provided to individuals?
- How individuals' rights will be implemented and supported?
- Measures to ensure data processors comply.
- Safeguards for international transfers.
- Measures to mitigate the risks.
- How the processing activity complies with the GDPR in all other respects?

The following is a suggested DPIA report template outlined in Table 6.5.

Phase 3 Risk assessment

A risk is a scenario describing an event and its consequences, estimated in terms of severity and likelihood. Similarly, "risk" is sometimes broadly used to refer to a risky processing activity or a "threat" that could result in harm for the individual, or to the harm itself, or to both. That is also the approach that appears to be taken in Recital 75 of the GDPR, which seems to conflate the concepts of risky processing activity and harm under the rubric of "risk".

CNIL defines privacy risk as: "the probability that a data processing activity will result in an impact, threat to or loss of (in varying degrees of severity) a valued outcome (e.g., rights and freedoms)". Privacy risk is also described as the likelihood that individuals will experience problems resulting from data processing, and the impact of these problems should they occur. An unacceptable privacy risk, therefore, would be a threat to, or loss of, a valued outcome that cannot be mitigated through the implementation of effective controls and/or that is unreasonable in relation to the intended benefits.

Privacy risks can apply to:

- Individuals or other third parties such as misuse or overuse of their personal data, loss of anonymity, intrusion into private life through monitoring activities, or lack of transparency.
- The organization such as failure of the project and associated costs, legal penalties or claims, damage to reputation, loss of trust of the public, or the cost of noncompliance.

Table 6.5 DPIA report template

Describe the nature of the processing:
1. How will you collect, use, store, and delete data?
2. What is the source of the data?
3. Will you be sharing data with anyone? You might find it useful to refer to a flow diagram or other way of describing data flows.
4. What types of processing identified as likely high risk are involved?

Describe the scope of the processing:
5. What is the nature of the data, and does it include special category or criminal offence data?
6. How much data will you be collecting and using? How often?
7. How long will you keep it?
8. How many individuals are affected?
9. What geographical area does it cover?

Describe the context of the processing:
1. What is the nature of your relationship with individuals?
2. How much control will they have?
3. Would they expect you to use their data in this way?
4. Do they include children or other vulnerable groups?
5. Are there prior concerns over this type of processing or security flaws?
6. Is it novel in any way?
7. What is the current state of technology in this area?
8. Are there any current issues of public concern that you should factor in?
9. Are you signed up to any approved code of conduct or certification scheme (once any have been approved)?

Describe the purposes of the processing:
1. What do you want to achieve?
2. What is the intended effect on individuals?
3. What are the benefits of the processing – for you, and more broadly?

Consider how to consult with relevant stakeholders:
1. Describe when and how you will seek individuals' views – or justify why it's not appropriate to do so.
2. Who else do you need to involve within your organization?
3. Do you need to ask your processors to assist?
4. Do you plan to consult information security experts, or any other experts?

Describe compliance, necessity and proportionality measures, in particular:
1. What is your lawful basis (or bases) for processing?
2. Does the processing achieve your purpose??
3. Is there another way to achieve the same outcome?
4. How will you prevent function creep?
5. How will you ensure data quality and data minimization?
6. What information will you give individuals?
7. How will you help to support their rights?
8. What measures do you take to ensure processors comply?
9. How do you safeguard any international transfers?

Privacy risk includes but is not limited to technical measures that lack appropriate safeguards, social media attacks, mobile malware, third-party access, negligence resulting from improper configuration, outdated security software, social engineering, and lack of encryption.

Consider the potential impact on individuals and any harm or damage your processing may cause – whether physical, emotional, or material. Look at whether the processing could contribute to:

- Inability to exercise rights (including but not limited to privacy rights).
- Inability to access services or opportunities.
- Loss of control over the use of personal data.
- Discrimination.
- Identity theft or fraud.
- Financial loss.
- Reputational damage.
- Physical harm.
- Loss of confidentiality.
- Loss of availability.
- Re-identification of pseudonymized data.
- Any other significant economic or social disadvantage.

Assessments should include the privacy and security risks, including sources of risk and the potential impact of each type of breach including illegitimate access to, modification of, or loss of personal data. This is where it is beneficial to connect with security people in your organization.

To assess whether the risk is a high risk, you need to consider both the likelihood and severity of the possible harm. Harm does not have to be inevitable to qualify as a risk or a high risk. It must be an unlikely/improbable risk of serious harm which may still be enough to qualify as a high risk or a highly likely/probable widespread risk of minor harm which may still count as high risk.

Risk assessment must be conducted objectively, albeit this can be very difficult as a certain level of subjectivity is inherent in the assessor. It is helpful to use a structured matrix to think about likelihood and severity of risks. See Figure 6.7 for an example of a structured risk matrix.

The above matrix shows a structured way to assess risk. Much of the time organizations don't use these risk matrices as there is little understanding of the likelihood levels and impact levels. Figure 6.8 and Figure 6.9 present illustrations of how these ranges of values can be defined and thus more easily interpreted and applied.

Your organization may use a different method which can be adapted for the same purpose. Individual company-specific corporate risks, such as the impact of regulatory action, reputational damage, or loss of public trust should be considered.

Likelihood (Threat Event Occurs and Results in Adverse Impact)	LEVEL OF IMPACT				
	Very Low	Low	Moderate	High	Very High
Very Low	Very Low	Very Low	Very Low	Low	Low
Low	Very Low	Low	Low	Low	Moderate
Moderate	Very Low	Low	Moderate	Moderate	High
High	Very Low	Low	Moderate	High	Very High
Very High	Very Low	Low	Moderate	High	Very High

Figure 6.7 Risk matrix example.

Likelihood of Occurrence	Adversarial	Non-Adversarial
Very Low	Adversary is highly unlikely to initiate the threat event.	Error, accident, or act of nature is highly unlikely to occur, or occurs less than once a year, or occurs less than once every 10 years.
Low	Adversary is unlikely to initiate the threat event.	Error, accident, or act of nature is unlikely to occur, or occurs less than once a year, but more than once every 10 years.
Moderate	Adversary is somewhat likely to initiate the threat event.	Error, accident, or act of nature is somewhat likely to occur or occurs between 1 and 10 times per year.
High	Adversary is highly likely to initiate the threat event.	Error, accident, or act of nature is almost highly likely to occur or occurs between 10 and 100 times per year.
Very High	Adversary is almost certain to initiate the threat event.	Error, accident, or act of nature is almost certain to occur or occurs more than 100 times per year.

Figure 6.8 Suggested "likelihood/probability" ranges.

Impact	Threat Event Description
Very High	The threat event could be expected to have multiple severe or catastrophic adverse effects on organizational operations, organizational assets, individuals, other organizations, or the Nation.
High	The threat event could be expected to have a severe or catastrophic adverse effect on organizational operations, organizational assets, individuals, other organizations, or the Nation. A severe or catastrophic adverse effect means that, for example, the threat event might: (i) cause a severe degradation in or loss of mission capability to an extent and duration that the organization is not able to perform one or more of its primary functions; (ii) result in major damage to organizational assets; (iii) result in major financial loss; or (iv) result in severe or catastrophic harm to individuals involving loss of life or serious life-threatening injuries.
Moderate	The threat event could be expected to have a serious adverse effect on organizational operations, organizational assets, individuals, other organizations, or the Nation. A serious adverse effect means that, for example, the threat event might: (i) cause a significant degradation in mission capability to an extent and duration that the organization is able to perform its primary functions, but the effectiveness of the functions is significantly reduced; (ii) result in significant damage to organizational assets; (iii) result in significant financial loss; or (iv) result in significant harm to individuals that does not involve loss of life or serious life-threatening injuries.
Low	The threat event could be expected to have a limited adverse effect on organizational operations, organizational assets, individuals, other organizations, or the Nation. A limited adverse effect means that, for example, the threat event might: (i) cause a degradation in mission capability to an extent and duration that the organization is able to perform its primary functions, but the effectiveness of the functions is noticeably reduced; (ii) result in minor damage to organizational assets; (iii) result in minor financial loss; or (iv) result in minor harm to individuals.
Very Low	The threat event could be expected to have a negligible adverse effect on organizational operations, organizational assets, individuals other organizations, or the Nation.

Figure 6.9 Suggested impact ranges.

HOW DO WE IDENTIFY MITIGATING MEASURES AND REDUCE RISKS?

To conduct a proper risk assessment, it is important that the appropriate stakeholders are included so important details are not left out of the assessment. Individuals may be interviewed separately or as a group. However, if reviewed as a group, utilize the "soft skills of interaction" as explained in the privacy leader soft skills chapter, especially if there is a mix of management and employees. Some employees may be uneasy speaking up about the true risks within the organization if interviewed alongside their management, as they may feel that this reflects upon the performance of the job they are doing, which may or may not be the case. The objective of risk assessment is to obtain a clear picture of the current state, so the appropriate controls can be selected to enhance the environment to keep up with the privacy threats (or alternatively reduce redundant controls not adding significant value and representing unnecessary cost). The following individuals will be useful in the risk analysis process:

- Chief Information Officer
- Chief Security Officer, Chief Information Security Officer
- Data Protection Officer/Privacy Officer
- Chief Marketing Officer/Chief Communications Officer
- Senior Management, Middle Management
- Internal Audit
- Chief Risk Officer/Legal/C-Suite
- System and Information Owners
- Business and functional support owners
- IT security practitioners
- Infrastructure personnel
- Physical security personnel

In certain circumstances, it may also be appropriate to consult with "data subjects or their representatives" as part of the DPIA. This is a judgment call, but it may be appropriate to seek the input of any recognized trade union or other staff representatives, as part of carrying out the DPIA. Collaborating with key stakeholders, against each risk identified, record its source, and consider options for reducing the risk. A template for performing the privacy risk assessment part of the DPIA is outlined in Table 6.6.

HOW TO IDENTIFY CONTROLS AND PROTECT DATA

Privacy controls can be categorized into four distinct groups:

- Directive controls guide an institution toward its desired outcome. Most directive control activities take the form of laws, regulations, guidelines, policies, and written procedures. For example, GDPR, CCPA, Privacy Policies, Privacy Procedures, etc.
- Preventive controls prevent the occurrence of an undesirable event. The development of these controls involves predicting potential problems before they occur and implementing ways to avoid them. For example, access management, authentication and authorization, and data loss prevention tools.
- Detective controls identify undesirable events that do occur, and alert management about what has happened. This enables management to take corrective action promptly. For example, SIEM, Audit Log Monitoring, data loss detection tools.
- Corrective controls are processes that keep the focus on undesirable conditions until they are corrected. They may also help in setting up procedures to prevent recurrence of the undesirable situation. For example, Awareness Training.

Table 6.6 DPIA: risk report template

Describe source of risk and nature of potential impact on individuals.	Likelihood of Harm Remote/ Possible/ Probable	Severity of harm Minimal/ Significant/ Severe	Overall risk: Low, Medium, or High	Options to Reduce, Mitigate, or Eliminate Risk	Effect on Risk Eliminated/ Reduced/ Accepted	Residual Risk Low/ Medium/ High	Measure Approved Yes/no
Lawfulness, fairness, and transparency. Example: Inadequate privacy information provided to data subjects	Remote	Significant	High	Example: Privacy notice information provided to data subjects and where appropriate GDPR-compliant consent obtained and recorded.	Reduced	Medium	No
Purpose limitation. Example: Data is processed for a purpose unrelated to and incompatible with why it was collected				Example: Appropriate policy document and training for relevant staff.			
Data minimization Example: More data is collected than is necessary to meet defined purpose. For example, individuals may submit details of irrelevant offences.				Example: Policy document to prescribe what data can be collected and processed. Process to remove irrelevant information submitted by data subjects.			

(Continued)

Table 6.6 (Continued)

Describe source of risk and nature of potential impact on individuals.	Likelihood of Harm Remote/ Possible/ Probable	Severity of harm Minimal/ Significant/ Severe	Overall risk: Low, Medium, or High	Options to Reduce, Mitigate, or Eliminate Risk	Effect on Risk Eliminated/ Reduced/ Accepted	Residual Risk Low/ Medium/ High	Measure Approved Yes/no
Accuracy Example: Inaccurate data is collected and processed which may be used to make decisions about individuals.				Example: Verification process where data is to be used to make admissions decision. Guidance for data subjects but difficult to mitigate where false information is deliberately provided by data subjects.			
Storage limitation Example: Data kept for longer than is necessary				Example: Approved retention schedule and process to securely delete records in a timely fashion according to this schedule.			
Security Example: Breach resulting from insecure storage of data.				Example: Records to be stored only in UWE secure storage.			
Accountability Example: Accountability principle not met: no record of processing or appropriate policies in place.				Example: Updated record of processing, approved DPIA, and relevant policies in place.			

To select a control that will adequately protect the data of an organization, one must consider several key components first before selecting the control. Why re-invent the wheel? There are several frameworks that include controls such as the NIST framework and ISO 27701. For example, ISO 27701 has 135 controls that extend or modify ISO 27001, and there are also 49 controls that outline new guidance regarding PII (these additional PII security controls are what make ISO 27701 a privacy framework). The five categories of controls in ISO 27701 are:

- Security management: These controls are related to creating and maintaining an efficient security management system.
- Information security controls: This includes the use of technical and organizational standards that safeguard information from unauthorized permits, usage, disclosure, or destruction.
- Information security risk management: This category entails procedures for identifying, evaluating, and responding to data security risks.
- Information security incident management: These controls address how to manage incidents that endanger data security.
- Business continuity management: This category aims to ensure that an organization can continue to operate in the event of an incident.

But before deciding on the most appropriate controls to have in place ("the technical and organizations measures"), one must consider the status – where is the data, how is it classified, and what controls are already in place. These are discussed below.

DATA DISCOVERY (WHERE IS THE DATA?)

The typical answer to this question when first asked is "I don't know" or "everywhere!" Even those organizations that have structured data stores and databases where the main customer information is held may think they know where all the information is stored and could point to a data store containing the "master record" for the information. However, without an explicit approach to data protection, the real location of this information is likely to be identified as only a subset of where the real information is stored.

Documents (Word, Excel, PowerPoint, PDFs, etc.)
How much information is extracted from the master databases or files and placed in Microsoft Excel files to be distributed across the organization? Information retained in databases is often difficult to access, as requests need to be processed by the access management team, resulting in minimally a one- or two-day delay in many organizations. Even if the access is promptly granted through a web interface, accessing the information in a database through the structured screens or via writing SQL queries is beyond the general skill level for most users. Most users within a company will have familiarity at a basic level with

Excel and for this reason, this has become a primary mechanism for exchanging information. Once information is extracted into this format, the privacy and security controls once in place are now removed unless the end user has taken steps to secure the individual files with passwords, encryption, and so forth. In the fast pace of organizations today, this step is often missed as end users are busy trying to complete their jobs and after all, they are exchanging the files with people with only a need to know, right? Unfortunately, these files typically end up on public internal company servers with limited protections implemented. Departments such as human resources, finance, and legal may implement protections at a department level or the proactive organizations at a more granular folder/file level. However, this is typically the extent of the departments that secure their information from others.

PCs, laptops, backups.

Corporate end user policies may state "No information may be stored on personal computers; all information must be stored on corporate servers or through company-approved cloud-based storage mechanisms". This would be a great policy – if only it was followed consistently by users. The policy usually gets adjusted, or people are given a pass if they "temporarily need the information on the laptops". This is a valid request, considering the auditor working on some files on the train with limited or no Wi-Fi capability trying to finish reports before the closing meeting or the business executive travelling by airplane for eight hours overseas wanting to access their files with spotty, unreliable satellite Wi-Fi access. If the organization does not provide a secure way to access files and data, employees will find a way that may be less secure. These policies allowing exceptions for PC or laptop storage, without thinking about the types of information that will be stored on the devices, add to the risk of not protecting critical data. When a laptop is lost it becomes very difficult to know what was on the device other than by the user's recollection of what information may have been on the device. One method to ascertain this is through the examination of the PC backup logs, as they record the files and changes that were on the device, assuming the organization had a strategy to back up the PCs. Knowledge of the full contents is usually unknown by the user.

Few organizations teach the end users about where the best place to store information may be. Users may not recognize that a document on their device was sitting in the temporary directory, or that the file was not really deleted on the hard drive, but rather marked for deletion.

Internal Databases/Applications/Servers and their backups
SharePoint/Intranet

Companies need to be able to share information across departments to accomplish their mission. Imagine the extreme where information within a department was not shared outside of the department – this would result in a siloed approach to business, where one department would not be able to know what was going on in another department. This would create large problems in communication across the company. For example, how effective would a privacy and security awareness program be if there was not the ability to share policies, procedures, standards, guidelines, news articles, and contact information for the rest of the organization?

SharePoint, and sharing by a common intranet, provide the company with the ability to broadly communicate information and that is a great improvement from the prior generation of printed newsletters, institutional knowledge maintained by a few go-to people, and the occasional email or memo to communicate relevant information the organization needed to know. The SharePoint site or Intranet becomes the "hub" for much corporate information and the reason why it is the home page for most people as they arrive to work. In the spirit of sharing, companies may have "gone too far" in "what" is shared. These intranet sites contain very capable search engines, like the Google search, whereby information is pulled from massive data stores and individuals may unintentionally have access to information they should not have. Since information to be useful needs to be found quickly, these powerful search engines default to returning as much information as possible, unless the information is specifically locked down. In the rush to make information immediately accessible outside of a department, these controls may not have been evaluated. For example, something as innocuous sounding as meeting minutes for a department may be posted to the department's intranet site for the department to share among themselves. However, the search engine will display the content of those minutes unless the files have been explicitly secured to only that department, as search engines are designed by default to return as much information as possible. Furthermore, unless there is clear guidance as to the level of detail that should be represented within the minutes with the note taker, embarrassing details of an employee discipline matter, salary discussion, or the divulging of an upcoming acquisition could be revealed.

Information that is shareable should be shared and encouraged. Unfortunately, the assessment for these sites usually comes after someone notices they have access to the information after it has been posted to the site, indicating a lack of policies and procedures regarding data protection.

Email Systems

Just as the information sprawls from the master files or databases to documents located on servers and intranet sites, information is passed from user to user across the internal and external email systems. Where did this file end up? How is the system/user receiving the information protecting it? As with the prior infrastructure discussion, how do we know that the platform the document is now stored in has the appropriate infrastructure controls? This is what gives rise to the M&M analogy for how most organizations are protecting their information – hard on the outside and soft and chewy on the inside! Internally, we want information to flow quickly, and as such, we limit the number of controls on the individual files and want to "trust" our internal infrastructure. Externally, we do not have that luxury, as we do not have visibility into the security and privacy of external systems and must assume that they are neither appropriately secure nor appropriately private. This is one of the primary reasons we encrypt files for external distribution – so we add SSL or Secure Socket Layer encryption and secure the files themselves by adding file-level encryption and distribute the keys through (preferably) another channel.

If the organization has not addressed data retention within the email system, imposed limits on the amount of storage available per user, or developed an archival strategy – excessive emails are likely stored within the email system. This can cause issues for e-discovery whereby large amounts of email would unnecessarily need to be presented to the court, potentially creating a disadvantage in the cost to acquire and analyze the information. As in the well-known case of a Sony Pictures breach (2014), embarrassing emails were revealed because of the breach causing reputational harm to the company.

Email systems used to be classified as a noncritical resource in business continuity/disaster recovery plans. Today, since email is still the primary means of communication within and externally by many organizations, the system and the contained information become critical information.

USB Drives

The inexpensive nature of USB drives makes retaining a backup of information easier than ever before. With capacities in recent years of multi-terabyte storage capacities for portable hard drives becoming the norm, company users are taking multiple backups (a good thing for disaster recovery) and storing copies of sensitive company confidential information (a bad thing for data proliferation). While some companies have resorted to blocking USB storage from their work computer systems, even those blocking these USB ports generally have an exception process for users needing to exchange information externally or create external presentations. In these cases, the focus tends to be more on "protecting the information" from external viewing vs managing the location of the information. In other words, while an organization may put in protection mechanisms, there is a strong likelihood that data flow diagrams of where the information is resident does not exist. In other words, the USB drive becomes just another infrastructure component of the company with no visibility as to what type of information is stored on the device. This could be mitigated somewhat with Data Loss Prevention (DLP) to track the writing of sensitive information. Even at this level, this becomes a detective control vs. an organization proactively understanding why external storage needs to be used for a piece of information used in a business process.

Cloud Storage

Cloud storage could be viewed as the evolution of USB drives. USB drives were the evolution of CDs/DVDs which were the evolution of floppy disks. The only real difference was the amount of storage – the effect was the same, passing information through "sneaker-net". This worked well when information was being exchanged in a local office or time expectations permitted mailing of the disks. However, in today's instant gratification world of same-day shipping and instant web transactions, the USB is rapidly becoming an outdated medium. The replacement technology that meets the need to communicate between disparate parties across the Internet is cloud storage. The enhanced capabilities of cloud storage provide better access control to the information, much like a "big database in the sky". The advantage of this platform with respect to data protection is that controls may be placed on the information to protect it while worrying less about losing or misplacing the actual (USB) device containing sensitive information.

The downside of this medium is that companies are typically surprised when a vendor offers to scan the environment to determine how many applications are being used outside of the "expected number of IT applications", only to find files are being stored in many external applications using cloud storage the organization is unaware of or has no visibility into.

Mobile Devices

More and more transactions are processed through mobile applications today as the platform of choice. Company user's login through mobile devices to portals, SharePoint sites, time and expense applications, cloud storage, Microsoft/Google office productivity applications, email, etc. With the Internet becoming ubiquitous, the model of "data access anywhere, anytime" can become a reality. Some of these applications provide access to other databases/files, while others retain access to information. What information is contained within the application? What information is contained on the device? How is this information being protected? Aside from the infrastructure of the mobile device – the pertinent question is – what data flowing to the device and being retained on the device needs to be protected? Is this information represented in a data inventory or data flow diagram? If the device is lost, is the information still protected (encrypted) or can it be wiped (eliminated).

Storage Space is Cheap

With all the places to store information and the ease with which we can drag/drop, cut/paste, and move information from one place to another, it should be no surprise our information exists in more places than we initially think within our companies. Additionally, since storage has become very inexpensive, organizations have been less sensitive about the costs of the storage and in some cases have decided that buying more storage is cheaper than having employees spend extra time organizing and deleting their files. This may be true from an operational sense in the short term; however, as the information grows and backups increase in size, more information must be searched, a greater cost appears – more information is at risk of disclosure – it also becomes more difficult to comply with the industry regulations, as the premise of these regulations are that there is control over the information entrusted to the company.

RESPONSIBLE AND ACCOUNTABLE DATA USE WITH APPROPPRIATE CONTROLS DRIVES DATA SUSTAINABILITY AND BUSINESS RESILIENCY

Barbara Lawler

President, the Information Accountability Foundation

In the observational data-centric world in which we live, work, and play, privacy – responsible and accountable data use with appropriate controls – drives data sustainability and business resiliency. Forward-looking organizations are applying and enhancing strategic frameworks to meet the demands of an observational world, responsible and resilient data use, and the expectations for fair AI. Corporate boards often consider privacy in the legal compliance bucket of corporate governance, and instead should treat privacy as a data sustainability issue, which in turn shapes business resiliency and strategy.

Business resiliency is one of the core governance responsibilities of a corporate board. Business resiliency is dependent on data sustainability. Data sustainability – whether PI or non-PI – is dependent on how external stakeholders see risk and how the company manages that data risk and evaluates people-beneficial data uses. Data risk and benefit assessment and oversight in the context of multiple stakeholders is becoming a primary function of privacy, security, and adjacent functions. It's also becoming a compliance requirement thanks to US state and international fair AI regulations.

Data risk comes from unrestricted use of data about people. Often the focus is on compliance driven by regulator statements and actions and court decisions. Data risk from unrestricted use also impacts its resiliency, where stakeholder influence arises from customers, employees, civil society, the media, and others.

Achieving data benefits to people, groups, or society requires us to understand the digital innovation path. The digital innovation path constitutes data, information, knowledge, action. The digital innovation path is shown in Figure 6.10.

The pathway to innovation is clear. Break the path at any point, then actions taken will be less than optimal – creating risks to individuals and to the organization. Data value disruption couples compliance and business resiliency issues.

There are no new actions – such as cancer therapies, smart car safety, pollution abatement, and specialized education – without the ability to think and act with data. At the same time, there is increased pressure and scrutiny on digital economy activities, from AI applications, to AdTech, from increased cybersecurity threats to international data transfers, and fundamental issues about individual body autonomy and safeguarding our youth.

Financial penalties may be the least of your problems. For example, recently a company with poor data use and security practices was penalized at the company business operations and CEO levels, and the board was warned by the US FTC. Another company was forced to stop using certain algorithms and purge all data created by those algorithms. These represent fundamental data sustainability issues in a nutshell, with direct impact on business strategy, governance, and resiliency.

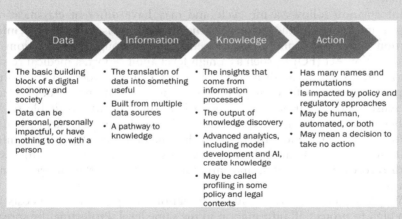

Figure 6.10 Digital innovation path.

CPOs and their peers can impact the business strategy discussion with corporate boards by framing data risk and benefit considerations as data sustainability and business resiliency governance. To do that, privacy leaders need to have fingertip view of data inventories and flows across the organization and be able to describe succinctly how those data sources feed into business-critical operational processing and serve as input to product or business model changes or development. CPOs can also have in place processes and assessments that prove responsible and ethical data processing occurs.

DATA CLASSIFICATION (WHAT CLASSIFICATION IS THE DATA?)

Data classification is distinct from data type (personal or sensitive or special category or PII, etc.). Data can be classified into 3–4 categories to specify how the information should be handled. The categories usually involve terminologies such as restricted, sensitive or confidential data, private or company internal data, and public data. Some organizations will have two categories of restricted or sensitive data to denote the differences between say health or financial information requiring a higher level of protection and company confidential information. One approach is to regard all information processed or controlled as private data requiring baseline protection unless it is specifically denoted as highly sensitive or sensitive information. In this manner, a thought process to deliberately identify the higher level of risk has been carried out or the information was deliberately viewed as available for public consumption. The intention of these categorizations is to have a set of information handling rules associated with each category so that those processing the data know exactly what conditions need to be in place.

Information follows a life cycle and may have different classifications depending upon who the recipient of the information is. For example, information requested from a government entity through the Freedom of Information Act (FOIA), such as a high-level audit report, a medical record for insurance purposes, or a criminal report, can be made available to the requesting entity by following a process. This information may be classified as sensitive information, even though it is subsequently available to the public upon completing a request. A mistake would be to classify this information as "public" under the pretense that the public can "obtain the information anyway". Because there is a process of law that must be followed with records of the request and information delivered, this information is not public.

Why is it important to classify information? Simply stated, the costs are too high to protect all information to the same level. Protecting the spreadsheet containing the company's diversity program events would not rise to the same level as protecting an individual's health record. However, each organization needs to evaluate the risk of information disclosure, destruction, or modification to the organization. For example, the log of the company's upcoming diversity efforts could be classified as private/confidential in the event the company was targeted by activist groups perceiving them to have less than stellar records in promoting minorities or maintaining a low percentage of women in leadership positions. The knowledge of the timing of these events could be targeted with demonstrations representing a reputation risk to the company. The point here is that even those files that may seem on the surface to not contain confidential information should be reviewed on a periodic basis as the risks may have increased and changed the data classification. For most of the data within the organization, the challenge is not the changing classification of the information, but rather agreeing on the correct classification and implementing the appropriate security controls for the data classification.

Data stewards or data owners are charged with the responsibility to maintain the correct classification of the information, as well as ensure that the information is being handled across the business appropriately. This may include who has access to the information, how the information is protected, and a periodic re-certification that access to the information is still required by each business area.

HOW IS THE DATA SECURED?

The answer will be different depending upon the classification of the data and the application that processes it (i.e., how it is to be used). The data classification of the information and the application/technical platform processing the information will drive the level of protection afforded to the information requiring protection. This should be recorded in the ROPA if one exists. Otherwise, a simple matrix can be created showing the classification on one axis and the technique to protect the information on the other axis and can guide the level of protection necessary.

If the privacy protection controls on one platform do not rise to the level the information is classified, then there is risk at this point in the system. For instance, information encrypted while residing within the database system of record is not sufficiently encrypted if exported to a spreadsheet without encryption controls and password protection. By assigning different technologies to the methods of protection, these can subsequently be reused when other data types are added to the organization. It may require a substantial initial investment to identify all the information, where it is located, and how it is/is not being protected; however, the long-term ramp-up time should be considerably less. This information can also often be found in the ROPA, where they exist. If not, this information can often be recorded in the ROPA once the exercise is completed.

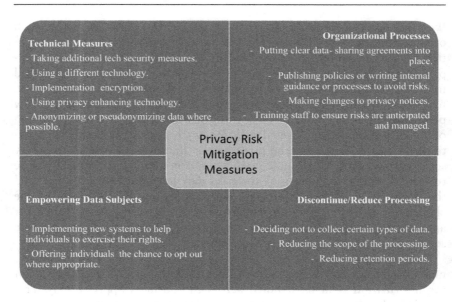

Technical Measures
- Taking additional tech security measures.
- Using a different technology.
- Implementation encryption.
- Using privacy enhancing technology.
- Anonymizing or pseudonymizing data where possible.

Organizational Processes
- Putting clear data- sharing agreements into place.
- Publishing policies or writing internal guidance or processes to avoid risks.
- Making changes to privacy notices.
- Training staff to ensure risks are anticipated and managed.

Privacy Risk Mitigation Measures

Empowering Data Subjects
- Implementing new systems to help individuals to exercise their rights.
- Offering individuals the chance to opt out where appropriate.

Discontinue/Reduce Processing
- Deciding not to collect certain types of data.
- Reducing the scope of the processing.
- Reducing retention periods.

Figure 6.11 Privacy risk mitigation measures.

DATA FLOW (RELATING DATA TO OTHER INFORMATION)

Understanding how the data flows throughout the system enables the opportunity to not only ensure that security is being maintained end-to-end, but also to enable the improvement of business processes. The process of documenting data flows can highlight inefficient processes, such as manual hand-offs to email systems and manual preparation of Word documents vs. leveraging the system to create the information. Gaps in access control may also be identified, whereby users are requesting access through decentralized means and the tracking of access is insecure (i.e., an application's logon and password information stored unprotected on a data owner's PC).

The privacy risk mitigation measures shown in Figure 6.11 are not an exhaustive list and other ways may be devised in conjunction with company business partners to help reduce or avoid the risks. Record whether each measure would reduce or eliminate the risk. The costs and benefits of each measure are evaluated when deciding whether they are appropriate.

Phase 4: Validation. What should I do once I have conducted the DPIA?

Unless specifically called out in particular legislation, there is typically no mandated requirement to publish the outcomes of a DPIA, however the process should be documented. Any record/documentation should include the privacy issues and potential solutions identified, as well as the reasons why a particular processing activity went ahead or was abandoned. It is important to keep a paper trail in the event of a claim and/or investigation by the supervisory authority.

In the event that the DPIA shows high "residual risks" to data subjects, the organization is obliged to consult with the relevant supervisory authority before any processing takes place. Broadly speaking, a high residual risk is one that cannot be sufficiently addressed by the measures put in place to protect the rights of the data subjects. If, during the DPIA process, the data controller has identified and taken measures to mitigate any risks to personal data, it is not necessary to consult with the relevant supervisory authority before proceeding with the project. If the DPIA suggests that any identified risks cannot be managed and the residual risk remains high, the relevant supervisory authority must be consulted before moving forward with the project.

Regardless of whether consultation with the relevant supervisory authority is required, the obligations of retaining a record of the DPIA and updating the DPIA in due course, remain. Even if consultation is not required, the DPIA may be reviewed by the relevant supervisory authority later in the event of an audit or investigation arising from your use of personal data.

The outcomes of the DPIA, and management risk acceptance, should be documented and the report should be signed and approved by the internal stakeholder responsible for privacy accountability. Table 6.7 presents a template to be used in a DPIA report for the purpose of management signoff.

Table 6.7 DPIA management signoff template

Item	Name/date	Notes
Measures approved by:		Integrate actions back into project plan, with date and responsibility for completion
Residual risks approved by:		If accepting any residual high risk, consult the ICO before going ahead
DPO advice provided:		DPO should advise on compliance, step 6 measures, and whether processing can proceed
Summary of DPO advice:		
DPO advice accepted or overruled by:		If overruled, you must explain your reasons
Comments:		
Consultation responses reviewed by:		If your decision departs from individuals' views, you must explain your reasons
Comments:		
This DPIA will be kept under review by:		The DPO should also review ongoing compliance with DPIA

Phase 5: Implementation

According to Article 35(1), it is ultimately the responsibility of the data controller to conduct a DPIA, though this must be done in consultation with the DPO, if the organization has appointed one. The designated team nominated by the data controller bears the responsibility for carrying out and documenting the DPIA. Even if the process is outsourced, the data controller remains responsible.

So, what about the DPO? There is much discourse on whether the DPO should "do" the DPIA. For clarification – the DPO's responsibility for the DPIA is to advise the controller. Following the principle of data protection by design, Article 35(2) specifically requires that the controller "shall seek advice" of the DPO when carrying out a DPIA. Article 39(1), in turn, tasks the DPO with the duty to "provide advice where requested as regards the DPIA and monitor its performance pursuant to Article 35". Guidance suggests that the controller should seek the advice of the DPO, on the following issues, among others:

- Whether or not to carry out a DPIA (threshold assessment).
- What methodology to follow when carrying out a DPIA (risk assessment methodology)?
- Whether to carry out the DPIA in-house or whether to outsource it.
- What safeguards (including technical and organizational measures) to apply to mitigate any risks to the rights and interests of the data subjects?
- Whether or not the data protection impact assessment has been correctly carried out and whether its conclusions (whether to go ahead with the processing and what safeguards to apply) are in compliance with the GDPR.

If the controller disagrees with the advice provided by the DPO, the DPIA documentation should specifically justify in writing why the advice has not been considered. Finally, if the processing activity is carried out entirely or partly by a data processor (such as a payroll provider or a background checking company), the processor should provide the controller with any necessary assistance or information.

CHALLENGES WITH THE IMPLEMENTATION PHASE

No matter who is assigned the responsibility for conducting and completing the DPIA, senior management owns the risk decisions made within it. So, it would seem appropriate they should sign-off to accept the risk. After all, ensuring things get done within an organization requires someone to be ultimately accountable or the result is no one is accountable. It should be easy to find the management person responsible for the risk, right? Unfortunately, in practice, this is more difficult for three key reasons outlined below.

I. CROSS-FUNCTIONAL BOUNDARIES

Business functions and projects typically cross organizational boundaries and as such, by definition, would have multiple people with a role in the risk acceptance. One person may be uncomfortable accepting the risk when the business function is not completely within his/her control. Second, when the risk item involves a business function and technology, which it most always will, who is responsible? Take, for example, the case where a key application used by a business, say a transaction to conduct wire transfers from one bank to another, is compromised because one of the underlying systems is using unsupported vendor software past its end of life. Who is responsible for managing this risk? One could argue that the issue lies with the CIO for lack of upgrading the infrastructure to support the current version of the software. Or one could argue the responsibility lies with the business executive that failed to influence the management team to provide additional funding to the CIO to upgrade the infrastructure over the other project priorities being considered. From this example, it is easy to see how both individuals could feel they were "right" in the decisions made; however, neither may desire to wholly own the risk for the software being exploited.

2. LACK OF FUNDING

Accepting the responsibility for the risk without being provided the necessary funding to fix it can occur even when the function is contained within one department. The question of "why should I accept responsibility for an unsecure product, when I have asked for funding during each of the past 3 budgeting sessions and was always turned down" appears to be a valid concern. There will be a reluctance to accept the risk. In this scenario, it would be important to document these requests as evidence other higher probability risks were mitigated before this risk would be allocated any funds.

3. CONTROLLABILITY

The senior executive may also have the sense they cannot control the risk, even if provided the funding and do not want to be held accountable. To these executives, this would be analogous to signing off that there should be two major storms this year vs six. While their assessment of the privacy risk may be their best estimate, they may not be comfortable at accepting the risk.

CIPP/US, CIPM: WANT TO DRAFT A TRANSPARENT PRIVACY POLICY? THINK ABOUT MOM!

Paul E. Clement

Privacy Program Manager, HP, Inc.

So, you need to draft a privacy policy that's transparent and gives individuals the ability to control how their personal information is used. You communicate daily by email, text, and in other written forms. Easy enough, right?

Distilling text for a privacy policy into something that's easy to understand and doesn't fatigue the reader is challenging. I learned this the first time I had to draft a privacy policy that was compliant with the EU's General Data Protection Regulation (GDPR).

For me, the most important factor is one I think often gets overlooked. Know your audience! Policies and procedures are written by professionals trained in the art of using words to satisfy requirements. The audience for your privacy policy is not that.

No doubt you can include what is legally required. Translating that into something that's easy to understand is the challenge. What's transparent to you, the author, may not be transparent to the reader. I tell people to ask themselves a question I've asked myself, if your parents read your privacy policy would they understand it? The reaction is usually laughter because the answer is almost always "no".

What can you do?

- Limit the number of words you use. Doing this will sometimes feel like an impossible task. When it does, try to present your content in a more easily digestible manner. Use methods that readers are familiar with like a table of contents, bullet points, and short-content descriptions that link to longer form content. Use pictures and videos to capture the attention of the reader and help guide them.
- Be intentional about word choice. As professionals, far too often we use words that we're comfortable using in our daily jobs. Instead, think of a conversation with your parents or friends and try to use words they relate to.
- Create clear and obvious controls. Develop processes and tools that make it easy for individuals to exercise their privacy rights, like opting-out or submitting a request under GDPR. Create groups to test your processes before you implement them. Make sure YOU are a tester.

SUGGESTED READING

CNIL. A methodology and tool for PIAs and DPIAs. https://www.cnil.fr/sites/default/files/atoms/files/cnil-pia-1-en-methodology.pdf

CNIL. A privacy maturity model. https://www.cnil.fr/fr/la-cnil-propose-une-auto evaluation-de-maturite-en-gestion-de-la-protection-des-donnees

CNIL. A template for ROPAs. https://www.cnil.fr/en/record-processing-activities

EDPS Commentary. Accountability on the Ground. https://edps.europa.eu/sites/default/files/publication/19-07-17_accountability_on_the_ground_part_i_en.pdf

ENISA. Evaluating the level of risk for a personal data processing operation. https://www.enisa.europa.eu/risk-level-tool/risk

ENISA. (2013). Recommendations for a methodology of the assessment of severity of personal data breaches. https://www.enisa.europa.eu/publications/dbn-severity

Krisper, M. (2021). Problems with risk matrices using ordinal scales, 2103.05440. arXiv.org

SOME SUGGESTED/HELPFUL LINKS FOR PRIVACY RISK ASSESSMENT

- Explanation of Risk Based Approach: *https://www.informationpolicy centre.com/uploads/5/7/1/0/57104281/cipl_gdpr_project_risk_white_paper_21_december_2016.pdf*
- *Free Tool Covering All Phases: https://www.cnil.fr/en/open-source-pia-software-helps-carry-out-data-protection-impact-assesment*
- *Risk Assessment Templates: https://gdpr.eu/wp-content/uploads/2019/03/dpia-template-v1.pdf*
- *Threshold Assessment Template: https://www.hiqa.ie/sites/default/files/2019-02/pia_threshold_assessment_0.pdf*
- *DPIA Template: https://iapp.org/media/pdf/resource_center/dpia-template.pdf*

Section V

Shared values

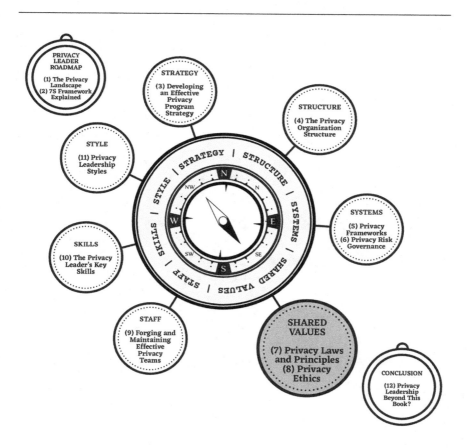

Chapter 7

Privacy and data protection

Laws and principles

> Privacy laws must prevent arbitrary or unlawful interference, but privacy is not absolute. It is an established principle that appropriate government authorities should be able to seek access to otherwise private information when a court or independent authority has authorized such access based on established legal standards.
>
> 2018: Five Eyes Nations (US, UK, Canada, Australia, New Zealand)

Laws are created to stand the test of time due to the lengthy process to pass a regulation or law. Laws are formed by committees in response to a need, given enough visibility for a legislator to see it in their best interest to act upon it. Then these law proposals are debated, voted on, and then pass the protocol for review and acceptance defined by the legal structure. For example, in the United States, for Federal regulations, Congress (legislative branch) first proposes a bill and if approved, will become a law. If Congress approves the bill, it goes to the President who can approve the bill or veto it. The new law, if approved, is then called an Act or a Statute. The House of Representatives standardizes the text and publishes it in the United States Code (USC) once every six years, with supplements issued in the interim.

Concerns about privacy risk have triggered several new privacy and data protection laws across the globe, and we will discuss these and the history of privacy regulation in this chapter.

LAWS AND REGULATIONS VS CONTROL STANDARDS AND FRAMEWORKS

In the United States, laws are pieces of statutory legislation that begin as bills and are then passed to certain governmental bodies as proposed acts to ratify them as laws. Regulations are supplementary to acts. They link to existing acts, and they are designed to aid in applying the principles of the act. Codes of Practice (often referred to as 'guidance') are positioned in the legal framework just beneath acts and regulations. While codes of practice are not the laws themselves, they often help to interpret the legislation and can provide additional clarity.

DOI: 10.1201/9781003383017-12

In the EU, a "regulation" is a binding legislative act that must be applied in its entirety across the EU and a "directive" is a legislative act that sets out a goal that all EU countries must achieve (however, it is up to the individual countries to devise their own laws on how to reach these goals). We would like to highlight the confusion that can often be associated with the term "regulation" as the term is often used to also describe mandatory industry standards that are not linked directly to acts of laws per se but are rather industry self-regulation formulated by an industry body. The Payment Card Industry Data Security Standard (PCI DSS) is a good example of this, whereby the standard was formed by the major credit card issuers to ensure security and privacy between the merchants and card processors. Even though the standard is not a law, it is a requirement established by the issuers which must be complied with to participate within the industry. Sometimes these are referred to as regulations, giving deference to the requirements that our organizations are held to, just as formal laws passed by legislative bodies, and sometimes they are referred to as control frameworks or standards, in deference to their ability to be used to guide the security and privacy programs to a more effective state. Hence, some of these regulations will often appear interchangeable when discussing the overarching law or regulation and when discussing the controls used to achieve compliance with the regulation, control framework, or standard.

Confused? That is understandable and is most likely why the terms Law, Act, Legislation, Regulation have come to be used interchangeably – reflecting the mandatory nature of the instructions within them. Frameworks, standards, and guidelines have also come to be used interchangeably to describe the sets of rules, procedures, or beliefs intended to make clear or structure a series of tasks and are not typically mandatory (with some exceptions in industry self-regulation).

CIPP/E: STRATEGY FOR COMPLYING WITH MULTIPLE LAWS

Rob Norris

Chief Privacy Officer, Cushman & Wakefield

Globally, privacy laws are changing at a significant rate, and it can sometimes feel overwhelming trying to be informed about these new laws and manage each new compliance requirement whilst competing against other business and regulatory priorities. Whilst this may be seen as an issue for large multinational organizations only, this is not the case. The absence of a federal privacy law in USA has prompted individual states to legislate and most international privacy laws include some form of extra-territorial reach to ensure their citizen's personal data is protected regardless of the location in which data processing occurs.

Rather than trying to comply with every single privacy law on a piece-meal basis, it is far more efficient for organizations to build a principles-based approach to privacy compliance.

Most privacy laws are congregating around the same core objectives: giving transparency to individuals; providing individuals with real, actionable rights, and ensuring personal data processing is secure, fair, and proportionate.

Establishing a principles-led privacy program greatly helps establish a "privacy bedrock" or a minimum level of data protection across an organization that helps insulate from knee-jerk reactions to new privacy laws.

Privacy principles can be simple to understand and align with the ethos, ethics and culture of the organization, anchored in the same language used by senior leaders to communicate the strategy and direction of the organization as a whole. By aligning the two together, it greatly helps with cut-through and understanding across the workforce and helps employees use their own judgment in assessing privacy risk.

A well-established and robust principles led privacy program allows new privacy laws to be benchmarked against these principles so that specific gaps can be identified, and small-scale changes designed and delivered quickly without affecting the fabric of the entire privacy program in the organization. Below are examples of privacy principles, including some practical examples of how they translate into tangible objectives for a privacy program:

Stand up for our customers	• We will be fully transparent in how we process personal data and ensure our notices are in plain language and easy to understand. • We will implement robust procedures to ensure data subject rights are fulfilled. • Privacy by Design and Default is a fundamental part of our change management practices and no change is rolled out without privacy approval.
Build sustainability into our supply chain	• Privacy assessment is included in all our RFP/vendor onboarding procedures. • We regularly verify our vendors are adapting to new privacy laws and emerging privacy and information security risks. • We partner with our vendors to learn, share, and continuously improve our privacy compliance program.
Invest in our culture	• We will continuously train our employees in privacy, so that it is integral to our daily operations and our employees feel comfortable in assessing privacy risk for themselves. • We will share examples of data incidents and be transparent about our failures so the entire organization can learn and improve. • We will ensure privacy is discussed regularly in board/audit committee meetings, so the tone is set from the top.

EVOLUTION OF DATA PROTECTION AND PRIVACY LEGISLATION

Before we discuss the evolution of privacy legislation, let us first discuss the data protection principles that underpin most data protection regulation today.

Key data protection principles

These principles are broad rules about conduct or desired outcomes – and are an important part of data protection law, and are, in fact, at the core of the GDPR. They should be understood as the fundamental overarching principles which aim to ensure compliance with the spirit of data protection law and the protection of the rights of individuals ("data subjects"). These are the key principles related to the processing of personal data, which controllers (i.e., those who decide how and why data are processed) need to be aware of and comply with when collecting and otherwise processing personal data:

Lawfulness, fairness, and transparency

Any processing of personal data should be lawful and fair. It should be transparent to individuals that personal data concerning them are collected, used, consulted, or otherwise processed and to what extent the personal data are or will be processed. The principle of transparency requires that any information and communication relating to the processing of those personal data be easily accessible and easy to understand, and that clear and plain language be used.

Purpose limitation

Personal data should only be collected for specified, explicit, and legitimate purposes and not further processed in a manner that is incompatible with those purposes. In particular, the specific purposes for which personal data are processed should be explicit and legitimate and determined at the time of the collection of the personal data. So, if personal data is collected to send an e-receipt, do not use the data for marketing purposes.

Data minimization

Processing of personal data must be adequate, relevant, and limited to what is necessary in relation to the purposes for which they are processed. Personal data should be processed only if the purpose of the processing could not reasonably be fulfilled by other means. This requires ensuring that the period for which the personal data are stored is limited to a strict minimum. For instance, is an individual's date of birth required for the processing of the data? If not, then do not collect it.

Accuracy

Controllers must ensure that personal data are accurate and, where necessary, kept up to date; taking every reasonable step to ensure that personal data that are inaccurate, having regard to the purposes for which they are processed, are erased or rectified without delay. Controllers should accurately record the information they collect or receive and the source of that information. For instance, names and addresses of employees need to be up to date, and the employee needs to change these details on request or enable the employee to do so directly themselves. Where details are recorded by telephone these should be confirmed via email.

Storage limitation

Personal data should only be kept in a form which permits identification of data subjects for as long as it is necessary for the purposes for which the personal data are processed. To ensure that the personal data are not kept longer than necessary, time limits should be established by the controller for erasure or for a periodic review. For instance, hospitals may hold records understandably for your lifetime, but online shopping retailers may not.

Integrity and confidentiality

Personal data should be processed in a manner that ensures appropriate security and confidentiality of the personal data, including protection against unauthorized or unlawful access to or use of personal data and the equipment used for the processing and against accidental loss, destruction or damage, using appropriate technical or organizational measures. An example of this would be a medical clinic implementing password encryption of files or two-factor authentication to access financial personal data.

Accountability

Finally, the controller is responsible for, and must be able to demonstrate, their compliance with all the aforementioned principles of data protection. Organizations must take responsibility for their processing of personal data and how they comply with data protection and privacy legislation and be able to demonstrate (through appropriate records and measures) their compliance. In other words, as a privacy leader – when making a privacy-related decision – imagine that the commissioner of the local supervisory authority is sitting across the table and asking you – "can you show me evidence of how this decision was made, by whom, how, and what risks were considered?". You need to be able to be accountable for the decisions made and how they came about and be able to evidence that.

Beyond the above-mentioned data protection principles, there are also other related rules and principles (which are enshrined in the GDPR and other legislation), such as the principles of proportionality and necessity, and the principles of data protection by design and by default. More details on these elements are discussed in the following sections.

Necessity and proportionality

Necessity is a fundamental principle when assessing the restriction of fundamental rights, such as the right to the protection of personal data. According to case law, because of the role the processing of personal data entails for a series of fundamental rights, the limiting of the fundamental right to the protection of personal data must be strictly necessary.

Necessity should be justified based on objective evidence and is the first step before assessing the proportionality of the limitation. Necessity is also fundamental when assessing the lawfulness of the processing of personal data. The processing operations, the categories of data processed, and the duration the data are kept shall be necessary for the purpose of processing. For instance, in Ireland the government had to roll back on its decision to introduce a public services card for all public services, as the Irish Data Protection Commission (DPC) determined that such an initiative breached individuals right to privacy and forced them to share information without an appropriate legal basis. Additionally, biometric information (photo) was stored alongside crucial identifying information (name and signature) in a database that was typically insecure, and the government had not published the required security protocols that would be in place. And finally, the card targeted economically vulnerable people, such as those in receipt of social welfare, pension, child benefit, or state grants.

Proportionality is a general principle of the EU law and is the bedfellow of the necessity principle. It requires authorities and organizations to strike a balance between the means used and the intended aim. In the context of fundamental rights, such as the right to the protection of personal data, proportionality is key for any limitation on these rights. More specifically, proportionality requires that advantages due to limiting the right are not outweighed by the disadvantages to exercise the right. In other words, the limitation on the right must be justified. Safeguards accompanying a measure can support the justification of a measure. A pre-condition is that the measure is adequate to achieve the envisaged objective. In addition, when assessing the processing of personal data, proportionality requires that only that personal data which is adequate and relevant for the purposes of the processing is collected and processed. Proportionality is often most clearly explained through the expression "don't use a sledgehammer to crack a nut". In the case of "Digital Rights", the EUCJ Court annulled the 2006 Data Retention Directive, which allowed data to be stored for up to two years. It concluded that the measure breached proportionality on the grounds that the Directive had too sweeping a generality and therefore violated, inter alia, the basic right of data protection. The Court pointed out that access by the competent national authorities to the retained data was not made dependent on a prior review carried out by a court or by an independent administrative body whose decision sought to limit access to the data to what was strictly necessary for the purpose of attaining the objective pursued. Nor did it lay down a specific obligation on member states designed to establish such limits. The EU legislator had provided insufficient justification – it was simply not good enough from the perspective of EU fundamental rights protection. The EUCJ Court also annulled a pending Agreement between Canada and the EU on the transfer and processing of Passenger Name Record (PNR) data, citing that the agreement granted too sweeping a purpose of fighting terrorism without concrete justification in the individual case just simply a general concern of public security and without respecting private life and data protection and proportionality.

When evaluating these principles, the privacy leader should be asking the following types of questions:

- What is the lawful basis for processing? Does the processing achieve that purpose?
- Is there another way to achieve the same outcome? Do other ways provide effective solutions with less invasion of individual rights?
- How will function creep be prevented?
- How will data quality and data minimization be assured?
- For AI, how will bias be avoided and its use explained?
- What information will be provided to individuals?
- How will we help to support their rights?
- What measures do we take to ensure processors comply?
- How do we safeguard any international transfers?

THE RIGHT TO DATA PROTECTION NEEDS TO BE BALANCED AGAINST OTHER RIGHTS AND INTERESTS

Dr. Tim Walree

Assistant Professor, Radboud University, Nijmegen (NL)

Too often I (still) see in headlines that the GDPR restricts certain data use or sharing, leaving organizations unable to do their jobs properly. Unfortunately, I also see such statements regularly from commercial parties or government agencies. Apparently, there is a perception that the GDPR mostly prohibits data processing, and that not much is allowed with personal data. As a result, many organizations are afraid to share or use personal data, also prompted by the risk of fines, liability, or reputational damage. This fear may cause data controllers to avoid certain data processing activities, which in turn may lead to disruption of (crucial) business processes.

The perception that the GDPR mainly prohibits is incorrect. Actually, the GDPR grants a lot of room to process personal data if there is a good reason for doing so and if, of course, the data controller complies with the various obligations of the GDPR. And that is a good thing. After all, many data processing activities are necessary in our democratic and capitalistic society such as the data processing that takes place when ordering products online, paying taxes or doing scientific research. What must be kept in mind is that the right to data protection is not an absolute right. That implies that if this right "clashes" with other interests or rights, it must be weighed against them. If that other right prevails, it means there is a good reason for the data controller to process personal data.

It is essential to realize that the right to data protection is not an absolute right and interacts with other interests and rights. It enhances (business) opportunities and prevents unnecessary disruption of business processes. Furthermore, awareness of that interaction ensures that a data controller can make a better risk analysis, such as in a DPIA or in determining what security measures a data controller should take. If the data controller has a better view of the relevant interests, he is more capable of assessing the risks with respect to those interests and can also more accurately assess what mitigating measures he must take to minimize those risks.

A good example of the challenges with proportionality and necessity (and beyond) can be represented by the following hypothetical case example relating to an organization's proposed use of a biometric systems as an identification and authorization tool:

An organization may be considering the implementation of a biometric identification and authorization system which uses facial recognition together with a one-time passcode generator device. This enables the organization to provide secure access to their systems, with little admin overhead, and provides ease of use for the user. The alternative for the organization is to use a simpler two factor authentication such as mobile phone generated one time passcode and a password. However, the organization chooses to use the biometric system as it is far more effective and does not require anyone to remember passwords, and they want to reduce the resources required to admin password changes.

Seems reasonable right? Well, not under GDPR (and many other data protection regulations), as it presents (amongst others) several challenges with:

- The principles of proportionality and necessity. The Council of Europe recommends promoting proportionality when dealing with biometric data, notably by "1) limiting their evaluation, processing and storage to cases of clear necessity, namely when the gain in security clearly outweighs a possible interference with human rights and if the use of other, less intrusive techniques does not suffice; 2) providing individuals who are unable or unwilling to provide biometric data with alternative methods of identification and verification; (...)". CNIL for instance notes that "the constitution of a fingerprint database can only be admitted in particular circumstances where the identification of individuals is required by a pressing security need". Cases of "pressing security need" have further been interpreted as situations where a biometric system aims at controlling access to a "delineated area" representing a "major stake, which surpasses the strict interest of the organization". In simple terms, the use of sensitive data in this way can only be justified where the need to protect the organization's sensitive crown jewels (e.g., access to a pharmaceutical lab where multibillion research into a new life saving drug is being undertaken) may weigh heavier in the balance.

- The legal basis for processing: Biometric data used to uniquely identify individuals is considered a "special category" of personal data under the GDPR and as such requires not only a legal basis from Article 6, but also one from Article 9. In most cases, this will be "explicit consent" (except for public bodies, legal, or health purposes). But how can consent be fair when the employee-employer power relationship is imbalanced? Employees can be considered vulnerable individuals because of this imbalanced power dynamic, and therefore their consent is considered invalid. In Sweden, a school was fined 200,000 Krona (about €19,000) by the supervisory authority for processing biometric data for identification purposes. Further afield, related to the Illinois Biometric Information Privacy Act (BIPA), there was a case regarding the use of biometrics with employee data (Cothron v. White Castle System Inc.). The suit alleges that White Castle violated sections 15(b) and 15(d) of BIPA by using a system that required its employees to scan their fingerprints to access their pay stubs and computers, which led to the collection and disclosure of employees' biometric data without their consent and without providing the disclosures required under BIPA (since 2004!!). The Illinois Supreme Court in a landmark decision concluded that every individual scan or transmission of biometric data made without the proper disclosures and consent amounts to a separate violation of BIPA.

Finally, another hypothetical case example is the use of Automatic Number Plate Recognition (ANPR) applications by certain public authorities (e.g., city councils). *These public sector organizations are often mandated by statutory instruments to ensure that (for example) they can prosecute those who are illegal dumping in a particular area.* So, while the principle of necessity is met in this scenario, the authority must adequately describe how the principle of proportionality is also met. The use of this type of ANPR surveillance must have a DPIA given the invasion of individuals privacy, and a really good real-world example of a DPIA in this area is from the UK's National Police Chiefs' Council, who published their DPIA on the use of ANPR – link in suggested reading.

DATA DEFENSE AND COMPLIANCE WITH GLOBAL PRIVACY REGULATIONS

Roland Cloutier

Global Security and Risk Executive, The Business Protection Group

The increasing complexity of operational executives to adhere and ensure compliance with global privacy regulations has accelerated at breakneck speeds. From regional jurisdictional requirements within the United States on a state-by-state basis to the changing and evolving requirements specific to data and privacy in their European Union and aligned countries like the United Kingdom; executives at companies of every size that operates on a global platform must now ensure the survival of their business through the interpretation of law and quite often the successful application of technical controls. The assortment of privacy laws and the abundance of new data protection laws differ considerably across the globe. Some countries may align to the European model, while others create their own. From Brazil to South Korea to India, sovereign nations are ensuring the protection of their citizens through the applicability of laws that affect any business that touches their citizens data.

So, the obvious question is, how do companies adhere to so many different requirements and are they really all that different? The black and white answer to the latter is absolutely yes. From definitions about data, data residency, access, and all the other terms used in the legal realm to define and enforce these laws, each culture, country, and jurisdiction often has varying definitions and requirements that the legal community is charged with understanding and ensuring their businesses achieve compliance. But to the first question, on operational adherence to data and privacy regulations, organizations can begin their path forward by coalescing around the four basic questions that regulators are asking.

- Where is the data?
- Who has access to it?
- Where did it go?
- What is it being used for?

Now before we jump into the process of how organizations can begin to approach these questions, leaders must look at why they're being asked these questions, and in that define their approach to solving with a Common Core capability across all markets they operate in. You see, the question about "where is the data" may be just as simple as insuring companies have minimum due care on the protection of consumer data or perhaps, there may be a broader requirement in countries with strict data residency requirements. And the issues and reasons behind those may be as complex as the laws themselves. For instance, one country may be focused on the economic benefits of data localization and residency to ensure businesses that operate within their countries support their GDP through localized operations. Others may be solely focused on the protection of the privacy of their citizens and so each business for the appropriate reason must take a different approach to the required controls, enforcement, and industry oversight based on their specific issues.

This is why partnership within your organization between the Chief Privacy Officer, the Chief Data Officer, and the Chief Security Officer are critically important to accelerating not only the compliance that you may face but also in advancing your time to market and the monetization of the data you have or even your ability to serve different markets around the globe.

There are five basic components that organizations can coalesce around that are fundamental to answering the questions above that are the basic pillars of all data and privacy enforcement actions. The first of these is **Jurisdictional Mapping and Requirements Documentation**. Simply put, a) where am I doing business, b) whose data do I have, c) and what are the laws that we accountable to? Think of this as a map of sorts, that helps your partners within your legal organizations and your business unit leaders understand the complexity of how data moves, is used, and what your legal requirements may be around the globe. This is a fundamental document that is living and breathing that all interested parties in your company can utilize to ensure everyone is operating with the same information.

The second major component is **Data Transparency**. In the world of global business protection operations and in defense organizations around the globe there's a simple saying that states "if you can't see it, you can't protect it". There is a truism to that but even more importantly, when organizations have data or privacy incidents, they are often looked at through the eyes of "reasonable" and "due care". Data transparency provides the basic tenancies of due care through understanding data mapping, data use, data localization, and data flow. In most cases, each of these are major undertakings. However, as organizations get more mature and introduce privacy and security by design programs, these efforts become easier through earlier documentation of the product and technology building cycle, addressing and documenting these basic tenets of data defense.

The third component is probably the most transcendent across all global regulations and that is **Controls**. Now this chapter is not meant to be a deep dive into every potential control, rather a basic understanding of the criticality that controls have across different laws and your ability to implement and adhere to them. Controls come in all different types such as policy, technical, monitoring, audit, and many other flavors. The important fact is that every law requires your ability to apply controls to protect the information. As important to the controls themselves is your ability to create a standard set of controls utilized across the globe that enables you to be compliant in a cost-effective and measured manner. The critical part of course is understanding the spirit of the regulation and required controls and matching those to your catalog of controls you have created to manage your business's ability to enforce data lineage inclusive of location, access, and use.

The fourth component is actually a subcomponent of the third but is so important it stands on its own, which is Access. **Access** is a broad term, and it requires a broad understanding. These are just basic conditions of defending the environment which operates and manages your information itself like network access, data center access, administrative access. Then there's access to the systems themselves that manage and process data or manage the applications that interact with humans. And then of course there's the independent access of people to the data either structured or unstructured either directly to the data itself or through applications. And the complexity goes even further because identity and access aren't necessarily one in the same. Most organizations focus on "people's" access to data but often organizations find themselves in trouble because of machine access to data. And whether this is as complex as microservices enabling access to other microservices that provide data exchange or the replication of large data stores to other data stores it was not intended for, the results are often the same; Data assets exposed to machines or people for use they were never intended for. It is imperative for organizations to map out a strategic approach to access control and assurance that considers their information, their architecture, their technology, and the people that use it.

The 5th component Is a cross functional capability for organizations that supports controls assurance, process integrity, trust development, and authoritative management oversight. That component is **Evidence & Reporting**. Many organizations have made broad and bold control capability statements that were later proven untrue with closer analysis by internal and external entities. The basis of a good management framework involves a continuous assurance capability and a formalized lifecycle management of any operation; and it is no different with data defense and privacy compliance. Organizations should seek to have an overall capability that collects and provides data analytics on the controls in place to show that they are in fact operational and working as intended. Secondarily, they should be able to compile a multi-tier framework of reports that starts with reports focused on operations assurance, leadership oversight, management attestation, and industry or regulatory compliance validation. This fifth component is important because it does not matter what country or jurisdiction is requiring what control, rather that you have the ability to prove it, show it, and provide evidential material necessary to reduce unnecessary and costly legal and compliance issues that come from an organization's inability to prove their claims.

Although these appear to be broad brush requirements, they are truly foundational elements found in every regulatory consideration specific to data defense, access assurance, data integrity, and data privacy around the globe. Companies and Agencies should take the time to understand the complexity and impact these will have to their organization as they begin the path to achieving not only compliance, but an operationally effective capability to ensure long term success in client trust, brand integrity, and data monetization through the appropriate handling of data assets. Organizations should consider parallel paths and staged implementation of programs and projects to achieve their goals as there are some significant uphill battles on the way to success. Security, Compliance, and privacy leaders should not underestimate the extraordinary requirements and effort necessary to achieve the basics of finding the data, implementing access control, implementing data lineage programs, and instilling dynamic control capabilities that understand what type of data they have, how it should be protected, and where it should live. Those are the four of the most critical projects any organization will have to achieve operational success in this space, and in many cases, it will take years to achieve. Additionally, industry is still coming to grips with newer requirements and in critical areas such as data lineage technology. This market is still evolving, leaving companies with limited options.

Although daunting, there are some basic steps that will help companies start the path, drive alignment, deliver new capabilities, and become proficient in this new world of data defense and privacy compliance. The first is simply to **set a destination**. Easier said than done but by aligning the entirety of the organization on a framework, the components necessary to achieve the strategic business vision, and this success opportunity, you will create a focused business imperative that will be necessary at all levels of the organization to achieve this goal. This goal should not be set on compliance alone but should be focused on the success of the organization from a market perspective. Through aligning your program to the businesses ability to succeed or achieve their longtime goals, you will have broad partnership in making the necessary changes to the company, organizationally, and technologically that will ensure success.

Another incredibly important point is that you don't have to go this alone. Seek partners both internally and externally that understand your mission, can help you develop a reasonable implementation model, and help you implement it. This may be as simple as an executive oversight committee for data and privacy or an Internal task force on technology advances to support strategic business efforts. Externally, find partners that can help you develop and implement programs (not just technology) they have done this before in similar industries and in similarly size companies that can accelerate your time to delivery.

Finally begin your journey with the basics. You can start before any major business project is even approved through iterative and consistent addition to services your operational teams deliver such as data cataloging, data scanning, and information gathering on your digital environment, the data therein, and the infrastructure that manages it. Look at easy threat surface reduction opportunities such as removing duplicative data that is found in backups, copies, in unnecessary locations that only complicate your ability to comply. Often organizations can find that they reduce their net threat surface of data defense up to 65% by simply removing duplicative and unnecessary copies of information around their organization. Take the opportunity for your teams and organizational wins through the remediation of simple issues and technical problems you find along the way. Celebrate those, highlight your organization's ability to overcome, and when bigger problems arise your team, company, and partners will have the confidence to push forward and achieve true data defense in global privacy compliance.

Privacy by Design (PbD)

Privacy by Design incorporates privacy into projects and data compliance activities keeping privacy in mind from the beginning of the effort. Too many times organizations are reactive and add on privacy in the back end, resulting in added unnecessary cost. The concept was developed in the 1990s by Ann Cavoukian, Ph.D., who was then serving as the Information and Privacy Commissioner in Ontario, Canada. Seven foundational principles were developed to address the impact of growing information systems and communication systems, recognizing that the privacy of information could not be adequately protected by implementing compliance activities focused on regulatory frameworks alone. Instead, privacy needed to be a way of doing business if it was to succeed. Privacy by Design incorporates information technology systems, accountable business practices, and physical design and network infrastructure. The principles may be applied to all types of information, however particular care should be taken with sensitive information such as healthcare and financial information. Privacy by Design principles provide a pathway for organizations to exercise control over the information under their control.

The Privacy by Design principles may have been first introduced several decades ago, so the focus was on IT systems and their infrastructures; however, the same principles can be applied today to Big Data, proliferation of mobile devices, Internet of Things (IoT), cloud storage across borders, etc., where there is a need to ensure privacy of the data contained within these applications and platforms.

The annual assembly of International Data Protection and Privacy Commissioners gathered in Jerusalem, Israel in October 2010, and unanimously approved a resolution recognizing Privacy by Design as a fundamental component of privacy protection. What did this mean? The adoption of the principles should be encouraged as part of an organization's default mode of operation and invited the Data Protection Authorities and Privacy Commissions to promote the incorporation of the seven principles into privacy policies and legislation and encouraging research into furthering Privacy by Design. Subsequently, the US Federal Trade Commission recognized Privacy by Design in 2012 as one of three practices for protecting online privacy, in addition to Simplified Choice for Business and Consumers (permitting users to make choices about their data at a relevant time and context), and Greater Transparency (pertaining to data collection and use). These principles have been translated into over 40 languages.

Privacy by Design principles have been built into GDPR, in Article 25. In this way, GDPR specifically calls out PbDs second principle of "privacy by default" – and combines it so that we have data protection by design and by default DPbDD. Essentially the default element implies that privacy is the default position and that a consumer can make something "unprivate", but that by default it must be configured with privacy settings configured as default. It also means that an organization must implement appropriate technical and organizational measures for ensuring that, *by default*, only personal data which are necessary for each specific purpose of the processing are processed.

In February 2023, PbD also became an international privacy standard for the protection of consumer products and services known as ISO 31700. ISO 31700 provides high-level requirements and recommendations for organizations that use PbD in the development, maintenance and operation of consumer goods and services, and includes general guidance on

- designing capabilities to enable consumers to enforce their privacy rights,
- assigning relevant roles and authorities,
- providing privacy information to consumers,
- conducting privacy risk assessments,
- establishing and documenting requirements for privacy controls,
- how to design privacy controls,
- lifecycle data management and preparation and
- managing a data breach.

The seven Privacy by Design (PBD) principles

These principles, when part of the general operation of a business, in other words, when thoughtfully evaluated when designing new products and services and conducting daily operations, should reduce the number of issues resulting from lack of privacy and should also go a long way toward remaining compliant with the emerging regulations. The Privacy by Design foundational requirements are illustrated in Figure 7.1.

1. **Proactive not Reactive; Preventative not Remedial.** The Privacy by Design approach is characterized by proactive rather than reactive measures. It anticipates and prevents privacy invasive events before they happen. Privacy by Design does not wait for privacy risks to materialize, nor does it offer remedies for resolving privacy infractions

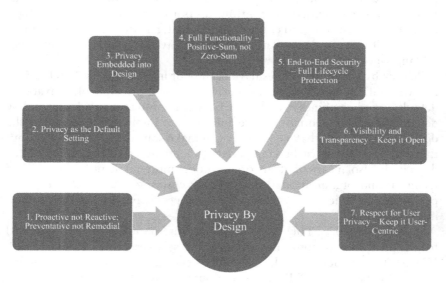

Figure 7.1 Privacy by Design principles.

once they have occurred – it aims to prevent them from occurring. In short, Privacy by Design comes before-the-fact, not after.

2. *Privacy as the Default Setting.* We can all be certain of one thing – the default rules! Privacy by Design seeks to deliver the maximum degree of privacy by ensuring that personal data are automatically protected in any given IT system or business practice. If an individual does nothing, their privacy remains intact. No action is required on the part of the individual to protect their privacy – it is built into the system, by default.

3. *Privacy Embedded into Design.* Privacy by Design is embedded into the design and architecture of IT systems and business practices. It is not bolted on as an add-on, after the fact. The result is that privacy becomes an essential component of the core functionality being delivered. Privacy is integral to the system, without diminishing functionality.

4. *Full Functionality – Positive-Sum, not Zero-Sum.* Privacy by Design seeks to accommodate all legitimate interests and objectives in a positive-sum win-win manner, not through a dated, zero-sum approach, where unnecessary trade-offs are made. Privacy by Design avoids the pretense of false dichotomies, such as privacy vs. security – demonstrating that it is possible to have both.

5. *End-to-End Security – Full Lifecycle Protection.* Privacy by Design, having been embedded into the system prior to the first element of information being collected, extends securely throughout the entire lifecycle of the data involved – strong security measures are essential to privacy, from start to finish. This ensures that all data are securely retained, and then securely destroyed at the end of the process, in a timely fashion. Thus, Privacy by Design ensures cradle-to-grave, secure lifecycle management of information end-to-end.

6. *Visibility and Transparency – Keep it Open.* Privacy by Design seeks to assure all stakeholders that whatever the business practice or technology involved, it is in fact, operating according to the stated promises and objectives, subject to independent verification. Its component parts and operations remain visible and transparent to users and providers alike. Remember, trust, but verify.

7. *Respect for User Privacy – Keep it User-Centric.* Above all, Privacy by Design requires architects and operators to protect the interests of the individual by offering such measures as strong privacy defaults, appropriate notice, and empowering user-friendly options. Keep it user centric.

By embracing these principles, there is increased possibility that information will be sufficiently collected, used, and stored in a manner as designed. This should give a competitive advantage to those organizations embedding trust in privacy practices, as well as gaining some efficiencies by not requiring the bolt-on to existing processes. Many organizations today are scrambling to meet regulatory privacy requirements, as privacy controls were not designed into the applications sufficiently to begin with.

LEAD WITH PRIVACY BY DESIGN AND GAIN A COMPETITIVE ADVANTAGE

Dr. Ann Cavoukian

Executive Director, Global Privacy & Security by Design Centre

We are witnessing massive technological changes in all things connected. The creation of digital information is accelerating and attaining near immortality on the Internet. We know the value of personal information has increased – that it is being sold to others for profit and for purposes not always known to the individual. Its value also makes it a target for attack vectors. The explosion of social media has revived the "end of privacy" chants. What I submit without question is that there is little evidence to change our view that privacy remains a valued social norm. Privacy relates to freedom of choice and personal control in the sphere of one's personal information – choices regarding what information you wish to share and, perhaps more important, information you may not wish to share with others. What has changed, however, is the means by which personal information is now readily exchanged. I admit that these trends carry profound implications for privacy, but we cannot give up. We need to change the paradigm – Privacy by Design is becoming essential to preserving our privacy now, and well into the future. From a privacy perspective, ICTs start off as being neutral. What matters are the choices made in their design and use – technologies may be designed to be privacy-invasive or privacy-enhancing. The framework of "Privacy by Design", that I developed in the late 1990s, emphasizes the need to embed privacy, proactively, at the design stages of information technologies, architectures, and systems. It highlights respect for user privacy and the need to embed privacy as the default setting. It also preserves a commitment to functionality in a doubly enabling "win-win" manner or positive-sum strategy. This approach transforms consumer privacy issues from a pure policy or compliance issue into a business imperative. Organizations that proactively embed privacy into the design of their operations will benefit in a number of sustainable ways from the resulting "privacy payoff". Gain a competitive advantage by leading with Privacy by Design.

Operationalizing Privacy by Design and Default

The EDPS provides a set of guidelines on operationalizing Privacy by Design and Default into an organization's processing operations, and we summarize these in Table 7.1.

Table 7.1 Key design elements of Privacy by Design and by Default

Transparency: Key design and default elements for the principle of transparency may include:	
Clarity	Information shall be in clear and plain language, concise, and intelligible.
Semantics	Communication should have a clear meaning to the audience in question.
Accessibility	Information shall be easily accessible for the data subject.
Contextual	Information should be provided at the relevant time and in the appropriate form.
Relevance	Information should be relevant and applicable to the specific data subject.
Universal design	Information shall be accessible to all data subjects, include use of machine-readable languages to facilitate, and automate readability and clarity.
Comprehensible	Data subjects should have a fair understanding of what they can expect with regard to the processing of their personal data, particularly when the data subjects are children or other vulnerable groups.
Multi-channel	Information should be provided in different channels and media, not only the textual, to increase the probability for the information to effectively reach the data subject.
Layered	Information should be layered in a manner that resolves the tension between completeness and understanding, while accounting for data subjects' reasonable expectations.
Lawfulness: Key design and default elements for lawfulness may include:	
Relevance	The correct legal basis shall be applied to the processing.
Differentiation	The legal basis used for each processing activity shall be differentiated.
Specified purpose	The appropriate legal basis must be clearly connected to the specific purpose of processing.
Necessity	Processing must be necessary and unconditional for the purpose to be lawful.
Autonomy	The data subject should be granted the highest degree of autonomy as possible with respect to control over personal data within the frames of the legal basis.
Gaining consent	Consent must be freely given, specific, informed, and unambiguous. Particular consideration should be given to the capacity of children and young people to provide informed consent.

(Continued)

Table 7.1 (Continued)

Consent withdrawal	Where consent is the legal basis, the processing should facilitate withdrawal of consent. Withdrawal shall be as easy as giving consent. If not, then the consent mechanism of the controller does not comply with the GDPR.
Balancing of interests	Where legitimate interest is the legal basis, the controller must carry out a weighted balancing of interest, giving particular consideration to the power imbalance, specifically children under the age of 18 and other vulnerable groups. There shall be measures and safeguards to mitigate the negative impact on the data subjects.
Predetermination	The legal basis shall be established before the processing takes place.
Cessation	If the legal basis ceases to apply, the processing shall cease accordingly.
Adjust	If there is a valid change of legal basis for the processing, the actual processing must be adjusted in accordance with the new legal basis.
Allocation of responsibility	Whenever joint controllership is envisaged, the parties must apportion in a clear and transparent way their respective responsibilities vis à the data subject, and design the measures of the processing in accordance with this allocation.
Fairness: Key design and default fairness elements may include:	
Autonomy	Data subjects should be granted the highest degree of autonomy possible to determine the use of their personal data, as well as over the scope and conditions of use or processing.
Interaction	Data subjects must be able to communicate and exercise their rights in respect of the personal data processed by the controller.
Expectation	Processing should correspond to data subjects' reasonable expectations.
Non discrimination	The controller shall not unfairly discriminate against data subjects.
Non exploitation	The controller should not exploit the needs or vulnerabilities of data subjects.
Consumer choice	The controller should not "lock in" their users in an unfair manner. Whenever a service processing personal data is proprietary, it may create a lock in to the service, which may not be fair, if it impairs the data subjects' possibility to exercise their right of data portability in accordance with Article 20.
Power balance	Power balance should be a key objective of the controller data subject relationship. Power imbalances should be avoided. When this is not possible, they should be recognized and accounted for with suitable countermeasures.
No risk transfer	Controllers should not transfer the risks of the enterprise to the data subjects.
No deception	Data processing information and options should be provided in an objective and neutral way, avoiding any deceptive or manipulative language or design.

Table 7.1 (Continued)

Respect rights	The controller must respect the fundamental rights of data subjects and implement appropriate measures and safeguards and not impinge on those rights unless expressly justified by law.
Ethical	The controller should see the processing's wider impact on individuals' rights and dignity.
Truthful	The controller must make available information about how they process personal data, they should act as they declare they will and not mislead the data subjects.
Human intervention	The controller must incorporate *qualified* human intervention that is capable of uncovering biases that machines may create in accordance with the right to not be subject to automated individual decision-making in Article 22.

Purpose Limitation: Key design and default purpose limitation elements may include:

Predetermination	The legitimate purposes shall be determined before the design of the processing.
Specificity	The purposes shall be specified and explicit as to why personal data is being processed.
Purpose orientation	The purpose of processing should guide the design of the processing and set processing boundaries.
Necessity	The purpose determines what personal data is necessary for the processing.
Compatibility	Any new purpose must be compatible with the original purpose for which the data was collected and guide relevant changes in design.
Limit further processing	The controller should not connect datasets or perform any further processing for new incompatible purposes.
Limitations of reuse	The controller should use technical measures, including hashing and encryption, to limit the possibility of repurposing personal data. The controller should also have organizational measures, such as policies and contractual obligations, which limit the reuse of personal data.
Review	The controller should regularly review whether the processing is necessary for the purposes for which the data was collected and test the design against purpose limitation.

Data Minimization: Key design and default data minimization elements may include:

Data avoidance	Avoid processing personal data altogether when this is possible for the relevant purpose.
Limitation	Limit the amount of personal data collected to what is necessary for the purpose.
Access limitation	Shape the data processing in a way that a minimal number of people need access to personal data to perform their duties and limit access accordingly.
Relevance	Personal data should be relevant to the processing in question, and the controller should be able to demonstrate this relevance.

(Continued)

Table 7.1 (Continued)

Necessity	Each personal data category shall be necessary for the specified purposes and should only be processed if it is not possible to fulfil the purpose by other means.
Aggregation	Use aggregated data when possible.
Pseudonymization	Pseudonymize personal data as soon as it is no longer necessary to have directly identifiable personal data and store identification keys separately.
Anonymization and deletion	Where personal data is not, or no longer necessary for the purpose, personal data shall be anonymized or deleted.
Data flow	The data flow should be made efficient enough to not create more copies than necessary.
"State of the art"	The controller should apply up to date and appropriate technologies for data avoidance and minimization.

Accuracy: Key design and default accuracy elements may include:

Data source	Sources of personal data should be reliable in terms of data accuracy.
Degree of accuracy	Each personal data element should be as accurate as necessary for the specified purposes.
Measurably accurate	Reduce the number of false positives/negatives, for example, biases in automated decisions and artificial intelligence.
Verification	Depending on the nature of the data, in relation to how often it may change, the controller should verify the correctness of personal data with the data subject before and at different stages of the processing (e.g., to age requirements).
Erasure/ rectification	The controller shall erase or rectify inaccurate data without delay. The controller shall in particular facilitate this where the data subjects are or were children and later want to remove such personal data.
Error propagation avoidance	Controllers should mitigate the effect of an accumulated error in the processing chain.
Access	Data subjects should be given information about and effective access to personal data in accordance with the GDPR articles 12 to 15 in order to control accuracy and rectify as needed.
Continued accuracy	Personal data should be accurate at all stages of the processing, and tests of accuracy should be carried out at critical steps.
Up to date	Personal data shall be updated if necessary for the purpose.
Data design	Use of technological and organizational design features to decrease inaccuracy, for example, present concise predetermined choices instead of free text fields.

Storage limitation: Key design and default storage limitation elements may include

Deletion and anonymization	The controller should have clear internal procedures and functionalities for deletion and/or anonymization.
Effectiveness of anonymization/ deletion	The controller shall make sure that it is not possible to re-identify anonymized data or recover deleted data, and should test whether this is possible.
Automation	Deletion of certain personal data should be automated.

Table 7.1 (Continued)

Storage criteria	The controller shall determine what data and length of storage is necessary for the purpose.
Justification	The controller shall be able to justify why the period of storage is necessary for the purpose and the personal data in question, and be able to disclose the rationale behind, and legal grounds for the retention period.
Enforcement of retention policies	The controller should enforce internal retention policies and conduct tests of whether the organization practices its policies.
Backups/logs	Controllers shall determine what personal data and length of storage is necessary for backups and logs.
Data flow	Controllers should beware of the flow of personal data, and the storage of any copies thereof, and seek to limit their "temporary" storage.

Integrity/Confidentiality: Key design and default integrity/confidentiality elements may include:

Information security management system (ISMS)	Have an operative means of managing policies and procedures for information security.
Risk analysis	Assess the risks against the security of personal data by considering the impact on individuals' rights and counter-identified risks. For use in risk assessment; develop and maintain a comprehensive, systematic and realistic "threat modelling" and an attack surface analysis of the designed software to reduce attack vectors and opportunities to exploit weak points and vulnerabilities.
Security by design	Consider security requirements as early as possible in the system design and development and continuously integrate and perform relevant tests.
Maintenance	Regular review and test software, hardware, systems and services, etc. to uncover vulnerabilities of the systems supporting the processing.
Access control management	Only the authorized personnel who need should have access to the personal data necessary for their processing tasks, and the controller should differentiate between access privileges of authorized personnel.
Access limitation (agents)	Shape the data processing in a way that a minimal number of people need access to personal data to perform their duties and limit access accordingly.
Access limitation (content)	In the context of each processing operation, limit access to only those attributes per data set that are needed to perform that operation. Moreover, limit access to data pertaining to those data subjects who are in the remit of the respective employee.
Access segregation	Shape the data processing in a way that no individual needs comprehensive access to all data collected about a data subject, much less all personal data of a particular category of data subjects.

(Continued)

Table 7.1 (Continued)

Secure transfers	Transfers shall be secured against unauthorized and accidental access/changes.
Secure storage	Data storage shall be secure from unauthorized access and changes. There should be procedures to assess the risk of centralized or decentralized storage, and what categories of personal data this applies to. Some data may need additional security measures than others or isolation from others.
Pseudonymization	Personal data and backups/logs should be pseudonymized as a security measure to minimize risks of potential data breaches, e.g., using hashing or encryption.
Backups/logs	Keep backups and logs to the extent necessary for information security, use audit trails and event monitoring as a routine security control. These shall be protected from unauthorized and accidental access and change and reviewed regularly and incidents should be handled promptly.
Disaster recovery/ business continuity	Address information system disaster recovery and business continuity requirements to restore availability of personal data following up major incidents.
Protection according to risk	All categories of personal data should be protected with measures adequate with respect to the risk of a security breach. Data presenting special risks should, when possible, be kept separated from the rest of the personal data.
Security incident response management	Have in place routines, procedures, and resources to detect, contain, handle, report, and learn from data breaches
Incident management	Controller should have processes in place to handle breaches and incidents, in order to make the processing system more robust. This includes notification procedures, such as management of notification (to the supervisory authority) and information (to data subjects).

Source: EDPS.

Enforcement, redress and recourse

The core principles of privacy protection can only be effective if there is a mechanism in place to enforce them, together with self-regulation regimes and recourse. Absent an enforcement and redress mechanism, a privacy code such as FIPPs is merely suggestive rather than prescriptive and does not ensure compliance with core privacy principles. Among the alternative enforcement approaches are industry self-regulation; legislation that would create private remedies for consumers; and/or regulatory schemes enforceable through civil and criminal sanctions.

- Industry Self-Regulation
  To be effective, self-regulatory regimes should include both mechanisms to ensure compliance (enforcement) and appropriate means of

recourse by injured parties (redress). Mechanisms to ensure compliance include making acceptance of and compliance with a code of fair information practices a condition of membership in an industry association audits to verify compliance; and certification of entities that have adopted and comply with the code at issue.

Appropriate means of individual redress include, at a minimum, institutional mechanisms to ensure that consumers have a simple and effective way to have their concerns addressed. Thus, a self-regulatory system should provide a means to investigate complaints from individual consumers and ensure that consumers are aware of how to access such a system.

If the self-regulatory code has been breached, consumers should have a remedy for the violation. Such a remedy can include both the righting of the wrong (e.g., correction of any misinformation, cessation of unfair practices) and compensation for any harm suffered by the consumer. Monetary sanctions would serve both to compensate the victim of unfair practices and as an incentive for industry compliance. Industry codes can provide alternative dispute resolution mechanisms for appropriate compensation.

The most famous self-regulation codes were Safe Harbor, followed by Privacy Shield, followed by the US-EU Transatlantic Data Privacy Framework. Notably, privacy shield was invalidated based on a shortfall in both these mechanisms – enforcement and redress.

- Private Remedies
  A statutory scheme could create private rights of action for consumers harmed by an entity's unfair information practices. Several of the major information practice codes, including the seminal 1973 HEW Report, call for implementing legislation. The creation of private remedies would help create strong incentives for entities to adopt and implement fair information practices and ensure compensation for individuals harmed by misuse of their personal information. Important questions would need to be addressed in such legislation, for example, the definition of unfair information practices; the availability of compensatory, liquidated and/or punitive damages; and the elements of any such cause of action.

- Government Enforcement
  Finally, government enforcement of privacy, by means of civil or criminal penalties, is a third means of enforcement. Fair information practice codes have called for some government enforcement, leaving open the question of the scope and extent of such powers. Whether enforcement is civil or criminal will likely depend on the nature of the data at issue and the violation committed.

US ARMY, ESQ: PRACTICAL TIPS FOR WORKING WITH GENERAL COUNSEL

Colonel (Retired) Lawrence D. Dietz

General Counsel, TAL Global Corporation

The Chief Privacy Officer (CPO) and General Counsel (GC) are natural allies. Each has skills and knowledge that complements the other. The role of GC is to identify and anticipate legal issues. GC can help CPOs by helping them understand legal issues and potential liabilities, particularly when dealing with data breaches and privacy issues where there can be dire legal consequences.

A good example of where the CPO needs to work with GC is in the area of data breach, for example, California requires disclosure when the organization discovers a breach, given notice or where there is reasonable belief that an encryption key or security credential securing PII has been breached <u>Cal Civ Code § 1798.82(a)</u>. Massachusetts, on the other hand, requires disclosure when the entity (1) knows or has reason to know of a breach of security or (2) knows or has reason to know that the personal information of an affected resident of the Commonwealth of Massachusetts was acquired or used by an unauthorized person or used for an unauthorized purpose. <u>Mass. Ann. Laws Ch. 93H, § 3(b)</u>.

The GC provides legal expertise to understand the law while the CPO helps the GC understand what the entity is doing to ensure that compliance. The CPO needs to work with GC to ensure that compliance is achieved in spite of confusing and conflicting laws.

However, bear in mind that GC is the company's lawyer, not the CPO's lawyer. This means that GC's duty is to take all actions necessary to protect the company and minimize its legal liability. This duty does not mean to protect the CPO from personal liability – either civil or criminal.

Here are some practical tips for a successful relationship.

1. Be sure that you understand what data you have, how it is protected, and your mechanisms for triggering an analysis if breach disclosure notice is required.
2. Have a clear understanding of what jurisdictions are involved, both domestic and international.
3. If you think you may be personally liable in any way, retain your own counsel.

Early privacy laws

Entick vs. Carrington (1765)

In the 1765 English case of Entick vs. Carrington involved the principle that the prerogative powers of the monarch were subordinate to the law of the land. This assured that government officials could not exercise power unless there was a law authorizing the activity. The government suspected that Entick was writing derogatory material against the majesty and about both houses of the Parliament. A warrant was created, and Carrington and three others broke into Entick's house with force of arms and against his will, spending more than four hours looking at his personal papers and causing damage to his property. Documents were also removed, Entick latter sued, and Lord Camden found the defendants liable, stating,

> if this is law it would be in our books, but no such law ever existed in this country; our law holds the property of every man so sacred, that no man can set foot upon his neighbors close without his leave.

William Pitt echoed this response in his 1763 speech on the excise bill, very eloquently by stating,

> the poorest man may in his cottage bid defiance to all the force of the Crown. It may be frail; its roof may shake; the wind may blow through it; the storms may enter, the rain may enter, – but the King of England cannot enter; all his forces dare not cross the threshold of the ruined tenement!

These early ideas of privacy within our homes having the protection from outsiders gave rise to privacy laws and the separation between the Executive and Legislative branches of government to ensure that there was an existing law of the land decided before an executive of the law could act.

Warren and Brandeis (1890)

Regarded as the publication in the United States positing privacy rights, Samuel Warren and Louis Brandeis wrote a paper called the "Right to Privacy" published in the 1890 Harvard Law Review. In the paper, "recent inventions and business methods" were called out as a threat to the "right to be left alone". What were these "recent inventions and business methods?" These were referred to in the paper as the "instantaneous photographs and newspaper enterprise have invaded the sacred precincts of private and domestic life; and numerous mechanical devices threaten to make good the prediction that 'what is whispered in the closet shall be proclaimed from the housetops'". Warren and Brandeis were alluding to the invention of the camera and the use by the newspapers to publish photos! In the past, there were the "gossip columns" whereby gossip could be printed, however it was subject to someone's belief that it happened. With the camera, it would be difficult to refute the "evidence". We can see similarities with the discussions today with widespread availability of cameras and video recording capabilities in smartphones. Brandeis and Warren felt that individuals had "the right to be left alone".

In the paper, the protections for privacy are best stated by,

> ...the design of the law must be to protect those persons with whose affairs the community has no legitimate concern, from being dragged into an undesirable and undesired publicity and to protect all persons, whatsoever; their position or station, from having matters which they may properly prefer to keep private, made public against their will. It is the unwarranted invasion of individual privacy, which is reprehended, and to be, so far as possible, prevented.

This provides for the protection of all individuals from libel and slander.

Louis Brandeis served as an associate justice of the Supreme Court of the United States from 1916 to 1939. Louis was born in Louisville Kentucky in 1856. It is interesting how the introduction of new technology (cameras) brought about concerns over privacy, and over the years, introduction of new technology continuously re-energizes the focus on privacy as more information is collected, aggregated, and reviewed for appropriate use – all protecting the fundamental human rights of the individual for protection.

1948 article 12 of universal declaration of rights

In December 1948, the General Assembly of the United Nations adopted the Universal Declaration of Human rights to address,

> ...disregard and contempt for human rights have resulted in barbarous acts which have outraged the conscience of mankind, and the advent of a world in which human beings shall enjoy freedom of speech and belief and freedom from fear and want has been proclaimed as the highest aspiration of the common people.

The declaration provides for a right to private life in Article 12 stating, "No one shall be subjected to arbitrary interference with his privacy, family, home or correspondence, nor to attacks upon his honor and reputation. Everyone has the right to protection of the law against such interference or attacks".

The right to freedom is expressed in Article 19 as follows, "Everyone has a right to freedom of opinion and expression; this right includes freedom to hold opinions without interference and to seek, receive and impart information and ideas through any media and regardless of frontiers".

The individual rights articulated in Article 19 are not absolute, with constraints clarified in Article 29(2) stating,

> In the exercise of his rights and freedoms, everyone shall be subject only to such limitations as are determined by law solely for the purpose of securing due recognition and respect for the rights and freedoms of others and of meeting the just requirements of morality, public order, and the general welfare in a democratic society.

In other words, individuals have a right to their privacy and reputation, as well as the right to freely express their ideas, provided that existing laws and morality are followed by expressing these opinions.

1950 European Convention on Human Rights

The Council of Europe, in Rome, invited the individual European states to enter into an agreement known as the European Convention on Human Rights (ECHR), which among other provisions, provides for "respect for private and family life" in Article 8, like Article 12 of the Universal Declaration of Rights, but with the added enforcement by the European Court of Human Rights. These provisions protect the rights of citizens to maintain the privacy of their personal information.

First modern data protection/privacy laws

1970 Fair Credit Reporting Act

The 1970 Fair Credit Reporting Act, addressing the collection and processing of information related to consumer credit, is the first national law passed regarding privacy in the United States in response to the growing technological capabilities provided by the growth of mainframe computers in the 1960s and concern over surveillance activities. During the same year, the German state of Hesse enacted the first modern data protection law, a regional law, in part to prevent personal abuse during Hitler's Third Reich, particularly with the increased collection of personal information. Several European countries started putting data protection laws in place during this period. Sweden subsequently created the first European national data protection law in 1973; however, much energy toward privacy did not occur until the 1980s.

1974 US Privacy Act

The Privacy Act provides restrictions on the Federal Government in the collection, maintenance and use of the information collected on individuals. The Act provides protection from disclosure of information that is defined within a defined "record set". Information cannot be released unless it was specifically requested by a court and with an individual's express consent. While the Health Insurance Portability and Accountability Act of 1996 (HIPAA) provided protections for the release of healthcare information, for information contained within government systems such as Medicare and Medicaid, the release of information was already protected by the Privacy Act of 1974. The attempts to provide a balance between the Federal government's need to collect information to go about their business and at the same time does not collect so much information or release information that constitutes an invasion of privacy. From a historical perspective, the act was born during the aftermath of Watergate, where information was collected on individuals related to the Watergate scandal. Also, with the interconnectivity between systems and networks in the 1970s and the subsequent introduction of the PC that followed the Act in the early 1980s, there was concern over the potential aggregation of information using a single identifier, such as the social security number. The act established fair information practices by placing some structure on how agencies managed their records, provided individuals with increased access to the records held by Federal agencies, provided the means to amend records that were not accurate, relevant, timely, or complete and restricted their disclosure to appropriate individuals.

Late 1970s European data protection laws

Sweden introduced the first national data protection laws in 1973, followed by Germany in 1977 and France in 1978. These laws were introduced both in response to surveillance regimes imposed by the state (Germany) and as an expression of a strong privacy culture (France and Sweden). In May 1975, the European Parliament adopted a resolution on the rights of individuals to data protection, stating that the protection of these rights was a responsibility of the Member States. By 1979, data protection laws were established across Europe in seven member states (Austria, Denmark, France, Federal Republic of Germany, Luxembourg, Norway, and Sweden). Three countries (Spain, Portugal, and Austria) specified privacy rights within their constitution.

1980 Organization for Economic Cooperation and Development (OECD)

The Organization for Economic Cooperation and Development (OECD), established in 1948, is an international organization that originally included the United states and European countries, but has expanded to include Australia, Austria, Belgium, Canada, Chile, the Czech Republic, Denmark, Estonia, Finland, France, Germany, Greece, Hungary, Iceland, Ireland, Israel, Italy, Japan, Korea, Luxembourg, Mexico, the Netherlands, New Zealand,

Norway, Poland, Portugal, the Slovak Republic, Slovenia, Spain, Sweden, Switzerland, Turkey, the United Kingdom and the United States, along with European Union participation. The OECD provides the opportunity for countries to discuss issues such as the economic, social, and environmental challenges of operating in a global environment, with representation of 39 countries accounting for 80% of the world trade and investment.

The OECD most notably created the most widely known framework for establishing fair means of transferring and handling information. In 1980, the OECD published a set of guidelines entitled, "Guidelines Governing the Protection of Privacy and Transborder Data Flows of Personal Data". The guidelines contained eight principles standing the test of time to provide a privacy framework leveraged in the construction of many privacy laws (explained later in this chapter). While the definitions of what is personal data may vary by country and regulation, the definition offered by the OECD in 1980 specified personal data as "any information relating to an identified or identifiable individual (data subject)", which was left unrevised in the 2013 OECD modification, a testimony to the thoughtful privacy thinking at the time.

The OECD guidelines were not changed for several decades, until 2013 in response to a document released entitled, "2008 Seoul Declaration for the Future of the Internet Economy" articulating the need for revision due to changing technologies, market and user behavior, and the growing importance of digital identities. The environment where privacy principles worked in the past had changed significantly (note the 1980 principles pre-dated the general population use of the Internet and the existence of the World Wide Web as we know it today, along with other technical advances, and pre-dated the CPO and CISO roles). Attributes such as the volume of information processed, used, and stored had increased; a wider range of analytics provided insights; value of the information increased; threats to privacy increased; the number and variety of actors capable of putting privacy at risk changed; substantial changes in the complexity and frequency of interaction of personal data that individuals were expected to comprehend were all factors contributing to the need to revisit the guidelines.

As part of the revision, the OECD Guideline 2013 revision focused on risk management and global interoperability when considering privacy issues. New concepts were also introduced including the strategic importance of national privacy strategies, implementation of privacy management programs, data security breach notification, strengthening privacy enforcement, and defining what it means to be regarded as an accountable organization. For example, the OECD revision included specific guidance in the 2013 version to articulate how to implement accountability as follows: "A data controller should: a) Have in place a privacy management program that: 1) gives effect to these guidelines for all personal data under its control; 2) is tailored to the structure, scale, volume, and sensitivity of its operations; 3) provides appropriate safeguards based on privacy risk assessment; 4) is integrated into its governance structure and establishes internal oversight mechanisms; 5) includes plans for responding to inquiries and incidents; 6) is updated in light of ongoing monitoring and periodic assessment. b) Be prepared to demonstrate its privacy management program as appropriate, in particular at the request of a competent privacy enforcement authority or another entity responsible for promoting adherence to a code of conduct or similar arrangement giving binding effect to these guidelines. and c) Provide notice, as appropriate, to privacy enforcement authorities or other relevant authorities where there has been a significant breach affecting personal data. Where the breach is likely to adversely affect data subjects, a data controller should notify the affected data subjects. This revision enabled measurement of whether the organization has acted in an accountable manner with respect to privacy.

1990s–2000s privacy laws

Multiple laws were emerging in the United States in the late 1990s modelling some of the fair information practices evident in the European Data Directive. Laws were created on a "sectoral" basis, aligning to individual industry verticals vs the "comprehensive" law within Europe, which was more broad-based by focusing on the flow of information between the member states. This approach resulted in many different laws regarding privacy. Laws were developed to apply to the private sector (not for profit and commercial business entities) and the public sector for US government agencies. Some key laws developed during this time were revisions to the Fair Credit Reporting Act (FCRA) including extending the powers of the Federal Trade Commission (FTC) to levy fines for violations of the act (1996): Children's Online Privacy Protection Rule (COPPA); Gramm-Leach-Bliley Financial Privacy Rule went into effect (2000); First Data Security Case with FTC vs Eli Lilly & Company for disclosing 669 names of Prozac patients in an email shutting down a website (2002); CAN-SPAM Rule goes into effect (2004).

The subsequent sections present a brief synopsis of some of the key laws that have driven privacy in recent years, as well as some of the high-level controls that are required. These sections should be regarded as an executive guide to the laws impacting privacy decisions. Many times, individuals are working within their own vertical industry and are unaware of the laws, regulations, control frameworks, and standards that are being discussed in other industries. Each of the laws has a specific purpose, genealogy and differences with other standards, but after working with these different laws, it is also clear that by following a consistent framework, whether it be ISO27001/27701, NIST Privacy Framework, or some other framework, there are requirements in these frameworks which if followed, would more than likely satisfy the law or regulation in most cases. This is since many of these laws and regulations are grounded in privacy and data protection principles to begin with and it should be no surprise that these requirements are presented within the regulation. The difference will typically be that the control framework will be more prescriptive and granular than the higher-level law to permit changes in technology, as articulated earlier.

Electronic Communications Privacy Act of 1986 (ECPA)

The ECPA (Public Law 99-508), also known as the "Wiretap Act", was passed by Congress to extend the protections of the wiretap law to electronic communication forms, such as email, text, video, audio, and data. Under the law, messages may not be intercepted in transmission or in stored form while in transit. Law enforcement would need to obtain a court order to obtain information such as account activity logs showing the IP addresses that were visited by a subscriber of Internet services or the email addresses from whom the subscriber exchanged emails. Law enforcement can also obtain a court order to compel cellular phone companies to provide records showing the cell phone location information for calls made from a person's cell phone. To increase the foreign intelligence gathering activities after the events of 9/11, the US Patriot Act was made law by President George W. Bush on October 26, 2001. The US Patriot Act weakened the restrictions and increased law enforcement's ability to obtain telephone, e-mail communications, and records such as medical and financial. For example, a search warrant could be issued for voicemail communications, bypassing the more stringent Wiretap Act. In subsequent years, this ability came under fire in privacy circles for being able to obtain this information.

Gramm-Leach-Bliley Act (GLBA)

Public Law 106-102, also known as the Financial Services Act, was enacted on November 12, 1999, repealed part of the Glass-Steagall Act of 1933 and provided the ability for banks to function as an investment bank, commercial bank, and insurance company. The act also provided the Financial Privacy Rule, which permitted individuals to opt-out of having their information shared with unaffiliated parties. The policy needed to be published to the individuals, as well as republished each time the policy changed. As such, the Financial Privacy Rule established a privacy policy between the individual and the company. Section 501(b) of the GLBA required the FDIC, FRB, OCC, and OTS to develop standards for the examination to ensure that adequate safeguards are being implemented. The examination procedures were developed to determine the involvement of the board of directors, evaluate the risk management process, evaluate the adequacy of the program to manage and control risk, assess measures taken to oversee service providers, and determine where an effective process exists to adjust the program.

The Safeguards Rule of the Gramm-Leach-Bliley Act requires the development of a written plan that must protect the current and past client's financial information. Title 15, Chapter 94, Subchapter I, Section 6801(b) requires that the financial institution, "establish appropriate standards for the financial institutions subject to their jurisdiction relating to administrative, technical and physical safeguards (1) to insure the security and confidentiality of customer records and information; (2) to protect against any anticipated threats or hazards to the security or integrity of such records; and (3) to protect against unauthorized access to or use of such records or information which could result in substantial harm or inconvenience to any customer. The Federal Financial Institutions Examination Council (FFEIC) IT Examination Handbook, substantially revised in September 2016 (and specifics expanded on in control frameworks chapter) can be used as a basis to meet the GLBA requirements.

TWO AREAS OF CONFUSION WITH BREACH RISK ASSESSMENTS

Catherine M. Boerner, JD, CHC

President, HIPAA Consultant, Boerner Consulting, LLC

One challenge early on when conducting breach risk assessments was the shift from the "harm standard" to "low probability of compromise" standard. One common area of confusion new privacy officers may still make is to consider if a privacy violation caused harm to the patient. The Final Rule states: "…breach notification is not required under the final rule if a covered entity or business associate, as applicable, demonstrates through a risk assessment that there is a low probability that the protected health information has been compromised, rather than demonstrate that there is no significant risk of harm to the individual as was provided under the interim final rule". Confusion can still occur now with privacy officers that mistakenly refer to the "Interim Final Rule" from their research.

The Interim Final Rule provided that "compromises the security or privacy of the protected health information" means poses a significant risk of financial, reputational, or other harm to the individual. The Department included this standard regarding a significant risk of harm to the individual (i.e., harm standard)". The true goal now of the four-factor test is to help assess what the probability is that the protected health information (PHI) was compromised. "Compromise" does not mean poses a significant risk of any of the harms listed as before. If it is a "low probability" of compromise based on the four-factor test, then it is not a reportable breach. The meaning of "compromise" is assessing the four-factor test NOT the previous "harm standard".

Another area of confusion is when considering Factor 4 of the test regarding the extent to which the risk to the protected health information has been mitigated.

The Final Rule states: "We note that this factor, when considered in combination with the factor regarding the unauthorized recipient of the information discussed above, may lead to different results in terms of the risk to the protected health information. For example, a covered entity may be able to obtain and rely on the assurances of an employee, affiliated entity, business associate, or another covered entity that the entity or person destroyed information it received in error, while such assurances from certain third parties may not be sufficient".

Too much emphasis on an "attestation of destruction" of PHI from patients who received another patient's PHI was not the intent of this factor to mitigate the probability of the compromise of the PHI. The PHI was compromised and an attestation of destruction from the person who brought home another patient's discharge paperwork does not make this a "low probability" of compromise.

Health Insurance Portability and Accountability Act of 1996

The Health Insurance Portability and Accountability Act (HIPAA) of 1996 was enacted by Congress (Public Law 104-191) with two purposes in mind: 1) to reform health insurance to protect insurance coverage for their workers and families when they changed or lost their jobs and 2) to simplify the administrative processes by adopting standards to improve the efficiency and effectiveness of the nation's healthcare system. Title I of the HIPAA contains provisions to address health insurance reform, while Title II addresses national standards for electronic transactions, unique health identifiers, privacy, and security. Title II is known as Administrative Simplification and is intended to reduce the costs of healthcare through the widespread use of electronic data interchange. Administrative simplification was added to Title XI of the Social Security Act through Subtitle F of Title II of the enacted HIPAA law.

While the initial intent of the Administrative Simplification portion of the law was to reduce the administrative costs associated with processing healthcare transactions, Congress recognized that standardizing and electronically aggregating healthcare information would increase the risk of disclosure of confidential information, and the patient's privacy rights needed to be protected. Provisions were needed not only to protect the confidentiality of information, but also to ensure that information retained the appropriate integrity. Consider the situation where the diagnosis or vital sign information is changed on a medical record and subsequent treatment decisions are based upon this information. The impact of not being able to rely on the information stored within the healthcare environment could have life threatening consequences. Thus, privacy issues are primarily centered on the confidentiality of information to ensure that only appropriate individuals have access to the information, whereas the security standards take on a larger scope to ensure also address issues of integrity and availability of information. While this focus has been primarily on confidentiality, the WannaCry breaches of UK National Health Service in 2017 raised the awareness within healthcare environments regarding the disruption that could occur because of a massive breach, with patients moved to other facilities and treatments postponed. Until this time, much of the conversation within healthcare environments was oriented toward keeping confidential information from being disclosed vs. concentrating on the availability concerns. As Internet of Things (IOT) and medical devices receive more focus, the conversation then involves the integrity aspect of security, highlighting the importance of being able to rely on the information created by the medical device.

The proposed security and electronic signature standards were originally published in the <u>Federal Register</u> on August 12, 1998. The regulations became effective on April 21, 2003, and covered entities were required to comply with the requirements by April 21, 2005, and small health plans had until April 21, 2006.

The Administrative Simplification (Part C of Title XI of the Social Security Act) provisions state that covered entities that maintain or transmit health information are required to

> maintain reasonable and appropriate administrative, physical and technical safeguards to ensure the integrity and confidentiality of the information and to protect against any reasonable anticipated threats or hazards to the security or integrity of the information and unauthorized use or disclosure of the information.

The administrative, technical, and physical safeguards were divided into addressable and required implementation specifications. The addressable standards were more flexible; however, the required safeguards had to be implemented according to the rule. The contractors supporting Medicare claims processing, today known as Medicare Administrative Contractors, were given the directive that all the required and addressable security controls were to be regarded as required, setting a higher and more stringent standard for the protection of Medicare information maintained by the contractors.

The security rule and the Privacy Rule are aligned, with the focus of security standards applied to "health information" in support of the Administrative Simplification requirements shifted to *electronic* PHI. The applicability statement of the final security and privacy rule states "A covered entity must comply with the applicable standards, implementation specifications, and requirements of this subpart with respect to electronic protected health information". Covered entities are defined as (1) a health plan, (2) a health-care clearinghouse, and (3) a healthcare provider who transmits any health information in electronic form in connection with a transaction covered by Part 162 of title 45 of the Code of Federal Regulations (CFR).

Both the security and privacy rules were intended to be scalable such that small providers would not be burdened with excessive costs of implementation, and the large providers, health plans, and clearinghouses could take steps appropriate to their business environments. For example, a small office may be able to control access and enforce segregation of duties between the staff with a manually documented process with supervisory review, while a larger organization would most likely need automated support through an Identity Access Management system, management approval processes, and automated reporting tools to achieve the same level of assurance. Decisions must be made to reasonably protect the information and document how the decisions were determined.

One of the criticisms of the Final HIPAA Security and Privacy Rules since its mandated implementation has been the lack of enforcement. When the HIPAA law was first issued, many organizations were very focused on achieving HIPAA compliance and formed steering committees, hired consultants, and tracked compliance. Investigations were handled on a complaint basis only, which resulted in a small number of complaints given the number of healthcare providers. In February 2006, HHS issued the Final Rule for HIPAA enforcement, setting the civil monetary penalties and procedures for investigations. Since the Office of Civil Rights (OCR), who oversees the enforcement (since July 27, 2009), has tried to work out arrangements between the offender and the victim vs. pursue prosecution, there were few prosecutions under the law in the early days of HIPAA.

DATA PRIVACY IN HEALTHCARE: EXTENDING BEYOND HIPAA

Tom Walsh, CISSP

Founder and Managing Partner, TW-Security, LLC

By volume, most of the confidential information in healthcare relates to patients. Because of that, privacy policies within healthcare organizations tend to solely focus on protected health information (PHI). However, organizations have other data beyond PHI or patient data, which must be kept private and secure. Examples of the other data would be personnel, financial, and strategic data along with intellectual property and in some cases, research data.

For many healthcare organizations, the official definition of confidential information doesn't include any of the data types previously listed.

When conducting an evaluation, I'll often ask the privacy officer for their organization's policy on "Uses and Disclosure of Data". I am yet to find a policy that addresses personally identifiable information (PII) or any other type of confidential information that should be included. I'll challenge the privacy officer asking, "As an employee, I assume you had to give the organization your Social Security number and other personal information about yourself and your family – correct?" I'll continue with, "So it's permissible for the organization to use and disclose your personal information as they please? There is nothing written in policy to prohibit it".

My message is simple: Privacy officers in healthcare need to have a more holistic understanding of data privacy.

Tom's Tips:
- If the acronym "HIPAA" is in your job title, get it removed. It narrows the focus of your areas of expertise and responsibilities and limits your overall value to the organization. Ask your administrative leader to be involved in privacy on a broader scope than just HIPAA.
- Verify that the official definition of confidential information and confidentiality agreements that are signed by the workforce include more than PHI (Reference the examples listed earlier).
- Get involved with the organization's external website. Participate in creating and updating the website's privacy policy. Learn more about how websites interact with browsers, cookies, and the type of tracking information collected and analyzed about the website visitor. Who has access to this data? Who would answer any questions from a website visitor on this data?
- Get involved with IT and in particular, mobile device security technology. What types of confidential information are available via a personally owned smartphone?
- If the organization accepts credit card payments, learn about the Payment Card Industry Data Security Standard (PCI DSS).

1995 Directive 95/46/EC (EU Data Protection Directive)

1995 Directive 95/46/EC on the protection of individuals regarding the processing of personal data and on the free movement of such data, also known as the EU Data Protection Directive, is a significant law which has been viewed by many as the baseline for privacy laws created since. The Directive incorporated the eight privacy principles specified by the OECD.

The directive was drafted as there were emerging differences between the laws of the individual European member states, affording different levels of protection. The differences in the laws made it difficult to have a uniform flow of information across the borders without needing individual consent to pass the information between the borders. The European Union Data Protection Directive was passed to require each member state to develop laws that provided equivalent protection. Differences still existed within countries; however, the key issue of being able to export the information between countries was mitigated and information could move freely among European Union members. Since this was a Directive (requiring each country to implement national laws to implement the principles stated in the directive) vs a regulation (requirement of law by the European Union), it was up to each individual country to ensure they have created laws within their country.

The Directive is consistent with earlier history whereby privacy is noted as a fundamental human right, as well as preserving the need to conduct business, stated as follows:

> Whereas data-processing systems are designed to serve man; whereas they must, whatever the nationality or residence of natural persons, respect the fundamental rights and freedoms, notably the right to privacy, and contribute to economic and social progress, trade expansion and the well-being of individuals.

The objective of the directive was clear, as noted in Article 1:

1. In accordance with this Directive, the member states shall protect the fundamental rights and freedoms of natural persons, and in particular their right to privacy with respect to the processing of personal data.
2. Member states shall neither restrict nor prohibit the free flow of personal data between member states for the reasons connected with the protection afforded under Paragraph 1.

In other words, the intent of the Directive was to maintain privacy protections while enabling commerce. Other countries have adopted laws like the European Union, particularly to establish "adequate protection" for transborder flows with EU member states.

2018 General data protection regulation (GDPR)

The GDPR was approved by the European Union (EU) Parliament in April 2016, with a compliance date of May 25, 2018. This represents a largest change to the prior Data Protection Directive (titled as Directive 95/45/EC on the protection of individuals with respect to the processing of personal data and on the free movement of such data) guiding information privacy efforts for European Union citizens almost a quarter century. The new regulation, which superseded the directive, gained much attention and will have reverberations for years to come in the 2020s just as the EU Data Directive of 1995/98 impacted the privacy regulations adopted around the world. The GDPR, first draft proposed in January 2012, was created to provide a comprehensive reform of the EU data protection rules to strengthen online privacy rights and bolster Europe's digital economy. This resulted in an expanded territorial reach as organizations established outside the EU offering goods and services or monitoring individuals in the EU are required to comply with the GDPR and designate a representative in the EU. The focus is on protecting the personal data of the data subjects residing in the EU, no matter where the controller or processor is located.

The prior privacy protection in the European Union was in the form of a Directive vs. a Regulation, meaning that each of the individual member states of the European Union were required to achieve a result by a specified date, but each of the 28 member states was free to decide the mechanism by which they would implement a solution. This created variation between the member states' interpretation and enforcement of the directive. An EU Regulation on the other hand, as in the case of GDPR, is immediately applicable and enforceable by law. The member states can issue national laws to support the regulation and assign national authorities to administer the law; however, the law is in force without the passage of any additional laws in each member state.

Penalties of up to 4% of global annual turnover (revenue) or 20 million Euro, whichever is greater can also be imposed on both controllers and data processors (previously not deemed directly liable under the prior directive, as the controller was primarily responsible per the Directive).

Consent requirements were also modified, requiring clear consent for processing of personal data, in intelligible terms, and must have an affirmative response. Parental consent is also required for processing personal data for children under 16.

The law also includes the right to be forgotten and erased from records, as specified in Article 17 entitled "Right to erasure". The data subject has the right to have their data deleted "without undue delay" where the data is no longer necessary for the purposes for which they were collected or processed, consent is withdrawn by the data subject or data subject objects to processing, the personal data was not lawfully processed, or the data was required to be erased for the controller to comply with a legal obligation. There are some exceptions to the right, such as excising the right of freedom of expression and information, handling of legal claims, reasons of public interest, and archiving for public interest, scientific or historical statistical and research purposes.

Privacy by Design principles have been built into GDPR, as specified by Article 25, "Data Protection by Design and by default". This article requires that the controller implements appropriate technical and organizational measures for ensuring that, *by default*, only personal data which are necessary for each specific purpose of the processing are processed. For the privacy leader, this provides another impetus for integrating privacy (and security) into the product, system, or service development lifecycle for the processing of personal data and extending these practices to critical applications at a minimum. Tracking by application of how the application implemented Privacy by Design principles should be retained for audit purposes.

Controllers are required to report a data breach within 72 hours unless the data breach can be shown to have a low risk to individual's rights. In supporting vendor risk management practices, the data controller must ensure they have contracts in place with the data processors. The data processors can be held directly liable for the privacy and security of personal data.

Data Protection Officers are required for companies that will be processing high volumes of personal data or "require regular and systematic monitoring of data subjects on a large scale" as articulated in Article 37. The DPO may be contracted and needs to be identified to the Data Protection Authority. International data transfers involve the concepts of Binding Corporate Rules (BCRs), Model Contract Clauses, etc.

GDPR prompted changes in business practices to ensure consent was obtained where required, data was retained for a reasonable amount of time, data protection officers were recruited/retained as necessary, the right to be deleted could be supported, data could be reproduced in a machine-readable data format, and incidents could be responded too quickly. Those organizations not aware of where the personal data was being stored had much extra work to discover and map the flows of this information. Tim Clements provides a concise infographic highlighting some of the key provisions of GDPR, as illustrated in Figure 7.2.

PRIVACY SELF-REGULATION

Industry-supported self-regulatory programs

The early industry-supported privacy self-regulatory efforts included:

- The Individual Reference Services Group was announced in 1997 as a self-regulatory organization for companies providing information that identifies or locates individuals. The group terminated in 2001, deceptively citing a recently passed regulatory law as making the group's self-regulation unnecessary.
- The privacy leadership initiative began in 2000 to promote self-regulation and to support privacy educational activities for business and for consumers. The organization lasted about two years.
- The Online Privacy Alliance began in 1998 with an interest in promoting industry self-regulation for privacy. OPA's last reported substantive activity appears to have taken place in 2001, although its website

Explaining GDPR

What organizations have to do

Keep records of all processing of personal information

Institute safeguards for cross-border data transfers

Implement Data Protection-by-Design (Privacy "baked-in")

Maintain appropriate data security

Take responsibility for the security and processing activities of third-party vendors

Conduct Data Protection Impact Assessments on new processing activities

Collect personal data lawfully and fairly and provide notification of personal data processing activities

Appoint a Data Protection Officer (if you regularly process lots of data or particularly sensitive data)

Get a parent's consent to collect data for children under 16

Consult with regulators before certain processing activities

Be able to demonstrate compliance on demand

Provide appropriate data protection training to personnel having permanent or regular access to personal data

Notify data protection agencies and affected individuals of data breaches in certain circumstances

What individuals can do

Withdraw consent for processing

Request a copy of all of their data and request corrections if wrong

Request that their information is deleted when there's no purpose to retain it

Request the ability to move their data to a different organization

Object to automated decision-making processes, including profiling

What regulators may do

Ask for records of processing activities and proof of steps taken to comply with the GDPR

Impose temporary data processing bans, require data breach notification, or order erasure of personal data

Suspend cross-border data flows

Enforce penalties of up to €20 million or 4% of annual revenues for non-compliance

purposeandmeans.io

Figure 7.2 Explaining GDPR to the workforce.

Source: Purpose and Means, Tim Clements Reprinted with Permission.

continues to exist and shows signs of an update in 2011, when FTC and congressional interest recurred. The group does not accept new members.

- The Network Advertising Initiative had its origin in 1999, when the Federal Trade Commission showed interest in the privacy effects of online behavioral targeting. By 2003, when FTC interest in privacy regulation had diminished, the NAI had only two members. Enforcement and audit activity lapsed as well. NAI did not fulfill its promises or keep its standards up to date with current technology until 2008, when FTC interest increased.
- The BBB Online Privacy Program began in 1998, with a substantive operation that included verification, monitoring and review, consumer dispute resolution, a compliance seal, enforcement mechanisms, and an educational component. Several hundred companies participated in the early years, but interest did not continue and BBB Online stopped accepting applications in 2007. The program has now disappeared.

Government-supported self-regulatory efforts

Not all privacy self-regulatory efforts were solely industry supported. Some were government sponsored, and there is one effort that involved consumers, academics, public interest groups as well as industry – the data transfer agreements between the United States and the European Union.

These efforts began with the US-EU Safe Harbor Framework (referred to as Safe Harbor). Safe Harbor began in 2000 to ease the export of data from Europe to US companies that self-certified compliance with specified Safe Harbor standards. Safe was a form of government-supervised self-regulation but with little evidence of active supervision.

The European Court of Justice declared the safe harbor principles as not being adequate for protection of the information in October 2015. This decision resulted in declaring the US-EU Safe Harbor Framework as an invalid mechanism for satisfying the data protection requirements of the 95/46/EC Data Protection Directive. At the time, more than 4,400 US companies depended upon the Safe Harbor framework to transfer information between the countries.

2000 EU-US safe harbor

The Data Protection Directive (95/46/EC) required the transfer of personal data to countries that lacked adequate data protection to be forbidden. The United States was one of those countries determined by the EU to not have adequate privacy laws. To facilitate commerce between the United States and the European Union member states, the US Department of Commerce worked with the European Commission to develop a "safe harbor" framework, whereby companies desiring to transfer personal data would agree to fair trade practices and certify to the US Government their compliance on an annual basis. Two regulatory agencies, the Federal Trade Commission (FTC) and the Department of Transportation" (DOT), agreed to facilitate this process. A set of principles were developed, modeling fair information practices such as those articulated within the Data Protection Directive including notice, choice, onward transfer, security, data integrity, access, and enforcement. The Department of Commerce maintained a listing of the companies certifying to safe harbor on their website.

The case against Safe Harbor started when Max Schrems (Schrems) filed a complaint in 2013 with the Irish Data Protection Commission (DPC) stating that his information in Facebook was being transferred to the United States and was not adequately protected. Information was also resident on Facebook's European servers; however, they were not the focus of the complaint. The complaint was lodged after knowledge about surveillance information captured by the US National Security Agency (NSA) was disclosed by systems administrator Edward Snowden. The reason for the ruling against Safe Harbor was that the agreement places "national security, public interest or law enforcement requirements" over the privacy principles. This was deemed to conflict with the fundamental human rights of persons the European law was predicated on.

2016 EU-US Privacy Shield Framework

To resolve the Safe Harbor logjam that could have been very detrimental to international trade, the US Department of Commerce and the European Commission worked together in early 2016 to create a replacement to the EU-US Safe Harbor Framework. Since the United States was deemed to not have adequate privacy practices, primarily due to the government being able to access the information, controls beyond the principles stated in the original EU-US Safe Harbor Framework needed to be strengthened. On July 12, 2016, the new framework entitled "EU-US Privacy Shield Framework" was announced as the replacement for the EU-US Safe Harbor Framework as an agreed-upon legal mechanism available for transferring personal data from the European Union to the United States. These new certifications started to be accepted on August 1, 2016, and the Safe Harbor certifications ceased being accepted as of October 31, 2016. On January 12, 2017, the Swiss government announced a similar framework, the US-Swiss Safe Harbor, for transfer of information between Switzerland and the United States.

The key enhancements of the Privacy shield over the Safe Harbor Framework were to address the concern over lack of oversight and transparency by implementing:

1. EU Individual rights and legal remedies: Individuals may bring a complaint to the company and the company has 45 days to respond. The individual may also submit a complaint to the data protection

authority in the EU. The FTC will also provide vigorous enforcement of the new framework.

2. Program oversight and cooperation with EU data protection authorities: Verify completeness of company self-certifications and work together with the EU authorities, as well as conduct assessments of the program.

3. New requirements for participating companies: Privacy policies must state a commitment to the privacy shield principles, along with links on the website to a complaint submission form. They must also disclose any information provided in response to a lawful request by public authorities. Onward transfers to third parties must also include contractual provisions that the information will be processed consistent with the consent and specified purposes provided by the individual, and that the information will be provided at the same level of protection as in the principles.

4. Limitations and safeguards on national security and law enforcement access to data: Multiple layers of constitutional, statutory, and policy safeguards applying to US Intelligence, along with active oversight by all three branches of the government have been communicated in writing to the EU Commission. Limits to access were also provided by the US Department of Justice. An Ombudsperson was committed to be made available through this process for EU citizens to inquiry regarding United States signal intelligence practices.

The Article 29 Working Party is a non-binding group made up of representatives from each of the EU data protection authorities from each member state, the European Data Protection Supervisor, and the European Commission. This group reviewed the proposals to come to the final resolution, as they have done with other areas where there is uncertainty in the direction. In the earlier review of the privacy shield, they noted several areas with a need to be addressed before the final approval, specifically: 1) massive collection of personal data by the US was not fully excluded, 2) independence of the ombudsperson, 3) lack of a data retention principle, 4) inconsistency in the terminology, 5) protection for onward data transfers, and 6) need for a simple process for EU citizen redress. The party also suggested that the EU-US Privacy Shield be reviewed after the EU GDPR became effective in May 2018 to ensure the new higher level of protection is also reflected in the Privacy Shield.

2022 The Transatlantic Data Privacy Framework

On July 16, 2020, the Court of Justice of the European Union (CJEU) published its judgment in the Data Protection Commissioner v. Facebook Ireland Limited, Maximillian Schrems (C-311/18) (the Schrems II case). In its judgment, the CJEU declared the EU-US Privacy Shield – one of the primary data transfer mechanisms for the safe and free flow of data between the EU and US organizations – invalid. On 25 March 2022, President von der Leyen and President Biden announced that they had reached an agreement in principle on a new EU-US Data Privacy Framework called The Transatlantic Data Privacy Framework. On 7 October President Biden signed an Executive Order (EO) on "Enhancing Safeguards for United States Signals Intelligence Activities". For Europeans whose personal data is transferred to the US, the new EO provided for:

- Binding safeguards that limit access to data by US intelligence authorities to what is necessary and proportionate to protect national security;
- The establishment of an independent and impartial redress mechanism, which includes a new Data Protection Review Court ("DPRC"), to investigate and resolve complaints regarding access to their data by US national security authorities.

The EO required US intelligence agencies to review their policies and procedures to implement these new safeguards. A new two-layer redress mechanism was also established, with independent and binding authority. Under the first layer, EU individuals were able to lodge a complaint with the "Civil Liberties Protection Officer" of the US intelligence community. Under the second level, individuals had the possibility to appeal the decision of the Civil Liberties Protection Officer before the newly created Data Protection Review Court. The Court is composed of members chosen from outside the US Government, appointed based on specific qualifications, and can only be dismissed for serious causes (such as being convicted of a crime, or being deemed mentally or physically unfit to perform the tasks) and cannot receive instructions from the government. The Data Protection Review Court has the powers to investigate complaints from EU individuals, including to obtain relevant information from intelligence agencies, and will be able to take binding remedial decisions.

The adequacy of the EO, the proposed framework, and the structures underpinning it had to be evaluated and ratified by the European Commission, and in July 2023, the European Commission formally adopted a new adequacy decision on the framework. The long-awaited adequacy decision provides EU companies transferring personal data to the U.S. with an additional mechanism to legitimize their transatlantic data transfers.

The adequacy decision allows self-certified companies that adhere to the EU-U.S. Data Privacy Framework and commit to a set of privacy obligations to receive EU personal data without having to put in place additional transfer safeguards. Now referred to as The EU-U.S. Data Privacy Framework, it will be subject to periodic reviews by the European Commission and representatives of European data protection authorities and competent U.S. authorities.

The lifespan of the framework may be brief however, for two key reasons. First, the EDPB said that the latest agreements falls short and urged the commission to do more to protect Europeans' privacy. Second, Max Schrems claims that the latest revision is inadequate and expects this to be back at the Court of Justice by the beginning of next year

Toward global data protection

By 2023, 65% of the world's population will have its personal data covered under modern privacy regulations, according to Gartner. Lawmakers' efforts have intensified in the last couple of years, with many data protection law initiatives being passed and adopted. This trend is likely to continue, with regions such as Europe, the Middle East, the United States, and the Asia Pacific introducing or amending data privacy and protection laws.

In 2021, US states Virginia and Colorado followed California and passed data protection laws which came into effect in 2023. In 2021, more than 160 consumer privacy-related bills were introduced in the United States in 38 states, highlighting the growing concern with adopting laws that guarantee the protection of consumers' personal information. California, New York, Virginia, and Colorado are the first states to enact broad legislation that create national impact, but many other US states are also considering data privacy laws. The passing of the Virginia Consumer Data Privacy Act (VCDPA) and the Colorado Privacy Act (CPA) in 2021 is likely to increase momentum in other states and lead to further legislation being passed in 2023 and beyond. At least 12 US states were set to consider comprehensive consumer privacy legislation in 2022–2023, and at least three US state privacy laws were set to come into effect in 2023 (California Privacy Rights Act of 2020, Colorado Privacy Act, and the Virginia Consumer Data Protection Act).

The IAPP notes that big regulatory movements in privacy and data protection will continue in 2023, and the jurisdictions to follow are India, Australia, Argentina, Canada, and South Korea. Companies are also working to address new or anticipated privacy laws across the globe (Brazil, China, India, and Saudi Arabia). Below we present the progress of some of these legislative movements around the world.

SOUTH KOREA

South Korea is set to review some key aspects of its existing data protection legislation and it may grant PIPC the power to impose severe fines up to 3% of their "total annual turnover" as opposed to "relevant turnover" as defined by the current law, which is making its way through the country's legislature. The Bill, introduced in 2021, was recently passed by the National Policy Committee and at time of press was for review by the Legislation and Judiciary Committee and a vote in the Plenary session. Most notably, in 2022 Google and Meta were levied the largest fines on record for privacy violations under South Korea's Personal Data Protection Act (the equivalent of 50 million $ against Google and of 22 million $ against Meta, in cases involving behavioral advertising).

CHINA

China also passed its first omnibus data protection legislation, the Personal Information Protection Law (PIPL), which seeks to protect personal data and regulate its processing, which came into effect on November 1, 2021. The PIPL is similar to, and partly based on, the European Union's GDPR and builds on top of both China's Cybersecurity Law ("CSL") and China's Data Security Law ("DSL"). However, one key difference is that PIPL has a state-backed regulator, while GDRP is regulated by independent regulators in EU member states.

JAPAN'S ACT ON THE PROTECTION OF PERSONAL INFORMATION

Japan modernized the Act on the Protection of Personal Information (APPI) in 2017 to bring it closer to European standards. Thanks to these changes, Japan secured the first adequacy decision issued by the European Commission under GDPR. Further amendments to the law were enacted on June 12, 2020 (came into force on April 1, 2022), based on the results of the Personal Information Protection Commission's (PPC) review and public consultation. The new changes, among other things, expanded the scope of Japanese data subjects' rights, made data breach notifications mandatory, and limited the range of personal information that can be provided to third parties. Penalties also saw a significant increase.

BRAZIL'S GENERAL LAW FOR THE PROTECTION OF PERSONAL DATA (LGPD)

Brazil's data protection law (Lei Geral de Proteção de Dados Pessoais in Portuguese, or LGPD) came into effect in 2020. It contains provisions like the GDPR and aims to regulate the treatment of personal data of all individuals or natural persons in Brazil. That means, like the GDPR, even if a company isn't based in Brazil, and Brazilian resident data is processed, the law applies.

Companies and groups that do not follow the law's terms and directives may receive a fine such as 2% of their sales revenue and up to $50 million Brazilian Real (approximately $12 million USD).

INDIA'S DIGITAL PERSONAL DATA PROTECTION (DPDP) BILL

India's DPDP bill (August 2023), has been gathering momentum since India's Supreme Court ruled in 2017 that Indians had a fundamental right to privacy. The law proposes penalties of up to 2.5 billion rupees ($30 million) for violations and non-compliance. The law allows companies to transfer some users' data abroad while giving the government power to seek information from organizations and issue directions to block content on the advice of a data protection board appointed by India's government. It also gives the government powers to exempt state agencies from the law and gives users the right to correct or erase their personal data. One provision allows the government to bypass aspects of the bill on broad grounds relating to the "sovereignty and integrity of India, security of the state, friendly relations with foreign states, maintenance of public order". As such these exemptions are somewhat controversial as they can facilitate a potential greenlight for government state surveillance.

EU PROPOSALS TO WATCH IN 2023 AND BEYOND

The landscape of digital services is significantly different today from 20 years ago. Online intermediaries have become vital players in digital transformation. Online platforms have 1) created significant benefits for consumers and innovation, 2) facilitated cross-border trading within and outside the Union, and 3) opened new opportunities to a variety of European businesses and traders. At the same time, online platforms can be used as a vehicle for disseminating illegal content or selling illegal goods or services online. Some very large players have emerged as quasi-public spaces for information sharing and online trade. They have become systemic in nature and pose risks for users' rights, information flows, and public participation. Thus, these regulations are intended to accomplish two goals: first, to create a safer digital space in which the fundamental rights of all users of digital services are protected and then second, to establish a level playing field to foster innovation, growth, and competitiveness, both in the European Single Market and globally.

These new regulations include the Digital Services Act, the Digital Markets Act, ePrivacy Regulation, and the Data Governance Act.

A DIGITAL SOCIETY CALLS FOR SUSTAINABLE TECH SOLUTIONS

Lena Lindgren Schelin

Director General, Swedish Authority for Privacy Protection

In 2018, the GDPR entered effect in EU/EEA. All of a sudden there was talk about privacy, data protection, and stronger rights for citizens regarding how companies and authorities can collect and process their personal data. And not least buzz about the data protection agencies' new tool to impose administrative fines.

Fast forward to 2023. The buzz word now is digitalization. In every corner of society, work is being done to develop new IT-systems, apps and hardware, that build on collecting and processing our personal data. The development of new technology is exponential – which of course challenges our privacy in the core.

I also support digitalization, but I also feel the need to stress the importance of future tech development being sustainable from a privacy perspective.

In 2021 we started an initiative to increase knowledge of privacy and data protection issues within the innovation eco system. We have since developed our ability to follow and analyze developments in the tech sector and have held hearings with researchers and start-ups in order to identify their challenges when it comes to developing privacy-friendly digital products and services. Today, we have collaborations with several organizations in the field of innovation.

Recently, we finished a pilot project involving regulatory testing activities regarding decentralized AI in healthcare and have launched an "Innovation Portal" on our web site, giving specific guidance to start-ups and organizations developing new, innovative tech solutions.

By this, I hope the Swedish Authority for Privacy Protection (IMY) can be a trusted party in moving the tech sector toward more sustainability from a privacy perspective.

I have a firm belief that companies that actively work with privacy protection in mind will gain future competitive advantages and that users will more actively choose products and services with the least impact on their privacy.

Digitalization is often promoted as driving environmental sustainability and this is of course something good. However, building privacy protection as an integral part of new techniques and developments is important to also obtain sustainability from a fundamental rights perspective.

The EU Digital Services Act (DSA) and the EU Digital Markets Act (DMA)

The European Commission aims to upgrade its rules on digital services in the EU using two proposed laws to form a single set of rules. They're called the Digital Services Act (DSA) and the Digital Markets Act (DMA). Together, they aim to protect users and establish a "level playing field to foster innovation, growth, and competitiveness". The new regulation addresses illegal and harmful content by getting platforms such as Google and Meta to rapidly remove such content. The primary principle noted by the Council of the European Union is "what is illegal offline must be illegal online".

The DSA regulates everything from "dark patterns" and algorithms to public safety threats and illegal content. The DSA prohibits misleading interfaces that prompt users to make decisions they might not otherwise make and compels large platforms to comply with stricter obligations on disinformation, political ad transparency and hate speech, among other things. It also provides options for users to opt out of behavioral algorithms, bans micro-targeted advertising, and requires large platforms to undertake annual analysis and reporting with respect to what the EU says are the systemic risks of their services. The Act applies to Very Large Online Platforms (VLOPs) and Very Large Online Search Engines (VLOSEs). Services with more than 45 million monthly active users in the EU fall into this category. Think of anything delivered via the internet when you think of digital services. That could be a music streaming service or an e-book or a website.

The DSA would cover

- Intermediary services (e.g., network infrastructure services, internet access providers, domain name registers)
- Hosting services, such as cloud and web services

- Online platforms, bringing together sellers and consumers such as online marketplaces, app stores, collaborative economy platforms, and social media platforms.
- Very large online platforms (platforms reaching more than 10% of 450 million consumers in Europe).

The obligations vary depending on an organization's size, but they can include monitoring of third-party vendors, external risk auditing, and codes of conduct. The European Commission summarizes the key principles enshrined in these regulations in Table 7.2.

Table 7.2 Obligation summary under the DSA

New obligations	Intermediary services (Cumulative obligations)	Hosting services (Cumulative obligations)	Online platforms (Cumulative obligations)	Very large platforms (Cumulative obligations)
Transparency reporting	●	●	●	●
Requirements on terms of service due account of fundamental rights	●	●	●	●
Cooperation with national authorities following orders	●	●	●	●
Points of contact and, where necessary, legal representative	●	●	●	●
Notice and action and obligation to provide information to users		●	●	●
Reporting criminal offences		●	●	●
Complaint and redress mechanism and out of court dispute settlement			●	●
Trusted flaggers			●	●
Measures against abusive notices and counter-notices			●	●
Special obligations for marketplaces, e.g., vetting credentials of third-party suppliers ("KYBC"), compliance by design, random checks			●	●

(Continued)

Table 7.2 (Continued)

New obligations	Intermediary services (Cumulative obligations)	Hosting services (Cumulative obligations)	Online platforms (Cumulative obligations)	Very large platforms (Cumulative obligations)
Bans on targeted adverts to children and those based on special characteristics of users			●	●
Transparency of recommender systems			●	●
User-facing transparency of online advertising			●	●
Risk management obligations and crisis response				●
External and independent auditing, internal compliance function, and public accountability				●
User choice not to have recommendations based on profiling				●
Data sharing with authorities and researchers				●
Codes of conduct				●
Crisis response cooperation				●

The Digital Markets Act (DMA) would cover the largest digital platforms, known as "gatekeepers", under the proposal. The Act would cover companies such as Facebook, Apple, Microsoft, and Google. The aim is to level the playing field for digital companies of all sizes. Rules would be created for major Internet platforms that would prevent them from imposing "unfair conditions on businesses and consumers". For example, a company like Amazon wouldn't be allowed to rank products on its site in a way that gives Amazon's own products and services an advantage. The European Commissioner would have the power to carry out investigations and sanction bad behavior and update the law's obligations as needed.

Unlike prior discretionary standards, both the DMA and DSA come with teeth. The European Commissioner is given the power to carry out investigations, sanction breaches, and update the law's obligations as needed. For the DSA, platforms that reach more than 10% of the EU's population (45 million users) are considered systemic in nature and are subject not only to specific obligations to control their own risks but also to a new oversight structure. This new accountability framework will be comprised of a board of national Digital Services Coordinators, with special powers for the Commission in supervising very large platforms including the ability to sanction them directly. This is a move under the country-of-origin principle – a similar enforcement regime applied under the GDPR. However, this enforcement regime also recognizes a number of layers of accountability and auditability. The first being the power of the commission and the local authorities themselves to directly influence audit (mandated annually), meaningful reporting, and enforcement. The next level recognizes the importance of researchers' output, journalist investigations, and civil society investigations, for example, ProPublica as transparency and accountability levers have been built into both the DSA and DMA. And then finally the users themselves who have also been empowered with rights under the DSA.

The IAPP suggests that competition and data protection laws are increasingly intertwined in the world of digital marketplaces. Privacy professionals need to be aware of these developments to ensure that companies comply with these requirements in a manner that satisfies not only the DMA and the DSA but also the EU GDPR. Some examples presented by IAPP of these crossovers are:

- Growing concerns about targeted advertising based on tracking online behavior have led to an obligation to "refrain from combining personal data sourced from these core platform services with personal data from any other services offered by the gatekeeper or with personal data from third-party services, and from signing in end-users to other services ... in order to combine personal data, unless the end-user has been presented with the specific choice and provide consent."· A prohibition to require "business and end users to subscribe to or register with any other core platform services ..." offered by the gatekeeper, thereby obviously limiting the amount of personal data that gatekeepers can accumulate.
- An obligation to "allow end-users to un-install any preinstalled software applications" on the platform.
- An obligation to "provide effective portability of data generated through the activity of a business user or end user ... and in particular to provide tools for end-users to facilitate the exercise of data portability".
- An obligation to provide "real-time access and use to aggregated and non-aggregated data with a specific reference to the need to comply with the GDPR and its consent requirements for access to personal data."
- An obligation for gatekeepers to provide third-party providers of online search engines with access to "query, click, and view data", subject to anonymization for personal data.
- A requirement for gatekeepers to "take the necessary steps to either enable business users to obtain (any) required consent to their processing (of personal data) where required or to provide duly anonymized data where appropriate".

E-privacy regulation

The e-Privacy Regulation has been a long time coming, as it aimed to come into force alongside the EU's GDPR in 2018 but has stalled for years. In March 2022, the EU Council agreed on a draft, but regulation isn't expected until at least 2023/2024.

The e-Privacy Regulation, if passed, would create privacy rules for traditional electronic communications services and entities that weren't covered by the former law, the e-Privacy Directive, such as WhatsApp, Facebook Messenger, and Skype.

It would create stronger rules on electronic communication's privacy, and it would apply to not only communications content but "metadata", that is, data that describes other data. Under ePrivacy, service providers and electronic communications networks must get prior consent from the user before processing their electronic communications metadata.

The regulation would also, importantly, create simpler rules on cookies. It would allow users to consent or deny tracking cookies at the browser level, and it would also clarify that websites do not need to get consent for what is called "non-privacy intrusive cookies". Those cookies allow website features like "shopping carts" to keep track of what a user has ordered. It would also require that organizations allow end-users to withdraw their previously granted consent at least once per year.

The Artificial Intelligence Act

According to the EU Council charged with developing harmonized AI rules

> Artificial Intelligence (AI) is a fast-evolving family of technologies that can bring a wide array of economic and societal benefits across the entire spectrum of industries and social activities. By improving prediction, optimizing operations and resource allocation, and personalizing service delivery, the use of artificial intelligence can support socially and environmentally beneficial outcomes and provide key competitive advantages to companies and the European economy. Such action is especially needed in high-impact sectors, including climate change, environment and health, the public sector, finance, mobility, home affairs and agriculture. However, the same elements and techniques that power the socio-economic benefits of AI can also bring about new risks or negative consequences for individuals or the society. In light of the speed of technological change and possible challenges, the EU is committed to strive for a balanced approach. It is in the Union interest to preserve the EU's technological leadership and to ensure that Europeans can benefit from new technologies developed and functioning according to Union values, fundamental rights and principles.

The AI Act has the following specific objectives:

- ensure that AI systems placed on the Union market and used are safe and respect existing law on fundamental rights and Union values;

- ensure legal certainty to facilitate investment and innovation in AI;
- enhance governance and effective enforcement of existing law on fundamental rights and safety requirements applicable to AI systems;
- facilitate the development of a single market for lawful, safe, and trustworthy AI applications and prevent market fragmentation.

The regulation lays down:

(a) harmonized rules for placing on the market, putting into service, and the use of AI system in the EU;
(b) prohibitions of certain AI practices;
(c) specific requirements for high-risk AI systems and obligations for operators of such systems;
(d) harmonized transparency rules for AI systems intended to interact with natural persons, emotion recognition systems, and biometric categorization systems, and AI systems used to generate or manipulate image, audio, or video content;
(e) rules on market monitoring and surveillance.

The EU's AI Act would apply to any company doing business in the EU that develops or adopts machine-learning-based software. It would apply extraterritorially, meaning the law will cover companies based elsewhere if they have customers or users inside the EU and effectively making it a global regulation.

Included in the AI Act are the following limitations:

- Techniques used to manipulate a person's behavior in a manner that could cause mental or physical harm.
- AI systems that could exploit vulnerable groups based on age, physical, or mental disability.
- AI systems that provide real-time remote biometric data in publicly accessible spaces by law enforcement.

A ROBOT, A HUMAN, AND A HORSE WALK INTO A BAR ...

Peter T. Davis

Principal, Peter Davis+Associates

Most likely you have tried out, or should I say, played with, a generative artificial intelligence (AI) chatbot like ChatGPT. These programs are ubiquitous and spread like wildfire. People are making all sorts of predictions about where this ultimately ends. Some talk of a dystopian future like Blade Runner or a legal quagmire, while others cite Polanyi's Paradox. Regardless, there is no doubt these tools will provide substantive value just like the Internet, World Wide Web, and social media did. But what we learned about those tools was that they were double edged: we could use them for good or evil. Similarly, generative AI is a double-edged sword cutting both ways. Undoubtedly, AI has unique abilities but there are potential risks associated with technology, such as responsibility, attribution and ethics. Companies can use AI to process large amounts of data and improve privacy within their company. But AI has the potential to replicate, reinforce, or amplify harmful biases or to promulgate information disorder.

So, what should you do as a Privacy Leader when thinking about integrating AI into your business? Like with most things in your organization, you need some rules. Following are my Top 5 tips:

- Familiarize yourself with all the laws and regulations for AI and your business. Understandably, many of the evolving statutes focus on healthcare, but this will rapidly evolve. Once you understand the laws and regulations and the need for AI, you must develop, socialize, approve and publish an AI Policy. In the Policy, address ethical and privacy issues, compliance, data governance, and data sharing. Incorporate AI language into existing policy, standards and procedures. Your *Code of Conduct* should stress the need to remove biases and discrimination from applications and to use AI ethically and responsibly. Remember Spider-Man's adage: "*With great power comes great responsibility*".
- Ensure AI apps follow principles of trustworthiness: fairness, accountability, transparency, and explainability. Don't tempt FATE. And don't overlook non-discrimination, human oversight, robustness, and security of the system. Depending on the nature of your model, you might need to set and validate safety thresholds and provide a kill switch. For example, a high-speed automated trading system could destabilize the financial system, so someone needs to pull the emergency brake.
- Follow data privacy principles in AI design. Bake privacy and data protection into your model or application lifecycle. Retrofitting is hard and expensive. Data collected by means of AI raises privacy issues like informed consent, opt-in and out, limiting data collection, and identifiability of individuals. Apparently, employees are entering company confidential information into ChatGPT. Hopefully it's not personal information!
- Practice good data hygiene and only collect necessary data types. This is true of any application but is especially true as you amass mounds of data to train your system.
- Ensure the privacy of any personal data and ensure that it is not possible to identify any individual who was not identifiable from the input dataset's perspective. Consider the use of differential privacy that enables companies to access sensitive data for research and business purposes

without privacy breaches and allows businesses to share their data with other organizations to collaborate with them without risking their customers' privacy.

Clearly, I have offered but a snippet of what you need to consider, so check out ISO/IEC 42001 for more implementation guidance and AI control objectives and controls.

You might be curious about the trio in the title. I fed the title into a generative AI program, and it responded: The bartender looks up and says, "What is this, some kind of joke?" It found the punchline on a Wikipedia page for bar jokes. Keep your sense of humor as it is what distinguishes humans from AI.

SUGGESTED READING

Breitbart, Paul. (2018). On large-scale data processing and GDPR compliance. https://iapp.org/news/a/on-large-scale-data-processing-and-gdpr-compliance/

Cavoukian, A. (2011). Privacy by design. https://www.ipc.on.ca/wp-content/uploads/resources/7foundationalprinciples.pdf

CNIL: Data Protection Impact Assessment Methodology. https://www.cnil.fr/sites/default/files/atoms/files/cnil-pia-1-en-methodology.pdf

CNIL: Template for Records of Processing Activities. https://www.cnil.fr/en/record-processing-activities

EDPS Commentary. (2019). Accountability on the ground. https://edps.europa.eu/sites/default/files/publication/19-07-17_accountability_on_the_ground_part_i_en.pdf

EU Artificial Intelligence Act. https://artificialintelligenceact.eu/the-act/

EU Commission. (2019–1024). Strategyhttps://commission.europa.eu/strategy-and-policy/priorities-2019-2024/europe-fit-digital-age/digital-services-act-ensuring-safe-and-accountable-online-environment_en

EU Digital Markets Act. https://commission.europa.eu/strategy-and-policy/priorities-2019-2024/europe-fit-digital-age/digital-markets-act-ensuring-fair-and-open-digital-markets_en

EU Digital Services Act. https://commission.europa.eu/strategy-and-policy/priorities-2019-2024/europe-fit-digital-age/digital-services-act-ensuring-safe-and-accountable-online-environment_en

EU E-Privacy Regulation. https://digital-strategy.ec.europa.eu/en/policies/eprivacy-regulation

European Data Protection Supervisor. (2017). Necessity and proportionality toolkit. https://edps.europa.eu/sites/edp/files/publication/17-06-01_necessity_toolkit_final_en.pdf

European Data Protection Supervisor. (2020). Guidelines on article 25 data protection by design and by default. https://edpb.europa.eu/sites/default/files/files/file1/edpb_guidelines_201904_dataprotection_by_design_and_by_default_v2.0_en.pdf

IAPP. (2022). Developments on the DMA and DSA and why this should be of interest to privacy professionals. https://iapp.org/news/a/developments-on-the-dma-and-dsa-why-this-should-be-of-interest-to-privacy-professionals//

ISO 31700. Consumer protection – Privacy by design for consumer goods and services – Part 1: High-level requirements. https://www.iso.org/standard/84977.html

Reuters. (2022). EU Lawmakers pass landmark tech rules. https://www.reuters.com/technology/eu-lawmakers-pass-landmark-tech-rules-enforcement-worry-2022-07-05

The Swedish Authority for Privacy Protection (IMY) Innovation Portal. https://imy.se/innovation

UK Police Chief's DPIA on ANPR Technology. https://assets.publishing.service.gov.uk/government/uploads/system/uploads/attachment_data/file/1079855/ANPR__DPIA_V3.0_approved.pdf

Chapter 8

Privacy, ethics, and responsible privacy

Although sometimes described as the new oil, because of the way data, and data science, are revolutionizing society just as fossil fuels did earlier, data have unique properties, leading to correspondingly unique ethical challenges... Such considerations do not permit simple formulaic answers since these must be context-dependent and dynamic. Instead, solutions must be principles-based, with higher-level considerations guiding decisions in any particular context.

David J. Hand, *Handwriting: Right, legitimate and proper? The new world of data ethics*

Privacy and ethics are intertwined because privacy is fundamentally about respecting the autonomy and dignity of individuals. When individuals provide personal information, they are placing their trust in organizations to use that information in a responsible and ethical manner. Privacy violations can lead to significant harm to individuals, including loss of autonomy, reputational damage, financial harm, and discrimination. Individuals are confronted with a constant reconfiguration of norms that regulate what information is known about them, observed, decided, processed, shared, etc. and what private decisions they can influence. Organizations are thus confronted with the challenge of having to weigh the benefits of processing data against associated risks beyond regulatory risks. Thus, the emergence of ethics as a needed bedfellow of privacy is omnipresent. This is reflected by the growing number of key privacy events and advocates calling for the inclusion of ethical frameworks for privacy, for example:

- The European Data Protection Supervisor (EDPS) has been calling for a broad understanding of privacy and data protection as core values central to protecting human dignity, autonomy, and the democratic functioning of our societies. For instance – regarding how is digitalization changing people and society? Are digital platforms affecting the way we think, develop our opinions, and interact with others? What role do governments play in shaping digital governance? What are the incentives and criteria of tech companies in developing new digital technologies? Who benefits from them and who does not?

DOI: 10.1201/9781003383017-13

- In 2017, the United Nations Development Group (UNDG), a forum comprising more than 35 UN agencies, came together to craft an approach to big data that is based not only on privacy, but also on ethical and moral obligations concerning data use in development and humanitarian contexts, which it published in its UNDG Guidance Note on "Data Privacy, Data Protection and Ethics: Big Data for the achievement of the 2030 Agenda".
- In 2018, the theme of the 40th Conference of Data Protection Commissioners and Privacy Commissioners was ethics in privacy. In the conference report, the then European Data Protection Supervisor Giovanni Buttarelli highlighted that the aim of the conference was *"to interrogate the notions of right and wrong around the world and across different disciplines which underpin law, technology and how people behave.... to start a global conversation about sustainable approaches to developing and deploying digital technology, from machine learning to sensors to biotech".*
- In 2019, Gartner identified privacy and ethics as one of the Top Ten trends for 2020, arguing that "shifting from privacy to ethics moves the conversation beyond 'are we compliant' toward 'are we doing the right thing'".

PRIVACY, CYBERSECURITY, INNOVATION AND ETHICS – MUSINGS FROM THE KITCHEN TABLE

Ian Travers

Principal Cybersecurity and Data Protection Consultant, BH Consulting

In 1939, Einstein was visited at his home by the then renowned Hungarian physicist Leo Szilard. The story goes that Szilard sat at Einstein's kitchen table and explained the process of how an explosive chain reaction could be produced in uranium layered with graphite by the neutrons released from nuclear fission to which Einstein reportedly replied, "I never thought of that". A few questions later and Einstein had grasped the implications.

Throughout the centuries, ingenuity, and the drive to innovate, has been ever present in the human psyche. Although disproportionately distributed across the world, our ability to innovate has brought about unimaginable benefits. Unfortunately, due to the frailties of the human condition and the perpetual pursuit of commercial and geopolitical power, innovation has consistently been abused in pursuit of our many vices. One must look no further than the insatiable appetite for and misuse of personal data by many tech' companies in their perpetual pursuit of financial gain.

As we sit on the cusp of the roll-out of generative AI, and with quantum computing envisaged as being less than a decade away, how will these and other emerging technologies impact our society? The rate of acceleration of both the adoption and capabilities of new technologies is unprecedented in our history, and the implications have not been adequately considered. Many ethical questions remain, yet the race is on as we jump off the ledge in pursuit of advantage, both for the greater good and for bad.

Who will be the Szilard of our times? Who will be the voice to petition the ethical use of innovative technologies and endeavour to at least try and limit their use for the greater good?

Looking at how we have regulated public health by assuring the safety, efficacy, quality and security of medicines and medical devices may provide some insight. Identifying and effectively applying principles to regulate disruptive immerging technologies must be considered. The role of privacy and cybersecurity professionals advocating for, and contributing to, the development of such principles will be instrumental. When we sit at our kitchen tables in years to come, we as a professionals must be able to say we played our part in positively influencing how society interacted with the innovations of our time.

ETHICS DEFINED

> Ethics is knowing the difference between what you have the right to do and what is right to do.
>
>   Potter Stewart, associate justice U.S. Supreme Court

The term "Ethics" is derived from the Greek word *ethos* which can mean custom, habit, character, or disposition. Ethics is a system of moral principles – often referred to as a "moral philosophy" and have been derived over centuries from religions, philosophies, and cultures. Through ethics, society establishes standards of right and wrong that prescribe what humans ought to do, usually in terms of rights, obligations, benefits to society, fairness, or specific virtues. At the heart of ethics is a concern about something or someone other than ourselves and our own desires and self-interest.

Philosophers nowadays tend to divide ethical theories into three areas: meta-ethics, normative ethics, and applied ethics. Meta-ethics deals with the nature of moral judgment. It looks at the origins and meaning of ethical principles. Examples would be ethical statements such as "lying is wrong", or "friendship is good" true or false? Normative ethics is concerned with the content of moral judgments and the criteria for what is right or wrong. For example, claims such as "it is wrong to kill someone even when they make you angry" – this is normative ethics. Normative ethics are represented by several theories such as Kantian Deontology (rights theory, utilitarianism, egoism). For example, utilitarianism is used to explore the moral rights and wrongs of war – the loss of the few to save the many. Where normative ethics studies what features make an action right or wrong, applied ethics attempts to figure out, in actual cases, whether certain acts have those features. Applied ethics looks at controversial topics like animal rights, capital punishment, and abortion.

Table 8.1 lists and describes the most common ethics (relevant to privacy).

Table 8.1 Common types of ethics relevant to privacy

TRADITIONAL ETHICS	Concerns relationships between individuals. Person to person sharing of data.
CORPORATE ETHICS	Concerns relationships between companies and customers and revolves around the practices of online platforms collecting sensitive/large volumes of information about users.
RESEARCH ETHICS	Governs the standards of conduct for scientific researchers. Discussion of the ethical principles of benevolence (i.e., having the individual's best interest at heart), justice and autonomy are central to ethical review. Typically, purpose, consent, and data minimization are in question in research ethics.
PROFESSIONAL ETHICS	Typically referred to as a code of ethics and professional conduct, it outlines the ethical principles that govern decisions and behavior for a particular professional or association of professions. For instance, the IAPP has adopted a code of ethics in collaboration with its members and national and international governments. The subjects covered include research, personal rights, truthful reporting, and the separation of editorial content and advertisements. The goal of the code of ethics is to clarify to every member his responsibility to media consumers and to appeal to his obligation to report professional and well-founded news.
DIGITAL ETHICS	The field of study concerned with the way technology is shaping our political, social, environmental, and moral existence. Digital ethics concerns how should we employ technology, what risks new tech may bring, and what the arrival of these new futures means to us as humans.
DATA ETHICS	The norms of behavior that promote appropriate judgments and accountability when acquiring, managing, or using data, with the goals of protecting civil liberties, minimizing risks to individuals and society, and maximizing the public good. Oxford professor and ethicist Luciano Floridi defines data ethics as "the branch of ethics that studies and evaluates moral problems related to data, algorithms and corresponding practices …, in order to formulate and support morally good solutions (e.g., right conducts or right values)".

WHAT ARE PRIVACY ETHICS?

> Ethics comes before, during and after the law....
> Giovanni Buttarelli, European Data Protection Supervisor

The current discourse regarding privacy and ethics most often falls to data ethics rather than the specific of privacy ethics. The IAPP suggests that data ethics incorporates privacy and encompasses the protections an organization puts in place around how the data is collected, used, and shared. However, data ethics also aims to reconcile the tension between these competing public goods – individual privacy protection vs. societal benefit. Data ethics also highlights the equally important ethical concern – the price of failing to use certain technologies or data for the public good in cases when the possibility to do so responsibly exists. Data ethics involves organizations investing resources to build internal programs to weigh and balance benefits and risks to individuals from big data and AI uses. According to Emory University ethicist Paul Root Wolpe, data ethics addresses considerations of bias (often inherent in the choices made when selecting data subjects, building a dataset, and deciding on research methods); ownership, and the rights to control data use; and power imbalances between an organization collecting data and individual data subjects. The simplest way to understand the relationship between privacy and ethics is to consider the phrase "Just because you can doesn't mean you should". Famously in 2010, the then CEO of Google, Eric Schmidt said that Google gets right up to the creepy line but never cross it. The creepy line is essentially a metaphorical representation of privacy and ethics. The problem is that profit associated with maximized use of data (right up at the creepy line) results in maximized profits. Choosing an ethical approach to data privacy can often result in less profit, as data-use may not be maximized. However, this may indeed be short-term thinking rather than long-term sustainable thinking. Organizations who apply ethical approaches to privacy frameworks may not make maximum return from their data but instead focus on maximizing loyalty and engagement from their customers while leveraging corporate privacy reputation as a competitive edge. This in turn leads to increased levels of trust, which in turn leads to increased data provision by consumers.

PRIVACY AND TRUST

Dr. Chris Dimitriadis

Chief Global Strategy Officer, ISACA

Thinking of regulations, like GDPR, privacy is so much more than protecting data subjects from breaches. It is about giving them rights to decide on who and for what purpose is processing their data. So, is it a data management issue, rather than a cybersecurity one? I have always considered Privacy as a key component of the wider notion of digital trust. According to ISACA, *digital trust is the confidence in the integrity of the relationships, interactions and transactions among providers and consumers within an associated digital ecosystem.* So how do we achieve such trust in practice, with privacy as a key enabler? One of the issues that organizations are facing globally is the siloed approach between their digital transformation efforts, audit, privacy, risk, cybersecurity and other digital trust-related domains. How can one be effective in privacy without understanding the business goals and P&L of a digital transformation program? I have seen many times privacy, technology and business professionals speaking three different languages (legal, technical and business/financial). How can one establish privacy without creating a balance with cybersecurity and without having cybersecurity enable privacy in a way that covers all privacy requirements on top of protection from breaches (data retention, deletion requests, consent etc.). How can one create a robust privacy program without understanding new technologies like AI and without taking into account the frequent technology updates needed or without mastering the art of risk management. What about the supply chain or the broader ecosystem dependencies and may impact privacy. Finally, doesn't privacy have a strong assurance requirement? How are audit programs shaped to address privacy as an embedded component of an ecosystem?

My point is that we need to create more holistic professionals that have a vertical expertise in privacy but also horizontal knowledge in adjacent digital trust professions, as well as strengthen the collaboration of several actors of a digital ecosystem under a common framework.

THE CHALLENGE FOR PRIVACY ETHICS

There are two key challenges associated with privacy ethics. The first is that while many current privacy regulations, such as the CCPA and the GDPR, take a risk-based approach, underpinned by data protection impact assessments that are focused on compliance and accountability, the ethical and social dimensions of privacy are often absent. This is because data protection legislation is largely focused on how organizations process personal data, rather than what organizations strategically do to extend, or shape conditions for that processing. Much of the recent advancement in technology associated with big data and AI also require consideration of human rights concepts beyond individual privacy, extending assessment to ethical implications of data use not only on individuals but also on society. The second challenge is that no two moral compasses are the same. Our ethical or moral position is influenced by our local legislative landscape, our culture, our religion, our personality, our nation's history, our personal beliefs, our values, and so on. Even our political beliefs. For example, a study on surveillance from the Annenberg School for Communication at the University of Pennsylvania found that Americans are deeply divided over tracking, both online and in real life. Political affiliation is a main predictor of Americans' emotional reactions to surveillance, the researchers found. Among people who identified themselves as Democrats, for instance, 62% said they felt "creeped out" by the idea of companies checking job applicants' credit history before hiring them. By contrast, half of independents and just 29% of Republicans felt creeped out. "The Republicans are most likely to be positive about surveillance", said Joseph Turow (a professor at the University of Pennsylvania and the lead author of the study). Turow also noted that "the Democrats are most likely to be negative, and independents are always in the middle".

Ethical privacy landscapes and perspectives also differ greatly between organizations, industries, jurisdictions, departments, and individuals. What is considered ethical in one context, may not be ethical in another. In other words, ethics is not black and white and is often grey. This greyness is particularly true across jurisdictions. For instance – the US privacy framework is based on a discretionary regime, underpinned by FIPPs as its ethical backbone, where the EU privacy framework is based on a mandatory regime based on GDPR. The principles of FIPPs are incorporated and thus enshrined into the data protection principles of GDPR and breaching them can result in penalties or fines. Therefore, in the EU – principles such as transparency, fairness, etc. are not considered ethical requirements but are instead considered legal mandates.

This moral/ethical grey area extends beyond organizations to individuals who, as previously noted, all have an individual moral compass where an action can be interpreted as honorable by one person, while another can interpret it as unethical or immoral. For instance, in 2013, after Edward Snowden brought mass surveillance by governments into question, the public were split 50/50 on whether his actions served the public interest or harmed it (Pew, 2013) and whether he was a hero or a traitor. Privacy and accountability advocates agreed with Snowden. Jesselyn Radack of the Government Accountability Project argued that "Snowden may have violated a secrecy agreement, which is not a loyalty oath but a contract, and a less important one than the social contract a democracy has with its citizenry". The Attorney General of the United States, Eric Holder argued "He broke the law. He caused harm to our national security, and I think that he has to be held accountable for his actions". Journalists too were conflicted about the ethical implications of Snowden's actions. The editorial board of The New York Times stated, "He may have committed a crime…but he has done his country a great service". In an Op-ed in the same newspaper, Ed Morrissey argued that Snowden was not a hero, but a criminal who should be prosecuted for his actions, arguing that his actions broke a law "intended to keep legitimate national-security data and assets safe from our enemies; it is intended to keep Americans safe".

In this greyness – a uniform universal ethics framework across all organizations, industries, jurisdictions, departments, and individuals is unlikely. The approach evolving appears to be the emergence of ethical frameworks for specific technologies, specific governments, or specific sectors/industries, etc. some of which we outline below:

- **Federal Data Ethics Framework**: The Framework's purpose is to guide federal leaders and data users as they make ethical decisions when acquiring, managing, and using data to support their agency's mission. The Framework does not include requirements or mandates of its own but rather provides guidance in the form of tenets to encourage ethical decision-making at all levels of the Federal Government.
- **UK Data Ethics**: The UK Data Ethics Framework guides appropriate and responsible data use in the government and wider public sector. It helps public servants understand ethical considerations, address these within their projects, and encourages responsible innovation.
- **Google AI Ethics**: Google AI Ethics Principles are a series of seven principles that Google believe AI should comply with together with a statement of what AI applications Google will not pursue.
- **FIPPs**: (outlined in Chapter 5).

Extending the risk-based approach typically in privacy regulation, to include the adoption of a more ethics and values based approach, would include a focus on the societal impact of data use. This impact encompasses the potential negative outcomes on a variety of fundamental rights and principles and considers the ethical and social consequences of data processing. Mantelero presents an excellent starting point for policymakers in this regard, by combining the Human Rights Ethical Impact Assessment (HREIA) framework with the GDPRs Data Protection Impact Assessment framework.

AI – PRIVACY'S NEW FRONTIER

Dan Or-Hof, ADV., ESQ., CIPP/E, CIPP/US, CIPM

Owner, Or-Hof Law

February 2, and March 31, 2023, will be remembered as the first realizations of the tension between data protection and artificial intelligence. In both dates, the Italian data protection supervisory authority (Garante), has initiated an investigation and issued an order to block the use of AI services – the first – Replika, an AI-powered chatbot and the second – OpenAI. The Garante orders were soon followed by an investigation launched by the Canada Office of Privacy Commissioner, on April 3, 2023, into OpenAI, following a complaint on collection and use of personal information without consent. No doubt, there is a growing attention of privacy regulators to generative AI.

According to the Garante latter order, OpenAI will either implement measures to stop data protection violations or face a fine of up to 20 million euros or up to 4% of annual global turnover.

The Italian regulator highlights four aspects of data protection violations that have already been addressed by privacy commentators and practitioners. The first, the lack of a disclosure to users and all stakeholders whose data is collected by OpenAI; the second, the absence of a legal basis to justify the massive collection and use of personal data for the algorithmic training; the third, the information generated by ChatGPT does not always correspond to the actual data, thus leading to inaccurate processing of personal data; and the fourth, the absence of any age verification or filters to prevent the exposure of minors to outputs unsuitable to them.

AI, as evidenced by the highly popular Generative AI services, raises novel legal and ethical questions. Ethics, responsibility, explainability and accountability in AI processing become important factors when neural networks can produce discriminating, offensive, IP infringing, privacy violating or otherwise unlawful outputs. Specifically, these applications have a substantial potential impact on privacy in a number of ways.

Generative AI requires masses of data to train on. Some data could contain personal information, such as head shots and personal details in texts. There are a number of privacy considerations associated with Generative AI.

For example, false, abusive, inaccurate or biased AI-generated published personal details can result in serious damage to the privacy of the respective individuals.

Transparency associated with the collection of the data is an additional obvious risk, as individuals do not receive genuine and accessible notice that data related to them is used for machine learning. Consent and other lawful grounds of processing would be additional factors to weigh. Must collecting personal information to train machines be based on individuals' consent, or can it be based, for example, on legitimate interests as a lawful ground? Can the generative AI processing of special categories of data governed by the GDPR be acknowledged as necessary for scientific or statistical purposes? Would AI-processing be regarded under the CPRA as a non-compatible purpose which requires a separate consent? These questions indicate the growing debate on whether AI data processing requires prior permission.

Sharing AI-based outputs raises another privacy consideration, as personal details can be transferred and used by those who were not the intended recipients of the original data. Data sharing beyond the individual's reasonable expectations could also be viewed as a privacy violation.

Another challenge relates to the ability of individuals to exercise their privacy rights, and the ability of generative AI applications to comply with such requests. Presumably, the rights of access and deletion are manageable. Conversely, including a human in the loop to effectuate the GPDR right not to be subject to automated decision making, or limiting the use of sensitive personal information, as required under the CPRA, would likely be harder to implement.

Generative AI systems use mases of data, which could be highly lucrative for hackers and therefore susceptible to cyber-attacks. Unauthorized access and use of the data, and concerns related to the security of mega-databases are another factor that requires attention.

Lastly, an interaction with a generative AI application requires the user to input text describing the user's wishes, e.g., a certain textual result or an image. The input is uploaded, processed and stored, and can contain sensitive personal information, which becomes part of the AI application's datasets (ChatGPT's privacy policy clearly indicates that they use data inputs to improve the service). Given the extent of sensitive information that individuals share across social networks and other online services, it is very likely that they will share the same with generative AI services, even when warned not to.

New technologies challenge existing norms. They generate the need to rethink where to strike the right balance between innovation and protection against adverse effects. In most cases, laws strive to be technology neutral, to maintain a broad and long-lasting application of the law when technology changes. However, some argue that AI in general and generative AI specifically are not just another technology, as they introduce a dramatic impact on norms and social mechanisms, and therefore require specific regulatory attention. This approach is at heart of current attempts to regulate AI, such as the EU AI Act which is planned to be finalized by the end of 2023 and the October 2022 White House's Blueprint for an AI Bill of Rights.

There are a variety of additional attempts to offer 'soft laws', i.e., guidelines, rather than laws, for responsible and ethical AI, that may serve both AI users and policy makers for potential future legislation. These include, for example, the May 2019 OECD AI principles, the January 2023 NIST AI Risk Management Framework and the October 2022 Israeli Ministry of Innovation, Science and Technology Principles for AI Policy, Regulation and Ethics.

Three main aspects describe current efforts to regulate AI: The first, regulation will mandate human intervention and oversight over AI-based processes. The second, regulation will focus on the uses and the users of AI, rather than on the technology itself. The third, AI regulation aims at setting out principles, some of which codify ethical norms (e.g., transparency), while others are aimed at managing risks properly (e.g., security and resilience).

From a privacy compliance perspective, regulation will heavily focus on two main aspects – design and control:

Showing that a machine learning-based system complies with the necessity and proportionality principles requires substantial effort. Alongside, generative AI services are becoming systems that process trillions of words, images and audio recordings, with billions of users worldwide that use these systems on daily basis. Meaningful and effective privacy controls to these systems require 'Scalability-by-Design'. Therefore, the need to use privacy enhancing technologies (PETs) and to promote privacy by design will probably be the most important aspect of AI privacy compliance. Especially, designers and users of AI will need to embed and be able to demonstrate data minimization and obfuscation practices, including de-identification, aggregation, control over retention periods and automated deletion processes, use of synthetic data, blurring, truncating, cropping and pixelating content. They will also need to design and embed methods to detect and treat algorithmics infected with bias and avoid other harmful inaccuracies.

An individual's control over AI processing of personal information related to that individual, will be manifested through disclosure requirements such as detailed privacy notices, through setting the right lawful grounds of processing (consent or others) and through exercising privacy rights, mainly access, deletion, limiting the processing, requiring human intervention in automated decisions, and transferring data under portability rights.

A provider of a generative AI service will also need to demonstrate control through algorithm reviews and sound information security management.

Some argue that regulating privacy in AI data processing should not be any different from privacy compliance efforts in relation to any other types of data processing. The norms, principles and obligations are already there. Yet implementation of practical solutions to manage privacy risks could be fundamentally unique when implementing them on AI. For example, minimizing algorithmic bias requires an interdisciplinary effort for designing solutions that will review algorithms before and during deployment and could provide an effective on-going oversight. The regulatory probe against AI has started. The outcome is yet to be seen.

PRIVACY AS PART OF THE ESG AGENDA

The rise in magnitude and frequency of high-profile privacy breaches and cybersecurity threats presents a challenge for organizations, governments, and policymakers – to balance the tension between the need to process data versus the impact such processing may have on the data subject and society.

Privacy legislation appears to dominate as the solution to address these tensions; however, the legislative solution appears to be ineffective. This is because the regulatory response to privacy presents two key challenges that are increasingly difficult to overcome. First, mandatory breach disclosure – a core element of privacy regulation – is predicated on detecting or prosecuting a violation, only after it has occurred, and the damage is done. Second, regulations are often reactive and lagging technology by the time they are enacted. For instance, the GDPR was in discussion for four years, before being approved by the EU parliament in 2016, coming into force then only two years later. These breaches not only impact an organization financially through penalties, fines, and remediation costs, they also have wider negative consequences on an organization's reputation, the wider stakeholder community, and is seen as a key element in loss of consumer trust.

In 2015, the then European Data Protection Supervisor Giovanni Buttarelli (RIP) suggested that simple compliance to regulation would no longer suffice and that organizations must adopt an ethical approach to the collection and processing of data. More recently at RSA 2022, key privacy leaders from Apple, Google, and LinkedIn concurred that privacy and security are set to join environmental, social, and governance (ESG) as important criteria that consumers use to determine if an organizations values align with their own, and investors use to determine the financial health and sustainability of the organization. For example, Kalinda Raina, LinkedIn CPO, said that the inclusion of privacy into ESG has been a shift conducted over the past decade. "We've been really trying hard to grow the awareness of privacy, the understanding of privacy in our organizations, and now we are beginning to see the public show interest as well," Raina said.

> And I think that the really exciting shift that has been happening is people's awareness and judgment of companies based on how they're handling data, how we're thinking about these issues, how they are treating privacy, and quite honestly all the things that go into trust, security, safety, privacy, how you're approaching the environment, how you're approaching diversity.

Keith Enright, Google CPO, noted that technology has an important role in protecting "democratic values and democratic institutions around the world. … The responsibility of technology providers in that conversation has never been more front and center". Finally, Jane Horvath, Apple CPO, highlighted that privacy was an "ESG value at Apple. Privacy is a corporate value at Apple. All of our execs are held to account for privacy as part of our ESG values".

Recent studies demonstrate that investing in privacy beyond mere regulation pays off. The 2020 Cisco Privacy Benchmark Study ascertained that for each pound spent on privacy and data protection, "companies are getting

£2.70 worth of improvements to their data loss mitigation, agility, innovation, customer loyalty and other key areas". By investing privacy and embedding it into organizational practices, strategies, and stakeholder communication, both company finances and the greater public can benefit from increased protections and sustainability.

However, what does privacy as an ESG look like and how can we address it as privacy leaders? The following section outlines in detail what privacy looks like when shaped as part of the ESG agenda.

What is ESG?

ESG means using Environmental, Social, and Governance factors to evaluate companies and countries on how far advanced they are with sustainability. The terms ESG and sustainability are often used interchangeably, yet it is incorrect to do so.

The current definition of corporate sustainability in the Oxford English Dictionary is:

> The property of being environmentally sustainable; the degree to which a process or enterprise is able to be maintained or continued while avoiding the long-term depletion of natural resources.

We prefer the definition from the 1987 Brundtland Report (Published by the World Commission on Environment and Development (WCED), in 1987 the Brundtland Report, named after the Norwegian Prime Minister Gro Harlem Brundtland who chaired the production of the report, first introduced the concept of sustainable development and described how it could be achieved):

> development that meets the needs of the present generations without compromising the ability of the future generations to meet their own needs.

In 2004, Kofi Annan, then the UN Secretary, asked major financial institutions to partner with the UN and the International Finance Corporate. The resulting 2005 study, titled *Who Cares Wins*, marked the first use of the term ESG. The main difference between ESG and sustainability is that ESG sets specific criteria to define environmental, social, and governance systems as sustainable. As we know, in a business context, *sustainability* may mean different things to different entities and is applied as an umbrella term of *doing good*. This translates into ethical and responsible business practices. Embedded into this term are concerns for social equity and economic development. ESG points to a specific set of criteria that removes the ambiguity surrounding the term sustainability. As such, ESG is a preferred term for investors.

ESG programs can be considered the next step in the evolution of corporate social responsibility (CSR). CSR programs tend to focus on qualitative issues and policies, while ESG programs quantify a company's impact on the environment, the value of relationships it builds in its community, and the controls it has in place to ensure ethical operation.

ESG environmental

Environmental factors include the contribution a company or government makes to climate change through greenhouse gas emissions, along with waste management and energy efficiency. Given renewed efforts to combat global warming, cutting emissions and decarbonizing have become more important.

ESG social

Social includes human rights, labor standards in the supply chain, any exposure to illegal child labor, and more routine issues such as adherence to workplace health and safety. A social score also rises if a company is well integrated with its local community and therefore has a "social license" to operate with consent. Socially responsible activities can reduce an organization's exposure to risk and improve firm reputation, consumer trust, and long-term loyalty.

ESG governance

Governance refers to a set of rules or principles defining rights, responsibilities, and expectations between different stakeholders in the governance of corporations. A well-defined corporate governance system can be used to balance or align interests between stakeholders and can work as a tool to support a company's long-term strategy. Governance can also refer to the standard of government of nations.

What is privacy as part of the ESG agenda (ESGp)

ESG rankings have proven that companies with below-average performance on governance standards are more likely to take on unnecessary risk through mismanagement. Data breaches resulting from poor or non-existent privacy programs are textbook examples of this kind of risk. Problematic privacy practices may also lead investors to question a company's accounting, labor, and environmental protocols. The shaping of privacy as part of the ESG suite reflects Dr. Lyons's view of privacy which she calls "doing privacy right not doing privacy rights" – and five years ago she embarked on a substantial piece of research into privacy as an ESG, to determine 1) a taxonomy of privacy as an ESG, 2) an understanding of key approaches to privacy as an ESG undertaken by organizations and their potential influence on firm performance and the wider stakeholder community, and 3) measuring the influence that different privacy as ESG had on consumer purchase behaviors. The remainder of this chapter outlines a summary of how privacy fits into the ESG suite, how it can be approached by organizations, and how it can be reported.

ESGp environmental

Privacy's inclusion in environmental ESG concerns is a relatively new development. From an IT perspective, many organizations have been exploring how to save energy related to the building and/or operation of their data centers, offices, and server farms. More recently, employers have started to shape full or partial work-from-home positions as pollution-reducing, and health enhancing, as it reduces from employees commuting every day and enables employees to have more time to exercise, study, or spend with their families. While these are not privacy specific, as data management technology continues to improve, it's probable that companies will have more environmentally friendly options for their privacy practices in terms of electronic waste, particularly regarding data retention. Th new EU Corporate Sustainability Reporting Directive (CSRD) starts in Jan 2024 (for all large companies in the EU/ with significant activity in the EU plus turnover over €150 million). Privacy and security teams are very much involved with organizational initiatives such as the implementation of hybrid and remote working models, and their involvement in these initiatives should be monitored and tracked.

ESGp social

Privacy and data protection requirements, such as those embedded in GDPR, have been well absorbed into current governance frameworks; however, they focus on such requirements as the "end-goal" instead of merely the "baseline", with little emphasis on engaging with more sustainable values such as consumer trust. This has given rise to the birth of three more recent strategies for privacy: privacy as social responsibility, privacy as a political responsibility, and privacy as a socio-political responsibility. In this way, organizations approach data protection beyond GRC, by building a sustainable and socially responsible information protection strategy that is founded on engendering and nurturing consumer trust.

Privacy as a corporate social responsibility (privacy as a CSR)

Corporate Social Responsibility (CSR) is defined by the European Commission as the responsibility that companies take with respect to their

Figure 8.1 CSR Pyramid of responsibilities.

(Source: Carroll, 1979.)

societal impact. The "father" of Corporate Social Responsibility (CSR) theory Archie B. Carroll (1979) categorized corporate social responsibilities into four pillars of responsibility. This was referred to as Carroll's CSR Pyramid of Corporate Responsibilities (see Figure 8.1).

Carroll argued that making a profit, within the boundaries of the law, is the quintessential responsibility of organizations, at which point organizations can consider both their ethical and philanthropic responsibilities. The CSR Pyramid of responsibilities should be evaluated as a whole, for an organization to remain sustainable. An organization should therefore be profitable and make sensible strategic decisions, be compliant and adhere to regulations, be ethical and operate above the minimum standard of the law and be philanthropic by contributing positively to the society.

In 1983 Mintzberg suggested that CSR activities are most appropriate where existing legislation requires compliance with the spirit as well as the letter of the law and where the organization can fool stakeholders through its superior knowledge; many organizations are known to conceal information practices from consumers, effectively keeping consumers "in the dark" and thus privacy fits into Mintzberg's description. Then, in 1998 Carroll suggested that the protection of online privacy rights was a discipline where legislation lags behind ethics, and morality comes into play – thus fitting into the ethical component of the CSR Pyramid – as it involves the pursuit of organizational interests such as profitability or market share, at the expense of those who provide personal information. Privacy also meets Mason's (1995) test of what constitutes an ethical problem, i.e., whenever one party in pursuit of its goals engages in behavior that materially affects the ability of another party to pursue its goals.

More recently, in 2013, Savitz identified privacy as a key social measure within the triple bottom line theory of CSR. Societal concerns regarding social issues often shape an organization's CSR and during the last decade, a concept referred to as CSR 2.0 emerged. CSR 2.0 is a reference to the influence of Web 2.0 on CSR behavior (Web 2.0 is a term used to describe the second stage of development of the Internet, characterized especially by the change from static web pages to dynamic or <u>user-generated</u> content and the growth of social media such as Twitter, Facebook, LinkedIn, etc.). CSR 2.0 is defined as socially responsible behaviors that generate positive changes in society. Privacy has been identified as one of the key social issues for CSR 2.0 (Scherer, 2018). These evolving societal concerns, together with organizational CSR practices, have given rise, in part, to privacy activities exceeding an organization's legal, financial, and ethical responsibilities, such as advocating for strengthened privacy, developing open privacy standards, or collaborating with privacy advocacy groups.

The interest in privacy as a CSR appears to be gaining momentum in the literature, in industry and in organizations:

- In the literature, more recent studies referencing privacy as a CSR are increasingly emerging (see suggested reading section for several recent studies in this area).
- In industry, Privacy as a CSR is also included in several standards for CSR reporting. For example, Section 6.3.4 of the International Standards Organization for Social Responsibility "ISO 26000" refers to privacy as a Human Right and Section 6.7.7 refers to consumer privacy (International Organization of Standards, 2021). Section 418 of the Global Reporting Initiative (GRI) also addresses consumer privacy (Global Reporting Initiative, 2021).
- The number of organizations undertaking privacy as a CSR is on the rise. For instance, Forrester (2018) found that of the Fortune 100 organizations in 2016 and 2017, 21 framed privacy as a CSR in their corporate publications, growing in 2018 to 28. My own research in 2022, using the same index, found 65 organizations in the Fortune 100 index to frame privacy as a CSR.

Bringing together these theoretical ethical principles of CSR into tangible and practical privacy guidelines, The Maastricht University Data Protection as a CSR (UM DPCSR) Project completed in 2021 presents a framework for organizations to apply to foster transparency, accountability, fair, secure, and sustainable data processing activities that positively contribute to the greater good. The UM-DPCSR Framework (link in the Suggested Reading section) presumes GDPR compliance and goes one step further to require that organizations process personal data in a fair, transparent, ethical, secure, and sustainable manner with a clear commitment to actively promote data protection rights and cybersecurity hygiene within the digital society.

Privacy as a corporate political responsibility

Privacy regulations (such as the CCPA or the GDPR) are rules enacted by governments that can limit markets and access to data. Organizations typically try to shape these rules using lobbying to make it more favorable for them. This type of activity is referred to as Corporate Political Activity (CPA). Organizations can lobby for privacy regulations that support their business, or lobby to block privacy regulations that harm their business. Large technology organizations have aggressively lobbied governments regarding privacy – for instance in 2018 Apple invested $8.9 million in privacy specific lobbying (VpnMentor, 2019). There have been concerns that privacy-specific lobbying is associated with organizations exerting undue control over governments, legislation, and policies and is consequently distrusted. For instance, after CCPA was launched, Facebook, Google, IBM, and Microsoft aggressively lobbied officials to start outlining a federal privacy law to overrule the California law, and instead enact a set of privacy rules that would give these organizations more control over how personal information was handled. Such lobbying can lack the altruism associated with privacy as a CSR; however, it can be incorporated where an organization tries to shape the rules [for privacy] in a way that balances the common good together with the corporate good or in a way that aims to resolve a public issue. For example, in 2019 Cisco lobbied for the US government and global citizens to establish privacy as a human right.

Privacy as a sociopolitical responsibility

While privacy as a social responsibility and privacy as a political responsibility aim to enhance an organization's competitive position or reputation, some organizations have more recently engaged in privacy-specific sociopolitical activities that demonstrate their support for, or opposition to, privacy as a politically charged social issue. Sociopolitical issues are by definition salient unresolved social matters on which societal and institutional opinion is split, thus potentially engendering acrimonious debate among groups. Such issues are often partisan, yielding polarized stakeholder responses. Involvement in sociopolitical issues is referred to as Sociopolitical Involvement (SPI), a corporate responsibility that has emerged alongside shifting societal expectations about the roles and responsibilities of business and government. SPI signals an organization's sociopolitical values, thus enabling stakeholders to evaluate the congruence of the organization's values with their own.

The Edelman Trust Barometer highlights that the current trend toward CEOs taking the lead for sociopolitical change has increased steadily from 65% in 2018 to 67% in 2020 (Edelman, 2020). The attention from both scholars and practitioners toward CEO activism has also risen in recent years, as more CEOs take a public stance on sociopolitical issues (McKinsey, 2020).

An example of privacy specific SPI comes from Apple who, in 2015 and 2016, challenged at least 12 orders issued by the FBI compelling Apple to enable the decryption of phones involved in criminal investigations and prosecutions (PEW, 2016). Apple noted in their corporate reports at the time that they "refused to add a backdoor into any of our products". In the United States, Apple did not garner widespread support for their decision, with 51% of American smartphone users against Apple's decision and only 38% supporting it (PEW, 2016). Another example comes from Salesforce whose Chairman and CEO, Marc Benioff, called for a national privacy law despite that this would require significant investment for Salesforce to address such legislation.

Notably, in 2018 over 70% of respondents to a Weber-Shandwick survey selected privacy and data protection as one of the top five issues that they expect CEOs to speak out about and express their opinion (Weber-Shandwick, 2018). Additionally, Amazon's shareholders, who in 2019, introduced two voting proposals regarding their privacy concerns for a facial recognition system called Rekognition (Irish Times, 2019). One proposal asks Amazon's board of directors to prohibit sales of Rekognition to government agencies unless its board concludes that the technology does not facilitate human rights violations. The other proposal asks Amazon's board to commission an independent report examining the extent to which Rekognition may threaten civil, human, and privacy rights, and the organization's finances.

ESGp governance

Traditionally privacy was incorporated with IT Governance or Corporate Governance frameworks. Privacy is evolving, however, to require a governance framework of its own. Essentially this means having a formal corporate governing structure to determine the level of privacy risk appetite acceptable for senior management. Privacy governance consists of having some or all the following in place:

- A formal corporate governing structure to determine the level of privacy risk appetite acceptable for senior management.
- A privacy framework containing policies and procedures relating to privacy of personal information address data classification, record management, retention, purpose, and destruction.
- A Privacy Risk Management Framework including a risk register, to identify, analyze and evaluate, and treat privacy risks.
- A set of roles, responsibilities, and accountability documented and communicated that are related to the privacy program during its life cycle.
- An ongoing awareness program to provide employees the privacy awareness training and guidance on their specific responsibilities in handling privacy requirements, issues, and concerns.

- A Privacy Compliance Monitoring Framework (an ongoing assessment of privacy laws and regulations currently applicable for the organization or will be applicable in the future).
- A Privacy Incident Response Plan.
- Data-Flow Map(s).
- Set of Record of Processing Activities (ROPA).

For more comprehensive details on the governance element of ESG(p), see Chapter 6 on Privacy Risk Governance.

IMPLEMENTING ESGp

Organizations need to understand the impact their activities have on the extended stakeholder community, including the broader economy, the environment, and the society in which they operate. To gain this understanding, organizations undertaking ESG will assess the materiality of a topic as part of their overall governance program. A combination of internal and external factors can be considered when assessing whether a topic is material. These include the organization's overall mission and competitive strategy, and the concerns expressed directly by stakeholders. Materiality can also be determined by broader societal expectations, and by the organization's influence on upstream entities, such as suppliers, or downstream entities, such as customers. Assessments of materiality are also expected to consider the expectations expressed in international standards and agreements with which the organization is expected to comply.

A materiality assessment is the process of identifying, refining, and assessing numerous potential environmental, social, and governance issues that matter most to an organization and its key stakeholders and condensing them into a shortlist of topics that inform organizational strategy, targets, and reporting. A materiality assessment is designed to help the organization identify and understand the relative importance of specific ESG and sustainability topics to the organization. This involves looking at a variety of factors through two dimensions: (1) the significance of the organization's economic, environmental, and social impacts – that is, their significance for the economy, environment or society, as per the definition of 'impact' – and (2) their substantive influence on the assessments and decisions of stakeholders. A topic can be material if it ranks highly for only one of these dimensions of materiality.

Over 80% of the world's largest 250 companies include materiality assessments in their ESG reporting, and in 2021, over 60% of the Fortune 100 reported privacy in their materiality assessments (Lyons, van der Werff and Lynn, 2022). Below are a few examples of materiality assessments presented in CSR reports. The Verizon materiality assessment from their 2021 report is presented in Figure 8.2, and the CISCO materiality assessment from their 2022 report is presented in Figure 8.3.

| Approach | Governance | Environmental | Social | SASB index | Appendix |

High-priority impactful issues

Climate change	Reducing the climate impact of our operations through energy-efficiency efforts and low-carbon energy generation and sourcing, as well as managing risks to our company and customers presented by climate change.
Data protection and privacy	Providing a safe and secure online experience, including preventing fraud, identity theft, exploitation, and cyber attacks; protecting and respecting the privacy rights of our customers by employing strong policies and controls during the capture, storage, and transfer of personal information.
Digital inclusion	Extending high-quality access to communications services regardless of ability, specifically to underserved locations and populations.
Diversity, equity and inclusion (DEI)	Creating an engaging and inclusive culture by providing equal opportunities regardless of race, national origin, gender, sexual orientation, gender identity or expression, disability, veteran/military status, age, experiences, and ways of thinking.
Network reliability and resilience	Network reliability, and resilience; managing systemic risks from technology disruptions.
Talent attraction and retention	Providing opportunities for employees to engage in sponsored activities, as well as providing support for community activities important to our employees. Training and development of employees with a focus on upskilling, including responsible approaches to addressing changing workforce needs.

Impactful issues

Competitive behavior	Ensuring compliance with antitrust laws, protecting fair competition, protection of patents, IP and open internet.
Employee health and safety	Promoting employee health and well-being, particularly through employee benefits, and protecting employees from risk of injury.
Labor practices	Compliance with labor laws, upholding workers' rights and our relationship with organized labor.
Management of legal and regulatory environment	Our approach to engaging with regulators, influence on policy and political contributions.
Product end-of-life management (including e-waste)	Reducing the end-of-life environmental impact of products and network equipment (including e-waste), by managing the reuse, recycling, and disposal of products and component parts.
Supply chain management	Managing labor issues in our supply chain (e.g., working hours, health and safety, remuneration, sexual harassment, freedom of association, and collective bargaining).

| Foundational areas: | Business ethics | Governance | Human rights |

Figure 8.2 2021 Verizon materiality assessment.

(Source: Environmental Social and Governance (ESG) Report, Verizon, 2021.)

ESG REPORTING STANDARDS

An organization's performance in relation to the society in which it operates and to the impact on the environment has become a critical part of measuring its overall performance and ability to continue operating effectively. This is, in part, a reflection of the growing recognition of the need to ensure healthy ecosystems, social equity, and good organizational governance. In the long run, all organizations' activities depend on the health of the

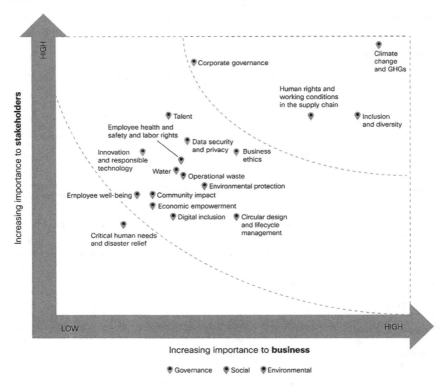

Figure 8.3 Cisco 2022 materiality assessment.

(Source: Cisco, 2022.)

world's ecosystems. Organizations are subject to greater scrutiny by their various stakeholders. The perception and reality of an organization's performance on social responsibility can influence, among other things:

- Organization competitive advantage.
- Organization reputation.
- Organization ability to attract/retain workers or members, customers, clients, or users.
- Maintenance of employees' morale, commitment, and productivity.
- View of investors, owners, donors, sponsors, and the financial community, and
- Organization's relationship with companies, governments, the media, suppliers, peers, customers, and the community in which it operates.

There are two key reporting standards that include privacy requirements: ISO 26000 and GRI. Both contain metrics related to privacy that help an organization to demonstrate its continued value of privacy and to demonstrate effectiveness of its privacy program, for example,

- Number of employees who have completed privacy training.
- Number of privacy incidents.
- Number of privacy complaints received from customers.
- Comparison of pre- and post-training assessment.

These reporting standards are discussed in further detail below.

ISO 26000

Launched in November 2010, ISO 26000 is the first real international standard about social responsibility. The standard was developed over five years of negotiations and represents a consensus between many different stakeholders across the world. The standard provides guidance on the underlying principles of social responsibility, recognizing social responsibility and engaging stakeholders, the core subjects and issues pertaining to social responsibility and on ways to integrate socially responsible behavior into the organization. Unlike management system standards, such as ISO 14001 or ISO 9001, which are subject to certifications and can supplement socially responsible approaches, ISO 26000 serves as a set of guidelines rather than requirements, meaning the standard is not intended for certification purposes.

ISO 26000 outlines the principles and themes that social responsibility encompasses, in line with international founding texts such as the Universal Declaration of Human Rights and the International Labor Organization's fundamental conventions. In particular, the standard clarifies the concept of social responsibility, defined as "the responsibility of an organization for the impacts of its decisions and activities on society and the environment, through transparent and ethical behavior".

ISO 26000 invites organizations to structure their approach around seven interlinked core subjects relating to social responsibility. This enables them to identify any relevant areas of action that they can then draw from to determine their priorities and implement measures.

Key principles and core subjects of ISO 26000

The Seven Key Principles, advocated as the roots of socially responsible behavior, are:

- Accountability
- Transparency

- Ethical behavior
- Respect for stakeholder interests (stakeholders are individuals or groups who are affected by, or can impact, the organization's actions)
- Respect for the rule of law
- Respect for international norms of behavior
- Respect for human rights

There are seven core subjects, which every user of ISO 26000 should consider which are:

1. **Core subject: Organizational governance**
2. **Core subject: Human rights**
   Issue 1: Due diligence
   Issue 2: Human rights risk situations
   Issue 3: Avoidance of complicity
   Issue 4: Resolving grievances
   Issue 5: Discrimination and vulnerable groups
   Issue 6: Civil and political rights
   Issue 7: Economic, social and cultural rights
   Issue 8: Fundamental principles and rights at work
3. **Core subject: Labor practices**
   Issue 1: Employment and employment relationships
   Issue 2: Conditions of work and social protection
   Issue 3: Social dialogue
   Issue 4: Health and safety at work
   Issue 5: Human development and training in the workplace
4. **Core subject: The environment**
   Issue 1: Prevention of pollution
   Issue 2: Sustainable resource use
   Issue 3: Climate change mitigation and adaptation
   Issue 4: Protection of the environment, biodiversity and restoration of natural habitats
5. **Core subject: Fair operating practices**
   Issue 1: Anti-corruption
   Issue 2: Responsible political involvement
   Issue 3: Fair competition
   Issue 4: Promoting social responsibility in the value chain
   Issue 5: Respect for property rights
6. **Core subject: Consumer issues**
   Issue 1: Fair marketing, factual and unbiased information and fair contractual practices
   Issue 2: Protecting consumers' health and safety
   Issue 3: Sustainable consumption
   Issue 4: Consumer service, support, and complaint and dispute resolution

Issue 5: Consumer data protection and privacy
Issue 6: Access to essential services
Issue 7: Education and awareness
7. **Core subject: Community involvement and development**
Issue 1: Community involvement
Issue 2: Education and culture
Issue 3: Employment creation and skills development
Issue 4: Technology development and access
Issue 5: Wealth and income creation
Issue 6: Health
Issue 7: Social investment

GLOBAL REPORTING INITIATIVE (GRI) SUSTAINABILITY REPORTING STANDARDS

The GRI is an international independent standards organization that helps organizations communicate their impacts on the economy, the environment, and society, such as governance, human rights, social impacts, corruption, and climate issues. The GRI Sustainability Reporting Standards are structured as a set of interrelated, modular standards. In the context of the GRI Standards, the social dimension of sustainability concerns an organization's impact on the social systems within which it operates.

In GRI, there are three universal standards that apply to every organization preparing a sustainability report: GRI 101: Foundation GRI 102: General Disclosures GRI 103: Management Approach. An organization then selects from the set of topic-specific GRI Standards for reporting on its material topics. These standards are organized into three series: 200 (Economic topics), 300 (Environmental topics), and 400 (Social topics). Each topic includes disclosures specific to that topic and is designed to be used together with GRI 103: Management Approach, which is used to report the management approach for the topic. In the context of the GRI Standards, the social dimension of sustainability concerns an organization's impact on the social systems within which it operates.

Disclosure 418-1 sets out reporting requirements on the topic of customer privacy, including losses of customer data and breaches of customer privacy. These can result from non-compliance with existing laws, regulations, and/or other voluntary standards regarding the protection of customer privacy. These concepts are covered in key instruments of the Organization for Economic Cooperation and Development.

To protect customer privacy, an organization is expected to limit its collection of personal data, to collect data by lawful means, and to be transparent about how data are gathered, used, and secured. The organization is also expected to not disclose or use personal customer information for any purposes other than those agreed upon, and to communicate any changes in data protection policies or measures to customers directly. This disclosure provides an evaluation of the success of management systems and procedures relating to customer privacy protection. The reporting organization shall report the following information:

- The total number of substantiated complaints received concerning breaches of customer privacy, categorized by 1) complaints received from outside parties and substantiated by the organization; 2) complaints from regulatory bodies.
- The total number of identified leaks, thefts, or losses of customer data.
- If the organization has not identified any substantiated complaints, a brief statement of this fact is sufficient.

PRIVACY, TRUST AND ETHICS

Amalia Barthel

Strategic Digital Leader, Privacy Advisor & Educator, Wareness Canada, Decode Series Leadership

As the modern business environment continuously evolves, a privacy savvy leader stands out as an invaluable asset. They foster growth by embracing the knowledge of their industry and technology advancements and understanding how data protection principles must factor into accountability for decision-making to ensure successful outcomes. By cultivating this essential comprehension, they help build trustworthiness with stakeholders while promoting responsible practices that safeguard valuable customer information.

Working across many industries, I realized that protecting the privacy of customers and service users is a crucial concern for business leaders in the modern age. Members of the public are very aware that they have a "right to know" what happens with their personal information from beginning to end and to be able to trust that it is in good and capable hands. A person's unique identity cannot be recreated if there was a mistake. Privacy of a person is intimately linked with their identity as a human being. But in this business-crazy state of affairs, we see many leaders prioritize profit over any human-centric ethical design decisions. And it all goes back to the consumer "right to know" and the Leader's obligation to "be in the know" and "do the right thing."

There is an increasing demand for digital services that are convenient yet secure, and privacy and business leaders alike must be able to strike the right balance between these two competing needs.

Lengthy privacy notices do not inspire trust. Having internal policies and procedures on a shelf without implementing them does not demonstrate the organization's practices are trustworthy. Because there is the intention, but the practices are not *really* implemented. Personal data must be protected throughout its lifecycle in every single processing operation undertaken by the organization. This translates into a solid governance framework and system of controls, reporting on how privacy (and data protection) obligations are embedded in processes, procedures, technology, escalations, risk logs, discussions, documentation, reviews, testing, QA etc., and Leaders must demand action when rules are not followed correctly or completely. A truly privacy and digital-savvy leader must know when there is potential for data to be used unethically and just because the law may be fuzzy on some requirements it does not mean they can operate "on the dark side."

As someone wise once said "To know and not to do, is not to know" - *Goethe*

For one of the heavily regulated organizations I worked with, I offered a so-called "controversial approach. The idea was to create an open dialogue between different departments and stakeholders regarding data protection and privacy matters, which helped them engage in a healthy exchange of ideas and reach consensus regarding complicated decisions regarding customer information.

By doing this, the company was able to *develop and build* trust and transparency with its customers, build a successful data protection strategy, comply with all applicable regulations, and *demonstrate they care to do the right thing*. Furthermore, this resulted in better customer engagement as customers were given a voice and they were heard.

> True Business Leaders are not wasting time building "privacy" into the functionality of their services and products, but rather invest time in delivering an invisible benefit: trust.
>
> Amalia Barthel

Overall, I believe that effective privacy leaders should take a holistic approach when working on digital services design. By combining a deep understanding of customer needs with a keen eye on the associated privacy challenges, they will be able to ensure that businesses can provide privacy-enhanced services while still maintaining their competitive edge.

So, where does a digital-savvy business leader start? With knowledge and acknowledgment. They need to be in the know and acknowledge the laws that apply to the information they are using in products and services. They need to know what can affect the business outcome so they can instruct their teams. I would recommend that any Leader encourage open dialogue between different departments and stakeholders when it comes to data privacy. Having all parties involved in developing a common strategy and way forward helps create transparency with customers, build trust inside and outside the organization, and comply with laws and regulations.

This is an area I am passionate about, and I believe that by working together, teams can create an environment that values transparency and open dialogue around privacy, leading to a more secure and trustworthy digital world. With the right support and guidance, business leaders have the potential to make an impact on the approach to privacy and data protection in their services. Privacy and data protection must become everyone's responsibility because "the organization" is every single one employee. And everyone holds in their hands valuable and precious personal data of individuals who count on the organization to protect it like they protect their own individual personal information. It's that simple.

SUGGESTED READING

A Brief History of Data Protection How Did It All Start? The International Network of Privacy Law Professionals. https://inplp.custom/latest-news/article/a-brief-history-of-data-protection-how-did-it-all-start/.

Bandara, R., Fernando, M., and Akter, S. (2020). Managing consumer privacy concerns and defensive behaviors in the digital marketplace. *European Journal of Marketing*, 55(1), 219–246.

Cisco. (2020a). Data privacy benchmark study: Discover how organizations are benefiting from data privacy investments. https://www.cisco.com/c/en_uk/products/security/security-reports/data-privacy-report-2020.html#~dataprivacy-report

Cisco. (2020b). Cisco data privacy benchmark study. From privacy to profit: Achieving positive returns on privacy investments. https://www.cisco.com/c/dam/en/us/products/collateral/security/2020-dataprivacy-cybersecurity-series-jan-2020.pdf?CCID=cc000160&DTID=esootr000515&OID=rptsc020143;

Cisco. (2022). CSR materiality assessment. https://www.cisco.com/c/m/en_us/about/csr/esg-hub/governance/materiality.html

Data Breach Report from the Identity Theft Resource Centre. (2022). https://notified.idtheftcenter.org/s/2022-data-breach-report

Digital Ethics: The Ethical Operating System (OS). https://ethicalos.org/

EU Commission. (2011). Corporate social responsibility & responsible business conduct. https://ec.europa.eu/growth/industry/sustainability/corporate-social-responsibility-responsible-business-conduct_en

EU Corporate Sustainability Reporting Directive (CSRD). (2022). https://finance.ec.europa.eu/capital-markets-union-and-financial-markets/company-reporting-and-auditing/company-reporting/corporate-sustainability-reporting_en

Federal Data Ethics Framework. https://resources.data.gov/assets/documents/fds-data-ethics-framework.pdf

Gartner Predictions for the Future of Privacy. (2020). https://www.gartner.com/smarterwithgartner/gartner-predicts-for-the-future-of-privacy-2020)

Global Reporting Initiative. (2016). Defining what matters in materiality assessments. https://www.globalreporting.org/resourcelibrary/GRI-DefiningMateriality2016.pdf

Global Reporting Initiative. (2021). GRI 418, Customer privacy reporting standards. https://www.globalreporting.org/how-to-use-the-gri-standards/gri-standards-english-language/

Google AI Ethics Principles. https://ai.google/principles/

Hand, David J. (2018). Handwriting: Right, legitimate and proper? The new world of data ethics.

Weber-Shandwick. (2018). CEO Activism in 2018: The Purposeful CEO. Available at https://www.webershandwick.com/wp-content/uploads/2018/07/CEO-Activism-2018_Purposeful-CEO.pdf

IBM and Ponemon Institute. (2022). Cost of a data breach report. https://www.ibm.com/security/data-breach

Irish Times. (2019). Amazon faces investor pressure over facial recognition. https://www.irishtimes.com/business/technology/amazon-faces-investor-pressure-over-facial-recognition-1.3900466

Lobschat, L., Mueller, B., Eggers, F., and Brandimartee, L. (2021). Corporate digital responsibility. *Journal of Business Research*, 122(2), 875–888.

Lyons, V. (2021). CISO stories podcast. Doing privacy right versus doing privacy rights. https://www.cybereason.com/blog/ciso-stories-podcast-doing-privacy-right-vs.-doing-privacy-rights

Lyons, V., van der Werff, L., and Lynn, T. (2022). Doing privacy right not doing privacy rights. https://doras.dcu.ie/27082/1/FinalPHDPDf.pdf

Maastricht University. European Centre on Privacy and Cybersecurity. (2020). The data protection CSR framework. https://www.maastrichtuniversity.nl/ecpc/csr-project/um-dpcsr-framework

Mantelero, A. (2018). AI and big data: A blueprint for a human rights, social and ethical impact assessment. *Computer Law and Security Review*, 34(4), 754–772.

Mantelero, A. (2021). An evidence-based methodology for human rights impact assessment (HRIA) in the development of AI data-intensive systems, *Computer Law & Security Review*, 41, 105561.

Martin, K. (2020). Breaking the privacy paradox: The value of privacy and associated duty of firms. *Business Ethics Quarterly*, 30(1), 1–32.

New York Times. (2018). Creepy or not? Your privacy concerns probably reflect your politics. https://www.nytimes.com/2018/04/30/technology/privacy-concerns-politics.html

Predictions for the US State Privacy Landscape. (2023). Future of Privacy Forum. https://fpf.org/blog/five-big-questions-and-zero-predictions-for-the-u-s-state-privacy-landscape-in-2023/

Reissman, H. (2023). Americans don't understand what companies can do with their personal data — And that's a problem. https://www.asc.upenn.edu/news-events/news/americans-dont-understand-what-companies-can-do-their-personal-data-and-thats-problem

Schultz, S., and Seele, P. (2019). Conceptualizing data-deliberation: The starry sky beetle, environmental system risk, and Habermasian CSR. *Business Ethics*, 29(2), 303–313.

Smith, A. (2022). Making the case for the competitive advantage of corporate social responsibility. *Business Strategy Series*, 8, 186–195.

Storer, K. (2021). Cisco calls for privacy to be considered a fundamental human right. /https://newsroom.cisco.com/press-release-content?articleId=1965781

Turow, J., and Lelkes, Y. (2023). Americans can't consent to companies' use of their data. https://www.asc.upenn.edu/sites/default/files/2023-02/Americans_Can%27t_Consent.pdf

UK Government Digital Service. Data ethics framework. https://www.gov.uk/government/publications/data-ethics-framework

UN The Global Compact. (2005). Who cares wins. Connecting financial markets to a changing world. https://www.unepfi.org/fileadmin/events/2004/stocks/who_cares_wins_global_compact_2004.pdf

Verizon. (2021). Environmental, social and governance (ESG) report 2021. www.verizon.com

VPN Mentor (2018). The issues that matter to the big tech lobby. https://www.vpnmentor.com/research/us-lobby-report/

Section VI

Staff

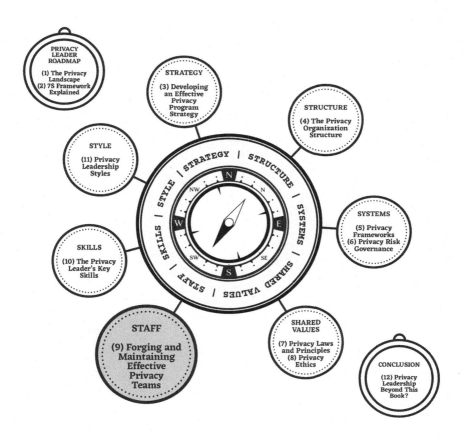

Chapter 9

Forging and maintaining effective privacy teams

> A musician must make music, an artist must paint, a poet must write, if he is to be ultimately at peace with himself. What a man can be, he must be.
>
> Abraham Maslow 1908–1970

Not all teams are alike – considering each team typically has a different composition of members. An effective team must have a combination of respected leadership and cohesive teamwork to work. We have distilled the characteristics of both these into six key qualities:

1. *Have open communication.*
   A good team should have honest discussions wherein they could share their thoughts and opinions. This makes the members feel that they are able to contribute.
2. *Have clear goals.*
   Setting a clear goal for the team helps in having a solid foundation and direction. A team that understands and focuses on their objectives is more likely to work effectively.
3. *Have good leadership.*
   A team needs a great leader to steer them toward the goal. A leader needs to provide constructive feedback to the members and learn to listen to them.
4. *Have trust and respect.*
   A team without trust and respect cannot work effectively as the members will constantly have conflicts with each other. Therefore, the leader must create an environment wherein the members are able to rely on each other and trust each other to work independently. Trust and respect must be top down, bottom up, and across peer relationships.

DOI: 10.1201/9781003383017-15

5. *Have diversity.*

As mentioned before, a team is made up of people with different expertise and knowledge. This is an advantage since members can contribute different ideas that can be beneficial for the team.

6. *Have good conflict management.*

Conflicts in the workplace are inevitable and it is the leader's responsibility to resolve them. Instead of creating heated arguments, it is better to have the members challenge each other in a constructive way.

THE CHALLENGE OF DIVERSITY AND INCLUSION

Kate Colleary

Founder and Director, Pembroke Privacy

The individual of the 2020s emerges into a digital plane beyond the conceptions of her predecessors with more participation, information, connection, ease of access and innovation than could have ever been imagined. This space defines a collective future for all of us, but its rules, values and boundaries are decided by a select few who may not be representative of global tech users.

The voices missing from the room may be the ones with the most to lose. A lack of representation creates a digital divide that perpetuates existing inequalities and widens the gap between the rich and the poor, the powerful and the vulnerable. This challenge is one that must be addressed.

We have the opportunity to create a more inclusive, diverse and innovative future. How can we do that? Here are some ideas:

- We can create more opportunities for diverse and inclusive participation in tech education, innovation and leadership. This means amplifying underrepresented voices, bolstering female leadership and ensuring that those around the table represent society as a whole.
- We can foster more dialogue and collaboration among different stakeholders in tech such as developers, users, policymakers, researchers and civil society. This means creating platforms and spaces where diverse groups of people can share their perspectives, experiences and ideas on how to use tech for good and address its challenges.
- We can advocate for more equitable policies and practices in the tech industry and beyond. For example, we can demand fair wages and working conditions for tech workers, promote ethical and responsible use of technology, or challenge biases and stereotypes in tech culture and media.

> • We can amplify more voices from the global south and other marginalized communities who are often left out of the tech conversation. This means listening to their needs, challenges and aspirations and ensuring that they benefit from the opportunities that tech offers.
>
> By ensuring that we have more voices around the table in deciding the future of tech, we can create a more diverse, inclusive and equitable tech ecosystem that reflects a more diverse set of values and serves our common good.

However, often teams form in such a way that the dynamic within them and around them changes. New people join, people leave, mergers occur, and people go through personal life crises. The list of change is endless. The need to nurture the team continuously is often considered nothing more than a twice annual dinner out in the town. This is ineffective. Nurturing an effective team is a daily task. The team leader needs to watch and observe the dynamics within the team and understand the dynamics "on the ground". Several tools can be used by the team leader to both analyze and enhance team effectiveness to create high performing teams. The tools focused on in this chapter that we have found most effective in practice are Belbin's team roles and Beckhard's GRPI model.

BELBIN'S TEAM ROLES

Meredith Belbin devised the Belbin Team Inventory test through a study at Henley Management College to establish the ideal roles for individuals to assume within a team. To measure personality traits with the Belbin test, participants evaluate their own behaviors, receive feedback from observers, and compare the two.

The results then show which of the nine roles each member of your team is best suited to. However, people may exhibit traits that enable them to assume more than one role, which means that you can build a well-balanced team from any number of people, if you include all the roles.

Often Belbin's test is conflated with the Myers-Briggs Type Indicator test. However, the latter is a psychometric test that reveals your personality type, whereas the Belbin test is a behavioral exam that establishes which traits you display of nine possible team roles. You can complete the Belbin test online, and a link is included in the suggested reading section at the end of this chapter. There are several free versions online and while they are effective – they are likely to present copyright issues.

The nine Belbin team roles are descriptions of job duties that fall into three broad categories: thought-oriented roles, action-oriented roles, and people-oriented roles. Understanding each role a team member can play, may help the team work more efficiently. Table 9.1 presents a summary of these team roles:

Now, let's look at each role in more detail:

Thought-oriented roles

Thought-oriented team members are critical thinkers. They may present new ideas or a new perspective, analyze ideas by weighing the pros and cons, or have specialized knowledge or skills. Thought-oriented roles include:

Table 9.1 Belbin's nine team roles

Role type	Role name	Role key action	Privacy activity ("suggested roles")
Action-Oriented Roles	Shaper	Challenges the team to improve.	Privacy program development and leadership (CPO)
	Implementer	Puts ideas into action.	(Privacy analyst)
	Completer Finisher	Ensures thorough, timely completion.	Subject access request process and responses
People-Oriented Roles	Coordinator	Acts as a chairperson.	Supervisory authority communications (DPO, Privacy Champion, Privacy Steering committee)
	Team Worker	Encourages cooperation.	ROPAs, Asset Inventory, policies, statements and notices (Privacy Analyst)
	Resource Investigator	Explores outside opportunities.	Privacy awareness Stakeholder engagement, Stakeholder influencing. (DPO, Privacy Researcher)
Thought-Oriented Roles	Plant	Presents new ideas and approaches.	Privacy By Design, Ethical Risk Assessment (DPO, Privacy Architect, Privacy Designer)
	Monitor-Evaluator	Analyzes the options.	Privacy audits and risk assessments (Privacy Auditor, Data Protection Auditor, GRC)
	Specialist	Provides specialized skills.	Privacy audits and risk assessments Privacy Enhancing technologies. (CPO, DPO, Privacy Auditor, Data Protection Auditor, GRC, Privacy Specialist, Privacy Expert)

Source: Meredith Belbin.

1. The Monitor Evaluator

    Monitor Evaluators make decisions based on facts and rational thinking as opposed to emotions and instincts. They are normally serious individuals who excel at critical thinking and strategic planning. If there is a challenge in a project, Monitor Evaluators will carefully consider all angles and possibilities and then devise an insightful solution. These individuals tend to be loners who prefer not to get involved in the lives of coworkers, which contributes to their objectivity. Monitor Evaluators work best when challenges arise that require advanced analytical ability and astute problem-solving. Thus, this role would seem best suited to the privacy audit functions.

2. The Specialist

    The Specialist is a team member who is an expert in a specific field. Since they have in-depth knowledge in a narrow subject, they will usually only contribute when a task requires their area of expertise. Like Monitor Evaluators, Specialists tend to be loners, so being part of a team does not often come naturally to them.

    Specialists are invaluable assets, as they provide expert technical knowledge that few else can. Often, senior management will create proposals and projects based on the knowledge of these Specialists. Although Specialists find the idea of being in a team challenging, they become very engaging and helpful when it comes to their field of expertise and will likely have no issues in sharing their knowledge with junior members who want to learn. There are those who know a little about a wide range of topics and there are those in privacy who know a lot about a specific subject. So, where a privacy advocate may know much about the E-Privacy challenges associated with the Ad tech industry, they may not know how to respond to a Subject Access Request – as a generalist might do. Specialists are typically the privacy enhancing technologists, the experts in key areas of privacy.

3. The Plant

    Plants are free-thinkers and creative people who produce original ideas and suggest innovative new ways of doing things. As is the case with the other two thought-oriented roles, Plants prefer to work alone. However, most teams and companies accept this, as the Plant's creative thinking typically leads to innovative solutions and ground-breaking concepts. Although Plants may not fit into the traditional concept of how a team member should act, they are nevertheless invaluable to a team or organization. As the name suggests, Plants are the team members who bring about growth and progress. Privacy researchers are often Plants, for example, those undertaking large research projects in privacy, or those working on groundbreaking technologies, those writing books, white paper or journal articles, those proposing new ways of thinking about old challenges.

Action-oriented team roles

Action-oriented team members strive to get things done. They can be counted on to complete a task, meet a deadline, and see a challenge as an exciting opportunity. Action-oriented roles include:

4. The Shaper

   Shapers are extroverts who tend to push themselves and others to achieve results. They are dynamic and driven individuals who can motivate and inspire passion in team members. Despite any challenges that may come their way, Shapers remain positive and seem to thrive under pressure. They enjoy challenging norms to create unique goals and strategies. It is usually vital to have one Shaper to help the team progress in its mission. Because Shapers are born leaders who tend to get results, they quickly move upward in organizations. They are ideal management material, as they act decisively in crises and drive progress. The CPO is best suited to the shaper role. Because of their comfort and decisiveness in a crisis, they are also best suited to dealing with a data breach and communicating it to key stakeholders.

5. The Implementer

   Implementers are organizers who like to structure their environments and maintain order. Because they are practical people, Implementers like to make concrete plans from abstract ideas. Implementers are highly disciplined and self-controlled individuals who can disregard their self-interest to focus on the needs of a team or an organization. Although Implementers normally prefer established ways of doing things, you can likely persuade them to change if you can prove that it would yield positive results. Implementers are usually the backbones of organizations since they implement workable strategies to ensure the team completes tasks quickly and effectively. These practical and diligent team members are the ones who ensure that goals become tangible successes.

6. Completers

   Also called Finishers, Completers are introverted individuals who perform quality assurance during key stages of a project. They are often perfectionists who can notice fine details, which enables them to scrutinize finished tasks or products for errors. Since these individuals strive for perfection, they tend to expect the same from those around them. Organizations need these individuals to ensure that teams produce high-quality work. Completers are especially valuable in work environments where precision and adherence to deadlines are essential. Implementors and completer finishers are vital roles on a privacy team. You can have the best leader in the world, but if they don't tick boxes, close projects, kick off new ones, monitor deadlines, etc., the team is doomed to be very ineffective.

People-oriented team roles

People-oriented team members use networking and relationship-building skills to complete tasks. They may be excellent active listeners and provide support to other team members to build cohesion in the group. People-oriented team roles include:

7. The Coordinator

   Coordinators are mature individuals who have excellent interpersonal and communication skills. They are normally in management positions, but their management styles are very different from those of Shapers. Where Shapers manage through directives, Coordinators prefer a more democratic approach that includes open communication. Instead of focusing on the achievement of the organization's goals, Coordinators tend to concentrate on helping team members accomplish their individual objectives. They are normally good at identifying talent in a team and utilizing it to achieve the group's objectives. Coordinators are normally calm and trusting individuals who are adept at delegating work. Coordinators are necessary to ensure that the team utilizes each member's strengths appropriately. As they tend to have broad perspectives, Coordinators can direct teams with diverse personalities and skills.

8. The Team Worker

   Team Workers are normally extroverts with mild and friendly dispositions. They tend to be good listeners and are adept at getting a team to function well together as a unit. If Team Workers notice that other team members are not coping with their workload, they are likely to step in and assist. These individuals are highly adaptable and versatile, which enables them to interact effectively with diverse people and cope with sudden changes. Team Workers are indispensable team members as they establish harmony within a team. They are adept at solving interpersonal issues within a team and support members who may feel neglected. Because of this, Team Workers tend to be popular with colleagues and often rise to senior positions.

9. The Resource Investigator

   Resource Investigators are extroverts who have a talent for networking. They are positive and enthusiastic people who like to explore new opportunities and investigate new developments. Although they may not necessarily come up with new ideas themselves, they are skilled at picking up ideas from others. Because of their outgoing personalities, Resource Investigators are good at making new business contacts and carrying out subsequent negotiations. They are also talented at finding new ideas and opportunities and bringing these back to the team. Resource Investigators are those people who "find answers"; however, they may not be the best at implementing them or finishing them.

One of the authors, Dr. Lyons, is a Resource Investigator – hence her interest in research and her ability to dig deep into elements of privacy. However, with this awareness she knows that she works best with Completers and Implementors, as these roles provide the skills she does not have strengths in.

Belbin's team roles summary

Knowledge of Belbin's team roles model can help to identify potential strengths and weaknesses within the team, overcome conflict between co-workers, and understand and appreciate everyone's contributions. Belbin suggests that a team filled with members that have similar styles of behaviors or team roles can become unbalanced. For example, if team members have similar strengths, they may compete for the projects, duties, and responsibilities that complement their natural skill set. A team made up of members with similar weaknesses may exhibit that weakness as a whole. Applying the Belbin model to the team can help create a more balanced team and identify opportunities for growth based on the team role. When you understand your own role within a team, personal contributions can be improved by developing your strengths and managing your weaknesses.

DEVELOPING THE RIGHT TALENT FOR YOUR PRIVACY TEAM

Caroline Louveaux
Chief Privacy Officer, Mastercard

When I stepped into the role of CPO in 2018, it was to lead a small team. We had just completed a massive GDPR compliance project, in which all parts and levels of the organization had been deeply involved. We thought the hardest part was behind us – yeah, right! Before we knew it, we were hit by a new wave of privacy laws – from Brazil to California to Thailand. Then major regulatory, business and technology changes came our way too, from open banking to the internet of things and AI.

Meeting increasingly high expectations from regulators, customers and investors required us to redefine our engagement model. We needed a new vision and mission to inspire and guide us. So, we came together as a team over a two-day offsite for a candid conversation about our future.

It became clear we had to become more than "just" privacy lawyers. There was a need to look at data holistically, working with business and technology partners to co-create innovations with Privacy *and Data* by Design. A team of true data experts would have to focus on four pillars: Protect, Enable, Influence and Educate.

This required investment in talent with the right skillsets, representing a diversity of gender, race, culture, geographies and backgrounds. We added people across the globe with expertise spanning cybersecurity, biometrics, AI, open banking, digital identity, human rights, data analytics and IT infrastructure. This included disciplines beyond the law, including compliance, communications and privacy engineering.

We also invested in our team's well-being. We launched a "privacy buddies" program to support new joiners and colleagues in remote locations. We started to organize rotations so our people could learn new geographies, new products and new customers. And importantly, we emphasized the value of humor and levity as core to our success, to help maximize fun, talent retention, creativity and business impact.

As a result, our team became the organizational Brain Trust on all data matters. We gained a seat at the table – at C-Suite and Board level – to help set strategic corporate priorities. We co-developed our Data Responsibility Principles which guide all our data practices at Mastercard. Privacy and data responsibility also became features of our ESG agenda. Policymakers and international organizations around the globe now come to us for data insights, to help shape the future of our global digital economy. Ultimately, our talent is our greatest asset and a key driver for building trust in our brand.

GOALS, ROLES, PROCESSES, AND INTERPERSONAL RELATIONSHIPS (GRPI)

Richard Beckhard first introduced the GRPI model in 1972. Goals, roles, processes, and interpersonal relationships are the four critical and interrelated aspects of teamwork. The GRPI is a four-step project planning tool to help team leaders ensure productivity, efficiency, and quality. It is often described as a team effectiveness "diagnostic" tool. A GRPI model aims to assess a team's effectiveness and determine which areas or dimensions still need improvement. Usually, the manager or leader is the first to assess the team's effectiveness in different aspects under the GRPI model. Then typically a team works together, led by the team leader – to agree on aspects within each of these four dimensions. Once agreed, a social contract is formed where everyone understands and agrees each goal/role/process and how interpersonal relationships should be navigated.

The GRPI model, as presented in Figure 9.1, is considered an excellent framework to facilitate a team's success.

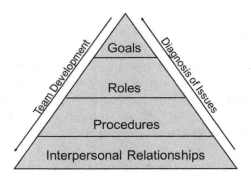

Figure 9.1 GRPI model, Beckhard, 1972.

It should be incorporated while developing a new team and planning the first steps, or revisit if a team starts to flounder. It eases the process of establishing and prioritizing the core mission of a team and framing it into a clear action plan. GRPI helps ensure that a team is productive, minimizing ramp-up time and rework. Team members might lose focus or be unproductive if goals are not clearly defined. People hesitate to exercise their roles and responsibilities if there is some ambiguity. This results in poor communication among team members affecting the productiveness of a project. Therefore, it is crucial to establish absolute clarity at each level. The model is most productive when addressed in order: effective goals first, then roles, then processes, and finally interpersonal relationships.

Goals

A goal lays the foundation for good teamwork by establishing the core mission of a team and framing its purpose. Just like a flock of geese, which fly together in the same direction forming a "V" or single line, they have a clear set of goals. Similarly, goals set direction for a team, helps them define where they want to be and unite each individual effort in getting there. Without a common goal which is clear, shared and agreed, any impact on the team would be limited. A fine goal is one that is Specific, Measurable, Attainable, Relevant, and Time-bound (SMART).

- What is our team's top goal? This is important because, of course, there will be other, smaller goals.
- How will we know when we have reached the defined goal? Goals need to be measurable, and success must be defined. If the goal is simply to "increase revenue" and you earn $0.01 more than last year, you are technically successful, but it doesn't feel like it. Therefore, setting SMART goals is helpful to provide clarity to the goal and know when the goal has been achieved.

- If the person's definition of the goal is different from yours, efforts should be focused on aligning everyone in the team.

Roles

A role statement clearly defines each team member's authority, responsibility, and tasks that need to be aligned to support the defined goal. To enable the team to function:

- Each team member should have a clear picture of who is doing what, who is responsible for what, and should know the extent of their authority.
- Each team member needs to understand, agree, and be satisfied with their roles and responsibilities.
- Each team member is also accountable individually and collectively.

Henceforth, it is crucial that team members have cooperative vision toward achieving the goals. Transparency among team member's roles enables them to effectively accomplish the goals. This is the foundation of a clear process in addressing, clarifying, and resolving issues.

Processes

Processes in organizations are a governance tool to overcome inefficiencies in the areas of decision-making, control, coordination, and communication. They try to ensure a repeatability of a certain level of output quality, while allowing enough operating flexibility so as not to constrain the process-users' work. This part of GRPI examines how work gets done and how the team makes decisions, allocates resources, communicates, or solves the inevitable problems that arise. If the processes are not understood or are ineffective, then frustrations grow, and the team develops the familiar symptoms of interpersonal strife. Defining processes is particularly important at the forming stage of a team – as this can effectively support the team's goals by determining the interactions within a team.

Setting standardized processes for actions, decision-making, conflict management, problem solving, communication procedures, resource allocations, etc., will effectively support the team's goals by determining the interactions within a team. While the amount and types of processes depend on team and task size and composition, certain processes for team development are recommended.

For a team to perform effectively, it is recommended that they have:

- Clear and frequent communication.
- Processes for group decision-making.
- Constructive ways of dealing openly with inevitable conflict.

Communication

Good communication is the singular most important facet of an effective team process. Without it all the other facets will fail. It is therefore important to know the communication channels and use them properly. Communication procedures are about providing space for team members, whether by means of a blog, coaching sessions, or regular meetings to enable the other team members to know what everyone is doing. By doing so, it provides measurements on how the team is progressing and gives team members and team leaders the information needed for adjustments. Good communications also build team trust as it establishes transparency and flow of information.

Decision-making

Clear role and authority definitions are the basis for decision-making. However, for decisions that must be made collectively, or where the decision-maker can invite input from other team members, a process should be defined. It is a question of how team members should interact to take decisions, set up formats (e.g., emails, meetings, etc.), and include a time frame. This will ensure rapid responses and reduce the delivery time.

Conflict management

There is no team without people, thus personal or interpersonal conflicts are natural and can arise. Conflict management is about following a clear process when conflicts occur. A clear process should be established for addressing issues to solve them quickly and to avoid escalation. Establishing clear processes provides a basis for success. By doing so, a team can gain significant insight into how work is actually completed, as a process flow will be identified. People will be able to work together efficiently by providing a rapid response to natural deficiencies within a team. The most important aspect of conflict is never to approach it in terms of right and wrong. Parties can both be right. Parties can both be wrong, and there is a gray area in the middle which is a "bot of both". The point of conflict management is to ensure that there is a safe and respectful place for people to air and address conflict within the team.

Interpersonal relationships

The Interpersonal Relationships section of the GRPI model is about establishing trust, open communication, and feedback to support a sound working environment. This encourages creative and diverse contributions from all members; however, this also discourages groupthink. Successful relations are built by understanding the strengths of team members and treating each other as people. Improving interpersonal relationships can be developed by simple gestures like smiling at someone to listening carefully, asking advice, passing on compliments, etc. Negative behaviors like threats or disrespect can immediately affect relationships. In this section, teams can agree on how conflict will be managed or how someone who is progressively late or absent will be managed. In a team I once worked in, it was agreed that when someone was late to a meeting or late for an event, this was a behavior we wanted to avoid. Rather than address this behavior with aggressive tactics like locked door meetings (i.e., late comers cannot enter), we would instead give a round of applause if someone arrived late. It made the moment "light" – it made everyone laugh. The latecomer would also laugh, but after a while people realized that lateness was "highlighted" and that people arriving late to a meeting were being "marked". Lateness to meetings reduced dramatically and no one was hurt or offended by the actions. If a team can find a way to deal with these behaviors in a positive way, we can reprogram how the team interacts.

The GRPI process

Host a meeting in a private room or office, where the entire team is invited to attend. Discuss each GRPI dimension and what that means for the team. We tend to use flipcharts/whiteboards for this exercise, as they tend to be less formal; however, this can also be accomplished digitally or in remote environments using a collaboration tool such as Zoom, Microsoft Teams, or Cisco's GoToMeeting platform. Using the checklist below, ask your team to fill in each section of the model. What do they believe their goals are? Guide the conversation and let them fill in the quadrants. They design the team cultural mores in accordance with the culture existent already. Listen carefully to any actions or behaviors that you feel do not align with the expected culture. Beckhard provides a series of questions to prompt discussion for each quadrant, and these are summarized in Table 9.2.

When the discussion regarding these questions is finished – the results should be written into a document. This document should be distributed as the "team contract" – outlining how we behave in this team. Human beings like to know what the boundaries and rules of engagement are, and this process really helps to clear this up.

OTHER TEAM ASSESSMENT TOOLS

While the GRPI model is a useful tool in determining the status of a team or determining a team-related problem, there are also other models that managers can use to shed light on a team's efficacy. Some of these team effectiveness models are listed below.

Table 9.2 The GRPI model: Questions to prompt discussion

G	**Purpose and Outcomes**
	• Does the team understand the project or team mission?
	• What is our team's top goal? (This is important because, of course, there will be other, smaller goals.)
	• If a team member's definition of the goal is different, the team leader should start working to align everyone.
	• Does the team understand and agree upon what is in and out of the project scope?
	• How will we know when we have reached the defined goal? (Remember, goals need to be measurable, and you must define success. This is why setting SMART goals is helpful.)
R	**Roles and Responsibilities**
	• Has the team defined and agreed on their roles, responsibilities, skills, and resources?
	• Does the team understand and agree the degree of authority of each role?
	• Does the team understand and agree the degree of empowerment for each role to meet our project mission?
	• Does each person have a defined and document job specification including roles and responsibilities
P	**Critical Success Factors/Plans and Monitoring Activities**
	• Do we the key factors/skills needed to meet the project goals and mission? What are the key tasks, are thy clearly defined and assigned to either a team member or a sub-team?
	• Do we have a monitoring process and specific metrics linked to progress and oversight?
	• Have we defined our project schedule, including the key phases and milestones?
I	**Team Operating Agreements**
	• Have we agreed the guidelines for how our team works and communicates?
	• How will we deal with team conflict?
	• What are our expectations for meeting structures and minutes, etc.?
	• How do we respond to latecomers at meetings?
	• How will we deal with underperformers?
	• How will we deal with overperformers?
	• What does trust look like? What will break trust for us?
	• What behaviors are unacceptable to the team?

Source: Beckhard.

The Katzenback and Smith model

This model was developed by Jon Katzenbach and Douglas Smith in 1993. Katzenbach and Smith studied teams in many companies that had different types of business challenges and co-wrote the book *The Wisdom of Teams*. The Katzenback and Smith model resembles a triangle with each point representing the team's goals or objectives, as depicted in Figure 9.2. These revolve around aspects of teamwork, including collective work products, performance results, and personal growth.

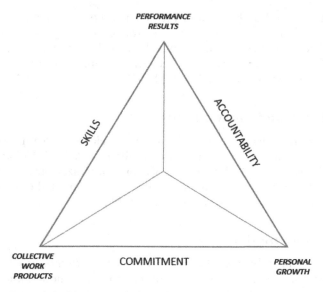

Figure 9.2 The Katzenbach and Smith model.

The three points of the triangle include:

- Commitment: Team members are more dedicated to their work when they are engaged and aligned to the mission of the organization, have clear goals and a shared team approach toward reaching them. A lack of commitment can have a negative effect on group dynamics.
- Skills: Every member of a team must be adept in problem-solving and teamwork and have the professional skills and adequate resources needed to accomplish goals.
- Accountability: Co-workers need to be steadfast in their commitment to their individual tasks and team goals. Avoidance of accountability can affect team success. For example, if an individual is unwilling to complete their task on time, this can have an impact on others who rely on their work to complete their own objectives.

In the Katzenback and Smith model, team development helps to increase accountability and engagement. Successful teams employ the use of performance management systems to increase adherence to a common goal.

The T7 model of team effectiveness

Michael Lombardo and Robert Eichinger crafted the T7 model in 1995 with the aim of better understanding the factors that contribute to team effectiveness. After all, you can't fix the problem if you don't know the causes of team dysfunction. Lombardo and Eichinger discovered there are five common internal factors and two external factors that highly impact team effectiveness. Each one begins with T, which earned it the name "T7 model". High performing teams ensure each of the five internal factors are active. The T7 factors are summarized in Table 9.3.

The LaFasto and Larson model

In 2001, Frank LaFasto and Carl Larson developed a team effectiveness model they coined "Five Dynamics of Teamwork and Collaboration". Through researching 600 teams in various organizations, they made a model of what an effective team looks like, which consisted of five elements for team effectiveness – as summarized in Table 9.4.

The Lencioni model

Patrick Lencioni published his book *The Five Dysfunctions of a Team* in 2005. This book suggested a new team effectiveness model, known as the Lencioni model, which looks at the underlying reasons why teams are dysfunctional. Table 9.5 summarizes Lencioni's five dysfunctions of a team.

Table 9.3 T7 model of team effectiveness

Factor type	"T" factor elements
Internal factors:	Thrust: Team members have a shared goal.
	Trust: Every employee is confident that their fellow team members have good intentions and are committed to the goal. For example, individuals may have trust in the rest of their team through working together previously, their noted skills/experience or status within the organization.
	Talent: Employees have the skills and resources to produce effective team performance and the best results.
	Teaming skills: The entire team works well together and has excellent problem-solving and decision-making skills.
	Task skills: Team members exhibit consistent/timely execution of tasks.
External team factors include:	Team leader fit: Does the team leader work for the greater good of the team and the goal? The leader must have a collaborative rather than dictating approach towards reaching team goals.
	Team support from the organization: Teams must have overall support at the right level across every tier of the organization and be provided with the resources needed to reach their goals e.g., team leaders should have access to administrative or project support as well as key project roles.

Source: Lombardo and Eichinger.

Table 9.4 Five dynamics of teamwork/collaboration

Element	Description
1. Team members	Your talent is your greatest asset, so choosing the right employees is key. Do team members have the proper skills and capabilities to work in a team environment? For example, you can select and build the right team by creating a skills matrix or reviewing the effectiveness of individuals against previous projects.
2. Team relationships	Like the importance of interpersonal relationships in the GRPI model, the right team building behaviors are key to maximizing team capabilities.
3. Team problem solving	When any group has good team connections and interactions, high levels of trust foster productive conflict resolution and problem-solving skills. Absence of trust can have the opposite effect.
4. Team leadership	An effective, proactive team leader that moves team members in a compelling direction is critical in any team effectiveness model.
5. Team organization environment	Collaborative work methods and organizational culture support team commitment and accountability.

Source: LaFasto and Larson.

Table 9.5 The five dysfunctions of a team

Dysfunction	Details
1. Absence of trust:	A lack of trust creates an environment where teams are unwilling to seek advice, support or assistance.
2. Fear of conflicts:	As conflicts can create space for new or better ideas, a fear of conflict can lead to an ineffective team. For example, a disagreement between two employees could encourage them to consider a third option that is beneficial for all.
3. Lack of commitment:	People who aren't committed to the work they've been assigned have an impact on the wider team.
4. Avoidance of accountability:	Team members are unwilling to hold themselves or others accountable for their work, which leads to team dysfunction.
5. Inattention:	A lack of attention to team goals and productivity can appear if individuals are too focused on their own goals.

Source: Patrick Lencioni.

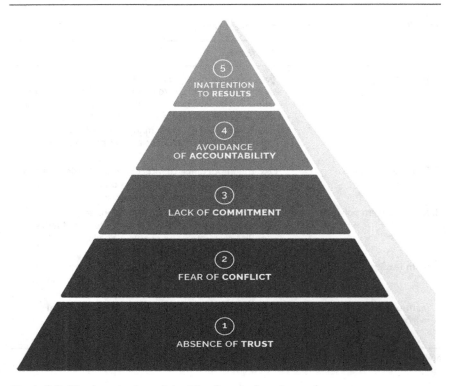

Figure 9.3 The Lencioni model – The five dysfunctions of team.

Lencioni's model is shown as a pyramid, see Figure 9.3, with the absence of trust at the bottom and suggests you need to tackle one dysfunction before you can work on the next.

Tuckman's FSNP model

In 1965, Bruce Tuckman introduced the Forming, Storming, Norming, Performing model, also known as FSNP. The model was enhanced in 1977 by Mary Ann Jensen to include a fifth phase known as Adjourning, creating the FSNPA model. Tuckman's team effectiveness model suggests that these five stages are necessary for teams to work at the highest possible levels of effectiveness and growth. The phases are:

- Forming: Team members get to know each other and develop a basic understanding from which they'll work throughout the project. At this stage, people are likely to avoid conflict and strive to feel included. For example, individuals may be more formal than they otherwise would.

- Storming: At this stage, team members are more open to challenging others and conflict is more likely. During this phase, the team navigates these challenges to progress.
- Norming: Individuals begin to feel they are part of a team and work together to agree and become more effective.
- Performing: The team is working well and performing against objectives. They are motivated to work together to reach goals.
- Adjourning: After the project has concluded, the team conducts a review that finalizes their time together and plans for any future necessities.

The Hackman model

J. Richard Hackman suggested a new team effectiveness model in his 2002 book, *Leading Teams: Setting the Stage for Great Performances*. Hackman identified five conditions that are believed to increase the likelihood of a team working effectively. These conditions are:

- *Real team*: This is defined as teams where everyone has a defined role with rights and tasks to carry out. For example, your team may have a clear document which captures everyone's roles and responsibilities.
- *Compelling direction*: The team has a clear direction or end goal that they are working toward. This may be set out as a series of smaller goals that help to motivate the team.
- *Enabling structure*: For a team to be truly effective, it needs to be supported by a structure, workflows, and processes that allow work to be completed as it needs to.
- *Supportive context*: An effective team needs access to the tools, resources, and support that's required to deliver a project or reach a goal.
- *Expert coaching*: Teams with access to a coach or mentor have a greater probability of working effectively, as they can access expert help when it's needed.

In 2015 a group of HR specialists from Google published the results of a longitudinal study they had undertaken over two years involving 200+ interviews with Googlers, looking at more than 250 attributes of 180+ active Google teams. They discovered that *who* is on a team matters less than *how* the team members interact, structure their work, and view their contributions. They highlighted five characteristics that set effective teams apart from others are presented in their blog on the findings outlined in Figure 9.4.

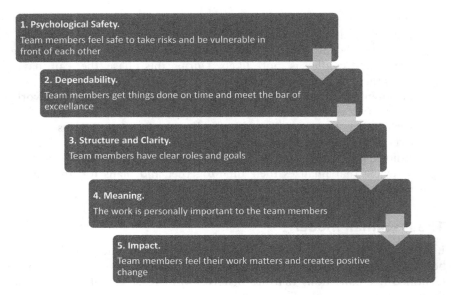

Figure 9.4 Google's five characteristics of team effectiveness.

SUGGESTED READING

11 Team Effectiveness Models to Build High-Performing Teams. https://www.aihr.com/blog/team-effectiveness-models/

Czernik, Annette B., (1972). GRPI model, Beckhard. https://www.inspired-executives.com/wp-content/uploads/2012/09/GRPI-Model.jpg

Google reWork. An introduction to understanding team effectiveness. https://rework.withgoogle.com/guides/understanding-team-effectiveness/steps/introduction/

Google reWORK. Five Keys to a successful Google Team. https://rework.withgoogle.com/blog/five-keys-to-a-successful-google-team/

Mastercard. Data responsibility principles. https://www.mastercard.us/en-us/vision/corp-responsibility/data-responsibility.html

Meredith Belbin. (1981). The Belbin team role test (can be found online at https://www.belbin.com/)

Raue, Steve, Tang, Suk-Han, Weiland, Christian, and Wenzlik, Claas. (2013). WHITE PAPER The GRPI model – An approach for team development | SEgroup. https://docplayer.net/1068425-The-grpi-model-an-approach-for-team-development.html

Section VII

Skills

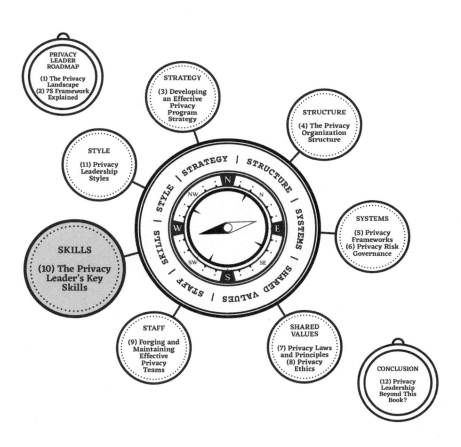

Chapter 10

The privacy leader's key skills

Knowledge is of two kinds. We know a subject ourselves, or we know where we can find information upon it.

Samuel Johnson 1709-1784

When GDPR came into force in May 2018, public bodies were required to appoint a new role of Data Protection Officer (DPO) and other organizations under certain conditions were also required to appoint a DPO. Beyond mandated appointments, many other organizations have bolstered their privacy efforts further by establishing a specific role responsible for privacy. The most common of these roles is the Chief Privacy Officer (CPO). In the United States, the CPO position was reportedly first established in 1999 when Internet advertising firm AllAdvantage appointed privacy lawyer Ray Everett-Church to the newly created role. The move sparked a trend that quickly spread among major corporations. But the CPO position was truly solidified within the US corporate world in November 2000 when Harriet Pearson was given the role with IBM. Many US states have employed privacy officers at the agency level for years. The Health Insurance Portability and Accountability Act (HIPAA) was a significant driver of those efforts, as it required states to appoint a privacy officer for each HIPAA-covered entity within a state.

The two roles (CPO and DPO) share many similarities and are often conflated. However, this can potentially lead to confusion, as the underlying aims and objectives of their duties are very different.

The *skills* factor of the 7-S framework applied to privacy leadership focuses on both the "hard" technical skills of privacy leadership and the "soft" skills required to navigate the organization. In this chapter, we describe both the CPO and DPO roles and discuss both their summaries and their differences and the key skills required for each.

THE CHIEF PRIVACY OFFICER (CPO)

CPO qualifications/experience/skills

First and foremost, a CPO should be highly articulate, as they'll be heavily engaged in communicating the company's privacy values and goals, both internally and externally.

As well as possessing exemplary communication skills, a CPO will be expected to be tech savvy, developing a deep understanding of data-related operational practices and technologies across the organization. While a number of CPOs come from legal backgrounds and have Juris Doctorate or equivalent degrees, the CPO role is a multidisciplinary one. The role requires an executive with an understanding of how data collection and usage, and the associated risks all factor into an organization's day-to-day business operations. CPOs also need to be aware of a range of legal, regulatory, contractual, and other factors that impact an organization's privacy risk strategy. For these reasons, many believe that a legal background is a requirement for a successful CPO. Others believe a legal background may result in too narrow of a focus, and CPOs should have more than just a legal background to be effective in leading and integrating the necessary privacy practices into the business operations.

Among other qualifications that are seen as valuable in CPOs are strong communications skills, particularly in public relations. This is mainly due to the fact they will need to deal with the PR fallout in the event of data breach or other personal data related incident and the development and execution of public outreach. They'll also likely be involved in publicity campaigns to support the wider privacy agenda. CPOs are also often called upon to function as lobbyists representing the organization's interests before lawmakers. CPOs are also increasingly required to have a deep knowledge of the organization's data-related operational practices and technologies, as well as the interaction between compliance measures that span the realms of privacy and security. The CPO must be knowledgeable about privacy and security laws and while some technical knowledge is important, he/she does not need to have the same level of expertise as say for instance the CISO. Most CPOs also have trained as technology, intellectual property, litigation, or regulatory attorneys. A smaller minority of sitting CPOs are non-attorneys with broad-based compliance and risk experience.

Given the cross-functional nature of this role – and the fact that many CPOs shift industries – we've found that certain "soft" skills are especially critical to success, including:

- **Collaborating and influencing skills** – This work is highly cross-functional, working not only with function leads, including the general counsel and chief compliance officer, but also with the rest of the

C-suite and key business leaders. Strong interpersonal skills and the ability to build relationships and consensus are critical, particularly with the CISO.

- **Project management and prioritization** – The best CPOs are those who can originate and implement an enterprise-wide project while understanding what to prioritize in an environment where decisions need to be made quickly based on data from multiple sources.
- **Crisis management** – CPOs who are familiar with crisis management and can mobilize and prioritize quickly in the face of a breach will be most successful.
- **Learning orientation** – Threats and regulations are always evolving, so chief privacy officers and their teams must be comfortable being constant students. It's also important to note that the privacy law landscape is new relative to centuries-old traditional legal doctrine, so the privacy leaders of today have largely learned their skill on the job.

PRIVACY INCIDENT AND BREACH INVESTIGATION

T. Andrew Reeder

AVP, Privacy Officer, Rush University Medical Center

Privacy incidents can have many consequences for an organization, including becoming a regulatory risk issue and a trust concern with clients, customers, patients, and stockholders. For these reasons and more, the Privacy Office must ensure that incident investigations are complete and accurate before a privacy breach determination is made. A privacy breach can be defined as an incident where a higher risk of compromise exists to personally identifiable information. Understanding federal, state, and international requirements for breach response and notification are important requirements for the Privacy Office. To successfully manage incident and breach investigations, a Privacy Office must have some essential elements in place. These include:

- Regulatory knowledge: whether it's HIPAA, FERPA, CCPA, GDPR or any other number of international, federal or state laws, the Privacy Office must have a good understanding of the laws which affect the organization at all levels. A solid understanding must exist of what constitutes personally identifiable information, how it can be used and disclosed, and what authorizations are needed. Incidents often arise from privacy policy violations in the absence of proper disclosure authorization.

- Investigatory approach: investigating an issue takes time and effort. A standard operating procedure should exist that identifies investigatory roles, how investigations will be conducted, and how reports will be shared. This is a great opportunity for the CISO and CPO to share information and determine the source and extent of any threat activity, whether internal or external
- Incident and breach support: when incidents seem large (such as over 500 affected individuals) it may be appropriate to notify the cyber insurance carrier and determine what type of forensics and response resources will be available if required. Having the right support during the investigation can help mitigate risk to make the right breach decision.

Since a privacy incident and breach investigation can have consequences for an institution it is important that the results be accurate and timely. The outcome can become not only a regulatory issue but a reputational one as well.

THE DATA PROTECTION OFFICER (DPO)

DPO qualifications/experience/skills

The GDPR does not define the professional qualities required or prescribe the training a DPO should undergo to be qualified to undertake the role. This allows organizations to decide on their DPO's qualifications and training tailored to the context of the organization's data processing. In any case, a DPO should have an appropriate level of expertise in data protection law and practices to enable them to carry out their critical role.

The appropriate level of qualification and expert knowledge should be determined according to the personal data processing operations carried out, the complexity and scale of data processing, the sensitivity of the data processed, and the protection required for the data being processed.

For example, where a data processing activity is particularly complex, or where a large volume or sensitive data is involved, such as an Internet or insurance company, the DPO may need a higher level of expertise and support.

- expertise in national and European data protection laws and practices including an in-depth understanding of the GDPR.
- understanding of the processing operations carried out.
- understanding of information technologies and security.
- knowledge of the business sector and the organization.
- ability to promote a data protection culture within the organization.

For example, a DPO may need an expert level of knowledge in certain specific IT functions, international data transfers, or familiarity with sector-specific data protection practices such as public sector data processing and data sharing, to adequately perform their duties. In evaluating the scale, complexity and sensitivity of their data processing operations, organizations should proactively decide on the qualifications and level of training required for their DPO. In undertaking such an assessment, organizations should be aware that there are various training options that may be pursued. Some training courses are one-day in-person sessions, while some are online only. Others lead to academically accredited certificates such as diplomas from national law societies. There are also other professional training programs which are recognized internationally and that offer professional qualifications that require an ongoing commitment to training to maintain the professional qualification. It is recommended that the following non-exhaustive list of factors be taken into consideration when selecting the appropriate DPO training program:

- Content and means of the training and assessment.
- Whether training leading to certification is required.
- The standing of the accrediting body.
- Whether the training and certification is recognized internationally.

It is important that the DPO enjoys a good understanding of the enterprise's business operation and the data handling needs of that specific industry. Experience within that organization and that industry are important qualifiers. The inherent benefits of employing a DPO with this specific company and industry knowledge apply significant pressure on senior management toward the acquisition of an in-house DPO rather than outsourcing that role.

While technical skills are not considered to be a primary requirement, a DPO should have practical experience in cybersecurity. The candidate should have dealt with real security incidents that will enable them to provide helpful guidance on risk assessments, countermeasures, and data protection impact assessments. Although security is an important component of GDPR, it is only one piece of the overall law. The DPO may still provide advice to the business on matters that are not the DPO's regulated tasks in Article 39, excluding risk assessment and DPIA advise, cooperation with the supervisory authorities, and liaison with the data subjects.

WHO'S THE D – WHO IS THE DECISION MAKER FOR THE TOUGH PRIVACY MATTERS?

Judy Titera

FMR Chief Privacy Officer, USAA

Making a decision can be easy, right? You collect the facts, assess the risks, consider alternatives and go. If only it was that easy! While decision making frame works are extremely important and necessary, and can get you to a decision you are comfortable with, at the end of the day who makes the final decision?

Depending on the size and type of the organization you work at, the regulatory geographical footprint you have, and where your privacy office sits, your results may vary but let's break this down.

Here's the situation, you are brought into a meeting as the Chief Privacy Officer for the company. The sales, marketing and data teams are super excited about a new initiative that they explain will be game-changing for the company and the industry. You complete your assessment and identify the use of data is clearly against the law in the jurisdictions where they want to implement. Easy – run it by your legal team decision made no go.

The next day the team comes back with an adjustment where it is not "really" against the law, but you believe it could quickly be a slippery slope to trouble and it clearly doesn't seem to align with your personal philosophy. Your next step is to point them to the company Privacy Policy that you have established. It is critical to have implemented a clear principle-based company Policy documenting what the organization will or will not tolerate is the cornerstone to your privacy program. Providing specifics on the violation of a policy provision will be your next approach.

Oh, wait you don't have a policy in place yet, or the team is very agile and comes back with another tweak to make this work. You still aren't fully aligned; however, the risk assessment comes back "moderate", legal, risk, compliance, and operational teams all agree that they are willing to move forward with the known risks but are waiting for your sign off. The final decision is that of the business that owns the risk – you decide to sign off that you understand the position and the risks, additionally you may also provide additional guidance to the business on what key metrics they need to implement to avoid crossing any legal or policy lines that are presented regularly to a management level.

Privacy is not about stopping business - it is about proper risk treatment. In the fast paced ever changing environment we live with privacy front and center is it critical to understand the laws that apply to your company, have well established policies in place that have been approved by the senior leadership and to always document and continue to track projects to ensure they continue to move forward appropriately aligned with the risk posture of the organization.

SOFT SKILLS OF THE PRIVACY LEADER

There are different styles of working, and different ways of interacting and responding to team members, subordinates, and seniors. The privacy leader must be able to interact with, and communicate with, individuals at different levels of the organizational hierarchy, from the Board of Directors to the end-users and everywhere in between. The privacy leader therefore needs to leverage and demonstrate a series of skills beyond their technical legal skills and knowledge. These skills are called soft skills and involve understanding and interacting with people from different experiences, backgrounds, and their own motivations and current life situations. Practicing soft skills increases the privacy leader's effectiveness to deliver on the technical aspects of the role. When the privacy leader was buried deep in the annals of the risk domain, it was possible to get by primarily on technical and regulatory knowledge. This model has clearly changed, with the privacy leader operating at all levels of the organization. To be trusted and viewed as a business partner, these skills must be viewed as just as important, if not more, than the regulatory and technical skills that advanced the technical privacy practitioner into the privacy leader role. The following soft skills can improve the ability of the privacy leader to communicate with others and to lead authentically.

Emotional intelligence

The first of these soft skills is emotional intelligence: popularized by psychologist Daniel Goleman, emotional intelligence (EQ) is defined as our capacity to be aware of, to control, and to express emotions. EQ enables us as leaders to handle interpersonal relationships judiciously and empathetically. EQ is considered a critical ability for leaders, as they are often required to manage multiple stakeholders with diverse opinions and needs. A leader with high emotional intelligence understands the importance of building trustful relationships with their team members. They know that trust is the foundation upon which all successful teams are built, and work hard to create an environment of mutual respect and understanding.

The ability to connect emotionally with employees and lead with emotional intelligence is essential for leadership effectiveness. Emotions can weave through every work situation, including:

- Change and uncertainty.
- Interactions with colleagues.
- Conflict and relationships.
- Effort and burnout.
- Achievement and failure.

Key components of emotional intelligence

Self-Awareness: The ability to know emotions, as well as your strengths and weaknesses, and recognize their impact on performance and relationships. Being self-aware and having the ability to control their emotions, even in challenging situations – is an invaluable trait for leaders in the business world. Self-awareness can be achieved in many ways.

Self-Management: The ability to control both positive and negative emotions and impulses and be flexible and adaptive as situations warrant.

Social Awareness: The ability to have empathy for others, navigate politically, and network proactively. Emotionally intelligent people can see things from other people's perspectives and respond accordingly. They know how to build rapport and create an environment where everyone feels valued and heard. As a result, they are more effective at motivating and inspiring their team members.

Relationship Management: The ability to inspire through persuasive communication, motivation, building bonds, and disarming conflict among individuals. A leader who is emotionally intelligent knows how to weigh up all the options before deciding. They consider not only the logical reasoning behind each option, but also the potential emotional impact of each decision on their team members. These four components are summarized in Table 10.1.

Table 10.1 Key components of emotional intelligence

Component	Definition	Elements
Self-awareness	• Ability to understand one's modes, emotions, and drives as well as its effect on others	• Self-confidence Realistic self-assessment Self-deprecating sense of humor • Positive Sense of self worth
Self-management/ Regulation	• Ability to control or redirect disruptive impulses or moods. Propensities to suspend judgment, think before acting	• Trustworthiness and integrity • Conscientiousness Comfort with ambiguity Adaptability • Initiative • Achievement orientation
Self-motivation	• Passion to work for reasons beyond money or status. Propensity to pursue goals with energy and persistence	• Strong drive to achieve optimism, even in the face of failure Organizational commitment
Empathy	• Ability to understand the emotional makeup of other people. Skill in treating people according to their emotional reactions	• Expertise in building and retaining talent Cross-cultural sensitivity Service to clients
Social skill	• Proficiency in managing relationships and building networks. An ability to find common ground and build rapport	• Effectiveness in leading change persuasiveness Expertise in building and leading teams

Source: Goleman 2004.

It's also important to understand that all emotion is *functional*. Whether our own behaviors or the actions of others are driving positive or negative emotions, both are impactful in different ways. Before we can apply new practices and strengthen the ability to lead with emotional intelligence, we must assess our current emotions and consider the outcome we want. Know that:

Laughter is reported to generate increases in positive emotion and produces self-reported improvements in immune system functioning.

- Positive emotions *broaden*:
  - Supporting resiliency. Resilience is characterized by flexibility in response to changing situational demands, and the ability to bounce back from negative emotional experiences.
  - Improving our thinking. The age-old expression "positive thinking". When we think positively – we make better decisions than when we think negatively.
  - Building new skills. Children, when they experience joy, are open to social learning social skills. Similarly, adults who experience happiness are more likely to learn new skills.
  - Creating psychological capital (PsyCap). Management professor Fred Luthans defined PsyCap as "an individual's positive psychological state of development". Essentially, PsyCap refers to our mental resources and their ability to help us get through tough situations.
  - Undoing negative emotions.

Emotionally intelligent leaders are less likely to let their emotions get the better of them, and as a result, are more effective at managing difficult conversations and conflict resolution.

Four ways to improve your emotional intelligence

Now that we have understood why emotional intelligence is important, let's examine some actionable ways privacy leaders can improve this key characteristic.

1. Be more self-aware
   The first step to improving your emotional intelligence is to become more aware of your own emotions. Start paying attention to how you feel in different situations and what triggers certain emotions. Once you have a better understanding of your own emotions, you will be better equipped to manage them. We outline in the previous chapter ways to become self-aware using Belbin's team roles. If you would like to dive deeper into self-awareness, there are also several other tools. The Myers Briggs Type Indicator (MBTI), for instance, is discussed in detail in the *CISO Compass: Navigating Cybersecurity Leadership*

Challenges with Insights from Pioneers. The Enneagram can also be used. If you use any of these tools, you may "warm" to one more than another. For example, because of his use of it in the past early career leadership training based on the MBTI, Todd warms to the MBTI program, whereas Valerie warms toward Belbin's for team awareness and the Enneagram for personal self-awareness. Perhaps you think that the enneagram and other personality labels have no validity? Perhaps you are right, however, it doesn't matter how you chose to find awareness of your strengths and weaknesses, it only matters that 1) you make the journey and 2) you find a kind way of exploring facets of yourself that maybe aren't so glorious. And then you address those facets. So, for instance, on my journey I discovered that I interrupt people all the time, and this can be quite irritating to others. Being interrupted never bothers me and I love a discussion that is electric, alive, and bouncing all over the table like electrons. Turns out not everyone else does. Bit of a revelation that was to me. So, bringing this new awareness with me now – I am more conscious to make sure I don't interrupt others. Corporately, there are also performance review-related processes called 360 reviews. A 360 review is a process of getting feedback on an individual's performance and/or potential from their manager and others who interact with them regularly, i.e., peers, direct reports, manager, etc. A 360 review has several different names – 360 evaluation, multidirectional feedback, peer feedback, etc. These reviews, where used effectively, can really help to provide insight into our triggers and the real-world view of our working persona, hopefully in a kind way (The Emotional Capital Report is one of these that we have found really effective). Whatever tool you use – it doesn't really matter; the tools are simply mechanisms in which a team or individual can identify and strengthen areas for improvement and leverage their strengths in a kind and compassionate way.

2. Manage your reactions

   It is important to acknowledge that we always have a choice in how we react to things. When something happens that gets us worked up, take a step back and pause before reacting. This will give you time to think about the situation logically and respond in a way that is constructive and helpful, rather than emotionally charged. How do you respond to anger? How do you respond to hurt? Can you remain calm? Are you a Barak Obama or a Gordon Ramsey in a crisis? If we are to lead teams, particularly during challenging circumstances such as privacy breaches, we need to be able to navigate such choppy waters with calm and structured demeanor.

3. Communicate effectively

   One of the key skills of emotional intelligence is effective communication. This involves being able to express yourself clearly, as well as active listening – hearing what others are saying and trying to understand their perspective. When communicating with others, always aim to be respectful and open-minded, even if you don't agree with them.

4. Develop/enhance empathy

Empathy is the ability to understand and share the feelings of another person. It is often conflated with sympathy; however, they are very different. Sympathy (which comes from the Greek word sym, meaning "together," and pathos, referring to feelings or emotion) is used when one person shares the feelings of another; an example is when one experiences sadness when someone close is experiencing grief or loss. Empathy is also related to pathos. It differs from sympathy in carrying an implication of greater emotional distance. With empathy, you can imagine or understand how someone might feel, without necessarily having those feelings yourself. Put simply, sympathy is when you share the feelings of another; empathy is when you understand the feelings of another but do not necessarily share them. As a leader, it is important to be able to empathize with your team members, so that you can better understand their needs and motivations. To develop empathy, we must try to put ourselves in someone else's shoes and see things from their perspective. This can be difficult to do at first, but you need to make a conscious effort to start with – and then it will slowly start coming to you as you make more and more of an effort.

Executive presence

Have you ever worked with an executive and noticed – they really seem together and in command of what they are doing – but you are not sure why you feel that way? Welcome to the club of executive presence. Want to know the answer why they are that way? It is simple – just do an Internet search – there are four traits, no wait, there a ten, oh, another says seven... and on it goes.

The bottom line executive presence is an elusive trait as to "what" it is. What is clear – executive presence is how one appears to others, and appears to be able to handle difficult situations, even when the individual is having a bad day. Executive presence is a set of behaviors and emotional intelligence that provide the ability to promote your ideas and influence others. People want individuals they can trust in uncertain and difficult times. The privacy leader's world may be calm today, but the organization needs to know it can rely on the privacy leader tomorrow when there is a crisis. Those with executive presence come across as calm, approachable and in control. The world may be in a hurry; however, the one with executive presence is not the flustered one in the room. The one with executive presence can take control of difficult situations, many times unpredictable. They can make tough decisions and hold their own with other members of a typically smart, motivated executive team.

The following is a distilled version of all those traits we believe create this confidence. After all, an individual may have an extensive amount of technical privacy knowledge, knowledge of the business, knowledge of all the privacy laws and regulations, certifications, and frameworks and these will all go to waste if a) the organization does not have confidence in their ability to move forward and b) the person does not seem to be in control of themselves.

1. Appearance – Do you dress like a senior executive? The dress should convey success, confidence, and respect. How do the executives in the company dress? Even on "Jeans Fridays", most likely, if the senior executives choose to participate, are they wearing tennis shoes or hoodies? How are the executives showing up on a remote video call? To be on the championship sports team, you need to wear the uniform of the team – this is no different.
2. Body Language – Stand with good posture, shake hands firmly, and speak firmly and with authority. This means believing in yourself and not being tentative. If speaking as if you are unsure of yourself, others will not have confidence in you. This doesn't mean you know it all, it just means being deliberate.
3. Elevator Pitch – The 60-second elevator pitch is great training. We should practice how we intend to add value the next time we see others and be able to articulate how we are adding value.
4. Listening Skills, knowing when to engage – Extraversion is not a requirement for success and listening and knowing when to enter the conversation can be very powerful.
5. Calmness – Exercising calmness when others are emotional increases respect for the individual. When challenged, a point can still be made without being confrontational, gaining the respect of others.
6. Presentation Skills – Public speaking to a large audience demonstrates the ability to handle pressure with other executives.
7. Be Genuine – Don't BS. Give people a reason to trust you.
8. Passion – Those that exude passion inspire others to see that you love what you do and in turn will trust you want to do the right thing.
9. Intelligence – People respect intelligence, and it will come through in the interactions.
10. Humility – We all make mistakes, and we need to be able to own up to and admit them. We also may be fearful and uncertain of some activities, and communicating the concerns shows we are real people also. Acknowledging these concerns can lead to solutions.
11. Humor – This is listed last; however, this is the secret sauce which can reduce tension and other people's defenses. Use it wisely and sparingly.

None of us will have all the strengths above, as we are all different individuals with different backgrounds, experiences, and strengths. Each of us needs to find what makes us authentic and unique to the point where we exude confidence. We may be nervous inside or wondering how we are going to do the task just assigned to us; however, we must be able to have enough confidence in our abilities, including our ability to reach out and partner with others in those areas we do not do so well, to project a "can do" attitude in having the back of our peers. Imagine being in an airplane that is having engine trouble and the pilot comes bursting into the passenger compartment screaming, "Help, we have an engine on fire!!!" How would we feel? Or would we rather receive an announcement, "Ladies and Gentlemen, we are experiencing some minor mechanical issues and expect the next couple minutes to experience some turbulent conditions, please remain seated with your seat belt fastened", even though they are trying everything possible up front in the cockpit to avoid disaster.

That is executive presence.

Practice stress management

Leadership can be a stressful job, so it is important to have effective stress management skills. This includes knowing how to relax and rejuvenate both physically and mentally. When we are feeling overwhelmed, we need to take a few minutes to yourself to breathe deeply and center ourselves. Relaxation techniques such as yoga or meditation can assist in centering ourselves. Some excellent techniques we have discovered over the years have been the breath app on apple watch, and the "take ten" app.

Stillness

While this may sound a bit hippy-dippy, we cannot emphasize the importance of finding stillness – especially for a demanding role such as that of the privacy leader. The mind it turns out (according to Eckhart Tolle in his book *The Power of Now*) likes to be kept stimulated. So, while we may try to quiet the mind....he/she loves to be kept awake. Thus, our job is to find a way to quiet the mind. Sleep does this (eventually); however, we need to find a way during the day to quiet the mind – to stop all the noise, particularly the overthinkers. This is not just for our mental well-being but also because as a leader we need to understand that the still mind makes far more effective decisions than the whirring one. Mark Nepo, in his wonderful book *Seven Thousand Ways to Listen*, uses the analogy of a bucket of water with a pebble dropped into it. The bottom of the bucket is not visible until the ripples in the water dissipate. Our job as leaders is to make sure that we manage the pebbles in our lives and work, so that our decision-making skills are razor sharp.

So many books are written on stillness and on silencing the monkey mind. Years ago – people found stillness without ever looking for it – it's simply a human condition. My mother knitted and crocheted and said the rosary every day. My father walked up the hills. Some people play golf, or walk along the beach, or read a book, or go for a cycle – the list is endless. How stillness can be cultivated for an individual is a very personal journey. No matter how someone cultivates stillness – it needs to become an everyday practice. In 2013, after completing a master's in leadership, I went on a journey exploring different ways to find stillness. I discovered that I was book perfect seven on the Enneagram – and was directed therefore to focus on finding stillness if I wanted to improve decision-making. I tried everything – yoga, mindfulness, even breathing techniques. None of these things worked (for me). And one day – I saw a group of people in the park doing Tai Chi and instantly I knew I would find stillness in movement. I have been practicing Tai Chi ever since and in fact am an advanced instructor now. Through Tai Chi I can still my mind over the course of the set (108 moves repeated for 40 minutes). The wonderful thing about learning how to still the mind without "gimmicks or gadgets" is you can take it with you anywhere and do it whenever you want or need to.

Talking vs Listening

Many people appear to believe that they are the best at communicating while they are talking, however when we are listening, and the other person feels they have been heard, our ability to communicate is much greater. Unfortunately, we block ourselves from effective listening by not paying full attention to the person speaking. Those that are good listeners tend to draw other people to them, people confide in you, and you become a trusted member of the team. By not listening, it sends the message that what they have to say is not very important. Critical information is then missed and opportunities to demonstrate that the person is cared about is also missed. True listening involves providing our full attention.

Blocks to effective listening

There are 12 blocks which get in our way of effective listening that make it hard for us to truly listen to what the other person is saying. Because listening is so crucial in communications, we should continuously be aware of our behavior when another person is speaking.

1. *Comparing* – While the other person is talking, you are trying to determine if you have had that situation before and was it worse or not. They may be talking about an issue that you have had before, and the thought is running through your mind, "hey, it isn't that tough to complete that, why are they having a problem". By comparing, it is difficult to listen to what their problem is, as the mind is busy analyzing our own past experiences.
2. *Mind Reading* – Instead of focusing on what the person is saying, the focus is trying to understand the meaning behind what they are saying

and interpreting a different situation and driving the comments. For example, they may be saying "I have worked long hours to review these privacy violation reports, and I am tired of re-working it", while the listener is thinking, "oh, they just had a long day because they are going to school in the evenings and are probably just tired". This may not be the case at all, and in fact the real issue is that the re-work is preventing other work from being performed.

3. *Rehearsing* – The mind is too busy thinking of what the listener will say next, that they are not focusing on the message that is being delivered. In this case, the listener "appears" to be interested in what is being said.

4. *Filtering* – The listener listens just long enough to hear whether the person is angry, unhappy, or in danger. Once the emotion is determined, then the listening stops and focuses on other activities or plans that the person is thinking about. The listener only hears half of what is being said.

5. *Judging* – Judging occurs when someone is prejudged before they even start talking. A negative label is placed on the person who devalues what they may have to say. If the person is seen as unqualified, incompetent, or lacking necessary skills by the listener, they may discount what they have to say. This causes insights to be missed that could provide valuable insight to the solution.

6. *Dreaming* – When the talker mentions a thought that causes you to think of something in your own life that is unrelated to what they are saying, this is dreaming. They may be talking about what happens if the contract that the company is bidding on is not won, what will happen to the privacy staffing levels, but before they get to ask the questions, your mind has drifted off to the last company that you worked for that lost a huge contract and how you hated going through the reduction in force motions with your staff.

7. *Identifying* – Similar to dreaming, in this case, everything the person is telling gets related back to by the listener to an experience in their own life. This is commonly shown when people are talking about a situation and then a similar situation is parroted back from the listener's life.

8. *Advising* – In this scenario, the listener is too busy thinking of the solution to the problem from the first few sound bites that they miss important information or fail to notice how the listener is feeling.

9. *Sparring* – Quickly disagreeing by the listener causes the listener to search for items to disagree with. This can take the form of a put-down where the talker does not feel listened to and possibly humiliated.

10. *Being Right* – This person will go to great lengths to demonstrate they are right, including standing by their convictions, not listening to criticism, making excuses, shouting, twisting the facts, and so forth.

11. *Derailing* – The conversation is ended by changing the subject and avoiding the conflict. This is sometimes done by joking to avoid the discomfort of having to discuss the subject.

12. *Placating* – The listener is very agreeable, as you want people to like you, see you as nice, pleasant, and supportive. Listening may be at the level just enough to get the idea of what is being said, however, you are not fully engaged.

By being conscious of these blocks, they can be avoided to become a better listener. Embedded in these actions above is our tendency to not really be listening, but rather trying to fix, control, confirm point of view, hear whether I'm liked, gain approval, avoid being dominated, avoid conflict, or be right. As a result, we are not present with the other person. While conducting "culture shaping workshops" at a major health insurer, we placed people into pairs for a coaching exercise and asked one person to speak and have the other person listen without interruption, except to ask, "how could you make this situation even more effective?", without providing advice. The experience for many people was a feeling of being heard, of being cared for. This act helped the other person work through the issue and process their problem.

There are also four steps to becoming a better listener:

1) Be Present – pay attention to the other person and give them your full attention, including putting distracting devices away, very challenging these days, but necessary to let the other person know you care,
2) Listen for Accuracy – practice paraphrasing back to the speaker and ask for confirmation so important details are not missed,
3) Listen for Empathy – try to understand the perspective and feelings from the other person's point of view,
4) Listen for Mutual creativity – only after listening with accuracy and empathy can we stand in the other person's reality and work together for a mutual solution.

These four steps can diffuse tension in a conversation and create more constructive conversations.

Generating a clear message

Effective oral communication depends upon generating a series of clear, straightforward messages that express the thoughts, feelings, and observations that need to be conveyed. Since over 90% of what we hear is not from the words, but from the volume, pitch, and rhythm of the message and the body movements, including facial expression, it is important that our messages are congruent. We cannot be verbalizing the need for a new, exciting privacy initiative, with our posture slouched in the chair and expect the recipient of the message to be as excited as we are (or potentially not!). Double messages should be avoided without hidden agendas. Over the long-term, hidden agendas serve to undermine the privacy department's credibility.

THE IMPORTANCE OF EFFECTIVE COMMUNICATION IN MITIGATING INCIDENTS BEYOND THE BREACH

Melanie Ensign
Founder and CEO, Discenable, Inc.

A common misconception about privacy incidents is that they're an inevitable cost of doing business and primarily related to security breaches. At the same time, communications are often considered a post-incident function, akin to traditional crisis communications, brought in to minimize a negative press cycle. However, just as strong technical teams are constantly engaged in proactive and preventative efforts, so too are the most effective communication teams. Not only can a dedicated privacy communications specialist help you avoid potential pitfalls as advisors in your product development process, but they can also help build a resilient reputation among potential supporters and ensure the work of your internal teams is known and accurately reflected in public reports.

As a byproduct of ongoing engagement with product and technical teams, privacy communicators force continuous stress-testing of an organization's anticipation and response capabilities for meeting (or even exceeding!) stakeholder expectations. Too often organizations wait until a privacy issue becomes a public crisis before addressing the underlying policies and procedures that caused it. In fact, it's the routine data governance mishaps like over-collection, surveillance, opaque third-party data-sharing, a lack of effective consumer choice or controls, burdensome processes for exercising data rights, etc. that erode customer trust faster than security breaches — and it can take years to repair the damage.

That's because these everyday incidents consistently chip away at the credibility of your technical capabilities and executive leadership.

It's rarely the major breaches that cause long-term impact on a brand's reputation. The greatest damage is caused by the sleeping giants that don't receive communications attention until it's too late. These high-frequency incidents have a greater potential to create a snowball effect regarding public perception. Additionally, your public response to a seemingly simple issue is critiqued more than the original cause.

The best way to prepare for these scenarios is to understand how to prevent them by considering public perception throughout every decision-making process, including product development. Here is a sample of communication questions to ask when reviewing a product or feature proposal:

- **What is the purpose of this feature/product?** *Be as specific as possible.*
- **Does it require collecting new types of data about people that**

we weren't collecting before? *Doesn't matter if it falls under a specific legal category of personal information or not, legality does not define public perception.*

- **Does it use data we already have in a new way than we've used it before?**
- **What is the customer benefit?** *If there's no meaningful customer benefit, the risk of violating expectations increases proportionally with the degree of potential harm to the customer, e.g., collecting personal data only for the benefit of your business without providing meaningful value from the customer's perspective. If your standard of "legitimacy" is simply whether it benefits your own business, get ready for people to get upset.*
- **Are any third parties involved and why did we choose them?** *If yes, check out the security and privacy reputation of each third party and prepare to explain why you believe they're trustworthy. If you run into red flags, share your concerns with internal teams and consider alternative partners. You will be judged by who you choose to do business with.*
- **Has our cybersecurity team reviewed this feature/product for potential risks and vulnerabilities?** *If yes, find out if and where the security team expects potential issues to occur as well as any mitigation measures taken to reduce the risk to customers, e.g., adding 2FA by default with more options than SMS.*
- **What industry standards, research, or best practices support our risk assessment?**
- **Have we done a data privacy impact assessment (DPIA) on this feature/product?** Communications and legal teams should work together to ensure the language is clear and precise for a non-legal audience. You may want or need to make a DPIA public someday, so it's important to be honest, thorough, and easy for non-legal/engineering audiences to understand. If you're nervous about a specific DPIA becoming public due to how you think the public will respond to your assessment or chosen mitigation path, it's time to reevaluate whether this feature/product is worth the reputation liability it creates.
- **What are the default security/privacy settings for this feature/product?** *Why did we choose them, i.e., what threat models are we considering?*
- **Are there relevant settings/controls that users can choose to exercise different privacy preferences than our defaults?**
- **Have we explored other design/business alternatives?** *If yes, why*

weren't they chosen? If not, how will you justify not considering other options?
- **What privacy commitments have we made publicly in our poli-cies, media interviews, presentations, or contracts?** *How does this product/feature honor those promises?*

Of course, no privacy professional can single-handedly control everything in an organization, but I've seen anticipating public reception prevent embarrassing and costly privacy incidents more times than I can count. Encouraging (and documenting!) critical and empathetic thinking throughout the decision-making process is often the proof you need to prove you cared long before a bad headline forced you to.

Influencing/negotiating skills

Not everyone is going to automatically sign up for the privacy initiatives, especially if this means spending money that could be allocated to other programs, involves an increase in the number of rules, or adds perceived overhead to their business operations. To successfully negotiate when discussing a position, the privacy leader must be able to separate the problem from the individual. Direct attacks based upon prior experience with a department will not help gain their support. The key is to look at the privacy initiative being proposed from the perspective of the person that you are trying to influence. It is also dangerous to try and read the other person's mind (as noted in the listening discussion) and come to pre-judged conclusions of their support or non-support of the project. It is ok to postulate in advance what the stakeholders may think about the situation to assisting the preparations; however, it is not prudent to come to foregone conclusions about their reaction.

Consider various options to implementing a strategy that may be pliable to the stakeholder. There is always more than one way to perform something. A request by a business manager may be met with resistance by the privacy leader. However, by brainstorming various options one of these solutions may be palatable, with some investigation, for both the business manager and advancing privacy initiatives to provide adequate protection. Once options are determined, these can be generated into requirements that are not demands, but rather where the solution is mutually agreeable.

SELLING PRIVACY TO EXECUTIVES AND STAFF

Jennifer Schack

CIPP-US/E, CIPM, FIP Privacy Engagement Leader, Google

According to the 2022 Cisco Consumer Privacy Survey, 89% of respondents care about privacy. On the news, we hear about new privacy laws, breaches or violations consistently. Your own company has annual privacy training. So, why is it so hard to get people within your company to treat privacy with priority? The issue isn't about understanding the importance of privacy, it's about communication.

Talking around each other. Many privacy professionals have a legal background and have been trained to use legal jargon. This can seem like a completely different language to those outside the field. Likewise, engineers have their own technical jargon which can leave legal and business scratching their heads. With these different languages, it is no wonder that it is hard to move the needle on building privacy into a product early in the design life cycle. Some companies have addressed this by introducing privacy liaisons that can help bridge the gap between legal, technology and the business. These individuals understand both 'jargons' and serve as a translator. This role may be defined as a technical project manager or privacy engineer. How does this work? When a policy is being updated, the liaison will coordinate with technology and legal to discuss risks and opportunities. Working together, the policy will include both the legal requirements and technical considerations to ensure the policy is not pushing requirements that are not achievable or misunderstood. From a business perspective, the liaison can help business teams practically apply the policy within their operating procedures. Having a privacy liaison can help eliminate confusion and bring about better privacy outcomes.

Talking at each other. Let's face it, executives have their own agenda and are compensated according to that agenda. When privacy comes knocking with a new project, the first question will be whether it will derail their pre-existing plans. Telling the executive, the project has to be done "because it's required" does not build trust. That is reminiscent of when my mother said, "because I said so." Queue eyeroll. When selling any product or service, trust must be developed. To build trust, establish a relationship. To start, initiate ongoing dialog to help you understand the executive's 3–5-year plans and share your own plans. During these discussions, talk about how privacy can help them achieve their goals and help their business overall. The goal is to find shared goals that can be built into annual plans. For instance, you agree to develop a shared goal to clean up the client servicing database. This helps the business focus their sales on relevant leads to improve sales volume and helps privacy remediate outdated personal data that is past its time to live. There will be situations where you are unable to develop shared goals. In these situations, leverage your privacy liaison and build a business case showing the business value of your privacy initiative while being transparent about regulatory obligations. If you believe there is no business value, I challenge you to look closer.

The overall goal is to bring along executives and staff by *talking with each other*. Knowing your audience, their goals, and building partnerships will help you move the needle in your compliance journey.

Building relationships across departments

To build effective relationships with other department stakeholders, it is critical to understand what is important to the management and technical staff in the organization. One approach when joining a new organization as the privacy leader, is to schedule one-hour meetings with each senior management member, middle management, front-line supervisor, and a cross-section of end users and key technical staff. In the first 20 minutes, the privacy leader discusses at a high level some of the privacy concerns today facing companies with respect to the privacy of personal information. It may be helpful to provide some statistical information, new stories of events within similar industries, external threats impacting the industry, and some specifics of events that have occurred with the company. This is followed by a brief ten-minute discussion of the functions of the privacy department and ways that the privacy department can help. The next 30 minutes are devoted to listening (leveraging the active listening skills noted previously) to the challenges of the business area and identifying where the privacy area may be able to help. Through this process, a champion or two for the privacy strategy may emerge in addition to learning what the issues are.

Face-to-face interviews also serve to build rapport with key people within the business. By just taking the step of demonstrating that the privacy department cares about their needs, concerns, and issues, begin to build the relationship. These are the same individuals that may be called upon later to support the implementation of the strategy by the departmental projects that are initiated.

WORKING WITH NON-PRIVACY TEAMS

Nubiaa Shabaka

Global Chief Privacy Officer and Chief Cyber Legal Officer, Adobe

Privacy done right is a cross-functional team effort!

Although the Chief Privacy Officer is responsible for setting the privacy strategy, it is impossible to build and maintain a mature privacy program without the partnership and collaboration of key cross functional stakeholders in IT,

Security, Legal, Compliance, Government Relations, and Business Units. Senior colleagues within these groups help reinforce a culture in which everyone at the company contributes to the privacy ecosystem designed for the benefit of the company, employees, and customers alike.

Everyone understanding their responsibilities and how the privacy puzzle fits together, is key to achieving privacy compliance and optimizing company success so 1) create a RACI document, and for key tasks involving privacy, explain who is responsible, accountable, consulted and informed. This clarity will reduce potential duplicative work and risk while allowing everyone to feel engaged.

When the CPO shares their vision, it motivates and grounds all workers that touch privacy, so 2) create and share a three-year strategy to be the North Star for maturing your program. It is easy to get caught up in business-as-usual tasks that are time sensitive but do not advance the strategic or material projects or products of your company. The light shining from that North Star can help people return to the more critical pathway.

Designing appropriate processes and training, drafting governing policies and notices, creating and periodically updating template contracts and runbooks as law and business change, are foundational building blocks for use by non-privacy teams, so 3) create and periodically revise documentation that translates privacy legalese into plain language and makes privacy accessible and easy to understand for all. Although the building blocks are necessary, different tools and tactics are needed to raise awareness and enable non-privacy teams to aid in privacy matters. Hosting live meetings in addition to providing written communication allows individuals to receive key, timely updates and ask questions in real-time, so 4) form a Privacy Committee and host regular meetings in which representatives from non-privacy teams have a seat at the table to share feedback, learn about privacy initiatives, laws, and develop a deeper understanding of important privacy matters.

The value of relevant and easy-to-use processes, training, communications, and tools will only be realized if individuals outside of the Privacy Office can find and use those resources in the moment when they need them most, so 5) ensure you create an easily findable and searchable repository of privacy information, such as accessed on or through a dedicated privacy page of your company's Intranet site.

The above practical tactics provide clarity, accessibility, and understanding to non-privacy team members about the vision and direction of your company's privacy program, the role they as individuals can play in achieving privacy compliance, and how to engage with the Privacy Office to take advantage of resources and contribute to future personal and company growth.

Written communication skills

Written communication takes on several forms in today's world from email, texting, twittering, social media posting, report writing, policy/procedure writing, and writing memos. Email is the predominant written form of communication and is much different than writing a memo or a policy and procedure. Care must be taken to know the audience and the purpose of the written communication. While email is a very quick method to communicate across the organization, it is amazing how many emails people send that have incorrect grammar, misspelled words, or use negative language. Since there is no tone button on the email that is sent, words must be chosen carefully to not alienate the recipient. A simple request may turn into hurt feelings if not written in a clear, non-confrontational manner. Emails are also received almost as quickly as the send button is pressed, so extra care needs to be made when constructing the message. While it may be easy to become emotional over an issue, these are best handled by picking up the phone if they cannot be addressed using a fact-based, diplomatic written approach. Typing an all-caps subject line or highlighting in red font may grab attention the first time, but to the recipient, this will portray an image of being frantic and not in control of the messaging. Long email messages are also ineffective – people don't read them, or they file them to "look at later", and "later" never comes. If a response is desired, a good technique is to have a question as the last line in the email, as this will be the last thought on their minds as they read the email.

Networking/mentoring skills

Networking is much more than sending out an email with your resume and asking if anyone knows of a privacy leader job available (bad idea anyway). Networking is not connecting to someone on LinkedIn or Facebook either. Networking is about building sustained relationships over time. While LinkedIn is a great professional tool to enable the privacy leader to stay connected, it is just that – a *tool* that enables that possibility. Networking is about helping others, sharing information, mentoring others and being mentored, as well as showing up at events well before you need a job. When someone is laid off at a company or decides to move on, it is interesting how the volume of connection requests suddenly increases. This is the wrong time to start building a network, as everyone knows you want something vs trying to build a relationship.

Successful networking is built by attending events and being part of the community. The privacy leader who remains solely in the office will be limited by only the thinking of the staff in the office. While the teams in the office may be excellent, they cannot replace hundreds of other privacy leaders whom they may meet – at just one event. Networking forums take different shapes, from breakfasts, awards programs, to conferences. Over time, privacy leaders come to know other privacy leaders who can help, or they can help to provide insights into an issue.

RESPONSIBILITIES AS A MENTOR AND MENTEE TO GROW PRIVACY AND SECURITY LEADERSHIP

Lynn Dohm

Executive Director, Women in Cybersecurity (WiCyS)

An estimated 3.14 million professionals are needed to fill the global cybersecurity workforce gap. At the same time, the Fortinet Training Institute's 2023 Global Cybersecurity Skills Gap Report found that the number of organizations experiencing five or more breaches jumped by 53% from 2021 to 2022.

It is a critical time for cybersecurity and for filling these essential roles. Women in CyberSecurity (WiCyS) was started in 2013 to address this problem, with the aim of getting more women working in the field. Currently, according to (ISC)2 only about 24% of cybersecurity professionals are female, but we know women and those underrepresented have a unique set of talents and perspectives to bring to the table. Our programs and initiatives – such as our skills training development programs, annual conference, job board, speakers' bureau, and more – are geared towards this end.

One of our highly engaged initiatives is our mentor/mentee program. Mentoring can be incredibly beneficial for helping to build leadership skills and self-confidence, especially important for career advancement in women at any age. Some studies have shown that individuals with a mentor are five times more likely to be promoted than those without a mentor and mentors are six times more likely to be promoted than those who aren't mentoring others. Paying it forward, defining your values, advancing your leadership skills, and leaning into crucial conversations add as much value to the mentor as the mentee.

The cybersecurity industry is at a critical workforce shortage, and we know that accessibility into the industry can sometimes be a challenging journey to navigate. But the journey is easier to work through when a community and network of support is available. Mentors play a valuable role in helping to mold future professionals and leaders and being a mentor is a leadership skill set itself. In our mentor/mentee program, we've designed and developed a curriculum to upskill and uplevel women, preparing them for their next level of advancement. We essentially mentor the mentor and create a mentoring community to lead the path. It's a win/win program for all involved.

Programs like this are much needed. It's not always easy for women wanting to get ahead in cyber. We recently conducted research on the roots of women's feelings of exclusion in the cybersecurity industry. Many women found that while their company inclusion policies were mostly in the right place, they did not feel respected and supported. Additionally, the fact that "career and growth" is the second-highest area where women felt excluded is something that our research partner, Aleria, has not seen in other industry studies. This has undoubtedly led to women turning away from a career in cybersecurity.

A good mentor can help overcome this problem, enabling women to grow their network, form a community, and be surrounded and supported by others like them advancing and thriving in a traditionally male-dominated field. Greater change in the cybersecurity workplace is needed, of course, but mentorship can help women new to the field understand both the challenges and the rewards.

I have seen first-hand the rewards that stem from mentoring, and many people have told me about their overwhelmingly positive experiences making new connections, learning new skills and, for mentors, advancing their leadership competence while giving back to the community. As the cybersecurity industry struggles to fill a yawning talent gap, and women in the industry battle against antiquated (but still very persistent) stereotypes, mentors can play a valuable role in guiding their mentees in the right direction and helping them understand the many rewards that come with a career in cybersecurity. Together, we thrive.

Get certified – for the knowledge!

A combination of both education and experience are needed. An increasing number of individuals seeking careers as CPOs and DPOs will seek training in multiple disciplines related to the field. Among the most common credentials seen in the space include:

- Certified Information Privacy Professional (CIPP) with regional specializations such as the United States, Canada, Europe, and Asia
- Certified Information Privacy Manager (CIPM)
- Certified Information Privacy Technologist (CIPT)
- Certified in Healthcare Privacy and Security (CHPS)
- Certified in Healthcare Privacy Compliance (CHPC)
- Certified Information Systems Security Professional (CISSP)

- Certified Data Privacy Security Engineer (CDPSE)
- Certified DPO (CDPO) (University of Maastricht)
- Certified Europrivacy practitioner (implementor/auditor)

A word of warning on certifications (both in cybersecurity and in privacy). There are too many so-called certifications in the marketplace that aren't actually certifications at all. They may say they are certified by the X Association or the Y Taskforce or the Z Forum, etc., but they are not real certification bodies. Take the IAPP for instance. This is a certification body. As is the ISC2. As is ISACA. And the University of Maastricht. If you are starting out in a career – don't listen to social media – go ask a long termer in the industry what are the tried and tested certifications that one should embark on achieving.

Certifications do not replace experience, just as a college degree does not make someone an expert practitioner in the discipline. The real value of certifications is not in the credential itself, but rather the investment of time to learn the subject matter at a deeper level than normal, knowing there is a test at the end on the material. The act of pursuing the credential drives knowledge enhancement for the privacy leader at a more rapid pace than would otherwise be learned. A good practice so "the years don't start to pass the knowledge by" is to obtain one certification a year, on something to ensure knowledge is continually increasing. This does not necessarily mean attending a seminar(s) either, although that's ok if that is the best learning method, as there are many online and self-study methods to achieve the same result.

Presentation skills

Presentations come with the territory and every privacy leader will find themselves in the position of having to deliver a presentation to senior management. Since they have limited time and need to "get to the point", presentations need to be focused on, "What do I hope to obtain or convey with this presentation". Sometimes presentations will be an impromptu type, such as the 30-second elevator pitch, or it may be at the other extreme in the form of a memorized presentation. Most presentations are a combination of the two – whereby the presentation slides serve to guide the presentation, with much of the material being an impromptu delivery, albeit prepared, by the presenter. Presentation DO's and DONT's are shown in Figure 10.1.

Privacy leaders should be actively engaged in public speaking internally and external to the company. The act of public speaking alone builds confidence in abilities and prepares for the critical presentations. Organizations are always looking for speakers on a topic. The preparation that goes into the making of an external presentation can be leveraged for internal presentations as well.

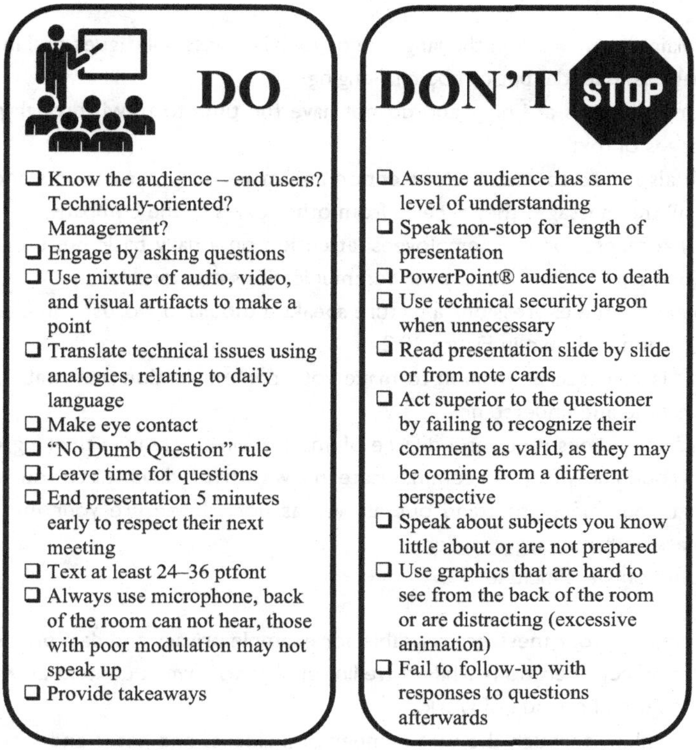

DO

- Know the audience – end users? Technically-oriented? Management?
- Engage by asking questions
- Use mixture of audio, video, and visual artifacts to make a point
- Translate technical issues using analogies, relating to daily language
- Make eye contact
- "No Dumb Question" rule
- Leave time for questions
- End presentation 5 minutes early to respect their next meeting
- Text at least 24–36 ptfont
- Always use microphone, back of the room can not hear, those with poor modulation may not speak up
- Provide takeaways

DON'T STOP

- Assume audience has same level of understanding
- Speak non-stop for length of presentation
- PowerPoint® audience to death
- Use technical security jargon when unnecessary
- Read presentation slide by slide or from note cards
- Act superior to the questioner by failing to recognize their comments as valid, as they may be coming from a different perspective
- Speak about subjects you know little about or are not prepared
- Use graphics that are hard to see from the back of the room or are distracting (excessive animation)
- Fail to follow-up with responses to questions afterwards

Figure 10.1 Presentation dos and don'ts.

GETTING ATTENTION BY VISUALIZING PRIVACY

Tim Clements

Business Owner and Privacy Professional, Purpose and Means

Privacy and data protection are complex professions to work in, and even more complex for the rest of our organizations to understand.

And it's the workforces of companies that really do need to grasp what our complicated notions and concepts mean in their unique contexts.

The temptation is to explain everything in data protection and privacy language. We do not want to get things wrong, yet this language is often indecipherable to most people outside of our profession.

Explaining our work in the language of your business colleagues, and in plain language, is essential but can be challenging.

Our colleagues are busy and do not have the time to trawl through pages and pages of text.

We also need to grab their attention and make our information stand out from all the messages they receive from other parts of the company.

You compete for your employees' attention on a daily basis but there is a way forward that help make your communications memorable.

You know the expression, "a picture speaks a thousand words?" An example visualization is shown in Figure 10.2.

This is your secret weapon to make your communication unmissable, easy to consume and understand.

This sometimes requires a degree of imagination or creative thinking, especially around how can you communicate in a way that is different to your peers so that your messages stand out, as well as how do ensure your messages resonate with the target audience.

Common ways include:

(i) making your messages relatable, for example privacy and data protection considerations while travelling applies to a work context as well as useful outside of work.

(ii) thinking through the vast number of incidents and cases and storytelling them in the context of your own company, either by asking "Could this have been us?" or "What would you have done?" typically in the form of a dilemma quiz on the intranet, or in department meetings.

(iii) applying a different perspective to privacy and data protection by personalizing messages to say, peoples' interests. Leaving a pile of data protection brochures titled "Data Protection for Coffee Lovers" next to the coffee machine, or in the kitchen areas will increase the likelihood of them being picked up, as opposed to a brochure with a boring image of the EU flag.

Every time you need to explain a complex topic, see it as an opportunity to create a visual explanation, whether it's explaining the GDPR itself using a visual one-pager, giving context to all the changes resulting from the Schrems cases or explaining to top management the complexities of your company's privacy program.

Figure 10.2 Visualization example: data protection while travelling.

(Source: Tim Clements, Purpose and Means, Reprinted with Permission.)

Budgeting

Budgeting is listed in this section as a "soft skill" because in practice, this is more of an art form than a science. While reports need to be made periodically with the Board of Directors indicating the cost of privacy and what was done with the money provided, first the funds need to be procured within the management structure of the organization. Obtaining funding requires making the case of why funds spent for privacy are more critical to allocate by the CEO and executive leadership team, than funds for a new marketing promotion or funds to upgrade a production facility – competition from the other business areas for the same pool of money. No matter what the company size is, there is a limit on the funding available.

Understanding trust

THE PRIVACY LEADER AND THE BOARD OF DIRECTORS (C-SUITE)

For the largest corporations, reporting to the Board of Directors (aka "The Board") by the C-level suite and executive management on strategic initiatives is not something new. The board has a fiduciary responsibility to protect the shareholders and other stakeholders such as regulatory agencies, customers, and the social and cultural environment from negative impacts resulting from the company's actions.

Increased visibility with the board

Over the last decade, the board of directors has become more interested in privacy issues. One could argue that the Target Breach starting the day before Thanksgiving 2013, extending until at least December 15 during the busy holiday season, impacting 40 million customers and costing upwards of $300 million, was the impetus for much of the Board of Directors attention in today's privacy and cybersecurity programs for businesses of all sizes. The following January Target reported the theft of personal information to 70 million additional customers. This was the first very visible instance of a CEO, Gregg Steinhafel, a 35-year company employee and leader of Target Corporation for the six years preceding the breach, being forced to step down. While there may be other contributing factors such as the under performance of the expansion of Target stores into Canada, the timing of the resignation was such that it was clear that breach clearly had an impact on the decision. In addition, the Target Board of Directors was under pressure as a proxy firm, Institutional Shareholder Services, was alleging that the board failed to protect the shareholders from the data breach and was recommending that seven of the board members be removed. The board was able to convince the shareholders to re-elect them and they continued;

however, it now became clear that privacy and cybersecurity, together with any future breaches, would be their responsibility.

In many privacy leaders' minds, the Target Breach was a very significant event, a watershed moment that was discussed at most privacy conferences at the time. Heretofore, there was some discussion about senior management in privacy; however, this was not generally a "board" topic for most organizations, other than to know that someone within the organization was designated with the responsibility and authority to appropriately manage the privacy risk. Having discussions at the board level regarding privacy for many organizations was not the modus operandi and far from commonplace. Chief Executive Officers, Executive Management, and board are now increasingly concerned with their responsibility to privacy from both a company and a personal liability level.

The focus here should not be to determine whether Target properly managed their privacy and security program, but rather what the impact on the rest of the industry was – initially the retail industry and subsequently other industries asking themselves hard questions such as, "could this have happened to us?" There were some fundamental lessons learned from the breach which has strengthened all our industries. Aside from the lessons learned that were more technical in nature, there were two key learnings at the management level:

1. Executive management is accountable
   Both the CEO and CIO resigned after the breach, albeit at different stages after the breach.
2. The Board of Directors must be involved
   The risk of loss due to the compromise of personal data can be substantial and needs to be given appropriate attention by the board of directors. Attacks are becoming more sophisticated and thus require increased investments requiring the support of the board of directors. Information technology has increased the complexity and interconnectivity of the systems being relied upon to carry out the mission of the business. Boards differ in where the involvement lies, whether the discussion should be the responsibility of the full board, viewing privacy as having a potential impact on the strategic direction and risk undertaking of the company, or by the audit committee, typically focused on the financial and compliance risk. In either case, the full board needs to have a line of sight of the incidents and the protection risk that is being accepted on a periodic basis (semi-annual or quarterly). Whatever be the involvement of the full board or the sub-groups, invitations to privacy discussions should be extended and there should be a minimum privacy discussion at a deeper level with the full board on an annual basis. Many organizations have determined annual is too infrequent and have discussions on a quarterly or monthly basis. A good practice would be to include the privacy topic on the agenda

of the full board or committee agendas, as well as being included in merger/acquisition, due diligence discussions, major investment decisions, and the creation of new products and services.

In 2018, the accountability principle in GDPR awoke the C-Suite to the need for increased understanding of privacy issues at the board level. Similarly, soon after the Target Breach, the National Association of Corporate Directors (NACD) published guidance for boards regarding their responsibilities for good cybersecurity governance. These principles have resonated with many corporate boards for cybersecurity, and just as boards must be in tune with impacts on privacy within their organizations (as discussed in prior chapters regarding ESG responsibilities), these responsibilities can be applied to the board of directors and executive management in the privacy context. Therefore, we have adapted these concepts into four principles that all privacy leaders should demand from their boards to improve the oversight of privacy risks:

1. **Directors serving on the board should understand the wider implications of privacy as they relate to their company's specific circumstances.** The laws are overlapping, sometimes conflicting, and can be confusing to those not involved with their interpretation daily. An organization would benefit from the homogenization of the laws applicable to the organization where possible and develop an institutional understanding of the laws mandating compliance. This is becoming increasingly important as companies venture into new global markets, where each country may have several laws pertaining to privacy, security, or conducting trade through digital means. Depending upon the country and the sector of the breach (financial, healthcare, manufacturing, government, etc.), different reporting requirements may apply. Discussions of the risks and mitigation strategies, privacy program discussions, and outcomes should be documented within the board meetings for possible later review by external parties to ensure compliance.

2. **Directors on the board should have adequate access to privacy expertise, and discussions on privacy risk management should be given regular and adequate time on the board meeting agenda.** This guidance points to the board being adequately informed on privacy issues and there are meaningful discussions vs checking a box indicating the subject was covered. The board should understand the risk level the organization is accepting with privacy and the impact of threats to the environment. Adequate access to privacy expertise could mean many possible avenues depending upon the company. They may choose to rely on their internal expertise or to obtain an external viewpoint by engaging a consultant to inform them on the efficacy of the privacy program and strategic privacy objectives, or by using the guidance of the CPO/DPO, Internal or External staff functions.

3. **Directors on the board should set the expectation that management will establish an enterprise-wide privacy-risk management framework with adequate staffing and budget.** Clearly the organization must evaluate the risk reward of initiatives competing for revenue from other parts of the business, and the allocation of funds must be adequate. These are subjective measures, and this is where external benchmarking may come into play to ensure that the spending is in line with other businesses within the same industry with a similar threat profile. Adequate spending for a financial or healthcare institution may be different than the expenditure allocated for an educational institution or a non-profit that doesn't process financial transactions or sensitive information.

   The organization should leverage a "privacy framework", such as one of the frameworks mentioned in this book. The key point here for consideration by the board of directors is that at least one framework needs to be selected, used, and progress continually reported and measured against this framework. The maturity of the privacy program should be increasing until the controls are at an acceptable level for the risk appetite of the organization, at which point the board can decide if additional investment is warranted as a strategic imperative. In any case, adoption of a framework is not a "one and done" initiative and there needs to have continued reporting and measurement to ensure that privacy risk is managed in a sustainable way.

4. **Board-management discussion of privacy risk should include identification of which risks to avoid, accept, mitigate, or transfer through insurance, as well as specific plans associated with each approach.** Once the risk appetite is discussed and those risks are identified which are unacceptable, the organization has the choice of which risks to accept, mitigate, or transfer some of the risk. These need to be thoughtful discussions resulting in plans of action to handle the risk. The board needs to be involved in understanding the risks being accepted by the organization. Risk acceptance processes need to be in place to continually review the risk accepted by the organization.

GETTING EXECUTIVE MANAGEMENT ONBOARD WITH PRIVACY REGULATIONS: DOES YOUR EXECUTIVE MANAGEMENT TEAM UNDERSTAND "PRIVACY?"

Caleb Cooper

Global Director of Data Privacy, Newell Brands, Inc.

Most Privacy Professionals have struggled at some point to obtain critical "buy-in" for Privacy efforts from Executive Management. One of the most overlooked reasons for this is a fundamental misunderstanding of "Privacy." Most

Executive Leaders who fail to support Privacy initiatives may hold an errant view that Privacy is solely a subset of Information Security. This usually results in an incorrect perspective; "if we are "secure," then we are compliant." It may seem elementary but to obtain the necessary "buy-in," it is imperative that an accurate understanding of "Privacy" is imparted to our Executive Management. Simply put, Privacy is not just Information Security or even a compliance program, but Privacy is the new business and operational model for modern organizations.

The purpose of Privacy Regulation is to compel organizations to utilize, collect, and share personal data in a responsible manner. Simply put, the regulations want organizations "to do the right thing" with individuals' data and individuals own their associated data. This means from the top down; organizations must view personal data as if it were on "loan" by the individual.

Data Privacy compliance sits at the intersection of each of the parts of your organization. It cannot be compartmentalized to an IT, Legal, Risk or InfoSec Department. Executive Management should understand that Privacy affects the entirety of how an organization interacts with individuals. A suitable place to start with your Executive Management Teams is to help them understand the "privacy as a business model" perspective. You can begin by helping them understand the impacts of the following questions:

Is your organization transparent with how data is collected?
What personal data is collected and why?
Can the average individual who interacts with your organization understand
    why and how personal data is collected?
If an individual interacts with an employee, can personal data be collected
    and be used for quality control?
Do we use data for direct marketing? Internal research?
Do we know which of our legal entities, employees, and 3rd parties access
    this data?

Personal data collection from a website or mobile application will increase complexity:

Is a valid and legal analytics method utilized?
Are cookies, pixels, scripts, etc. properly disclosed?
Will this personal data move internationally?

Each of these hypothetical questions may not be applicable to your organization but they should provide you with a start on how to facilitate a wholistic understanding of "Privacy" complexities for an Executive Leader. Privacy regulations are designed to change how information is utilized within modern organizations. This will invariably conflict with organizational objectives. Additionally, Executive Management must understand that Privacy "compliance" is the way an organization **must** operate and should be viewed as the **new operational model**. Setting a fundamental understanding of what "Privacy" is the key to building a successful Privacy Compliance Program and ensuring Privacy related initiatives are supported.

Driving effectiveness and efficiency

The board and management should be concerned with driving effectiveness (doing the right things) and efficiency (doing things right) when implementing the privacy program. All organizations have limited funds which must be allocated across multiple strategic and operational initiatives and increasing the privacy budget will likely result in the reduction of another budget to maintain the appropriate level of spending. As shown in Figure 10.3, there are multiple activities in the delivery of privacy to be taken to reduce the cost of privacy and demonstrating these activities to the board.

For example, by focusing the privacy investment on the crown jewels previously described, the organization can reduce the business impact due to privacy failures. Increasing focus on business resiliency can also reduce the

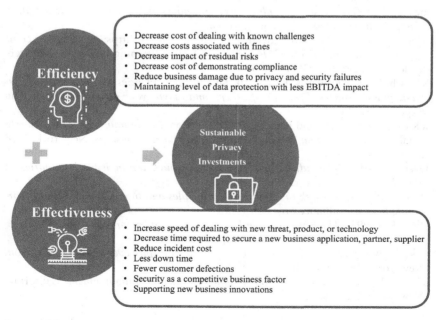

Figure 10.3 How privacy can contribute to cost efficiency and operational effectiveness.

business impact of an outage by quickly enabling the organization to return to the normal state of operations. Likewise, having policies, procedures, and training in place and tested for incident response, thus increasing the preparedness, can increase the speed of response and minimize response time in dealing with a new threat. These practices can lead to increased effectiveness of the privacy program.

SUGGESTED READING

Cisco Secure. Data transparency's essential role in building consumer trust. https://www.cisco.com/c/dam/en_us/about/doing_business/trust-center/docs/cisco-consumer-privacy-survey-2022.pdf

Duan, M. (2017). *Improve your executive presence.* Stanford Graduate School of Business. https://www.gsb.stanford.edu/insights/improve-your-executive-presence

Dweck, Carol Dr. (2008). *Mindset: The New Psychology of Success: How we can learn to fulfill our potential.* New York: Ballantine Books.

Goleman, D. (1995). *Emotional intelligence. Why it can matter more than IQ.* Bantam Books.

Google ReWork. What makes a great manager. https://rework.withgoogle.com/guides/managers-identify-what-makes-a-great-manager/steps/learn-about-googles-manager-research/

Lapid Bogda, G. Dr. (2009). *Bringing out the best in everyone you coach: Use the Enneagram System for Exceptional Results.* McGraw Hill.

Lewis, R. (2015). *When cultures collide: Leading across cultures.* 3rd ed. Boston: Nicholas Brealey International.

Littauer, F. (2005). *Personality plus: How to understand others by understanding yourself.* Grant Rapids: Fleming H. Revell.

Loder, V. (2015). 4 Steps to Effective Listening. *Forbes.* https://www.forbes.com/sites/vanessaloder/2015/07/01/4-steps-to-effective-listening-how-to-be-a-better-leader-overnight/2/#7c3b8a6c7067

McGrath, H. and Edwards, H. (2010). *Difficult personalities: A practical guide to managing the hurtful behavior of others (and maybe your own).* New York: The Experiment, LLC.

McKay, M., Davis, M., and Fanning, P. (1997). *How to communicate: The Ultimate guide to improving your personal and professional relationships.* New York: MJF Books.

Meyer, E. (2014). *The culture map: Breaking through the invisible boundaries of global business.* New York: Public Affairs.

NACD. (2020). *Cyber-risk oversight: Key principles and practical guidance for corporate boards.* Isalliance.org

Palmer, H. (1995). *The Enneagram in Love & work: Understanding your intimate & business relationships.* New York: Harper Collins.

Sinek, S. (2009). *Start with why: how great leaders inspire everyone to take action.* New York: Penguin Group.

Tolle, E. (2010). *The power of now: A guide to spiritual enlightenment.* California: New World Library.

Section VIII

Style

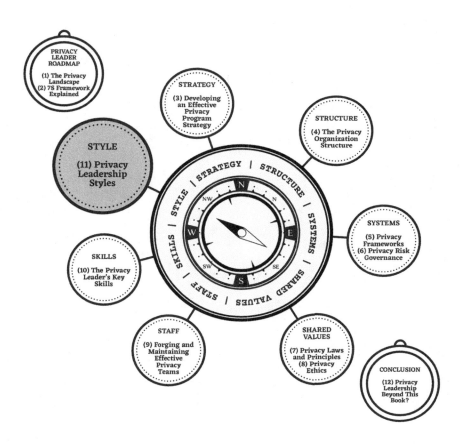

Chapter 11

Privacy leadership styles

TRUST AS THE FOUNDATIONS OF LEADERSHIP STYLE

> The best way to find out if you can trust somebody is to trust them.
> Ernest Hemingway 1899–1961

Trust is the willingness of one party (person, consumer, employee, patient, organization, etc.) to be vulnerable to the actions of another party. The individual may have some factors encouraging them to trust and others to distrust, such as dispositions toward trust (i.e., someone who "trusts easily" or someone who doesn't). Trust is a critical component of any successful organization. Without trust, relationships between employees, customers, and other stakeholders can quickly deteriorate, leading to a breakdown in communication and collaboration. A Gallup (2020) study found that trusted workplaces enjoy 56% higher productivity than lower trust environments, along with 106% more energy at work and 13% fewer sick days. Gallup also found that companies with high trust levels outperform companies with low levels by 186%. In 2022, a Harvard Business Review report (link in suggested reading) noted that the most trustworthy companies have outperformed the S&P 500, and high-trust companies are more than 2.5 times more likely to be high-performing revenue organizations. The research also shows that customers who trust a brand are 88% more likely to buy again and that 79% of employees who trust their employer are more motivated to work and less likely to leave.

There are different types of trust that exist each with its unique characteristics, relationship with privacy, and impact on the overall functioning of the organization, team, and employee, and some of these are discussed below.

Employee trust

Employee trust refers to the confidence that employees have in their employer, co-workers, and the organization as a whole. It is the belief that the employer will act in their best interests, respect their privacy, and provide a safe and fair working environment. Employee trust is crucial for fostering employee engagement, productivity, and commitment to the organization. Interestingly, according to the 2022 Edelman Trust Barometer, one in three people don't trust their employer. A breach of privacy, such as unauthorized access to an employee's personal data or monitoring of employee activities without their knowledge, can significantly erode employee trust and have negative consequences on the organization. The recent data breach at the NHS (UK's National Health Service), where a file containing employee's sensitive payroll information was sent in error to hundreds of NHS managers, is a good example of a breach of employee trust.

THE CHALLENGE OF BALANCING WORKFORCE PRIVACY WITH PROTECTING SENSITIVE INFORMATION

Dr. Larry Ponemon

Chairman and Founder, Ponemon Institute

A challenge all organizations face is protecting their business and operations while not infringing on employees' privacy in the workplace. This challenge has only been exacerbated with the shift to hybrid work, as many organizations desire more insight into workforce engagement beyond the office. Furthermore, data privacy regulations enacted during the past several years, such as the California Privacy Rights and Enforcement Act (CPRA), have focused on protecting the privacy of their customers' data but not so much employee data privacy.

A Ponemon Institute study on workforce privacy and risk found that organizations are very much aware about the importance of protecting employees' privacy in the workforce because of their concerns that tracking performance and productivity will affect morale and trust in the organization. However, organizations also understand they have a responsibility to stop data breaches caused by employees who accidentally disclose sensitive information on a website, mishandle it or send it to the wrong person.

The key takeaway from this research is that a new approach to protecting workforce privacy is needed to build employee trust and drive better data security and operational efficiencies. The following are actions organizations can take:

Empower employees to have more control over their privacy. The first step is to provide transparency about what employee information is collected onsite and in remote locations. Secondly, give employees a voice by enabling them to express any concerns about the protection of their privacy in the workplace and in remote locations. Thirdly, have a formal policy that describes your organization's workforce monitoring practices.

To mitigate risk without affecting employee trust, organizations should be mindful of how and what data is collected. Organizations should anonymize and minimize the amount of data collected. In addition, consider training and technologies that support employees' efforts to safeguard data and avoid phishing attacks.

Encourage the collaboration between IT/IT security and lines of business because a closer collaboration between these two functions would result in employees believing they are partners with their organization in both the improvement of data security and operational efficiencies.

Organizational trust

Organizational trust refers to the confidence that external stakeholders, such as customers, suppliers, employees, and investors, have in the organization. It is built on a reputation for integrity, ethical conduct, and a track record of delivering on promises. Organizational trust is essential for establishing long-term relationships and loyalty among stakeholders. There are three broad types of Organizational Trust: 1) trust within organizations (e.g., between employees or co-workers, or between workers and management), 2) trust between organizations and their customers, and 3) trust between organizations. A violation of privacy, such as a data breach that compromises customer data for instance, can severely damage organizational trust and lead to the loss of customers and business opportunities. A good example of a breach of organizational trust is the data breach at Equifax in 2017, where personal data of 147 million customers was exposed.

THE NEED FOR DIGITAL TRUST AMONG THE DIGITAL CHAOS

Conor Hogan

Global Director, Data Governance, Digital Trust Consulting Services, BSI Group

Organizational success relies on brand reputation. This in turn relies on stakeholder and customer trust in management and their actions. The most trusted companies in the world are not there by mistake. They have made a series of careful decisions to engender trust.

Building trust in drops

Brands rely on building stakeholder and societal trust, and then sustaining it. If you visit a familiar chain restaurant, you know the meal will taste exactly as you expect. Communication devices in your pocket or on your desk work as you expect them to when you need them to. These organizations have built trust in their brands over a long time. Sustaining trust is a critical measure of brand resilience. Most especially when facing modern societal digital chaos encompassing:

- Data proliferation.
- Technologies:
  - Large Language Models (LLM)
  - Artificial Intelligence (AI)
  - Virtual/augmented reality (VR/AR)
- Cyber-attacks.
- Digital supply chain issues.

Even the **potential** of an incident can erode trust. Reputations are built in "drops" over time but can be lost in seconds, becoming **harder** to regain.

Sustaining trust amongst the chaos

Many issues link to the rise of business digitalization in every sector. Modern business climates drive significant interest into broader risks. Enterprises, in response, build complex digital ecosystems. Many, discover that digital services become a primary determinant of performance. Yet, the understanding of bias, privacy, security, or ethical concerns leads to poor digital risk mitigation. This introduces novel, unknown risks and intensifies already complex ones.

At a socio-political and economic level, the need for a broader concept of Digital Trust is critical. Digital Trust is defined as *"Trust in the digital interactions and relationships between business, people and things"*, and builds on known concepts including:

- Kitemarks.
- Compliance certifications.
- Privacy-by-design.
- Sustainability.
- Management attestations.
- Audits.
- Independent verification.

Digital trust cannot be tied to any specific domain, instead it transcends its constituent elements. It is a product of multi-layered assurance and by-design approaches.

If governed and managed appropriately, digital chaos can pivot into real opportunity. Opportunities to power business operations; drive performance; foster innovation and benefit all stakeholders and wider society.

Institutional trust

Institutional trust is defined as the extent to which individuals accept and perceive institutions as benevolent, competent, reliable, and responsible toward citizens. It refers to the confidence that individuals have in government institutions and public organizations, such as schools, hospitals, and non-profit organizations – that these institutions act in the public interest, uphold democratic values, and protect the rights and privacy of individuals. Institutional trust is essential for the legitimacy and effectiveness of government and public organizations. A breach of privacy, such as government surveillance programs that infringe on citizens' privacy rights, can significantly erode institutional trust and undermine democratic principles. A good example of a breach of institutional trust is the revelation of the National Security Agency's (NSA) mass surveillance programs in 2013, which sparked a global debate on privacy and government surveillance.

HOW PRIVACY LEADERS CAN BUILD TRUST

In the context of privacy program leadership, trust plays a particularly important role. Trust is built over time through a combination of factors, including open communication, transparency, consistency, and reliability. Leaders who can demonstrate these traits are more likely to inspire trust among stakeholders. Leaders who are trusted by employees, customers, and other stakeholders are more likely to be able to effectively implement privacy programs that protect data while also meeting organizational goals and complying with regulations. For example, a leader who is seen as transparent and reliable is more likely to be able to successfully communicate the importance of privacy to employees and ensure that they adhere to established privacy policies and procedures. Trust is also important when it comes to complying with regulatory privacy requirements. A privacy program leader who can establish trust with regulatory agencies is more likely to be able to successfully navigate the complex regulatory landscape and ensure that the organization follows relevant laws and regulations. This can be particularly important in the event of a data breach or other privacy violation, as trust with regulators can also help mitigate potential legal and reputational damage.

The privacy leader sets the tone for the team culture and establishes norms of behavior. If the privacy leader isn't focused on trust, then communication, collaboration, and innovation will suffer. So how can the privacy leader build trust within their team? It starts with creating a safe environment where people feel comfortable expressing themselves and taking risks. It means being transparent and authentic. And it requires establishing clear expectations and following through on commitments. Abbey Lewis from

Harvard Business suggests that leaders can do several things to foster an environment of trust:

Be transparent
- Share information openly and candidly. Keep the team updated on what's going on in the company and at the senior leadership level. Don't withhold resources from employees or make decisions in secret.
- Provide regular feedback. Be clear about the team vision and expectations of team members. Share how employees are tracking toward their performance – both positively and constructively.
- Encourage open communication. Create an environment where employees feel comfortable speaking up and voicing their opinions – even if those opinions differ from leadership. Leaders can follow formal processes, such as anonymous surveys, as well as informal processes, such as asking employees for their thoughts on a workplace topic at regular check-in meetings.

Be authentic
- Start with self-awareness. Leaders become more authentic when they begin with knowing who they are – what they value, what they're good at, how emotionally intelligent they are – and how others perceive them.
- Show vulnerability. When leaders reveal their trip-ups and failures, they are seen as more approachable and less arrogant (Goleman's Leadership Styles, n.d.), but showing vulnerability isn't always easy. Start by sharing lessons from past mistakes or areas of development.
- Embrace the journey. The path to authenticity can be tricky. Nevertheless, the answer is not in pushing away difficult emotions or situations that might arise, but in embracing the ups and downs. And, above all, learning from them and sharing those learnings with team members.

Be reliable
- Follow through on commitments. To be reliable, leaders must ensure their actions line up with their words. Employees will quickly lose faith in a leader if they can't rely on the leader to do as they say.
- Establish expertise. Employees don't expect their leaders to know everything, but they do need to hold a certain level of confidence in their leaders' capabilities. To build their confidence, root ideas in sound evidence, suggest industry best practices, and share trends, insights, and resources relevant to the team's function.
- Demonstrate integrity and fairness. All team members should be able to rely on their leaders for fair treatment, especially when it comes to growth opportunities. Provide all team members with learning experiences so they can develop their skillsets, whether through projects, training programs, or other roles in the organization.

BUILDING TRUST USING LEADERSHIP THAT "GETS RESULTS"

Daniel Goleman (author of the book *Emotional Intelligence*) conducted a study involving the analysis of thousands of leadership styles, to develop an understanding of the influence that leadership styles had on culture, team dynamics, and trust. Goleman, along with Richard Boyatzis, and Annie McKee described six distinct emotional leadership styles in their 2002 book, *Primal Leadership* each one springing from different components of emotional intelligence. *[Emotional intelligence, and its importance to the privacy leadership function is described in the previous chapter on the soft skills of the privacy leader.]*

Each of these leadership styles has a different effect on people's emotions and trust, and each has strengths and weaknesses in different situations. Four of these styles (Authoritative, Coaching, Affiliative, and Democratic) promote harmony and positive outcomes, while two styles (Coercive and Pacesetting) can create tension and should only be used in specific situations. Goleman and his co-authors say that no one style should be used all the time. Instead, the six styles should be used interchangeably, depending on the specific needs of the situation and the people that you're dealing with. Anyone can learn how to use these leadership styles. In his subsequent HBR Article called "Leadership that Gets Results", Goleman argued that the most effective leaders used a collection of distinct leadership styles – each in the right measure, at just the right time. The styles, by name and brief description alone, will resonate with anyone who leads, is led, or as is the case with most of us, does both. Each style has a different effect on the emotions of the people being led, so a leader can choose the best style to use if they know how to "read" the emotions of those in their team together with the situation or context.

FOUNDATIONS OF GOLEMAN'S LEADERSHIP STYLES

Goleman's research suggested that successful leaders showed strengths in the emotional intelligence dimensions of self-awareness, self-regulation, motivation, empathy, and social skill. By taking on one of the more positive leadership styles, a leader can motivate employees and get them aligned with the company's mission through genuine enthusiasm and buy-in. When a leader opens communication and coaches the team, they help the team overcome obstacles quickly, by engendering trust.

Leadership styles are based on factors influencing a company's working environment:

- flexibility,
- responsibility,

- standards,
- performance,
- rewards,
- clarity,
- commitment.

Leadership styles reflect the degree of how much flexibility, trust, and freedom leaders are willing to give to their employees, how responsible they feel for the company or how important standards are. Moreover, different leaders expect different levels of performance, mission awareness, or commitment.

It is important to highlight that these styles are not prescribed to be one better than the other. Nor do the styles equate to one person – one style. Leaders will "lean" toward a favored style no doubt, but need to be able to demonstrate more than one style. Goleman compares leadership styles to the array of golf clubs in the golf player's bag. Just like the golf pro picks and chooses clubs based on the demands of the shot, the high-profile leader should pick and choose leadership styles based on the demands of the business situation. Every leader, Goleman notes, should be able to draw on at least four styles to be an effective leader. A leader, like a golfer, must be able to select the right club or style according to the terrain that lies ahead. According to Goleman, leaders who have mastered four or more – especially the authoritative, democratic, affiliative, and coaching styles – have the best climate and business performance.

Familiarizing oneself with different leadership styles can help leaders identify areas to improve and develop and eventually, expand the individual personal leadership style. A summary of Goleman's Leadership Styles is presented in Figure 11.1. In the section that follows, we include a "when to use" for each style, to keep the leader "on the fairway" so to speak.

While there have been many extensions to these styles over the years (such as the delegative style, the transformational style, the transactional style, etc.), these six styles of leadership remain undoubtedly the foundational styles that should be in every privacy leader's playbook.

The authoritative style of leadership (sometimes called visionary style)

People using the Authoritative leadership style are inspiring, and they move people toward a common goal. Authoritative leaders tell their teams where they're all going, but not how they're going to get there – they leave it up to team members to find their way to the common goal. Empathy is the most important aspect of Authoritative leadership.

When to Use: Authoritative leadership is most effective when the organization needs a new vision or a dramatic new direction, such as during a corporate turnaround. This style is useful to the privacy leader during

The Six Leadership Styles (Goleman)

	Commanding	Visionary	Affiliative	Democratic	Pacesetting	Coaching
The leader's modus operandi	Demands immediate compliance	Mobilizes people toward a vision	Creates harmony and builds emotional bonds	Forges consensus through participation	Sets high standards for performance	Develops people for the future
The style in a phrase	"Do what I tell you."	"Come with me."	"People come first."	"What do you think?"	"Do as I do, now."	"Try this."
Underlying emotional intelligence competencies	Drive to achieve, initiative, self-control	Self-confidence, empathy, change catalyst	Empathy, building relationships, communication	Collaboration, team leadership, communication	Conscientious-ness, drive to achieve, initiative	Developing others, empathy, self-awareness
When the style works best	In a crisis, to kick start a turnaround, or with problem employees	When changes require a new vision, or when a clear direction is needed	To heal rifts in a team or to motivate people during stressful circumstances	To build buy-in or consensus, or to get input from valuable employees	To get quick results form a highly motivated and competent team	To help an employee improve performance or develop long-term strengths
Overall impact on climate	Negative	Most strongly positive	Positive	Positive	Negative	Positive

Figure 11.1 Summary of Daniel Goleman leadership styles.

(Source: Goleman, Daniel. (March–April 2000). Leadership that gets results. *Harvard Business Review,* **pp. 82–83.)**

mergers and acquisitions, takeovers, and corporate restructuring and lay-offs. It is also useful when implementing or pushing forward with a new privacy strategy.

To amplify this style, consider the following:
- Formulate the vision, policy, strategy, and objectives. Test it out with others.
- Consult appropriately – with commitment and honesty. Keep true to the integrity of the vision.
- Explain, communicate, and influence others to understand and feel a part of the vision. Solicit input and consider it carefully. Respond to the input quickly and honestly. Provide a rationale for the vision. Delegate responsibility for delivering the vision.
- Avoid getting involved directly with the doing. The leader's job is to influence and check alignment. Ensure that the vision remains up to date and consistent with the current climate.
- Provide feedback on a regular and ongoing basis. Seek feedback on a regular and ongoing basis. Listen carefully. Act upon it where appropriate.
- Advance team members on merit only.

To de-amplify this style:
First of all, we must ask ourselves – why do I want to turn down this style? As Goleman says, "Any leader would be wise to grab for the visionary 'golf club' more often than not. It may not guarantee a hole in one, but it certainly helps with the long drive". If you're overplaying this strength – and it can happen – then ask yourself which of the other styles is appropriate for you to turn up. Ask others for their feedback on exactly which aspects you're overplaying. It may be that they're feeling you're too distant from them.

The affiliative style of leadership

"Come with me", "People come first". An affiliative leader is all about the people. They want to create a positive work environment for their team members and are big on giving praise. The downside, though, is that the team rarely receives actionable advice or correction, leaving team members feeling confused and leaderless. They manage by building strong emotional bonds and then reaping the benefits of such an approach, namely fierce loyalty. They drive up flexibility, resulting in high levels of trust, habitual innovation, and responsible risk taking. They offer ample positive feedback and build a sense of belonging.

When to use: The Affiliative style is a good all-weather approach. Employ the Affiliative style when trying to build team harmony, increase morale, improve communication, or repair broken trust. The Affiliative style should not be used alone, as it can allow poor performance to go uncorrected;

employees may perceive that mediocrity is tolerated. People need clear directives to navigate through complex challenges and the affiliative style often leaves them rudderless. From a privacy perspective, this style is useful in a long-standing team where members have worked together for a considerable amount of time and are experienced needing little direction or guidance.

To amplify the Affiliative style, try the following:
- Identify and act to resolve conflict. Recognize the individual positive traits in people and accept them for who they are. Resist judging them harshly for not being like you.
- Encourage and reward harmonious and appreciative behaviors. Sympathize and empathize with others.
- Trust your people to perform. Trust that people who are respected and given authority and resources will deliver. Initiate personal contact with your employees – find out what makes them tick, what they enjoy and hate, what's going on in their lives.
- Provide social activities and personal gifts.

To de-amplify the Affiliative style, try the following:
- Ask yourself how the team is performing. Are there any weak points and people? Is there anyone who needs some constructive and critical feedback that you're avoiding?
- Ask yourself what would allow you to provide that feedback? What's holding you back? Listen to your answers and act upon them.
- Force yourself to take a hard look at your range of leadership styles – are you relying too heavily on this one? What are the implications of that? If you're overplaying this strength – and it can happen – then ask yourself which of the other styles is appropriate for you to turn up.
- Focus on the "To increase..." section of that style. Ask yourself – what's the purpose of my role? How much time are you devoting to the people aspects? Track how much time you're devoting to the other aspects of your role. Be honest with yourself.
- Decide how to go forward. Ask for feedback from your team members. Encourage them to tell you how it really is as they won't be keen to hurt you. See it as an over-played strength that can be adjusted.

The democratic style of leadership (also known as the participative style)

Under democratic leadership, every team member has a valued voice that management genuinely wants to hear from. These workplaces are typically more flexible and collaborative, but that comes with a price: longer, more frequent meetings to discuss everyone's opinions and hash out ideas. They include people in the business issues of the organization. They ask for their ideas on ways to handle the difficult issues and spend much of the time just listening and allowing obvious conclusions to be accepted. By allowing each stakeholder to reach their decision collectively, none of the backlash that would have accompanied such a change. The drawback of this style is that its impact on climate is not as high as some of the other styles and it can have exasperating consequences such as endless meetings.

When to use: Ideal when a leader is uncertain about the best direction to take and when the leader needs ideas and guidance from able employees. Even if a leader has a strong vision, the democratic style works well to generate fresh ideas for executing that vision. Makes much less sense to apply this stye when employees are not competent or informed enough to offer sound advice, or during a crisis. In the context of privacy, this style is best applied when building the privacy strategy, building plans for the year embarking on new projects and most importantly dealing with ethical complexities associated with the panoply of privacy.

To amplify the Democratic Style, consider the following:
- Hold information-sharing meetings. Keep everyone involved and well informed. Always try to involve everyone who might be directly affected by any decisions.
- Demand excellent meeting management skills of yourself and others – otherwise you'll miss deadlines and defer making decisions.
- Don't, however, forget to allow people opportunities to explore ideas and ask questions. Differentiate between genuine exploration and deviation/time wasting. Ask employees to share the decision-making with you. Seek consensus. Allow everyone to be heard before making important decisions.

To de-amplify the Democratic Style, consider the following:
- Consciously differentiate between decisions that are most effectively dealt with through democracy and those that require a leader to act more authoritatively. Resist referring all/most decisions through the democratic process.
- Ask yourself what it will take to feel more confident in your own decision-making. Consider the consequences of over-reliance on this style. Ask yourself how you might address these short-comings and read up on that style's "To increase…" section.
- Ask yourself what opportunities are being missed by the long decision-making process. Are there other ways of retaining the advantages while losing the disadvantages? Catch yourself deferring a decision to a committee and decide instead.

The coaching style of leadership

Much like its name suggests, coaching leaders focus on the personal development of their team members, rather than just meeting work-related quotas or sales goals. They work one-on-one with their employees to achieve excellence, which works well for employees who are open to improvement. Of the six styles, Goleman's research found that the coaching style is used least often, with many of the leaders involved in his research noting that they don't have the time for the slow and tedious work of teaching people and helping them grow. Leaders who ignore this style are passing up a powerful tool: its impact on climate and performance are markedly positive. Coaching leaders help employees identify their unique strengths and weaknesses and tie them to their personal and career aspirations – coaching leaders excel at delegating. They give employees challenging assignments, even if that means the tasks won't be accomplished. They tolerate short-term failure if it furthers long-term learning. The coaching style focuses primarily on personal development, not on immediate work-related tasks. Even so, coaching improves results as dialogue (engaged through coaching) has a way of pushing up every driver of climate.

Leaders who ignore this style are passing up a powerful tool: its impact on climate and performance is markedly positive. However, the coaching style is used least often as most leaders don't want to give the time required.

When to use: The coaching style works particularly well when employees are already aware of their weaknesses and would like to improve their performance. Also works well when employees realize how cultivating new abilities can help them advance. By contrast, the coaching style makes little sense when employees are resistant to learning or changing their ways. The coaching style fails if the leader lacks the expertise or experience at coaching. In the context of privacy leadership, this style is most effective during performance reviews with your team members, and when dealing with interns and juniors.

To amplify the Coaching Style, consider the following:
- Establish professional and personal development goals.
- Try to reality check their suggestions and resist telling them what to do. Seek to understand their perspective and not enforce your own.
- Ask them how you can support them. Resist finishing the discussion in one session if they can't come up with any ideas.
- Ask them to book a follow-up session with you – show them you mean to support them and want their ideas.
- Resist telling employees what to do in any given situation. Encourage them to consult with you; but ask them questions, for example, how do you feel about this challenge and how do you want to feel about this challenge? How do you see your options? What would move you toward that? Have you ever had a situation like this before and what did you learn from it?
- Seek opportunities for their personal development. Offer them assignments that will challenge them but will move them toward their goals. This may involve you advocating their involvement in an area outside your immediate responsibility.

- Encourage partnership.
- Review employee's progress and share responsibility for it.

To de-amplify the Coaching Style, consider the following:

First of all, ask yourself – why do I want to turn down this style? As Goleman says, "The coaching style may not scream 'bottom-line results' but, in a surprisingly indirect way, it delivers them". If this style is an over-played strength – it happens – ask yourself exactly what's going wrong here. Seek feedback. Listen to the answers. What other styles need to be turned up? What's missing? Check that you've really been applying the coaching style effectively and have the skills for it. To quote Goleman again, "Leaders who are also pacesetters – focused exclusively on high performance – often think they're coaching when actually they're micro-managing or simply telling people how to do their jobs. Such leaders often concentrate solely on short-term goals that keeps them from discovering employee's long-term aspirations – and employees in turn can believe that the leader sees them as mere tools for accomplishing a task, which makes them feel underappreciated rather than motivated".

The pacesetting style of leadership

If you're a pacesetting leader, you walk the walk and talk the talk. You know the importance of setting a good example for your team and having high standards for the work they produce. The pacesetting leader sets extremely high-performance standards and exemplifies them. They are obsessive about doing things better and faster and ask the same from everyone around them – demands more from them. You would think such an approach would improve results, but employees often feel overwhelmed by the pacesetter's demands for excellence, and their morale drops in the long term. People often feel that the pacesetter doesn't trust them to work in their own way or to take initiative. Pacesetting leaders, who want to be able to use the affiliative style more often, may need to improve their level of empathy and, perhaps, skills at building relationships or communicating effectively. If the pacesetting leader should leave, people feel directionless – they're so used to "the expert" setting the rules.

When to use: The pacesetting style should be used sparingly. The approach works well when all employees are self-motivated, highly competent, and need little direction or coordination – for example, it can work for leaders of highly skilled and self-motivated professionals. In the context of privacy leadership, this style should be avoided as the default style. It tends to "rub" people up the wrong way and is unsuitable for teams where there are juniors or interns. However, this style can be useful during audits where the production of information in a timely manner is of paramount importance.

To amplify the Pacesetting Style, consider the following:
- Maintain and develop your technical/professional expertise.
- Teach by example and model the behavior you wish to see such as first into work, last out. When employees need assistance, tell them, or show them how you would handle the situation. Anticipate all potential obstacles and how to overcome them; and explain to what you would do in those situations.
- Insist on excellence, don't accept mediocrity.
- Delegate only those tasks about which you feel comfortable s/he can handle. If the outcome is critical, add some back-up support.
- Emphasize results. Tell your employees that you'll leave them alone if they get the results you're seeking, otherwise you'll be following up regularly.

To de-amplify the Pacesetting Style, try the following:
- Ask yourself how it feels to be led by you. Ask others who are led by you how they feel. Listen to their answers. Ask yourself how you wish to be led. How does the pacesetting style fit with your answer (s)?
- Offer support that doesn't include giving them the answer, saying "how can I help you go forward with this issue?".
- Let go of the idea that you are the only one who can do things properly around here. Instead ask yourself how you are contributing to this perceived situation.
- Learn to listen properly. Be fully present not just waiting for them to finish speaking so that you can speak. Adopting some of the active listening strategies earlier in this book would enhance this capability.

The coercive style of leadership

Commonly referred to as "directive" or "commanding" leadership, the Coercive leader uses an autocratic approach to leadership. This style often depends on orders, the (often unspoken) threat of punishment, and tight control. Because this leadership style is so often misused, it can have a profoundly negative effect on a team.

When to use: The coercive leadership style is best used in crisis situations, to jump start fast-paced change, and with problem employees. Always appropriate during a genuine emergency, during a turnaround or when a hostile takeover is looming. In the context of privacy, however, this style can be useful during or after a data breach, or during a supervisory authority audit or enquiry – as it ensures that everyone in the team is clear on direction and tasks to be completed.

To amplify the Coercive/Commanding Style, try the following:
- Get to know the job better than the individuals concerned.
- Give direct and unequivocal orders.

- Design rules and publicize them widely. Ensure that people understand the consequences of any deviation from them. Set strict standards of behavior and do not be swayed by others' opinions or demands/requests. Monitor everything closely.
- Criticize any deviation from the rules.

To de-amplify the Coercive/Commanding style, try the following:
- Ask yourself how it feels to be led by you. Ask others who are led by you. Listen to their answers. Ask yourself how you wish to be led. How does the commanding style fit with your answer(s)?
- Learn to ask others' opinions. Be clear that you're interested.
- Reserve the right to make your own decisions but make sure that you've given real attention and consideration to people who hold different views to your own.
- Don't be tempted to "consult" without any intention of changing anything – the situation will get significantly worse if people feel duped by you. Let go of the idea that you are the only one who can do things properly around here. Instead ask yourself how you are contributing to this perceived situation. Learn to listen properly and be fully present, not just waiting for them to finish speaking so that you can speak. Ask yourself why control is so important to you. Listen to your answer.
- Ask yourself – what it would take to trust others more?

Few leaders, of course, have all six styles in their "leadership arsenal", and even fewer know when and how to use the styles, or how to amplify/de-amplify them. Goleman notes that many of the leaders involved in his research commented that they only had two of the styles and that they would struggle to use and command all six styles. Goleman suggests two antidotes: 1) the leader can build a team with members who employ styles that the leader lacks or 2) leaders can expand their own style repertories by understanding which emotional intelligence competencies underlie the leadership styles they are lacking. They can then work to increase their quotient of them. For instance, an affiliative leader has strengths in three emotional intelligence competencies: in empathy, in building relationships, and in communication. So, if you are primarily a pacesetting leader who wants to be able to use the affiliative style more often, you would need to improve your level of empathy and relationships skills.

SUGGESTED READING

Brooks, Alison Wood, Huang, Karen, Abi-Esber, Nicole, Buell, Ryan W., Huang, Laura, and Hall, Brian. (2019). Mitigating malicious envy: Why successful individuals should reveal their failures. *American Psychological Association*. https://www.hbs.edu/ris/Publication%20Files/Mitigating%20Malicious%20Envy_b763904a-ac7a-4981-8e4e-52da0640efa9.pdf

Edelman Trust Barometer. (2022). Special report. Trust in the workplace. https://www.edelman.com/trust/2022-trust-barometer/special-report-trust-workplace

Fitzgerald/Krause. 2008. *CISO leadership essential principles for success*, ISC2® Press Series, Auerbach Publications

Frei, F., and Morriss, A. (2020). Begin with trust. *Harvard Business Review*. https://hbr.org/2020/05/begin-with-trust

Gallup. (2020). How to improve engagement in the workplace. https://www.gallup.com/workplace/285674/improve-employee-engagement-workplace.aspx

Goleman, D. (2000). Leadership that gets results. *Harvard Business Review* https://hbr.org/2000/03/leadership-that-gets-results

Goleman, D., Boyatzis, R., and McKee, A. (2001). Emotional intelligence. Primal leadership: The hidden driver of great performance. *Harvard Business Review*. https://hbr.org/2001/12/primal-leadership-the-hidden-driver-of-great-performance

Goleman, D., Boyatzis, R., and McKee, A. (2003). *The New Leaders. Transforming the art of leadership*. California: Harvard Business School Press.

Goleman's Leadership Styles. https://www.bfwh.nhs.uk/onehr/wp-content/uploads/2016/02/Leadership-Styles-V1.pdf

https://uk.indeed.com/career-advice/career-development/leadership-styles

Pasmore, W. (1988). *Designing effective organizations: The sociotechnical systems perspective*. New York: Wiley; Peters, T. J., and Waterman, Jr., R. H. (1982). *In search of excellence: Lessons from America's best-run companies*. New York: Harper & Row

Ponemon Institute and DTEX (2021). The 2021 State of Workforce Privacy & Risk Report. https://www.businesswire.com/news/home/20210623005171/en/DTEX-and-Ponemon-Institute-Survey-Reveals-Significant-Workforce-Privacy-Gap

Tannenbaum, R., and Schmidt, W. (1973). How to choose a leadership pattern. *Harvard Business Review*, 3(1), 162–175.

Van Voorhis, S. (2022). People trust business but expect CEOs to drive social change. *Harvard Business School Working Knowledge*. https://hbswk.hbs.edu/item/people-trust-business-but-expect-ceos-to-drive-social-change

Zak, P. (2017). The Neuroscience of Trust. *Harvard Business Review*. https://hbr.org/2017/01/the-neuroscience-of-trust

Section IX

Conclusion

Chapter 12

Privacy leadership
Beyond this book?

The greatest leader is not necessarily the one who does the greatest things.
He is the one that gets people to do the greatest things.

Ronald Reagan 1911–2004

THE PRIVACY LEADER – WHAT NEXT?

The privacy leader's role has certainly become more complex over the past several years due to many external and internal forces. As evidenced by this book, the modern privacy leader has a broad range of focus, and failure to pay attention to any one of these areas can result in the one "career limiting gotcha" that makes it difficult for the privacy leader to recover from within their organization.

By way of next steps, we would suggest that the privacy leader about to embark on instigating a privacy program should start with the MACRO approach – by establishing minimum baselines, signoff committees, and risk management forums, as outlined in Figure 12.1.

Moving on from there, then we would suggest that the privacy leader consider the MICRO elements, *by* addressing the key tasks outlined in Figure 12.2. We suggest asking yourself the "who, what, where, when, and how" questions for each task.

Then the privacy leader could integrate Steve Covey's landmark book, *The Seven Habits of Effective People*, method of using the Eisenhower Urgent-Important Principle and use the prescribed four quadrants to prioritize tasks. The system distinguishes between "Important" and "Urgency" by referring to important tasks as those responsibilities contributing to the achievement of the function's goals, and "urgent" as those responsibilities needing immediate attention. Urgent tasks are typically tied to the achievement of someone else's goal and there will be consequences if these tasks are not dealt with. The quadrants for prioritizing tasks are shown in Figure 12.3.

The 1st quadrant contains items of high importance and require high urgency – tasks and responsibilities needing immediate attention. The 2nd quadrant requires items that are important, but do not require immediate

DOI: 10.1201/9781003383017-21

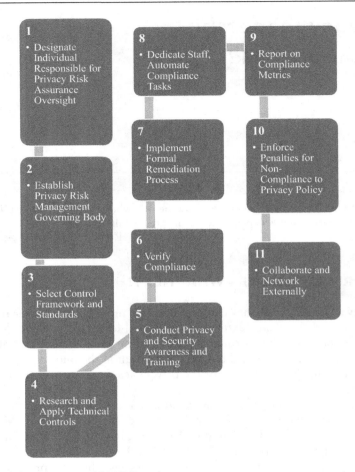

Figure 12.1 Next steps MACRO tasks.

attention. This quadrant is where long-term strategizing would come into play, as if this is not done today, an immediate effect will not be felt. The 3rd quadrant contains urgent tasks that are urgent, but not that important. These are the day-to-day distractions that do not contribute to your output – these may be an option to reduce, eliminate, or delegate to someone else. The 4th quadrant contains items that are unimportant and not urgent and therefore hold little value. These are time wasters that should be eliminated. Most of the activities that we perform are in quadrants I and III, those urgent tasks that are either important or unimportant. The urgency of the moment grabs our attention. Many people spend too little time in the 2nd quadrant, the long-term strategizing quadrant, as this quadrant is not urgent. When this happens, this means that we are most likely very operationally

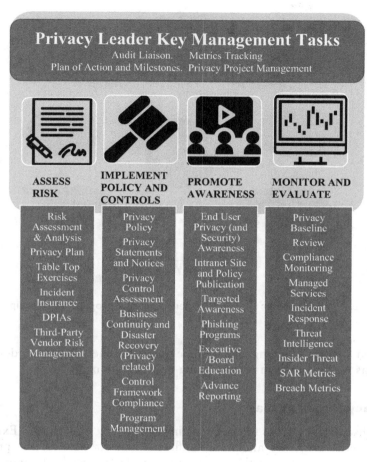

Figure 12.2 Next steps "MICRO" tasks.

	URGENT	NOT URGENT
IMPORTANT	*Quadrant I:* Urgent and Important	*Quadrant II:* Not Urgent and Important
NOT IMPORTANT	*Quadrant III:* Urgent and Not Important	*Quadrant IV:* Not Urgent and Not Important

Figure 12.3 Four-quadrant prioritization matrix.

Figure 12.4 Privacy forces that will influence privacy program leadership.

focused and not spending enough time on our business long-term development as well as our own personal long-term development.

Privacy forces at play

Let's discuss the various forces impacting the privacy leader's role. External and internal activities and trends influence the direction of the privacy leader, and subsequently, the prioritization of the privacy leader workload. Notice these forces occur at a higher level than the administrative, technical, and operational controls required to ensure the confidentiality, integrity, and availability of the systems and information. These forces can come from both internal and external sources and can shape the privacy program priorities, goals, and strategies of privacy leaders. Figure 12.4 outlines the key privacy forces that influence the privacy program.

1. *Increased Intersection between Privacy and Cybersecurity*
   Increased regulations and the emergence of proposals to place more control over privacy around the world have a larger effect on the ability of small and medium businesses to comply with the regulations to ensure the data protection environment is consistent with the regulation. The privacy leader should be aware of the emerging laws and how they may impact both current business operations and

strategic initiatives. Most privacy regulations mandate some form of technology evaluation be done, for example, GDPR mandates that sufficient "organizational and technical measures" are in place. The European Digital Operational Resilience Act (DORA) mandates that certain financial institutions must follow new rules regarding the protection, detection, containment, recovery, and repair capabilities against ICT-related incidents. Many of these rules have privacy implications where personal data is involved. This inter-relationship is only set to continue, given the nature of work and business has become so digitally connected. This now means that the privacy leader needs to skill up on all things cybersecurity. Both authors of this book have cybersecurity and privacy credentials, and for the privacy leader, we highly recommend undertaking the CISSP exam (or equivalent) to have the baseline cybersecurity knowledge required to understand how the two domains intersect.

2. *Privacy Compliance – Increased Legislative Requirements and Scrutiny*
Over the past several years, there has been an increased focus on privacy due to the amount of information collected and aggregated based on activity and location for targeted marketing and the AdTech industry. We also see the emergence of legislation in AI and its increased use in industry. The privacy leader needs to pay attention to the labyrinth of privacy laws not only on the ground but also all the legislation that is being "discussed" at a local or international level. In addition to this, the privacy leader needs to broaden their lens when considering the applicable legislation, as many regulations can have impacts outside the traditional borders. For example, the territorial scope mandated in GDPR (Art. 3) has two "legs" so to speak. The first being where data processing activities are conducted by organizations (controller or processor) established in the EU. The second being the extension of the territorial reach with two types of business activities, i.e., data processing activities relating to:

- offering of goods or services (even if for free) to data subjects in the EU *[Note: So many times, we have heard people refer to this territorial scope as being limited to 'EU citizens' – and we wanted to emphasize that the term EU Citizens is not mentioned in the GDPR]*; and
- monitoring of the behavior of such data subjects.

We see this extended territorial scope reflected in many of the more recent European regulations such as the EU's DSA and the EU's AI Act. The breadth of such provisions is intended to ensure comprehensive protection of data subjects' rights but mean that organizations operating internationally must conduct careful assessments of whether a specific piece of legislation applies to their processing activities.

MAKING PREDICTIONS IS DIFFICULT, BUT WE NEED TO BE PREPARED

Federico Marengo

Senior Data Protection Consultant, White Label Consultancy

Making predictions sometimes is usually very difficult, especially when so many changes and new developments are constantly happening. However, we can make informed guesses about what could occur in the future.

One obvious prediction is that processing personal data using AI systems will be part of the day-to-day challenges privacy pros will face. More particularly, we need to be prepared to answer this kind of question: can I use ChatGPT to work?

While AI chatbots can dramatically increase our productivity at work, at the same time, they may significantly increase the risks of processing personal data. In light of this, what should we do?

> First, consider whether the processing carried out by these tools is legal in the relevant country. For this, consider that these models may conduct data scraping, which is not allowed in some countries, as well as the difficulties in exercising data subject rights, and challenges regarding transparency and processing.
> Secondly, consider the different purposes for which you may use the tool. For instance, using the tool to write an informative blog entry poses fewer risks than using it to process personal data from the company.

Finally, consider the increased attention that Data Protection Authorities around the globe are putting on the processing of personal data using AI systems in general. Many decisions and procedures against companies developing or using AI systems have been issued, and the use of chatbots is one of the most notable targets (see, for instance, the cases "Iruda" in Korea, "Ticketmaster" in the UK and "Replika" in Italy). Further, many data protection authorities have announced the creation of programs to either promote AI awareness in civil society, assist developers or AI users to develop AI products (France, the UK, the Netherlands), or increase their capacity to address their enforcement powers (hiring personnel with specific AI knowledge in Italy). This will definitely increase their capacity to tackle new AI risks.

It is still too soon to give concrete answers, but we need to be prepared to assist businesses and support them in the use of these tools. So before using these AI systems, consider privacy implications from the beginning, conduct the required impact assessments, evaluate security measures, assess non-typical risk sources and impacts, and, crucially, document your decisions.

3. *Technical Advances*

As technology continues to advance rapidly, the privacy leader must consider the impact these new technologies have on both compliance to the regulation, and cybersecurity – both the technology being used internally for existing applications, as well as the new technology which could be leveraged to reduce costs, add functionality, or provide a strategic benefit. For example, less than a decade ago, access controls consisting of a logon ID and password were deemed sufficient for most operations. While this may seem questionable for current operations it was considered sufficient for many years. Today, with the prevalence of multifactor authentication (MFA), whereby something you know is also supported with something you have or are, this is becoming the emerging standard for authentications. The need for MFA was often driven by the IT or Risk department rather than by the privacy program. However more often now – privacy requirements drive the implementation of technical security measures such as MFA as they may be included as controls within the DPIA. In the case of MFA, the factors initially used were digital tokens, then mobile phones, emails, etc. We now see the emergence of biometrics in this space such as the use of fingerprints or facial recognition. While these technologies are no doubt hugely beneficial, legislation such as the EU's GDPR and Illinois' BIPA specify additional requirements for this category of personal information.

PRIVACY ENGINEERING

Stuart S. Shapiro

Principal Cyber Security and Privacy Engineer, the MITRE Corporation

Engineering specific properties into complex systems requires serious analysis. It's true for properties such as safety and security and it's just as true for privacy. A significant part of that analysis revolves around risk, and success or failure can depend on whether the tools brought to bear are up to the job. Those tools basically boil down to a privacy risk model (threats exploiting vulnerabilities to produce adverse consequences) and a privacy risk assessment method which leverages that model. Any attempt to identify and evaluate privacy risks invariably employs those two things. The trick is explicitly recognizing this and acting accordingly.

The oft-taken path of least resistance is to just stick with the standard, familiar (and likely required) stuff, which in most cases is some form of privacy impact assessment (PIA) or its GDPR cousin, the data protection impact assessment (DPIA). That's better than nothing and will identify some kinds of issues, but for a genuinely complex system may very well miss as much as it catches (e.g., social sorting via facial recognition, tracking and profiling of connected vehicles, micro-targeting and manipulation on social media). More expansive risk model components (for consequences in particular) and more capable assessment methods (that can surface unexpected interactions and failure modes) are necessary and available, but an organization needs the wherewithal and expertise to use them.

Equally important is integrating them into whatever systems engineering life cycle is being used. This is more involved than just assigning a PIA/DPIA to a particular milestone. (Actually, they're supposed to evolve with the system, but that's frequently wishful thinking.) Privacy risks may arise from both requirements and design; an appropriate risk assessment methodology working off a relevant privacy risk model should be applied to each and revisited as these change. Integration into incremental (e.g., Agile) and iterative (e.g., Spiral) life cycles can prove challenging, however, requiring factoring of activities and artifacts to align them with the specific life cycle. As a privacy engineer, though, one thing is certain: life cycles aren't going to fundamentally change to accommodate you, so you had better figure out how to accommodate them.

4. *New Products/Services*

Paying attention to the strategic direction of the organization and the products and services on the horizon are essential to long-range planning. Failure to understand these developments will result in the privacy leaders being out of the loop and ending up later supporting products not having the benefit of input by the privacy leader organization. The privacy leader must function as a business partner enabling the business, and this means being directly involved in ensuring their team is helping to "bake" privacy in early for the product or service under consideration. Bolting on privacy after the fact is not only expensive but also not in compliance with privacy by design requirements. By designing sufficient privacy controls from the start, the privacy leader may be able to improve the user experience through suggesting items such as biometric authentication (i.e., smartphone integration with Touch ID/Face ID, operating system integration with facial recognition, or usage of mobile devices as proximity badges) or ensuring that DPIAs are comprehensively conducted before investment decisions are made.

In this way, engaging with the applications management team is a must for any privacy leader. Understanding the application development life cycle and approaches to application development (such as the waterfall methods or Agile development methods) will also help the privacy leader understand how best to be engaged with the development of new products and services within the organization.

MANIFESTING THE VALUE OF PRIVACY

Michelle Finneran Dennedy

CEO and Co-founder, PrivacyCode, Inc.

Functionally defined, "Privacy" is the authorized processing of personal data from cradle to grave according to moral, ethical, legal and commercially sustainable principles and processes. Why then is privacy seemingly always under-resourced and under leveraged when it comes to value and trust creation in business? As Peter Drucker famously quipped, "we manage what we measure." And I shall add that, "we also measure and protect that which we treasure." Should we not treasure the stories about ourselves and to whom, and when and where we tell them? So, where we follow this functional definition for privacy and follow authorized data sets that relate to identified people across time, and throughout data supply chains and around the globe, we discover immense business and social value in protecting the stories that we observe and collect and share and analyze about our fellow humans. 2 Once we take on the responsibility, the operations (including security and audit and quality) and these positive benefits for privacy (including accuracy and good marketing and timely, personalized information) as valuable outcomes in this fashion, privacy can, and should, be understood and incorporated as a business driver rather than a cost center! Compliance must happen for an increasingly complex maze of regulatory compliance necessities, but such initiatives follow and are most often already incorporated into business requirements where data and data subject needs are measured first and harms are anticipated within a well privacy engineered model. Because privacy engineers build within and for soft systems, we know we must always build for resilience and resonance.

5. Social and Cultural Trends

As the world becomes more connected and the availability of shared information continues to grow daily, information can "go viral" and be shared by millions of people in a short period of time. As news of company activity, whether it be unpopular with a hacktivist group, or the changing demographics of the customer base, the privacy leader should be aware of how these changes may impact the way individuals' access and use technology. Different policies may need to be constructed to manage the privacy challenges. For example, post pandemic – more and more workers want flexibility in their working arrangements across all demographics, desiring flexible work-at-home arrangements or work-from-anywhere capabilities. The privacy leader must be responsive to implementing policies with a balance between security, privacy, and the ability to work remotely. We have progressed from desktop to laptop to personal digital assistant to smartphone to tablet era for the chosen device for our work. Offices have become smaller and no longer have large filing cabinets for paper files, and in some modern offices, the concept of hoteling, or "borrowing a hot desk" for the day has become the norm. These social trends are moving more toward a paperless, portable society. Both the security and privacy policies need to be able to support these changes. This book, for example, was written entirely in a home-office in Dublin, a home office in Chicago, a holiday home in Newry, on airplanes, on the road at conferences, and even in a shared workspace in Dublin. There was no storage of paper files in a big filing cabinet, and only a number of high-powered laptops. Many of the offices today are moving to open floor plans with no or very little personal permanent space. Privacy leaders today need to make sure they support this mode of working from anywhere – securely AND privately.

Social networks such as Facebook, Snapchat, WhatsApp, TikTok, Instagram, LinkedIn, Google, etc. have grown in popularity in just a little over a decade. This has changed the way we communicate with distant friends and acquaintances, even changing how we think of a "friend", and now encroaching on how we do business. This has given rise to changes to Acceptable Use Policies to ensure that appropriate content is posted externally and that when the individual posts information, that they recognize they are still, in some manner, are reflecting upon the organization where they work.

6. *Consumer Expectations*

Consumer expectations have also become a significant privacy force. Individuals are increasingly concerned about how their personal information is being used and are demanding greater transparency and control over their data. PEW publishes results from their annual survey results showing that consumer's concern for privacy is at its highest ever. A 2020 study, "Privacy Front and Center", from Consumer Reports' Digital Lab with support from Omidyar Network, found that American consumers are increasingly concerned about privacy and data security when purchasing new products and services (FPF, 2020), which may be a competitive advantage to companies that raise the bar for privacy. Privacy leaders must be responsive to these expectations and ensure that their organizations are meeting the needs of their customers. Changes in public opinion, cultural norms, and political agendas can also impact the way organizations approach privacy. We see this evidenced in marketing messages from Big Tech companies – which are starting to reflect consumers' privacy demands. For instance, Facebook CEO Mark Zuckerberg touted privacy features at the 2019 developer conference. Apple too had an Ad campaign in 2019 with the tagline "what happens on your iPhone stays on your iPhone". Finally, Google also launched a similar Ad campaign in 2019 which simply said, "Turn it on Turn it off – you control what data gets saved".

PRIVACY IN THE AGE OF BIG DATA: APPLE AIR TAG

Theresa Payton

Founder and CEO, former White House Chief Information Officer, Fortalice Solutions

Imagine this: As you walk down the street, you feel like someone is watching you, but you can't identify any suspicious individuals. You look around, but you don't see anyone suspicious. So, you brush it off and continue with your day, but the feeling lingers.

You may not know it, but you could carry a tracking device in your pocket or purse. The rise of tracking technology, such as Apple AirTag and its competitors, has made it easier than ever for people to track and monitor others. While these devices can be helpful in certain situations, they can also threaten personal privacy and security if misused.

Apple AirTag has become the tracker of choice among consumers and would-be stalkers alike. This small device connects to an app via Bluetooth and GPS, allowing users to locate lost items quickly. But it doesn't stop there. Apple's vast device network and long-standing "Find My Device" app means that the AirTag can identify the tag and any item nearby.

However, the convenience of tracking technology comes with potential risks. For example, the trackers can be used for malicious purposes like stalking or harassment. Our clients have reported finding trackers, including AirTag competitor models, in their belongings, such as jackets, bikes, purses, and even in-car glove compartments.

Individuals must be aware of the potential risks associated with these devices and take steps to protect themselves. Regularly checking your belongings for suspicious devices and being cautious when allowing others to handle your personal belongings, mainly if they are unfamiliar or untrusted individuals, can go a long way in preventing unwanted tracking attempts.

If you suspect you are a tracking victim, taking action to protect yourself is essential. Contacting law enforcement is one option, but there are other steps you can take as well. For example, suppose you own an Apple device. In that case, you can take advantage of the safety features built into the AirTag by receiving a notification if an unknown AirTag is detected in your vicinity. This can help you quickly identify and respond to any potential tracking attempts.

The future is full of possibilities, and tracking technology is no exception. We must be mindful of the potential risks and benefits of using this technology, but that doesn't mean we should shy away from it completely. With proper education and awareness, we can take advantage of the conveniences that tracking technology offers while protecting our privacy and security. By doing so, we can confidently enjoy the benefits that come with this technology without fear of unwanted surveillance. So, let's remain optimistic as we navigate the evolving world of technology together!

The text above is adapted from the second edition of Privacy in the Age of Big Data by Theresa Payton and Theodore Claypoole.

7. *Organizational Culture*

Management guru Peter Drucker is often credited with saying "Strategy eats culture for lunch" (however, this has been a topic of discussion as to who first said it), this is especially true for the plans of the privacy leader. Does everyone nod their heads in agreement in the meeting, however fail to provide the necessary funding or carry out their departmental security responsibilities? This is one of the priorities that is often not given much "thought" in the privacy leader's long-term strategic thinking – assuming that others are onboard. Have you ever left a meeting thinking everyone agreed, only to find out later that "silence" or "absence of verbal objection" does not mean agreement and commitment? Several issues may reveal themselves as conflicts requiring immediate attention or may not be visible until longer in the future when commitments of support were made but not delivered.

8. *Training and Development*

The tech industry is moving fast and professionals working in the sector need to keep pace with it. What do you know about AI? What do you know about algorithms? What experience have you with privacy-enhancing technologies? What do you know about the ePrivacy Regulation? What do you know about CCPA? If the answer is "I know what the abbreviation stands for", you may need to do some catching up if you want to remain relevant. Here are a few suggestions about how to progress your learning pace in line with technology:

- Reading white papers, journals, articles: just read, read, read.
- Attend conferences. Go to workshops. Attend professional development sessions. It's not just for learning, it's also for networking.
- Do a professional chartered qualification, for example, CIPP from the IAPP, or CISSP from (ISC)[2]. Or better still, an academic qualification such as a Masters or PhD. You don't have to complete

these in a year; you can progress them along together with your career. Choose a topic you know will interest you. Studying is hard enough, so it should be a subject you really enjoy and one that will be sustainable into the future.

- Move jobs/role. If you stay in a position for more than five years without challenging yourself in your role, you can quickly lose relevance.
- Speak at conferences. When you submit a paper to a conference, you are already committed to learning. We often schedule speaking events to speak on a topic that we are studying or have a research interest in, and this gives a goal to become more expert by. The act of setting a date creates a deadline and allows you to prepare for audience questions.
- You don't have to be Shakespeare to write a blog post, a LinkedIn article or a white paper. Share your knowledge. Identify what you know that others may not know. Submit proposals to conference calls for papers (CFPs). Perhaps you have a book in you. It will take a year to write it! Be patient.
- Apply for awards. Many of us are afraid to promote our career achievements loudly – (so read Brag!: The Art of Tooting Your Own Horn Without Blowing It, by Peggy Klaus). There are many organizations handing out honors within the tech industry. To focus your efforts, consider researching what accolades your role models have received and then apply for those awards or honors. Be warned that many awards are based on "sponsorships" rather than real merit, so try to find the awards that require a nomination and qualifying interviews.

The need for training and development is not an altruistic goal – in that it is also connected to another important challenge or force – the privacy leader's own personal reputation and brand. Madonna revisits her brand every five years and reinvents herself by updating her image, getting a new producer, and releasing a new single. In the music industry, this keeps her "relevant". Now we are not advocating that the privacy leader should start wearing eye patches and conical bras, but what we are advocating is a stock-take of your role and career every five years. Why is it important to "stay relevant"? First, your knowledge and experience may well be important to your organization, but is it important to the industry as a whole? If not, are you running the risk of pigeonholing yourself? Second, relevance brings well-being as it means we have knowledge that is "sought", we are understood, and we have a contribution to make to our community or our tribe. When we don't feel relevant, we feel isolated and left out, like the last person to be picked for the schoolyard football team.

TWO SIDES OF THE SAME COIN

Emerald de Leeuw-Goggin

Technology is ubiquitous and forms an integral part of our lives. Therefore, it is vital that we design technology in a way that respects our privacy and data protection rights. We know that privacy and data protection are about more than just legal compliance. They are critical elements of creating humane technology that promotes individual wellbeing and dignity. In order to be successful as privacy professionals, we are continually required to expand our knowledge into privacy-adjacent areas such as trust and safety, AI and machine learning, CSR and user experience design. This way, we can create technology that is not only privacy-friendly but designed with the wellbeing and dignity of the individual at its center. Technology should be designed in line with the individual's expectations. Staying up to date with the latest regulatory developments is crucial. However, this is not an easy task, as new laws and guidance are released almost every day. I would argue that it is more important to work on skills than simply acquiring more privacy knowledge. In many cases, you can find what you need through being adept at research. Your success will often depend on how well you can articulate your plans and how skillful you are at convincing people to come on the journey with you. If you are responsible for rolling out a global privacy program, it's especially important to upskill in areas such as project management, corporate finance, and business strategy. It's worth spending time learning how to communicate effectively and how to create a strong business case for investment in privacy. It can feel as if the work is never done. On days of self-doubt, during which you may feel like an imposter, remember that the Dunning-Kruger effect and Imposter Syndrome can be seen as two sides of the same coin. The more we know, the more we realize that there's always more to learn. This is a good thing, as it keeps us all moving forward. By staying curious and continuing to develop our skills, we can continue to support building a future in which technology is used for good.

Prioritizing the forces using the four quadrants

So how do we apply the matrix to the privacy leader's world? It would seem prudent to examine each of the forces contributing to the complexity of the role and examine how we are prioritizing the activities of each of these forces by quadrant. We may not be explicitly assigning quadrants to the activities we perform today; however, we are always implicitly assigning a priority to each of these forces and the resources we assign to them, whether we are conscientious of the prioritization or not.

	URGENT	NOT URGENT
IMPORTANT	**Quadrant I:** Urgent and Important Increased International Government Regulations and Scrutiny Privacy Compliance Breach Responses	**Quadrant II:** Not Urgent and Important Technical Advances New Products and Services Third Party Outsourcing Social and Cultural Trends Organizational Culture
NOT IMPORTANT	**Quadrant III:** Urgent and Not Important Internal/External Audits Day-to-day tactical fire- fighting	**Quadrant IV:** Not Urgent and Not Important Unnecessary reporting

Figure 12.5 Proposed quadrant positioning of privacy issues.

External and internal activities and trends influence the direction of the privacy leader, and subsequently, the prioritization of the privacy leader's workload. Combining these forces with the Four-Quadrant Prioritization Matrix results in placement along important/unimportant and urgent/not urgent lines and serves to focus the privacy leader as to where he or she should be spending most of their valuable time. Just because an item falls into the "not important" category, does not necessarily mean it is not important, although it may be, but rather that it is less important for the privacy leaders to deal with the issue than other more strategic issues, and could be eliminated or delegated depending upon the nature of the issue. A sample privacy leader Four-Quadrant Prioritization Matrix of where particular issues could be placed is shown in Figure 12.5.

The privacy leader future is cumulative

The privacy leader's role is still advancing and maturing; however, the "need for a privacy leader" is no longer a question for many of our organizations (and for those that don't think they need one – they will rethink that assumption after they have been breached). A decade ago, boardroom presentations were something only a few would get to present and were typically requested in response to a crisis. Today, the privacy leader is often in the boardroom with scheduled privacy updates and therefore presentation skills are even more vital competencies required. Privacy leaders also still manage all the other challenges associated with regulation, compliance, risk, control selection, cloud privacy, mobile privacy, social media privacy, privacy protection tools, emerging technology privacy, maturity mapping with privacy control frameworks, etc. And post-pandemic, they manage privacy in workplaces where the perimeter is blurred and expanded.

In short, each of the challenges and methods to combat these privacy challenges in an ever-increasing data breach environment are cumulative. More platforms and more places to put data, more AI and algorithms, increases susceptibility to a breach. The discussion for an organization to then recruit a privacy leader is not a "should we hire one", but rather, "let's get the right one for us".

The privacy leader's world has been gradually evolving through these phases over the past 25 years, adapting and adding new skills. The privacy leader of today and the future is expected to be the sum of all the parts of development which preceded them. To skip and under develop and not absorb the lessons learned of any of these parts will decrease the effectiveness of the privacy leader.

Never has the profession had a career path for those who want to seek it as there is today. The opportunities in this field will only increase in the future. The privacy leader is here to stay.

PRIVACY – WHAT NEXT?

In 1970 Milton Friedman argued that the "responsibility of business is to increase its profits"; however, organizations are also required to balance this responsibility with several other responsibilities including the responsibility to protect privacy. Organizations struggle to balance the need for this privacy with the need to monetize data and have traditionally considered privacy as a compliance cost, including costs associated with auditing, regulatory fines, and breach remediation. These responsibilities must be driven from the heart of the organization and can no longer be driven by governments and policymakers. In 2015, when discussing the then forthcoming GDPR, Giovanni Buttarelli (the then European Data Protection Supervisor) noted that organizations would need to adopt an ethical approach to the collection and processing of data, and not just adhere to the letter of the law but the spirit of the law.

Approaching privacy as merely compliance runs the risk of overlooking the benefits of privacy to the organization beyond compliance requirements, such as increased consumer trust and reputation, reduced privacy incidents, and increased firm value. For example, results from a 2020 Study "Privacy Front & Center: Meeting the Commercial Opportunity to Support Consumers Rights" found that customers were willing to pay more for both privacy and security across a number of categories, as outlined in Figure 12.6.

In a 2015 study from Accenture and Ponemon, it was found that organizations that exhibit a "culture of caring" with respect to information privacy were less likely to experience privacy breaches. These types of

	VPN	HEALTH	SECURITY CAMERAS	SMART SPEAKERS	STREAMING SERVICES	CARS
Price	236	190	153	253	201	287
Security	171	177	96	140	170	59
Privacy	160	135	79	118	118	107

These scores are indexed importance scores. An average impact scorer would sit at 100, with scores above 100 having greater impact and below 100 having less.

Figure 12.6 Product categories where customers are willing to pay more for privacy and security.

(Data from Consumer Reports in collaboration with Omidyar Network, *Privacy Front and Center*. 2020.)

organizations tend to view themselves as stewards, not owners of personal data, taking actions beyond regulatory compliance to protect information entrusted to them. To explore what potential impact this "culture of caring" might have, we suggest looking at the analogy of the pacemaker: For many years, if a patient had a heart attack and survived, surgery could be performed. However, tissue damage to the heart was often significant, irreparable and negatively affected life expectancy. Given that a heart attack occurs when the heart stops beating, pacemakers were introduced to stimulate a proactive, sustainable heartbeat. Surgeons could insert pacemakers without invasive surgery when symptoms indicated a heart attack was imminent. The key to its success was that the pacemaker was implanted PRIOR to the heart attack, thereby preventing tissue damage. This resulted in the number of heart attacks being significantly reduced (or delayed).

So, what might a "privacy-pacemaker" look like? We believe it is an approach to privacy that is established on engendering trust, not on avoiding regulatory fines or penalties, and considers all stakeholders rather than the shareholder only (see Figure 12.7).

Trust is a critical component of any successful organization. Without trust, relationships between employees, customers, and other stakeholders can quickly deteriorate, leading to a breakdown in communication and collaboration. The relationship between privacy and trust is complex and intertwined. Privacy is an essential element of trust, as individuals and organizations are more likely to trust those who respect their privacy and protect their personal data. On the other hand, trust is crucial for promoting privacy, as individuals and organizations are more likely to share personal information with those they trust. A breach of privacy can erode trust and lead to negative consequences on the organization's reputation, relationships, and overall functioning.

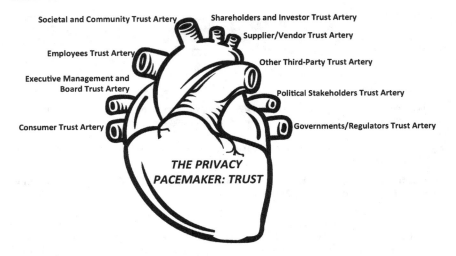

Figure 12.7 What might the privacy pacemaker look like?

SIGNALING TRUSTWORTHINESS AND BENEFITING FROM TRUST

Dr. Lisa van der Werff

Associate Professor of Organizational Psychology, Irish Institute of Digital Business at DCU Business School

As the material in this chapter suggests, the privacy activities that organizations engage in are likely to act as a signal as to how trustworthy (or otherwise) an organization is. Organizations that practice privacy right are likely to be seen as having more benevolence and integrity. Benevolence because they keep the needs and preferences of their various stakeholders at heart and are not solely focused on maximizing their own gain. And, integrity in that their practices are in line with fair and acceptable principles. While our integrity opinions are focused more generally on doing the right thing consistently and fairly, benevolence opinions involve a perception that the organization is going to do right *by me*. Together, these perceptions create a signal about the character and goodwill of an organization based on the kinds of privacy activities that they engage in or, perhaps more importantly, based on the kinds of privacy activities that their stakeholders are aware of them engaging in.

While not all stakeholders are likely to be well versed in privacy regulations and best practices, for well-informed stakeholders doing privacy right may act as a signal of an organization's competence as well. Going above and beyond minimum requirements for privacy compliance requires organizations to have more than good character. To achieve this, organizations need to also possess knowledge about ways to achieve best practice and act consciously and skillfully to protect their stakeholders. These competence perceptions are heavily dependent on the knowledge of the various stakeholder groups regarding what they can and should expect with regards to organizational practices.

While it is tempting to think of this as a relatively straightforward relationship where the type of privacy practices an organization uses will signal their trustworthiness, it is also likely that the reverse is true. Organizations that we believe to be trustworthy and are willing to share our information with gain the benefit of our doubt. Our trust provides a kind of rose-tinted glass through which we view the practices of the organization and, where there is any room for interpretation, we are more likely to be generous about their motivations and intentions. Two organizations that report the same privacy practices or data breach issues might receive a very different reaction from stakeholders depending on how much they are trusted (or not) when they make their report.

TIPS FOR BUILDING TRUST

Beyond the somewhat obvious advice to do more to protect stakeholders and actually *be* more trustworthy, organizations and their leaders can actively seek manage trust in a way that both maximizes the impact of any positive privacy practices they engage in and builds a trust bank that helps them if/when things go wrong:

1. Where you are exceeding minimum requirements for compliance, actively communicate this and the reasons behind it. Evidence suggests signals that influence stakeholder's perceptions of benevolence and integrity will be especially influential in building trust.
2. With more informed stakeholder groups, seek to demonstrate your organization's competence in terms of knowledge and creating of best practice.
3. Consider how more general perceptions of your organization's reputation might influence how your reports of privacy practice are received.

In the context of privacy program leadership, trust plays a particularly important role. Leaders who can establish and maintain trust among stakeholders are more likely to be successful in implementing effective privacy programs that protect sensitive data while complying with relevant regulations. Trust is also important when it comes to complying with regulatory requirements. A privacy program leader who can establish trust with regulatory agencies is more likely to be able to successfully navigate the complex regulatory landscape and ensure that the organization follows relevant laws and regulations. This can be particularly important in the event of a data breach or other privacy violation, as trust with regulators can help mitigate potential legal and reputational damage. We call the approach to privacy that is founded on trust rather than compliance "Doing Privacy Right, not Doing Privacy Rights".

Doing privacy "Right", not doing privacy "Rights"

For a business to be sustainable, privacy compliance should be the baseline and consumer trust should be the goal. Unfortunately, many organizations operate on the basis of targeting compliance as the goal. We need to consider revising this corporate approach to privacy to include other pillars of privacy that are equally important – pillars that engender and enhance the consumer-trust relationship. Bart Willemsen, Vice President at Gartner, highlights how building privacy programs that proactively address privacy in this way, rather than simply responding to regulation, increases consumer trust. We call such privacy programs "doing privacy right" rather than "doing privacy rights". This more holistic privacy program recognizes that useful or profitable does not equal sustainable and emphasizes responsibility over compliance. The following section describes such an approach to privacy ("doing privacy right") that can help organizations address the multiple pillars of a privacy program – not just the regulatory compliance pillars. This approach urges organizations to address the legal/regulatory and incident management pillars as a baseline, and the discretionary pillars as they apply to the organization. The pillars of "Doing Privacy Right" are summarized in Figure 12.8.

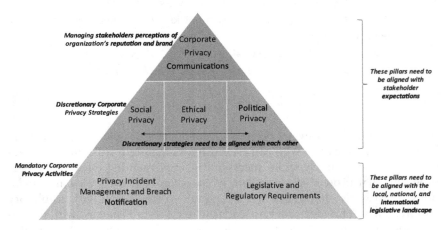

THE SIX PILLARS OF "PRIVACY BY ALIGN"

Figure 12.8 "Doing privacy right" model.

The six pillars of "Doing Privacy Right"

- Mandatory Pillars: The Incident Management and Breach Notification pillar relates to the reporting of incidents to supervisory authorities/ regulatory bodies/stakeholders, remediating privacy incident damage, managing possible lawsuits, financial penalties, or increased oversight/ audits that result. The Legislative and Regulatory pillar relates to consumer, privacy, data protection, and cybersecurity legislation.

  Discretionary Pillars: The Social pillar relates to privacy as a corporate social responsibility (CSR), for example, privacy advocacy, developing open privacy standards, and responding to the privacy expectations of multiple stakeholders (including employees, suppliers, consumers, surrounding communities, etc.). The process of reaching out to stakeholders to determine what matters most to them is called a "materiality assessment", and the Global Reporting Initiative (GRI) discussed earlier in this chapter provides a useful set of tools for conducting a materiality assessment. The Ethical pillar concerns the way technology is shaping political, social, environmental, and moral existence. Alessandro Mantelero's work combining the Human Rights, Social, and Ethical Impact Assessment (HRSEIA) with the Privacy Impact Assessment (PIA) can be a useful starting point to address ethical privacy. The UK Data Ethics Framework and the Omidyar Network's Ethical OS also provide useful tools for addressing this privacy risk. The Political pillar represents organizational activities such as lobbying for (or against) privacy issues such as national surveillance, freedom of speech, voting, democracy, and privacy regulation. Organizations invest millions lobbying governments to favorably shape privacy legislation, for example, privacy was the most frequently used word in US lobbying submissions in 2021 and 2022.

  Managing Stakeholder Perceptions Pillar: The Communications pillar relates to how an organization publishes its privacy values and activities, for example, privacy policies, transparency reports, privacy statements, CSR reports, lobbying databases.

Aligning the pillars of privacy

The first alignment process consists of aligning activities across privacy pillars (i.e., "to walk the talk"). For instance, organizations that undertake collaborations with privacy advocacy groups (reflecting the social privacy pillar) should ensure that their lobbying submissions (reflecting the political privacy pillar) are aligned. By way of example, in their CSR report, Cisco states that it is leading the development of the EU Cloud Code of Conduct while also lobbying for more comprehensive privacy laws that respect privacy as a fundamental human right (Storer, 2021). In this way, Cisco's pillars of social and political privacy are aligned. Misalignment of these pillars can result in reduced stakeholder trust and increased concern for privacy and negative reputational effects. The second alignment process consists of aligning the privacy activities in the pillars with stakeholder expectations toward privacy. Again, using Cisco's most recent materiality assessment, "data security and privacy", is reported to be of significant importance to Cisco stakeholders and to the organization. In this way, Cisco's privacy pillars are aligned with stakeholder expectations and will likely result in positive corporate outcomes such as increased consumer trust and reputation.

CONCLUDING REMARKS

By applying the 7S Model of Organizational Effectiveness to Privacy, we presented in this book a novel strategic framework for building a comprehensive and robust privacy program. Failure in any one of these seven areas can reduce the effectiveness of the privacy leader and their privacy program. In the spirit of collaboration, we also leveraged the lessons learned from 75+ prominent privacy leaders moving the needle in their organizations, professional privacy association leaders, and privacy standards setters/policymakers. We believe this framework is unrivalled and addresses many of the gaps outlined in the introduction. We are convinced that paying attention to both the 7S areas we have discussed in this book, along with trust and the pillar of "Doing Privacy Right" will minimize the privacy risk to the organization to meet today's privacy challenges and be resilient for tomorrow's emerging technologies and new threats presented. Thank you and the other privacy leader contributors (60+ number already mentioned above) for going on this journey with us and sharing insights for the benefit of us all. It was both an honor and a privilege to partner with you all on this collaboration and we hope you gain as much insight from this book as we had intended.

SUGGESTED READING

Covey, S. (1989). *The 7 habits of highly effective People*. Simon and Schuster Books.

Dennedy, M., Finneran, T., and Fox, J. (2014). The privacy engineer's manifesto: Getting from policy to code to QA to value.

Klauss, P. (2003). *BRAG! The art of tooting your own horn without blowing it*. Hachette Book Group.

Lyons, V. (2022). Doing privacy right or doing privacy rights https://doras.dcu.ie/27082/1/FinalPHDPDf.pdf

Lyons, V., van der Werff, L., and Lynn, T. (2016). Ethics as pacemaker – Regulating the heart of the privacy-trust relationship between organisations, their consumers, and their employees: A conceptual model, and future framework. *ICIS 2016 Proceedings*.

Payton, T., and Claypoole, T. (2023). *Privacy in the age of big data*. Maryland: Rowman and Littlefield.

PrivacyCode platform. https://www.privacycode.ai/

Privacy front & center: Meeting the commercial opportunity to support consumers rights (2020). https://thedigitalstandard.org/downloads/CR_PrivacyFrontAndCenter_102020_vf.pdf

Index

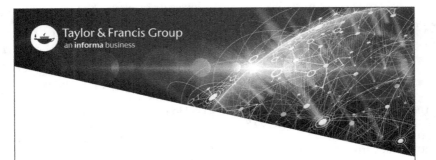

Printed in the United States
by Baker & Taylor Publisher Services